PENGUIN BOOKS

GR___ANATOMY

'A b___
David S___

'A very handy historical and philosophical guide to how we all got here, in a hefty, readable slab of glorious prescience'
Deborah Orr, *Independent*

'Invigorating' *Metro London*

'An ideal introduction for new readers and a useful overview for those already familiar with this most elegant, witty, incisive and quietly fierce commentator on our benighted time'
John Banville, *Guardian*

'Gray charts and interrogates decades of revolutionary change, exposing with clarity and a good deal of passion the betrayals of freedom, culture and peace committed on our behalf . . . a contribution to contemporary politics of a kind that is rarely heard' Ben Wilson, *Literary Review*

ABOUT THE AUTHOR

John Gray is most recently the acclaimed author of *Black Mass: Apocalyptic Religion and the Death of Utopia, Straw Dogs: Thoughts on Humans and Other Animals, Al Qaeda and What it Means to be Modern, Heresies: Against Progress and Other Illusions* and *False Dawn: The Delusions of Global Capitalism.* Having been Professor of Politics at Oxford, Visiting Professor at Harvard and Yale and Professor of European Thought at the London School of Economics, he now writes full time. His books and articles have been translated into over thirty languages

JOHN GRAY

Gray's Anatomy

Selected Writings

PENGUIN BOOKS

PENGUIN BOOKS

Published by the Penguin Group
Penguin Books Ltd, 80 Strand, London WC2R 0RL, England
Penguin Group (USA), Inc., 375 Hudson Street, New York, New York 10014, USA
Penguin Group (Canada), 90 Eglinton Avenue East, Suite 700, Toronto, Ontario, Canada M4P 2Y3
(a division of Pearson Penguin Canada Inc.)
Penguin Ireland, 25 St Stephen's Green, Dublin 2, Ireland (a division of Penguin Books Ltd)
Penguin Group (Australia), 250 Camberwell Road, Camberwell, Victoria 3124, Australia
(a division of Pearson Australia Group Pty Ltd)
Penguin Books India Pvt Ltd, 11 Community Centre, Panchsheel Park, New Delhi – 110 017, India
Penguin Group (NZ), 67 Apollo Drive, Rosedale, North Shore 0632, New Zealand
(a division of Pearson New Zealand Ltd)
Penguin Books (South Africa) (Pty) Ltd, 24 Sturdee Avenue, Rosebank, Johannesburg 2196, South Africa

Penguin Books Ltd, Registered Offices: 80 Strand, London WC2R 0RL, England

www.penguin.com

First published by Allen Lane 2009
Published in Penguin Books 2010
2

Copyright © John Gray, 2009

The moral right of the author has been asserted

All rights reserved
Without limiting the rights under copyright
reserved above, no part of this publication may be
reproduced, stored in or introduced into a retrieval system,
or transmitted, in any form or by any means (electronic, mechanical,
photocopying, recording or otherwise), without the prior
written permission of both the copyright owner and
the above publisher of this book

Printed in Great Britain by Clays Ltd, St Ives plc

A CIP catalogue record for this book is available from the British Library

978-0-141-03954-1

www.greenpenguin.co.uk

Mixed Sources
Product group from well-managed
forests and other controlled sources
www.fsc.org Cert no. SA-COC-1592
© 1996 Forest Stewardship Council

Penguin Books is committed to a sustainable future
for our business, our readers and our planet.
The book in your hands is made from paper
certified by the Forest Stewardship Council.

Contents

CONTENTS

Introduction

The law of chaos is the law of ideas,
Of improvisations and seasons of belief.
Wallace Stevens, 'Extracts from
Addresses to the Academy of Fine Ideas'[1]

The world changed out of all recognition during the period in which
the writings that are collected here were written. When the earliest of
them appeared, over thirty years ago, the international scene was
shaped by a struggle between two power blocs – a geopolitical freeze
that was mirrored in the realm of ideas. Europe was divided along
the boundaries established during the Second World War, Russia was
a Communist state and China ruled by Mao. The recent wave of
globalization had hardly begun. The rise of Asia was yet to come,
and America was by far the most powerful country. In Britain Labour
was negotiating a bailout from national bankruptcy with the International Monetary Fund, and Margaret Thatcher was leader of the
Opposition. The political classes took it as given that some version
of the post-war consensus on the mixed economy would remain in
place, while the intelligentsia were occupied in languid disputes over
the varieties of Marxism.

Behind this shadow play there were beliefs no one doubted. Liberal
democracy was spreading inexorably; the advance of science would
enable the affluence of some countries to be enjoyed by all; religion
was in irreversible retreat. The path might not be straight or easy, but
humanity was moving towards a common destination. Nothing could

stand in the way of a future in which 'Western liberal values' were accepted everywhere.

Not much more than thirty years later all these certainties have melted away. The Soviet state has ceased to exist and Europe has been reunified; but Russia has not adopted liberal democracy. In the years after his death in 1976 China shook off Mao's inheritance and adopted a type of capitalism – without accepting any Western model of government or society. The advance of globalization continued, with the result that America has lost its central position. The US is in steep decline, its system of finance capitalism in a condition of collapse and its vast military machine effectively paid for by Chinese funding of the federal deficit. All mainstream parties in democratic countries converged on a free-market model at just the moment in history when that model definitively ceased to be viable. With the world's financial system facing a crisis deeper than any since the 1930s, the advancing states are now authoritarian regimes. The bipolar world has not been followed by one ruled by 'the last superpower'. Instead we have a world that nobody rules.

The growth of knowledge has continued and accelerated. At the same time economic expansion has come up against finite resources, with peaking energy supplies and accelerating climate change threatening industrial growth. Rival claims on scarce resources are inflaming wars around the world, and these resource wars are intertwined with wars of faith. Far from fading away religion is once again at the heart of human conflict.

If the global scene at the start of the twenty-first century is different from any that was commonly anticipated, this was only to be expected. A weakness for uplifting illusions has shaped opinion throughout this period. No doubt intolerance of reality is innate in the human mind. Every age has a hallucinatory image of itself, which persists until it is dispelled by events. Secular thinkers imagined they had left religion behind, when in truth they had only exchanged religion for a humanist faith in progress that was further from reality. There is nothing wrong in taking refuge in a comforting fantasy. Why deny rationalists the consolations of faith – however childish their faith may be? The pretence of reason is part of the human comedy. But the decline of religion that occurred in the twentieth century was accompanied by the rise of faith-based politics, a continuation of religion by other means that has proved as destructive as religion at its worst.

Lenin's embalmed body and the saviour-cult orchestrated around Hitler are examples of the twentieth-century sanctification of power. Nazism and Communism were political religions, each with its ersatz shrines and rituals. The Nazi paradise was confined to a small section of the species, with the rest consigned to slavery or extermination, while that of the Bolsheviks was open to everyone – apart from those marked down for liquidation as remnants of the past, such as peasants and bourgeois intellectuals. In both cases terror was part of the programme from the start. Humans are violent animals; there is nothing new in their fondness for killing. The peculiar flavour of modern mass murder comes from the fact that it has so often been committed with the aim of creating a new world.

It is important to understand that faith-based violence has not been limited to totalitarian regimes. Starting with the French Jacobins, it has been a pervasive feature of modern democracy. It is not only revolutionaries that have turned politics into a crusade. Liberal humanists who say they aim for gradual improvement have done the same. Like the utopian projects of the far left and right, the liberal ideal of a world of self-governing democracies has spilt blood on a colossal scale.

Even in Britain – supposedly the home of a sceptical, pragmatic approach to government – politics has been understood in terms that derive from religion. The Thatcher experiment is an example. I cannot count the number of times people have asked why I 'stopped believing' in Thatcherism. The assumption is that there was once a body of thought that could be described as 'Thatcherism' – something I never encountered as a participant observer at the time. More to the point, the question assumes that politics is like religion – some parts of Western Christianity, at any rate – in requiring belief in a creed or doctrine. My view was quite different. Politics is the art of devising temporary remedies for recurring evils – a series of expedients, not a project of salvation. Thatcher was one of these expedients.

The Thatcher era began as a response to local difficulties, only to end by producing another political religion. To be sure, true believers gathered around Thatcher from the start. The right-wing think-tanks of London of the early 1970s were littered with former Communists and Trotskyites who had lost their belief in Marxism but not the need for a political faith. The trend was exemplified in figures such as Sir Alfred Sherman – a founder of the Centre for Policy Studies and an early adviser of Thatcher whose faith in the free market followed the same doctrinaire footsteps as the faith in central planning he had as a Communist in the 1930s. For Sherman and others like him the triumph of the free market was pre-ordained.

In the context of the Cold War these enthusiasts had their uses. Their doctrinal turn of mind offered clues to Soviet thinking, in which ideology was surprisingly persistent. The USSR contained fewer convinced Marxists than the average Western university. Even so Soviet perceptions of the world were heavily filtered by Leninist ideas, and ex-Communists who shared this framework were better guides to the Soviet mind than Western specialists. None of the Sovietologists grasped the illegitimacy of the Soviet system, or suspected it might suddenly implode. When the dissident writer Andrei Amalrik, author of *Will the Soviet Union Survive until 1984?* (1970), raised the prospect of its collapse his analysis was written off as wildly unrealistic. Yet he was closer to reality than the Western experts who were declaring the USSR unshakable right up to the moment when it collapsed.

As an anti-Communist I shared Amalrik's belief that the Soviet state was not a permanent fixture. During the Cold War, respectable opinion viewed anti-Communism as a grubby and at times shady business, and there are many who still see it that way. I am unrepentant. The defeat of Communism was as worthwhile a goal as the destruction of Nazism. The predominant Western view of the Soviet system was a mix of progressive wishful thinking and cultural prejudice. Western opinion attributed the totalitarian character of the system to Stalin, and then to Russian traditions of tyranny. Lenin – the system's true architect, and a faithful disciple of Marx – was absolved of responsibility. The fact that Soviet repression was from the beginning on a scale not dreamt of in the Russia of the tsars was never admitted. This was not a position confined to the far left. It was maintained throughout the intelligentsia, for whom the only permissible criticism of the Soviet system was that it was not authentically Marxian.

Western Marxism was the subject of the piece originally published in 1989 in the Royal Society of Philosophy journal *Philosophy* that is reprinted as Chapter 15 of the present volume. The Marxist linguist whose study of the labour theory of meaning the piece analyses is an invention, not a real figure. Revai's account of the primitive accumulation and expropriation of meaning, of surplus meaning and the atom of meaning, the *ergoneme*, are also invented. These absurd notions were meant to mimic the mumbo-jumbo of Western Marxism, but the parody escaped many readers. (Amusingly, Richard Dawkins has long promoted a rather similar theory of the basic unit of meaning – the meme – and not as a joke.) Among the many people who commented on the piece to me, only one – the late Isaiah Berlin – immediately recognized it as a spoof. When I disclosed that the review was a fiction – as the title of the piece indicated – I was not believed. It is true the fiction contained some elements of fact. Stalin did publish a pamphlet on linguistics in which he considered the position of deaf mutes, concluding that they lack anything that might be called a language. It is also true – though this fact is not mentioned in the piece – that during the purges members of deaf-mute associations were arrested and shot, or sent to the Gulag, after being found guilty of engaging in anti-Soviet conspiracies through the use of sign language. Events such as these are too far-fetched to be included in a spoof.

Anti-Communism had the merit of being a response to actual conditions. Obviously, it was not free markets that brought Communism down. Nationalism and religion in the Baltic States, Poland and Afghanistan, along with Reagan's technically flawed but politically effective Star Wars programme, destroyed the Soviet state. Equally, though the fact eluded most people at the time, a period of profound upheaval was bound to follow. As I wrote in October 1989, commenting on Francis Fukuyama's announcement of the end of history in the neo-conservative journal *National Interest* in August of that year:

Ours is an era in which political ideology, liberal as much as Marxist, has a rapidly dwindling leverage on events, and more ancient, more primordial forces, nationalist and religious, and soon, perhaps, Malthusian, are contesting with each other . . . If the Soviet Union does indeed fall apart, that beneficent catastrophe will not inaugurate a new era of post-historical harmony, but instead a return to the classical terrain of history, a terrain of great-power rivalries, secret diplomacies, and irredentist claims and wars.

Inevitably, given the prevailing view of things, this diagnosis – which can be found here in Chapter 16 – was seen as doom-mongering. In a delicious inversion, the observation that history was continuing its course was dismissed as apocalyptic. The truly apocalyptic notion that history had ended was embraced as realism.

It was only after the fall of Thatcher that 'Thatcherism' appeared on the scene. In the early days one of her close advisers used to refer to her as 'the reality principle in skirts'. Up to a point it was an apt description. Thatcher confronted the collapse of post-war British corporatism and imposed a new settlement on the country that would last a generation. Yet her initial programme was not devised in any right-wing academy of fine ideas. It was a succession of improvisations, whose aims were not much different from those that Labour had tried and failed to achieve in the late 1970s. Her first goal was curbing union power, with the defeat of inflation a close second.

Both were feasible objectives, and were in fact achieved. The semi-imaginary Britain Thatcher wanted to restore – a country of unshackled markets and conservative values – was further away than ever. Free markets overturn established ways of doing things, including traditional moralities. The revolution in the economy Thatcher wanted did take place, but the country it produced had no resemblance to the chintzy replica of 1950s Britain she had envisioned. Old hierarchies were dissolved, along with the monoculture of post-war Britain. Conservatism ceased to exist as a coherent political project, and the Conservative Party was forced to make peace with the society that, contrary to her intentions, Thatcher had helped bring into being. The pleasantly ironic upshot of her experiment was the liberal Britain that exists today – a country more diverse and more tolerant than in the past, if in some ways also more fragmented.

If Thatcher made Britain in some ways more liberal it was as an unintended consequence of pursuing other ends. The doctrinaires who invented 'Thatcherism' – the word, incidentally, was a coinage of the left – believed that free markets could be installed, throughout the world, by conscious design. Like Thatcher herself, they misread the fall of Communism. Certainly it was a major advance. In the authoritarian state established by Putin Russians are freer and living standards are higher than at any time in the history of the Soviet Union. That is why Putin is probably the most popular Russian leader since the last tsars. At the same time, however, the fall of Communism was also a defeat for the West.

Lenin and the Bolsheviks aimed to realize Marx's utopian project, while turning Russia into a modern Western state along the way. The neo-liberals who came to power under Yeltsin opted for a type of market Leninism rather than for central planning, but they too wanted to modernize Russia on Western lines. Central planning was replaced, but not by the free market. A new type of command economy controlled by a shifting coalition of oligarchs and the intelligence services emerged instead. Putin's Russia is not a regime committed to global expansion; it has abandoned the militant political religion that underpinned the former Soviet Union. Instead it is reasserting its claims over what it considers its historic sphere of influence, while using the energy resources it controls to promote its strategic interests. In geo-political terms Russia is once again what it has been for most of its history, a Eurasian empire warily positioned between East and West.

The end of the Cold War was followed by a period of triumphal delusion, with the victorious powers acting as missionaries for their own version of political religion – a belief in democracy as a universal panacea. It was not the first time something like this had happened. A similar response underpinned the ill-fated European settlement that was put in place after the First World War. Woodrow Wilson welcomed the collapse of the Habsburg Empire as leading the way to a Europe of self-governing nations. What followed was an era of xenophobia, ethnic cleansing and ultimately genocide.

Many circumstances led to disaster in inter-war Europe, but the savage logic of national self-determination was an integral part of the process. Enabling rulers to be held accountable and changed without violence, democratic government has definite advantages. But democracy does not always expand freedom, or even prevent atrocities. For the minority populations of Eastern and Central Europe the ramshackle empire of the Habsburgs was a protector. Joseph Roth, one of the most perceptive inter-war European writers, observed that it had come to be believed that 'every individual must now be a member of a particular race or nation' – in other words, a member of a group defined by the exclusion of others. A Jew from the Austro-Hungarian province of Galicia, Roth viewed the spread of ideas of national self-determination with foreboding. If the Habsburg monarchy collapsed, he feared, the result would be a type of modern barbarism. Mocked as a reactionary, he foresaw Europe's future with a clarity possessed by none of his progressive contemporaries.

The highly civilized Austro-Hungarian monarchy and the brutal despotism of Saddam Hussein have very little in common. Saddam's Iraq was a modern state, modelled on the Stalinist Soviet Union, while the Habsburg monarchy was a pre-modern survival. Saddam ruled with a degree of violence unimaginable in Habsburg Europe. But when these very different regimes were overthrown the results were not dissimilar. Replacing a secular dictatorship in Iraq with Islamist democracy has left women and gays, religious minorities and even the Shia majority at risk as never before. Outside the Kurdish Zone where a separate state has been set up, Iraqis are less free than at any point in the country's history.

Another debacle is under way in Afghanistan. The current Afghan war has been described as unwinnable and yet too important to lose. Certainly it cannot be won, if only because it has no achievable objectives. Here it resembles some earlier exercises in imperialism. When they expanded into Africa, Asia and Latin America, European colonists claimed to be advancing the cause of civilization. The process was in fact extremely violent, and at times overtly genocidal. In South-west Africa (present-day Namibia) at the start of the twentieth century, somewhere between half and three-quarters of the Herero people were exterminated under German colonial rule. The methods used included forced labour, starvation, mass poisoning and shooting, and death by disease while incarcerated in concentration camps (where captured Hereros also perished while being subjected to medical experiments designed to prove their racial inferiority). For these colonists subjugated peoples were expendable resources – if they ceased to be useful, they were destroyed. But imperialism of this kind was not only an exercise in predatory barbarism. Quite often it was also absurd.

In *Heart of Darkness* by Joseph Conrad, the subject of the essay that appears as Chapter 25, Marlow recounts how the French, who 'had one of their wars going on thereabouts', anchored a warship off the African coast. The ship was shelling the bush:

In the empty immensity of earth, sky, and water, there she was, incomprehensible, firing into a continent. Pop, would go one of the six-inch guns; a small flame would dart and vanish, a little white smoke would disappear, a tiny projectile would give a feeble screech – and nothing happened. Nothing could happen. There was a touch of insanity in the proceedings, a sense of lugubrious drollery in the sight . . .[2]

Afghanistan is being shelled from planes and helicopters whose firepower far exceeds that of the French warship. Many civilian casualties will be inflicted and the war will go on, but otherwise nothing will happen. Nothing *can* happen.

Promoting freedom by force is not so much impractical as nonsensical. Liberal fundamentalists believe freedom can be packaged into a system of rights that can be delivered anywhere in the world, but as the history of the West demonstrates, there is more to freedom, and for that matter to civilization, than a regime of rights. A society can be civilized without recognizing rights, while one based on rights may be tainted with barbarism. Austria–Hungary abolished torture in 1776 as the result of an edict by Maria Theresa, an absolute monarch. More than two hundred years later, the leader of the world's preeminent liberal democracy licensed the practice as part of a worldwide crusade to defend human rights. At the same time habeas corpus – a defence against arbitrary power dating back to medieval times – was indefinitely suspended. In effect the US has undergone a regime shift in which constitutional restraints on executive power that were in force during much of its history no longer apply. With a new president in charge the old regime may be restored, but there can be no guarantee. Regimes come and go.

The renormalization of torture illustrates a theme running throughout the pieces collected here. Progress in science and technology is a fact, whereas progress in ethics and politics is a fiction. There are universal human goods and evils; the abolition of slavery in the nineteenth century was a genuine gain. But advance in civilization is not like the growth of knowledge, which is cumulative and irreversible. Old evils return, usually with new names. What we see as unalterable features of civilized life vanish in the blink of an eye.

When 'Torture: a modest proposal', reprinted as Chapter 21 of the present volume, was first published in the *New Statesman* on 17 February 2003, a few weeks before the invasion of Iraq, many readers viewed it as an exercise in satire without much topical bite. Not all of the readers noticed it was a satire. Despite appearing under the title 'A Modest Proposal for Preventing Torturers in Liberal Democracy from Being Abused, and for Recognizing their Benefit to the Public (with Apologies to Jonathan Swift)' and featuring a photo-shop portrait of me wearing a Swift-like hairpiece, readers telephoned the magazine to cancel their subscription.

At the time I was struck by the loss of cultural memory these calls revealed. Whatever the merits of my own effort, Swift's *Modest Proposal* – suggesting that Irish families suffering from poverty could improve their condition by selling off their children to be eaten by the rich – was once the most celebrated satire in the English language. The indignant calls to the magazine suggested this was no longer the case. The argument that a universal right to be tortured should be enforced, with states that refuse to recognize it being subject to regime change, failed to arouse their suspicions. The proposal that torturers need counselling to overcome the psychological traumas that go with their profession sparked no sense of absurdity. Months and years later I continued to receive protests taking me to task for my indecent suggestions.

By that time reality had overtaken satire. The abuses of Abu Ghraib had been committed, exposed, denied, condemned and forgotten – consigned to the memory hole where awkward facts disappear in Orwell's *1984*. The techniques used to torture Iraqi detainees – sexual assault, simulated electrocution and attacks by dogs, among others – were no longer employed, as far as anyone could tell, in American centres of confinement. Redefined as stressful interrogation techniques, water-boarding and sensory deprivation were adopted as the methods of choice. An administration lauded by neo-conservatives for its stand against moral relativism ditched a moral prohibition that only a few years ago was regarded as absolute. Torture was taken up as a weapon in the fight for human rights, and the liberal torturer became a defining figure of the age.

My modest proposal was written in the belief that when Iraq was invaded torture would be used. The French had used it in Algeria and the Soviets in Afghanistan, in each case on a vast scale. It was on the cards that the Americans, who were fighting a similar neo-colonial war in Iraq, would also use it. The idea that torture might be needed in the 'war on terror' was in the air. Professor Alan Dershowitz, the distinguished Harvard civil libertarian, had already presented his elegantly reasoned arguments for 'torture warrants'. Tony Blair – an exceptionally talented politician with the priceless gift of never doubting his own sincerity – sold the Iraq war as the beginning of a liberal world order in which military intervention would be used to enforce human rights. For many liberals it was an easy sell. Toppling Saddam was part of the war against tyranny, a chapter in the story of human emancipation. If torture aids the noble cause of progress, how can any enlightened person fail to support it?

The ironies here are many layered. The result of a long campaign begun over two hundred years ago by Montesquieu and Voltaire, the prohibition of torture is one of the genuine achievements of the Enlightenment. Yet today partisans of Enlightenment values defend torture as part of the global struggle to defend Enlightenment values against Islamist fundamentalism. Militant liberal interventionists and belligerent neo-conservatives have been prepared to relax the prohibition on the ground that it may be necessary for the continuation of progress.

There are precedents for this position. A previous generation of Enlightenment militants was also ready to use torture as a means to progress. Lenin and Trotsky made the methodical use of terror the basis of Soviet power. Lenin's 'Hanging Order' of December 1918 instructed that capital punishment – which Kerensky's Provisional Government had abolished – be used on peasants who resisted grain-requisitioning, specifying that the hangings take place in full public view. Trotsky defended shooting hostages in the Russian civil war, dismissing criticism as 'Quaker–vegetarian chatter'. Neither Lenin nor Trotsky ever questioned the legitimacy of torture, which the Soviet regime used routinely from the time it came to power. For these progressives torture was an essential weapon in the cause of humanity.

Neo-cons and liberals of the militant tendency who defend the practice of torture are continuing an authentic Enlightenment tradition. Lenin was not mistaken in seeing himself as continuing a European revolutionary project. Soviet Russia and Maoist China were Enlightenment regimes in which progress and terror marched side by side. Even the Nazis were able to invoke a nineteenth-century Enlightenment tradition of 'scientific racism' to rationalize their crimes.

Of course the Enlightenment was a highly contradictory movement. It contained thinkers such as Spinoza, who despite his faith in reason knew that humans would always live by illusions; sceptics such as David Hume, for whom history was the working out of chance events; Schopenhauer, who used the work of Kant – the supreme Enlightenment philosopher – to argue that history is a kind of dream; and Freud – the greatest twentieth-century Enlightenment thinker – who showed that humans could only ever be partially sane. But it was the Enlightenment belief in progress that had mass appeal, and here religion comes back into the picture. Like much else in secular thought the idea of progress is a legacy of Christianity.

Most of the religions that have ever existed lack the idea of salvation. In animism, which is the primordial religion, humans are part of the natural world; they do not need deliverance from it. Even among salvation religions there are many visions of what salvation involves. Pre-Christian Europe contained cults such as the Orphics, who saw it as release from the burden of transmigration – a view also found among Hindus and Buddhists. For Manicheans and Gnostics, it meant emancipation from the material universe.

The belief that salvation is a type of historical event is an innovation, most likely originating around three thousand years ago with the Persian prophet Zoroaster. The belief that history is a battle between good and evil that good can win derives from Zoroastrian traditions. So does the belief, which is unknown in ancient Hebrew thought, in an approaching end-time. For Jesus, the heterodox Jewish prophet from whose teachings Paul invented the Christian religion, salvation meant a new world created by God in a final battle with evil. Despite Augustine's attempt to defuse this millenarian myth it persisted into medieval times, helping make the Middle Ages an era of constant warfare. In modern times the belief that God could defeat evil was translated into secular terms, and became a strand in the Enlightenment. Substitute for God a divinized humanity, and you have the myth that lies behind radical secular politics from the Jacobins onwards.

The impact of this vision went far beyond revolutionary movements. It also produced meliorism – the faith in gradual improvement of liberal humanists, who although they deny any belief in a single, world-transforming event still believe that the world can be remade by human action. Until some time around the second half of the eighteenth century no one believed 'humanity' could fashion the future. When this belief began to spread it was not, as secular humanists like to think, a departure from Christian religion. The Enlightenment was hostile to Christianity, but a Christian framework still shaped the view of history adopted by most Enlightenment thinkers. Ancient Greek and Roman humanists, such as the hedonist philosopher Epicurus and his disciple Lucretius, rejected the religions of their time (without denying the existence of the gods); but their goal was to achieve tranquillity by withdrawing from the world, not to change it. They had no dreams of universal human emancipation. The world-transforming hopes of modern humanism derive not from these ancient thinkers but from Christianity, with its promise that salvation is open to all.

There have been times when belief in progress has been a civilizing force. Before it is anything else civilization is the restraint of violence, and it was the belief in progress that inspired the Enlightenment thinkers who began the campaign for a ban on torture. But it was also belief in progress that fuelled many of the crimes of Communism and colonialism, and which energized the liberal struggle for self-determination that helped release ethnic savagery in inter-war Europe. Another version of the progressive faith licenses torture in the 'war on terror'. In its belief that violence can renew society Islamism is a prototypical modernist movement; it is not by accident that Islamists so often use ideas lifted from Lenin. Yet Islamism is not a threat of the order of Communism or Nazism, and there is no reason why it cannot be contained.

What is worth defending in liberal societies is not their belief in progress. As I argue in the first of the pieces collected here, originally published in my book *Two Faces of Liberalism* (2000), it is the practice of toleration – in other words, the attempt to achieve a civilized *modus vivendi* between different ways of life. The trouble with *modus vivendi* is that it demands a stoical commitment that may be lacking. Faced with the long haul of civilization there will be many who find barbarism more exciting.

At present the most powerful decivilizing force is resource war, which is ultimately a by-product of human population growth. The perennially unpopular Thomas Malthus is featured in the earliest of these essays, 'John Stuart Mill and the idea of progress', published in 1976 and appearing here as Chapter 2, while a Malthusian argument also features in 'An agenda for Green conservatism' (1993), reprinted here as Chapter 24. As Mill argued, it is only when human numbers are controlled that progress in science can be matched by lasting improvement in human affairs. A society in which scientific advance is used to enhance the quality of life rather than increase production or population could be more humanly fulfilling than any that exists today.

Since the essay on Green conservatism was written environmentalism has moved from the fringes of politics on to the centre ground in many countries. In Britain Green ideas have been part of the reinvention of the Conservative Party. But population control remains a taboo, and the stationary-state economy I advocated a decade and a half ago seems to me now just another utopia. As the American paleo-anthropologist and poet Loren Eiseley noted in 1969: 'Basically man's planetary virulence can be ascribed to just one thing: a rapid ascent, particularly during the last three centuries, of an energy ladder so great that the line on the chart representing it would be almost vertical.'[3] Human expansion over the past few centuries is a by-product of fossil fuels. Now these fuels are running out or are too dirty to use safely, and the energy-intensive civilization that enabled the spike in human numbers is no longer viable. A low-energy society using high-tech devices such as nuclear fusion and the artificial synthesis of food is theoretically possible, but humans have overshot the planet's capacity to support them. Whatever is done now cannot alter that fact.

A global resource war is already under way. The first Gulf conflict of 1990–91 was an oil war and nothing else. The conflict in Iraq is also in part an energy war, with the US and its allies, Iraq's several communities and Iran scrambling to secure control of the country's oil. So too are conflicts in post-Soviet regions such as the Caucasus and Central Asia. Again, water wars are brewing in many parts of the world. Behind the incessant rant about democracy and rights it is resource wars that are shaping the future.

A pervasive and probably incurable unreality permeates contemporary politics and culture. The record of the past century shows that incremental change is rare, whereas revolutionary upheaval is normal. Time and again entire societies have vanished and whole ways of life have been extinguished. Yet even the most radical critics of contemporary societies seem to believe their own societies are immortal. It does not occur to them that their civilization may simply disappear as so many others have done in the past. Scientific and technological advance makes this more rather than less likely.

The belief that knowledge is intrinsically benign is perhaps the definitive modern myth. The pacification of the world by canals and railways, the power of radio and television to conjure away tyrants, the role of the Internet in giving birth to a peaceful world – these and many other whimsical hopes have all foundered on the same intractable fact. Knowledge advances, while the human animal stays the same. *Homo rapiens* will not cease to be predatory and destructive, nor will *Homo religiosus* cease to pursue the intimations of faith.

Contemporary humanism is a religion that lacks the insight into human frailty of traditional faiths. In envisioning the universe as the work of a divine person Western monotheism has always been anthropocentric, but it has preserved a sense of mystery, the insight that the nature of things is finally unknowable. In contrast secular rationalists have promoted a type of solipsism. Like the Tlönists of Borges's fable, examined in Chapter 5, they think the real world and their intellectual constructions are – or can be made to be – identical. Hence the ornate theories of justice devised by credulous philosophers, the elaborate systems of incentives designed by *bien-pensant* economists and the recondite schemes for taxing emissions advanced by Greens – just the latest of many attempts to reorder human life by the use of reason.

Humankind is not a collective agent that can decide its destiny. If humans are different from other animals it is chiefly in being governed by myths, which are not creations of the will but creatures of the imagination. Emerging unbidden from subterranean regions, they rule the lives of those they possess. Many of the worst crimes of the last century were the work of people possessed by what they believed to be reason. Science is believed to confer a superior rationality on its initiates, but science cannot make us into a rational animal of the kind imagined by humanist philosophers. Humans can anthropomorphize anything, except themselves.

A little realism would surely be useful. Accepting that we are flawed and our problems not fully soluble need not be paralysing; it could make us more flexible and resourceful. But no realist will try to convert the world. The myth-free civilization of secular rationalism is itself the stuff of myth. Myths are fictions, which cannot be true or false; but fictions can be more or less truthful depending on how they capture human experience. No traditional myth is as untruthful as the modern myth of progress. All prevailing philosophies embody the fiction that human life can be altered at will. Better aim for the impossible, they say, than submit to fate. Invariably, the result is a cult of human self-assertion that soon ends in farce.

The line of thinking that is traced in this book runs in an opposite direction – not only in questioning the idea of progress but also, and more fundamentally, in rejecting the idea that it is only through action that life can be meaningful. Politics is only a small part of human existence, and the human animal only a very small part of the world. Science and technology have given us powers we never had before, but not the ability to refashion our existence as we wish. Poetry and religion are more realistic guides to life.

From one angle the writings collected here can be read as a vivisection of contemporary belief, and some readers are sure to demand a replacement for the creeds that have been dissected. In the current climate of needy uncertainty this is an inevitable reaction, but it also misses the point. In our everyday dealings we all rely on a kind of animal faith in the trustworthiness of things. But belief is dangerous in politics, while the core of religion has never been doctrinal. The life of the spirit is not a matter of subscribing to a set of beliefs, and only people bent on converting the world trouble themselves with creeds. The obsession of secular rationalists with true belief is an inheritance from Christian traditions deformed by Greek philosophy, which from Socrates onwards preached the fanciful dogma that reason, virtue and the good life are, in the end, one and the same. Keats's negative capability – 'being in uncertainties, mysteries, doubts, without any irritable reaching after fact and certainty' – seems to me a more interesting way to live, and more likely to yield glimpses of truth.

The point of showing the flimsiness of all that is seemingly solid is not to come up with an immovable truth, and persuade the reader to accept it. Persuasion is a missionary enterprise, the goal of which is conversion. Instead the aim is to present a record of what one observer has seen, which readers can use as they will.

PART ONE

Liberalism: An Autopsy

I

Modus vivendi

The liberal state originated in a search for *modus vivendi*. Contemporary liberal regimes are late flowerings of a project of toleration that began in Europe in the sixteenth century. The task we inherit is refashioning liberal toleration so that it can guide the pursuit of *modus vivendi* in a more plural world.

Liberal toleration has contributed immeasurably to human well-being. Nowhere so deep-rooted that it can be taken for granted, it is an achievement that cannot be valued too highly. We cannot do without that early modern ideal; but it cannot be our guide in late modern circumstances. For the ideal of toleration we have inherited embodies two incompatible philosophies. Viewed from one side, liberal toleration is the ideal of a rational consensus on the best way of life. From the other, it is the belief that human beings can flourish in many ways of life.

If liberalism has a future, it is in giving up the search for a rational consensus on the best way of life. As a consequence of mass migration, new technologies of communication and continued cultural experimentation, nearly all societies today contain several ways of life, with many people belonging to more than one. The liberal ideal of toleration which looks to a rational consensus on the best way of life was born in societies divided on the claims of a single way of life. It cannot show us how to live together in societies that harbour many ways of life.

Toleration did not begin with liberalism. In ancient Alexandria and Buddhist India, among the Romans, the Moors and the Ottomans, different faiths coexisted in peace for long periods. Yet the ideal of a common life that does not rest on common beliefs is a liberal inheritance. Our task is to consider what becomes of this patrimony in societies which are much more deeply diverse than those in which liberal toleration was conceived.

Liberalism has always had two faces. From one side, toleration is the pursuit of an ideal form of life. From the other, it is the search for terms of peace among different ways of life. In the former view, liberal institutions are seen as applications of universal principles. In the latter, they are a means to peaceful coexistence. In the first, liberalism is a prescription for a universal regime. In the second, it is a project of coexistence that can be pursued in many regimes.

The philosophies of John Locke and Immanuel Kant exemplify the liberal project of a universal regime, while those of Thomas Hobbes and David Hume express the liberalism of peaceful coexistence. In more recent times, John Rawls and F. A. Hayek have defended the first liberal philosophy, while Isaiah Berlin and Michael Oakeshott are exemplars of the second.

The ideal of toleration as a means to truth was stated canonically by Locke. In Locke's account, liberal toleration was far from being sceptical about truth in religion or morality. It presupposed that truth had been found, and imposed a duty on government to promote it. It was toleration of things that were judged to be bad or false.[1]

Locke understood toleration as a pathway to the one true religion. He did not extend toleration to Catholics or atheists, if only because he was not confident that persuasion would lead them to that faith. Locke's defence of toleration was that it enables us to discover the best life for humankind. He never doubted that there was such a thing. Throughout its history, the liberal ideal of toleration as a means to a universal rational consensus has rested on the same conviction.

Yet from the beginnings of liberal thought there was another understanding of toleration. Nothing in Hobbes suggests he favoured toleration as a pathway to the true faith. For him, toleration was a strategy of peace. Indifferent to belief, the sole concern of government was with practice. In this Hobbesian view, the end of toleration is not consensus. It is coexistence.[2]

For liberal thinkers who sought a rational consensus on the best life, toleration was a remedy for the limitations of human understanding. As Voltaire put it: 'What is toleration? It is the appurtenance of humanity. We are all full of weakness and errors; let us mutually pardon each other for our follies.'[3] Liberal thinkers have never been over-sanguine about the prospects of people reaching agreement in their beliefs about the good life. They have always been too conscious of the force of the passions to view reason as anything more than a frail power in human affairs.

It was this manifest imperfection of human reason that underpinned the ideal of toleration as a means to consensus. The hope of a rational consensus on values supports the liberal philosophies that prevail today. Yet the idea that the persistence of many ways of life is a mark of imperfection has little to support it.

Rational inquiry in ethics does not yield consensus on the best life. It shows that the good life comes in many varieties. The idea that the exercise of reason produces agreement is at least as old as Plato's Socrates. Even so, there has never been much to support it. Reason can enlighten us as to our ethical conflicts. Often, it shows them to be deeper than we thought, and leaves us in the lurch as to how to resolve them.

Liberal regimes are often viewed as solutions to a modern problem of pluralism. Yet what is most notable about the early modern societies from which liberal regimes emerged is how homogeneous they were. Few, if any, late modern societies display as much consensus in their values and beliefs. It is not only that they differ greatly from one another. Most of them contain several ways of life, honouring different goods and virtues.

The fact that society contains different forms of ethical life is far from being peculiarly modern. On the contrary, in their diversity of ways of life late modern societies have something in common with the ancient world. What is new in the modern world is not acceptance of diversity in styles of life. It is hostility to hierarchies.

The cultures from which European moral philosophy emerged contained many forms of ethical life. Greek polytheism expressed the belief that the sources of value are irreducibly plural. If it recognized the idea of the best human life, it was one in which many distinct and at times conflicting sources of value were honoured. In their acceptance of many sources of value, the Greeks were at one with other ancient cultures: ancient Judaism imposed few universal obligations;

Hinduism recognized different duties in different stations and stages of life.

Ancient societies were more hospitable to differences than ours. This is partly because the idea of human equality was weak or absent. Modernity begins not with the recognition of difference but with a demand for uniformity. There is nothing new in the idea that the good life may vary with different people. To think that it is distinctively modern is a mere prejudice.

Ancient pluralism found few echoes in Greek philosophy. The founders of European ethical theory were monists. Neither Plato nor Aristotle was in any doubt that one way of life was best for humankind. Whether the good for humans was finally one, as Plato imagined, or many, as Aristotle was sometimes ready to admit, the best kind of life was the same for everyone – even though they never doubted that it could be lived fully only by a few leisured Greek males. In this classical view, conflicting judgements about the human good are symptoms of error. For the founders of European ethical theory, as for the Christians who came after them, conflicts of value were signs of imperfection, not a normal part of ethical life.

From its beginnings, moral philosophy has been a struggle to exorcize conflict from ethical life. The same is true of political thought. European political philosophy has been deeply marked by the resistance to conflict that shaped Greek ethics. In the city, as in the soul, harmony has been the ideal. Most liberal thinkers have taken over the Socratic, Christian and Enlightenment faith in the harmony of values. But an ideal of harmony is not the best starting-point for thinking about ethics or government. It is better to begin by understanding why conflict – in the city as in the soul – cannot be avoided.

In the form that we have inherited it, liberal toleration is an ideal of rational consensus. As heirs to that project, we need an ideal based not on a rational consensus on the best way of life, nor on reasonable disagreement about it, but instead on the truth that humans will always have reason to live differently. *Modus vivendi* is such an ideal. It embodies an older current of liberal thought about toleration, and applies it to our own new circumstances.

Modus vivendi expresses the belief that there are many forms of life in which humans can thrive. Among these there are some whose worth cannot be compared. Where such ways of life are rivals, there is no one of them that is best. People who belong to different ways of life need have no disagreement. They may simply be different.

Whereas our inherited conception of toleration presupposes that one way of life is best for all of humankind, *modus vivendi* accepts that there are many forms of life, some of them no doubt yet to be contrived, in which humans can flourish. For the predominant ideal of liberal toleration, the best life may be unattainable, but it is the same for all. From a standpoint of *modus vivendi*, no kind of life can be the best for everyone. The human good is too diverse to be realized in any life. Our inherited ideal of toleration accepts with regret the fact that there are many ways of life. If we adopt *modus vivendi* as our ideal we will welcome it.

Ethical inquiry does not yield a single way of life or scheme of values for all – not even for a single individual. Instead it shows that people have reason to live in different ways. Different ways of life embody incompatible aspects of the human good. So, in different contexts, may a single human life. Yet no life can reconcile fully the rival values that the human good contains.

The aim of *modus vivendi* cannot be to still the conflict of values. It is to reconcile individuals and ways of life honouring conflicting values to a life in common. We do not need common values in order to live together in peace. We need common institutions in which many forms of life can coexist.

The span of good lives of which humans are capable cannot be contained in any one community or tradition. The good for humans is too beset by conflict for that to be possible. For the same reason, the good life cannot be contained in any one political regime. A theory of *modus vivendi* is not the search for an ideal regime, liberal or otherwise. It has no truck with the notion of an ideal regime. It aims to find terms on which different ways of life can live well together.

Modus vivendi is liberal toleration adapted to the historical fact of pluralism. The ethical theory underpinning *modus vivendi* is value-pluralism. The most fundamental value-pluralist claim is that there are many conflicting kinds of human flourishing, some of which cannot be compared in value. Among the many kinds of good lives that humans can live there are some that are neither better nor worse than one another, nor the same in worth, but incommensurably – that is to say, differently – valuable. Even so, there may be good reasons for preferring some incommensurable goods over others.

Value-pluralism is closer to ethical theories which affirm the possibility of moral knowledge than it is to familiar kinds of ethical scepticism, subjectivism or relativism. It enables us to reject some judgements about the good as being in error. At the same time, it means giving up a traditional notion of truth in ethics. To affirm that the good is plural is to allow that it harbours conflicts for which there is no one solution that is right. It is not that there can be no right solution in such conflicts. Rather, there are many.

The good is independent of our perspectives on it, but it is not the same for all. It is not just that different ways of life honour different goods and virtues. More, what one way of life praises another condemns. Value-pluralism is the claim that both may be right. This claim is paradoxical. It seems to imply a tolerance of contradiction that classical logic prohibits. There is paradox here, but not – or so I shall argue – of the kind that should concern us. It may be that the good cannot contain contradictions; but it shows itself in ways of life that are incompatible.

Conflicts of value need not express any uncertainty, practical or intellectual, about what is good. At their starkest, they exclude any such uncertainty. They are conflicts within the good itself. However variously they may be understood, peace and justice are universal goods; but sometimes they make demands that are incompatible. When peace and justice are rivals, which is worse, war or injustice? Neither has automatic or universal priority. Peace may be more urgent than justice; the claims of justice may override the immediate needs of peace. In conflicts of this kind, people need not differ about the content of the good or the right. Where they differ is on how their rival claims are to be reconciled.

Justice does not speak always with one voice. The communities that are locked in conflict in Israel and Ulster may claim that they invoke the same principles of justice. Yet their judgements of what is just and what unjust in the context of their contemporary conflicts are deeply at odds. In part, this reflects their different interpretations of their shared history. Partly, no doubt, it is also an expression of the fact that their interests are in many ways opposed. When communities contend for power over scarce resources, they are likely to seek to justify their rival interests by arguments of fairness. Where interests are at odds and political power is at stake, shared principles of justice are likely to yield incompatible judgements of what justice demands.

But conflicts over what justice demands do not come only from these familiar facts. Justice itself makes incompatible demands. When justice requires that restitution be made for injustice done to communities in the past, the result may be unjust to present generations. A claim for the return of land that was unjustly expropriated may collide with a no less just claim to the land that is based on generations of working it. Such conflicts do not arise from an imperfect sense of justice. They express the truth that justice itself encompasses conflicting values.

Even if a conception of justice could be formulated that received universal assent, it would make conflicting demands about which reasonable people could differ. Once again, this is not because human reason is imperfect. It is because incompatible solutions of such conflicts can be equally reasonable.

That conflicts between universal values can be settled in incompatible ways is one reason why people belong to different ways of life. The many ways in which humans can live well embody different settlements among discordant universal values. Contrary to the liberal ideal of toleration, the fact of divergent ways of life is not a result of the frailty of reason. It embodies the truth that humans have reason to live differently.

At the same time, some conflicts of value do arise from rival views of the good. They come not from rivalry among values that are universal but from the different goods that are honoured in particular ways of life. Some goods that are central in some ways of life are absent, or else marginal, in others. In late modern societies, personal autonomy and romantic love are highly valued; but these rival goods are far from being valued by everyone. Today, as in the past, there are ways of life that do not celebrate them, or which condemn them.

To be caught between the demands of different ways of life is a common source of moral conflict. Many people face conflicts among values for which there is no single right solution. The fact that ways of life honour different goods and virtues is not a mark of imperfection. It is a sign that humans can live well in different ways.

Yet not all ways of life allow humans to live well. There are universal human goods and evils. Some virtues are needed for any kind of human flourishing. Without courage and prudence no life can go well. Without sympathy for the suffering and happiness of others, the artefact of justice cannot be maintained. Forms of life that are deficient in these virtues are lacking in the conditions of human well-being. Such values are generically human. Because they are universal they can be used to assess any particular way of life.

That some values are incommensurable does not mean that all ways of life have the same value. The bottom line for value-pluralism is the diversity of goods and evils, not of ways of life. Different ways of life can be more or less successful in achieving universal goods, mitigating universal evils and in resolving conflicts among them.

Even so, universal values do not fit together to compose an ideal life – for the species, for particular societies or for individuals. Rather, if universal values can be rivals, there can be no such thing as an ideal life. There may be a best life for any individual; but not one that is without loss. In particular ways of life there may be better or worse solutions to conflicts of value; but none that meets fully every legitimate claim. There are better and worse regimes, and some that are thoroughly illegitimate; but none that fully realizes all universal values, and is thereby a model for all the rest.

The most fundamental differences among ways of life arise from the manner in which they deal with conflicts among values that are universal. Universal values enable us to assess particular ways of life; but they do not add up to a universal morality.

In the world as we find it, even the barest requirements of a life worth living cannot all be always met in full. Toppling a tyranny may trigger civil war. Protecting a broad range of liberal freedoms may result in the regime that guarantees them being short lived. At the same time, supporting a strong state as a bulwark against anarchy may worsen the abuse of power. Wise policy can temper these conflicts. It cannot hope to overcome them.

Conflicts of value go with being human. The reason is not that human beings have rival beliefs about the good life. Nor is it – though this comes closer to the nub of the matter – that the right action sometimes has wrong as its shadow. It is that human needs make conflicting demands. The idea of a human life that is without conflicts of value runs aground on the contradictions of human needs.

It is not only that, because they make incompatible demands on scarce material resources, human needs may be practically at odds. More, they can be met fully only in forms of life that cannot be combined. The lives of a professional soldier and a carer in a leprosarium, of a day trader on the stock market and a contemplative in a monastery, cannot be mixed without loss. Such lives embody virtues that do not easily coexist; and they may express beliefs that are contradictory. Yet each answers to a human need.

The best human lives are very different from one another, and often incompatible. This is not a truth of logic. It is a fact about human nature. As such it is not unalterable. Perhaps, as technologies of genetic engineering advance, human beings will be tempted to alter the biological endowments that have enabled them to live in so many different ways. There is nothing to say such attempts cannot succeed; but if they do they will destroy much that has hitherto been of value in human life.

Conflicts of value come from the competing needs of our common human nature. A kind of moral scarcity is built into the fabric of human life. It is because human needs are contradictory that no human life can be perfect. That does not mean that human life is imperfect. It means that the idea of perfection has no meaning. The idea of conflicting and incommensurable values is far from the Augustinian notion that all things human are imperfect. Augustine contrasted the imperfection of the human world with the perfection of the divine. By contrast, rivalry between incommensurable values destroys the very idea of perfection.

The fact that good harbours conflicts of value does not mean that the human condition must always be tragic. To be sure, tragic choices cannot be eliminated from ethical life. Where universal values make conflicting demands, the right action may contain wrong. When values clash in this way, there may be irreparable loss. Then there is surely tragedy.

But the plurality of values signifies more than simply tragedy. It means that there are many kinds of life in which humans can thrive. Where these lives are so different from one another that their worth cannot be compared, it makes little sense to speak of gain or loss. When such lives cannot be combined, they need not be antagonists; they may be alternatives. If we choose among them, as sometimes we must, the choice need not be tragic. It may simply bespeak the abundance of flourishing lives that is open to us.

If this is true, it has always been so. Value-pluralism is an account of ethical life, not an intepretation of pluralism in late modern societies. If it is true, it is a truth about human nature, not the contemporary condition. Nevertheless, value-pluralism has a special application to late modern societies.

In nearly all contemporary societies the coexistence of many ways of life is an established fact. Though distinct, these ways of life are not independent. They interact continuously – so much so that it may be hard to tell the difference between them. Indeed, since many people belong to more than one, it may be impossible to distinguish them completely. Ways of life are tricky things to get to know. They do not come ready labelled. There is no sure-fire method of enumerating them. And they come in many varieties.

There is the way of life of religious fundamentalists and secular liberals, of countryfolk and 'young urban professionals', of Taliban and Quakers, of first-generation immigrants and that of their children, of Homer's warrior-class, the Desert Fathers and twenty-first-century Hasids, and indefinitely many more. It is impossible to specify the necessary and sufficient conditions that must be met for a style of human activity to qualify as a way of life. Nor is it necessary. We can distinguish them by a loose bundle of criteria.

Ways of life must be practised by a number of people, not only one, span the generations, have a sense of themselves and be recognized by others, exclude some people and have some distinctive practices, beliefs and values, and so forth. Often these criteria do not yield a clear result. Two communities may honour many of the same values but be locked in an historical conflict. We might say of them that they have the same way of life but are divided in their allegiances to the regime under which they live. (Think of Ulster.) Or two communities may have distinctive and opposed beliefs about the historical sources of their present conflicts, contrasting attitudes to a number of social issues, and a strong propensity to exclude one another (by avoiding intermarriage, for example). Then we might be inclined to say they have conflicting ways of life. (Think again of Ulster.) What counts as a way of life may not always be decidable.

When the standard types of contemporary liberal thought refer to pluralism they mean the diversity of personal ethical beliefs and ideals. That is not the kind of pluralism that should most concern political philosophy. Late modern societies are notable for the diversity of ways of life they contain. Immigration and the partial erosion of the cohesive national cultures that were constructed earlier in the modern period have increased the number of ethnic and cultural traditions that coexist in the same societies. At the same time, continuing cultural experimentation has produced a number of new styles of life. *This* fact of pluralism was not foreseen in liberal thought. Even now it has not been fully comprehended.

The conflicts of value that rightly shape the agenda of political thought come not from the divergent ideals of individuals but from the rival claims of ways of life. Recent liberal orthodoxy passes over these conflicts because it takes for granted that one way of life is dominant in society. In contrast, value-pluralism has particular relevance to late modern societies in which, by choice, chance or fate, many ways of life have come to coexist.

Liberal thought needs revision if the ideal of toleration is to be refashioned to suit this circumstance. In standard liberal accounts, pluralism refers to a diversity of personal ideals. Liberal thought rarely addresses the deeper diversity that comes when there are different ways of life in the same society and even in the lives of the same individual. Yet it is this latter sort of pluralism that should set the agenda of thought about ethics and government today.

To think of this condition as a peculiar disability of modern times is mistaken.[4] The pot-pourri sometimes called Western civilization has always contained conflicting values. Greek, Roman, Christian and Jewish traditions each contain distinctive goods and virtues that cannot be translated fully into the ethical life of the others. The notion of a 'Western tradition' in which these irreconcilable elements were once fused cannot withstand philosophical – or historical – scrutiny. There was never a coherent synthesis of these values, nor could there have been. Still, for many centuries, these diverse inheritances were subordinated in European societies to a single ethical ideal. With all its doctrinal variations, and the many prudent allowances it made for the intractability of human nature, the Christian ideal of life succeeded in subjugating or marginalizing others that had been part of the European inheritance for centuries or millennia. Liberalism needs to be rethought to fit a context in which different ideals of life coexist in the same societies – and often the same individuals.

In recent liberal writings, the fact of pluralism refers to a diversity of personal ideals whose place is in the realm of voluntary association. The background idea here is that of the autonomous individual selecting a particular style of life. This type of diversity resembles the diversity of ethnic cuisines that can be found in some cities. Like the choice of an ethnic restaurant, the adoption of a personal ideal occurs in private life. But the fact of pluralism is not the trivial and banal truth that individuals hold to different personal ideals. It is the coexistence of different ways of life. Conventional liberal thought contrives to misunderstand this fact, because it takes for granted a consensus on liberal values.

In reality, though there is unprecedented lip-service to them, most late modern societies contain little consensus on liberal values. Many people belong at once in a liberal form of life and in communities which do not honour liberal values. At the same time, many who stand chiefly in liberal ethical life do not subscribe to some of its traditional values. The liberal ideal of personal autonomy is the idea of being part-author of one's life. For some, the pursuit of autonomy comes into conflict with allegiance to an established community. For others, it is in tension with the freedom to respond to the needs of the present. For all these kinds of people, 'traditional', 'liberal' and 'post-modern', ethical life is inescapably hybrid.

Most late modern societies are far from exhibiting an overlapping consensus on liberal values. Rather, the liberal discourse of rights and personal autonomy is deployed in a continuing conflict to gain and hold power by communities and ways of life having highly diverse values. Where it exists, the hegemony of liberal discourse is often skin-deep.

If it can be found anywhere, an overlapping consensus on liberal values should exist in the United States. And it is true that in the USA there is virtually no group that does not invoke liberal principles. Yet America is no different from the rest of the world in being riven by conflicts between ways of life. The quarter of the American population that espouses creationism, 'the right to life' and other fundamentalist causes does not repudiate liberal values explicitly – as people with similar beliefs might do elsewhere in the world. It appropriates them for its own purposes. The strategic deployment of liberal discourse for fundamentalist ends by a large segment of the population is not a consensus on liberal values. It is practically the opposite. Like other late modern societies, the United States is not hegemonically liberal but morally pluralist.

Recent liberal thinkers claim that the appropriate response to the fact of pluralism is a 'theory of justice'. The 'political liberalism' of John Rawls and his followers claims to advance an account of justice that can be accepted by people who have different conceptions of the good. According to this recent orthodoxy, the liberal state is not just one among a number of regimes that can be legitimate. It is the only mode of political organization that can ever be fully legitimate. In recent liberal thought this claim is conjoined with another – that what makes a liberal state legitimate is its protection of human rights.

For Rawls, as for Ronald Dworkin, F. A. Hayek and Robert Nozick, political philosophy is a branch of the philosophy of law – the branch which concerns justice and fundamental rights. The goal of political philosophy is an ideal constitution, in principle universally applicable, which specifies a fixed framework of basic liberties and human rights. This framework sets the terms – the only terms – on which different ways of life may coexist.

These thinkers claim that conflicts among goods and ways of life can be resolved by reading off the requirements of justice or rights. But the requirements of justice and rights can and do conflict. It is not just that the demands of one right may clash with those of another. A single right may make incompatible demands. There is no uniquely rational way of resolving these conflicts. This truth has large consequences. It means that there can be no such thing as an ideally liberal regime. Because rights make conflicting demands that can reasonably be resolved in different ways, the very idea of such a regime is a mistake.

To say that there cannot be an ideal political regime is not to mount a defence of imperfection in politics. It is to reject the idea of an ideal regime. Different regimes can rightly resolve conflicts among vital human rights in different ways. Some such settlements are better than others, but there is nothing which says that the best regimes will resolve conflicts among rights in similar ways.

On the contrary, because their circumstances and histories vary so much, the best regimes are very different from one another. (So are the worst.) Politics abounds in tragic choices. Even so, it is not because of the tragedies of politics that the idea of an ideal regime lacks sense. It is because the best regimes come in many varieties.

When we differ deeply as to the content of the good, an appeal to rights will not help us. For in that case we will differ as to which rights we have. Fundamental differences about rights express rival conceptions of the good. When rational inquiry leaves our views of the good deeply at odds, it is vain to appeal to rights. Basic human rights can be justified as giving protection against universal human evils; but even such rights clash with one another, and incompatible settlements of their conflicts can be equally legitimate. When universal evils clash, no theory of rights can tell us what to do.

It is the same with social justice. We cannot avoid judgements of fairness regarding the distribution of goods in society. The notion that fairness in procedures is all that society needs in the way of a shared conception of justice, which Hayek made familiar,[5] has little to be said for it. Yet no contemporary society contains a consensus on fairness that is deep or wide enough to ground a 'theory of justice'.

There is no more consensus on what justice means than there is on the character of the good. If anything, there is less. Among the virtues, justice is one of the most shaped by convention. For that reason it is among the most changeable.

When many ways of life share the same society, it is natural that the sense of justice should vary. It is therefore hardly surprising that liberal philosophers differ about the most fundamental requirements of justice. Today, most liberal thinkers affirm that justice is the supreme virtue of social institutions; but some declare that it demands equal distribution of social goods, others that it requires respect for the supposed fact that each of us owns his or her natural endowments, yet others that it involves matching resources with basic needs or merits – and still others that it has nothing to do with distribution at all. Such differences are to be expected. They mirror differences in moral outlook in the wider society. What is surprising is that they are not seen as an objection to the enterprise that most contemporary liberal thinkers have in common – the attempt to construct a theory of justice. When recent liberal thinkers claim that liberalism is a strictly political doctrine, they mean that it does not depend on any comprehensive conception of the good. They never tire of telling us that the demands of justice must take priority over any ideal of the good. They appear to have overlooked the fact that different views of the good support different views of justice.

Only this oversight can account for the fact that in 'political liberalism' nothing of importance is left to political decision. The basic liberties and the distribution of social goods are matters of justice, and in political liberalism what justice demands is a matter not for political decision but for legal adjudication. The central institution of Rawls's 'political liberalism' is not a deliberative assembly such as a parliament. It is a court of law. All fundamental issues are removed from political deliberation in order to be adjudicated by a Supreme Court. The self-description of Rawlsian doctrine as political liberalism is supremely ironic. In fact, Rawls's doctrine is a species of anti-political legalism.[6]

Liberal legalists differ about the rights we have. Egalitarian legalists, such as Rawls and Dworkin, think we have welfare rights to resources, whereas libertarian legalists such as Nozick and Hayek insist that the only human rights are rights against aggression and coercion. These are fundamental differences. They reflect different beliefs about whether human beings can be said to own themselves, how they acquire property rights in natural resources, and what their well-being consists in.

Liberal legalists are at one chiefly in their common illusion that their views on rights do not express rival views of the good. In reality, Rawls and Hayek have opposed conceptions of justice, not because they take different stances in the philosophy of right, but because they hold to antagonistic conceptions of the good life. In their accounts, as in all theories of rights and justice, differing views of rights spring from different views of the good.

What these egalitarian and libertarian variants of liberal legalism have in common is more fundamental than the points at which they differ. Each supposes that principles of justice and rights can be formulated that are at once highly determinate and ideally universal. (That the later Rawls appears to have retreated from the ideal of universality does not affect the present argument.)[7]

Libertarian liberals such as Nozick believe that a universal economic system is required by justice. For them, rights of property and laws of contract are not social and legal conventions, which can reasonably vary in accordance with the changing requirements of human well-being. They are direct applications of universal human rights. It is not merely that modern economies cannot prosper without well-functioning market institutions. Rather, the institutions of the market embody timeless dictates of justice. Indeed, on this strange view, only a single type of market economy – the highly singular type of capitalism found intermittently in some English-speaking countries over the past century or so – is fully compatible with the demands of justice.[8]

Thinking of market freedoms in this way, as derivations from fundamental human rights, is a fundamental error. Like other human freedoms, the freedoms embodied in market institutions are justified inasmuch as they meet human needs. Insofar as they fail to do this they can reasonably be altered. This is true not only of the rights that are involved in market institutions. It is true of all human rights.

The institutions of the market advance human well-being to the extent that they enable individuals and communities with different or incompatible goals and interests to trade with one another to mutual advantage. This classical defence of market institutions can be given another formulation. Individuals and communities animated by rival and (in part) incommensurable values can interact in markets without needing to reconcile these rival conceptions of the good. Market institutions assist personal autonomy and social pluralism by enabling such communities to replace destructive conflict by beneficial competition. In short, there is a value-pluralist defence of market institutions; but there is no one best variety of market institutions, either for every society or for every context in a single society.

Markets are not free-standing. They are highly complex legal and cultural institutions. They do most to promote pluralism and autonomy when they are complemented by other, non-market institutions. Without the 'positive' freedoms conferred by enabling welfare institutions, the 'negative' liberties of the market are of limited value.[9]

Egalitarian liberals such as Rawls do not claim that only one kind of economic system can be just. They recognize that justice can be realized in a variety of economic systems. Depending on historical circumstances, sometimes socialism may be best, at others some species of capitalism. In Rawlsian theory, justice is silent on the choice of economic systems. Despite this, whatever system is chosen must satisfy Rawls's principles of distribution.[10]

This last requirement presupposes that an overlapping consensus on distributive issues can be reached across the numerous ways of life that exist in late modern societies. But insofar as different ways of life are animated by different ideals of the good, they will think of issues of distribution differently. A strongly individualist way of life will take for granted that the social unit of distribution is the individual. Others will nominate the family or intermediate social institutions for that purpose.

The several ways of life that may be found in most contemporary societies do not share a conception of the primary goods of human life. They are animated by different conceptions of the good life, which may overlap enough to make compromise possible, but which have too little in common to permit the development of a single, overarching conception of justice.

For liberal legalists, when different ways of life clash, all that needs to be done is to ask what justice demands. Once the principles governing an ideally liberal constitution have been stated, they need only to be applied. Applying the law is applying a theory of justice to particular cases; and there are no hard cases that cannot be decided. But when society contains not one but many ways of life, each with its own conception of the good, will there not be as much divergence in views of fairness as there is in understandings of the good? When ways of life differ widely in their view of the good, will they not support different views of justice?

Liberal legalists aim to circumvent conflict about the good life by appealing to ideas of justice and rights. In this they claim a lineage that goes back to Kant, who sought to develop a political philosophy based solely on the right. Whether or not this is a correct interpretation of Kant, a pure philosophy of right is a quixotic enterprise. The right can never be prior to the good. Without the content that can be given it only by a conception of the good, the right is empty.

A strictly political liberalism, which is dependent at no point on any view of the good, is an impossibility. The central categories of such a liberalism – 'rights', 'justice' and the like – have a content only insofar as they express a view of the good. At the same time, insofar as they have any definite content, claims about rights and justice are enmeshed in conflicts of value. If we differ about the good life, we are bound to differ about justice and rights. Political liberalism presupposes that justice can stand aloof from conflicting claims about the good. In truth the enterprise of a theory of justice is undone by these conflicts.

Recent liberal political philosophy ascribes infinite weight to a value that is almost infinitely complex. The requirements of justice are not everywhere the same. Because expectations vary from society to society, what is just in one may be unjust in another. What justice demands is not a matter of subjective preference, but it varies with history and circumstances.

Universal human values do not generate a single view of justice. They frame constraints on what can count as a reasonable compromise between rival values and ways of life. In this way, universal human values set ethical limits on the pursuit of *modus vivendi*. Like liberal toleration, *modus vivendi* is far from being the idea that anything goes.

Peaceful coexistence is not an *a priori* value. In this it is no different from any other human good. It is desirable only insofar as it serves human goals and needs. There is no argument which shows that all ways of life are bound to pursue it. Nevertheless, nearly all ways of life have interests in common that make *modus vivendi* desirable for them. Even ways of life that do not recognize any ideal of toleration may have reason to seek peaceful coexistence. So, equally, do 'liberal' and 'non-liberal' regimes. Yet there are limits to *modus vivendi*.

Liberals and pluralists walk side by side in resisting totalitarian and fundamentalist regimes. *Modus vivendi* is impossible in a regime in which the varieties of the good are seen as symptoms of error or heresy. Without institutions in which different ways of life are accorded respect there cannot be peaceful coexistence between them. Where liberal regimes foster this coexistence, pluralists are bound to support them.

Nevertheless, when liberals set up one regime as a standard of legitimacy for all the rest, pluralists and liberals part company. For pluralists, a liberal regime may sometimes be the best framework for *modus vivendi*. At other times a non-liberal regime may do as well, or better.

The distinction between liberal and non-liberal regimes is not categorical; but that does not mean we cannot tell the difference between them. It means only that a liberal regime cannot be identified by reference to any set of common features. We distinguish liberal from illiberal regimes by a number of marks, none of which is possessed by all. We recognize liberal regimes not by their having any essential properties but by their family resemblances.

It is a mark of an illiberal regime that conflicts of value are viewed as signs of error. Yet liberal regimes which claim that one set of liberties – their own – is universally legitimate adopt precisely that view. They treat conflicts among liberties as symptoms of error, not dilemmas to which different solutions can be reasonable. Liberalism of this kind is a species of fundamentalism, not a remedy for it.

It is commonly held that value-pluralism supports liberalism as a political ideal. The truth is nearer the opposite. If a pluralist account of the human good is true, the claims of fundamentalist liberalism are spurious. From the standpoint of value-pluralism, all conflicts between rival claims about the best life for humankind are collisions of illusions. Universal religions fall into this category.[11] So do most Enlightenment political philosophies.

Inasmuch as they prescribe a single way of life, or a small family of ways of life, as being right or best for all humankind, universal religions are incompatible with the truth of value-pluralism. Common experience and the evidences of history show human beings thriving in forms of life that are very different from one another. None can reasonably claim to embody the flourishing that is uniquely human. If there is anything distinctive about the human species, it is that it can thrive in a variety of ways.

The truth that there are many varieties of human flourishing is no less incompatible with the universalist political projects that have emerged from the Enlightenment. Not only liberals but Marxists and social democrats have held that the human good is such that it can only be fully embodied in a single, universal regime.[12] In their different ways, each of these political philosophies is committed to the Enlightenment project of a universal civilization.

To affirm that humans thrive in many different ways is not to deny that there are universal human values. Nor is it to reject the claim that there should be universal human rights. It is to deny that universal values can only be fully realized in a universal regime. Human rights can be respected in a variety of regimes, liberal and otherwise. Universal human rights are not an ideal constitution for a single regime throughout the world, but a set of minimum standards for peaceful coexistence among regimes that will always remain different.

Liberal universalists are right that some values are universal. They are wrong in identifying universal values with their own particular ideals. Human rights are not a charter giving universal authority to liberal values. They are a benchmark of minimal legitimacy for societies whose values are different.

Liberal relativists are wrong in thinking there are no universal values. They are right that liberal values belong in one way of life, or a family of ways of life, and have no universal authority. At the same time, they are mistaken in supposing that liberal societies can abandon their universalist claims without being altered profoundly.

Liberal societies claim to be the only legitimate embodiment of universal values. All others are judged as approximations to themselves. This claim to universal authority has entered deeply into the self-image of liberal cultures. Insofar as a pluralist view of human values spreads, it is bound to undermine this self-understanding.

Value-pluralism does not leave everything as it is. It is a subversive doctrine. It undermines all claims about the best life for the species.

Accordingly, it is inimical to fundamentalism of every kind, whether it originates in religious faith or in the dogmas of the Enlightenment.

Totalitarian and fundamentalist regimes claim that conflicts of value are illusory – at any rate in the long run of history, or in heaven. If value-pluralism is true, that claim itself embodies an illusion. Pluralism about values undermines illiberal claims about harmony. At the same time, it works to subvert the self-interpretation of liberal cultures in which they are precursors of a universal regime or way of life.[13]

Universal values are not the ground of a universal civilization. Through their conflicts they explain the fact that no such thing has ever existed. The persistence of many ways of life is a natural response to species-wide conflicts. Humans are highly inventive animals. From universal conflicts they are continuously devising particular forms of life. Unless new technologies succeed in altering human endowments radically, this will always be true.

The belief that we are destined to live in a universal civilization is a commonplace in societies shaped by Enlightenment thinking. Yet it has scant support in history. In truth, it is not a result of historical inquiry, but rather the product of a discredited philosophy of history.

All political philosophies express a philosophy of history. This is most obviously true of those varieties of liberalism that deny possessing any such thing. The Rawlsian school affects a stance of neutrality or silence regarding questions in the philosophy of history. Yet Rawls's political philosophy can claim to be something more than the pursuit of the intimations of American academic liberals only if its account of the fact of pluralism fits a broad range of modern societies.

In truth, Rawls's interpretation of the fact of pluralism and his account of overlapping consensus are relevant to the majority of contemporary societies only if they are destined to become increasingly like the United States – as Rawls imagines it to be. In effect, this is to subscribe to a specific interpretation of history – an Americocentric version of a Positivist philosophy which affirms that as societies become more modern they are bound to become more alike.

Describing the Positivist interpretation of history, Stuart Hampshire writes:

The positivists believed that all societies across the globe will gradually discard their traditional attachments . . . because of the need for rational, scientific and experimental modes of thought which a modern industrial economy involves. This is an old faith, widespread in the nineteenth century, that there must be a step-by-step convergence on liberal values, on 'our values'.

The difficulty with this theory, as Hampshire concludes, is that it has been falsified by history: 'We now know there is no "must" about it and that all such theories have a predictive value of zero.'[14]

This Positivist interpretation of history has had a practical influence. Since the last decades of the twentieth century many governments and some transnational institutions have formed their policies on the unexamined assumption that only one economic system is compatible with the requirements of modernity. In this, they are influenced by neo-liberal ideologues who believe that in promoting the free market they are easing the birth of a universal economic system that history would anyway have made inevitable.

The idea that only one kind of economic system is compatible with modernity is of a piece with the notion that as different societies become more modern they are bound to become more alike. In fact, as different societies become more modern, they develop different modes of economic life. In Japan, modernization has meant not the replication of any other mode of economic life, but instead the development of an indigenous variety of capitalism which has many unique features. The same is true in India and China.

Subject to constraints of geography, competition and power, different societies develop modes of economic life that express their different ways of life. Where, as in most late modern societies, there are several ways of life, there tend to be a number of distinct types of productive enterprise, expressing different family structures, religious beliefs and values.

The notion that all modern economies are converging on a single mode of economic life does not square with history. It is a remnant of early nineteenth-century speculative sociology which became embedded in later thought. Like Marxists in the 1930s, contemporary neo-liberals are unwitting disciples of a defunct Positivist ideology.[15]

The belief that modern societies will everywhere converge on the same values does not result from historical inquiry. It is a confession of faith. In fact late modern societies show little evidence of any such consensus. They differ from each other too much.

There are many ways of being modern. Different societies absorb science and engender new technologies without accepting the same values. The idea that modern societies are much the same everywhere, which is still defended by Enlightenment fundamentalists, has scant support in history. Like many of the hopes bequeathed by the Enlightenment, it is a fleeting shadow of monotheism.[16]

Liberal toleration is an ambiguous inheritance. From one side, it is an ideal of rational consensus. From the other, it is a solution to a problem of peaceful coexistence. These are not variations on a single ideal. They are rival projects, expressing rival philosophies – not least, rival philosophies of history.

In practical life, seeking compromise among irreconcilable aims is a mark of wisdom. In intellectual life, it is a sign of confusion. In present circumstances, attempting to preserve the liberal ideal of toleration as a means of reaching a rational consensus is harmful. It makes the practice of coexistence contingent on an expectation of increasing convergence in values that is fated to be disappointed.

If the liberal project is to be renewed, the ambiguity that has haunted it from its origins must be resolved. The idea of toleration as a means to a universal consensus on values must be given up, with the adoption instead of a project of *modus vivendi* among ways of life animated by permanently divergent values.

Like any other political philosophy, *modus vivendi* articulates a view of the good. It is an application of value-pluralism to political practice. It tells us to reject theories which promise a final resolution of moral conflicts, since their result in practice can only be to diminish the goods that have generated our conflicts.

When it is applied to the ethical life of individuals, value-pluralism suggests that seeking a compromise among values and ways of life whose claims cannot be fully reconciled need not be unreasonable. On the contrary, the struggle to honour incompatible claims may be a mark of the richness of our lives. Yet *modus vivendi* is a political project, not a moral ideal. It does not preach compromise as an ideal for all to follow. Nor does it aim to convert the world to value-pluralism. In these respects *modus vivendi* is far from any of the conventional varieties of liberalism.

The pursuit of *modus vivendi* is not a quest for some kind of super-value. It is a commitment to common institutions in which the claims of rival values can be reconciled. The end of *modus vivendi* is not any supreme good – even peace. It is reconciling conflicting goods. That is why *modus vivendi* can be pursued by ways of life having opposed views of the good.

The ideal of *modus vivendi* is not based on the vain hope that human beings will cease to make universal claims for their ways of life. It regards such claims with indifference – except where they endanger peaceful coexistence. In this, *modus vivendi* harks back to Thomas Hobbes. A Hobbesian state extends to private belief the radical tolerance of indifference. Hobbes is thereby the progenitor of a tradition of liberal thought in which *modus vivendi* is central.

The idea that Hobbes is one of the authors of liberalism may be unfamiliar to political philosophers whose education has not included a study of the history of the subject. But liberal thought did not begin a generation ago. Only ignorance of the longer history of liberal thought supports the belief in a single, continuous liberal tradition.

The proposition that principles of justice must be neutral regarding rival views of the good is treated as an axiom in the liberal orthodoxy of the past generation; but neither the term nor – more significantly – the idea of neutrality is to be found in liberal writings before the 1970s. In this, as in other ways, recent liberal thinking is discontinuous with what went before. Such shifts are not new in liberal thought. They occur throughout its history.

Just as liberal regimes cannot be identified by a range of essential properties, so liberal theories and thinkers are not alike in having common ideas. It is a basic error to search for the essence of something as heterogeneous and discontinuous as *the* liberal tradition. Liberalism is not the kind of thing that has an essence.[17]

The dangers of seeking to define an essential liberal tradition are well illustrated by Hayek's attempt to identify 'true' or 'classical' liberalism as a Whiggish, 'English' tradition running from Locke to Adam Smith, which was swamped by a 'new' or 'French' liberalism towards the end of the eighteenth century.[18] Identifying David Hume and Adam Smith as English thinkers is only one of the oddities in this account. The Scottish Enlightenment to which Hume and Smith belonged was not a separate development, wholly detached from the French Enlightenment. Many of the formative influences in Hume's thought were French. Much in his thought is a response to the sceptical tradition of early modern Pyrrhonism to which Michel de Montaigne belonged.[19] It is a mistake to represent Hume's philosophy as part of an indigenous 'English' intellectual tradition. Rather, it is a development in European thought. If there is a formative English influence on Hume, it is Hobbes – whom Hayek consigns to the 'French' tradition of Cartesian rationalism.[20] Again, Hayek's attempt to define a tradition of 'true' or 'classical' liberalism deforms the thought of Adam Smith. True, if anyone was a liberal in the late eighteenth century, it was Adam Smith; but he was just as much a critic of liberalism. He was an early critic of the moral hazards of commercial societies. Many of the criticisms of capitalism that were later developed by Marx – notably those concerning its alienating and stupefying effects on workers – are prefigured in Smith's thought. In fact, so far is Smith from being an exemplar of 'true' or 'classical' liberal thought that one could just as well say of him that he is one of the chief sources of later critiques of liberalism.[21]

Contrary to Hayek, no useful purpose is served by seeking to separate out 'false' from 'true' liberalism. Even so, we can clearly identify some thinkers as liberals and others as critics of liberalism. (And some – such as Adam Smith and Michael Oakeshott – as both.) If it is clear that Constant and de Tocqueville were liberals, it is equally evident that Rousseau and de Maistre were not. If Kant is a paradigm of a certain type of liberal thinker, Nietzsche is no less exemplary as a critic of liberalism. When James Fitzjames Stephen attacked John Stuart Mill, his target was the leading liberal thinker of the age.[22]

As we do with liberal and non-liberal regimes, we recognize these thinkers as belonging to a tradition of liberal thought not in virtue of their exhibiting a set of defining features but by their family resemblances. As we move back from the eighteenth to the seventeenth century, recognizing any liberal tradition becomes trickier. Yet even then some thinkers were unmistakably liberal and others manifestly not.

Locke belongs in a tradition of liberal argument on the limits of political authority, whereas Filmer is an opponent of that emerging tradition. For Filmer, political authority comes by right, ultimately divine, unlimited by the consent of the subject. For Locke it depends on consent – however obscurely consent is qualified by his vestigial medieval notions about natural law. In seeking to ground the authority of government on hypothetical individual choice, Locke looks forward to later thinkers who are without question liberals.

So does Hobbes – in some ways more unequivocally. By making the authority of government contingent on its success in protecting the vital interests of its subjects, Hobbes belongs more clearly with later liberal thought than does Locke. In truth, if one of the core projects of liberalism is a form of peaceful coexistence that is not held together by common beliefs, Hobbes is a liberal thinker *au fond*. Hobbes understood better than most of the liberal thinkers who followed him what the problem of coexistence was, and how far it could be solved. As Michael Oakeshott put it, 'without being himself a liberal, Hobbes had in him more of the philosophy of liberalism than many of its professed defenders.'[23]

So, too, did David Hume. In contrast to Locke, Hume did not seek to found society on shared beliefs. For Hume, society stands not on any foundation of first principles or common belief but on shared practices. As I have noted, Hume was much indebted to French Pyrrhonism. His resolution of the sceptical paradoxes propounded by the Pyrrhonists was itself sceptical: it accepted that nature and convention, not reason, sustain morality and society. Radical scepticism of this kind can easily lead to quietism (as it did in Montaigne). In Hume, however, it produced a species of liberal philosophy in which the conviction that society needs shared beliefs has been largely abandoned.[24]

The two rival liberal philosophies help us understand what is new in our present circumstances. Throughout much of their history they had a crucial assumption in common. Both affirmed that human nature was constant and invariant. Both assumed that the good life was the same for all humankind. After Mill, this became increasingly difficult to take for granted. A new element of cultural difference entered the old ambiguities of liberal toleration.

For Hobbes, 'commodious living' means much the same wherever it can be achieved. For Hume, 'civilization' has always been animated by the same values. For both, politics was the pursuit of a peaceful accommodation of competing human interests; and, for both, the interests of human beings are everywhere much the same. In this last belief, Hobbes and Hume were at one with Locke and Kant, the chief exemplars of the rival liberal philosophy of rational consensus. None of these thinkers doubted that the good life was something singular, univocal and universal – even when they recognized, as Kant surely did, that its ingredients were often in conflict.

The faith that the good life is the same for all humankind is far from being universal or immemorial. In Europe, however, it prevailed until the time of the Romantics, when – led by such thinkers as Herder – it began to be questioned, then abandoned. As this faith gave way, the idea of 'civilization' was supplanted by that of 'culture'.[25]

The idea of 'culture' suggests that the forms of life in which humans can flourish are inherently various. It enters liberalism from German post-Romantic thought, notably that of Wilhelm von Humboldt. It becomes a central liberal theme only with John Stuart Mill.[26]

Mill's thought contains something of each of the rival liberal philosophies. At times, he is a militant partisan of an Enlightenment faith according to which the best way of life is the same for all – the form of life of autonomous individuals. At other times, Mill is a hesitant critic of this liberal Enlightenment faith. Influenced by Humboldt's arguments for 'the absolute and essential importance of human development in its richest diversity', which he quoted as the epigraph to *On Liberty*, Mill wrote: ' "Pagan self-assertion" is one of the elements of human worth, as well as "Christian self-denial". There is a Greek ideal of self-development, which the Platonic and Christian ideal of self-government blends with, but does not supersede.'[27] In such statements, Mill is not far from accepting that human beings can flourish in divergent forms of life whose worth cannot be compared.

Mill spent much of his life trying to reconcile his Enlightenment project of a universal civilization with his post-Romantic suspicion that it endangered freedom and diversity.[28] His suspicion was that if liberal toleration is based on the pursuit of such a consensus it might itself become illiberal. If diversity in ways of life has merely heuristic value as a means of discovering the best life, it is endangered by intellectual progress. A liberal society has no value in itself. It is no more than a stage on the way to a rational consensus. In that case, as humankind progresses, liberal values are bound to become obsolete. This was a result the French Positivists were happy to accept when they argued that freedom is no more necessary in morality than it is in chemistry.[29]

On Liberty was Mill's attempt to develop an argument for freedom that does not have this self-undermining effect. He was only partly successful. His *Essay* is haunted by the ambiguity that runs throughout the liberal tradition. Insofar as he held to the faith that one form of life is best for humankind, he sought to defend toleration of different ways of living as a path to truth. In this Mill held to a version of the Enlightenment project in which liberal institutions are defended not so much as embodiments of a particular conception of it as means of inquiry into it. At the same time he sought to avoid the self-undermining effect of justifying liberal institutions as a means to truth by claiming that humans can thrive in different and incompatible forms of life. In this view, which Mill imbibed from the German Romantics, rival values need not stand to one another in a relation of truth and falsity. They may point to different ways in which humans can live well. In favouring liberal institutions as instruments of inquiry, Mill looked forward to a rational consensus on the best way for humans to live. In affirming that humans can live well in a variety of ways he was a proto-value-pluralist. His project in *On Liberty* founders between these two philosophies.

Assessing Mill's argument in *On Liberty*, Isaiah Berlin wrote:

His argument is plausible only on the assumption which, whether he knew it or not, Mill all too obviously made, that human knowledge was in principle never complete, and always fallible; that there was no single, universally visible truth; that each man, each nation, each civilisation, might take its own road towards its own goal, not necessarily harmonious with those of others; that men are altered, and the truths in which they believe are altered, by new experiences and their own actions – what he calls 'experiments in living': that consequently the conviction, common to Aristotelians and atheistical materialists alike, that there exists a basic knowable human nature, one and the same, at all times, in all places, in all men – a static, unchanging substance underneath all the altering appearances, with permanent needs, dictated by a single, discoverable goal, or pattern of goals, the same for all mankind – is mistaken.[30]

By tacitly abandoning the assumptions that underpin the liberalism of rational consensus, Mill came close to affirming a philosophy of liberal pluralism, or *modus vivendi*. Yet in so doing he did not look back to Hobbes or Hume. He looked forward to a time when the common assumption not only of Hobbes and Hume but also of Locke and Kant – that humans flourish best in a single, universal civilization – could no longer be sustained. By affirming that the human good is found in divergent forms of life, Mill opened the way for a variety of liberal thought in which the idea of a universal civilization has no place.

In 'Two Concepts of Liberty' Berlin took up where Mill left off. Berlin sought to ground the value of liberty in the same plurality of ideals and forms of life that defeated Mill's enterprise in *On Liberty*. He defended liberty not because it enables the discovery of the one true way for humans to flourish, but because it allows people to flourish in different ways.

Nor was this merely a diversity of personal lifestyles. Berlin recognized that, for nearly all human beings, living well involved participation in particular ways of life. For Berlin, human flourishing required peaceful coexistence among different cultures, not their merging into a universal civilization. He never imagined that a world of distinctive ways of life could exist without deep and sometimes tragic conflicts.

There are many difficulties in the account of liberal thought that is implicit in Berlin's writings. At some points in 'Two Concepts of Liberty', he seems to suggest that a commitment to negative liberty in terms of non-interference embodies true liberal values, with positive conceptions of liberty as personal autonomy representing a departure from this position. Against this, some thinkers who are liberals by any standard, such as John Stuart Mill, hold to a more positive view of liberty, while others who stand outside of liberal thought, however laxly construed, such as Jeremy Bentham, adopt a negative view. It is legitimate to seek to understand liberal thought in terms of the ideas of freedom that are found in it, but none of them is the key that unlocks liberalism's 'true' values.

On the other hand, Berlin's recognition that conflicts of value break out within liberty itself marks a new development in liberal thought. Unlike most liberal thinkers, he understood that liberty is not one thing but many, that its various components do not all mesh together but often clash, that when they do conflict there is inevitably loss and sometimes no solution that all reasonable people are bound to accept. The result is a profoundly instructive philosophy of agonistic liberalism.[31]

Yet, despite its insights, Berlin's attempt to ground liberalism in a value-pluralist ethical theory breaks down in much the same way as did Mill's attempt to construct a liberal utilitarianism. If there are irreducibly many values which cannot be ranked or weighed on any single scale, negative liberty – which Berlin sees as the core liberal value – can be only one good among many. If, furthermore, there are incommensurable sorts of negative liberty, then different regimes can rightly protect different mixes of liberties. Yet again, if there are incommensurable kinds of liberty, there cannot be comparative, on-balance judgements about 'the greatest liberty'. In that case, it cannot be true that the best regime is that which promotes the greatest liberty. For if there are many incommensurable liberties, maximal liberty has no meaning.

The impossibility of deriving the priority of negative liberty over other values from value-pluralism can be seen as a defeat for liberalism. That was how Michael Oakeshott understood the failure of John Stuart Mill's enterprise of deriving a principle of liberty from utilitarianism. Oakeshott claimed that, because Mill could not defend the 'one very simple principle' he sought in *On Liberty*, he 'abandoned reference to general principles as a reliable guide in political activity'.[32]

Oakeshott understood this as a defeat for liberalism. In fact, his political philosophy was itself closer to liberalism than to any other – but it was a version of the liberalism of *modus vivendi*.[33] His mistake was to suppose that liberalism must be understood as a system of principles, and to seek to replace reference to principle by the guidance of tradition – as if any late modern society, least of all his own, contained only one tradition. If contemporary societies contain several traditions, with many people belonging to more than one, politics cannot be conducted by following any one tradition. It must try to reconcile the intimations of rival traditions. As Hobbes understood, it must seek *modus vivendi*.[34]

We need not see the failure of Mill's enterprise, or of Berlin's, as the failure of liberalism. Instead of seeing liberalism as a system of universal principles, we can think of it as the enterprise of pursuing terms of coexistence among different ways of life. Instead of thinking of liberal values as if they were universally authoritative, we can think of liberalism as the project of reconciling the claims of conflicting values. If we do this, liberal philosophy will look not to an illusion of universal consensus, but instead to the possibilities of *modus vivendi*. If we think of liberalism in these terms, we will take a further step in an intellectual pilgrimage begun by John Stuart Mill and continued in our own time by Isaiah Berlin, and resolve an ambivalence that has beset liberalism throughout its history.

Because *modus vivendi* rejects the claim of liberal values to universal authority, it is bound to be at odds with the prevailing philosophy of liberal toleration. Yet *modus vivendi* can still claim to be a renewal of the liberal project. For it continues the search for peace that liberal toleration began.

2000

2

John Stuart Mill and the idea of progress

If there is a consensus on the value of Mill's political writings, it is that we may turn to them for the sort of moral uplift that sustains the liberal hope, but we shall be disappointed if we expect to find in them much enlightenment about the urgent issues we face today. There are some, claiming access to new and greater truths, who do not hesitate to announce the obsolescence of that impassioned and reasonable liberalism which is the inspiration of all Mill's political writings. There are many others who will express their confidence that most of the causes for which he fought have now been safely won, and who accordingly deny to his writing that contemporary relevance they undoubtedly possessed for their original readers. Most significantly, perhaps, there is a widespread impression in progressive circles that Mill's tentative and humane liberalism has little to say to the perplexed citizens of societies whose manifold crises demand bold and drastic measures. Whether the news is greeted with regret, complacency or acclamation, there are not many who doubt the accuracy of the report that Mill's liberalism is as dead as any tradition of political thought can be.[1]

Obituaries of this kind may be premature, however, and their currency should be a matter of concern for all liberals. Mill's liberalism has a relevance which transcends the conditions of the age in which he wrote, and it meets needs which are enduring and widely felt. His writings contain an argument for an open society which has not yet been decisively refuted, and of which every generation needs reminding: they are especially relevant to those sceptical of the claims of collectivist and totalitarian systems, who remain dissatisfied with any kind of purely defensive conservatism and seek a form of radicalism which is not afraid to contemplate the necessity of massive changes in current policies and institutions but which keeps a clear head about the dangers of all such large-scale social engineering. Those who are looking for an open-minded radicalism of this kind will find that Mill addresses himself to some of the most pressing problems that we face today. It is hard to believe that contemporary debate has not suffered through neglect of his distinctive contribution to the liberal tradition.

MILL'S ARGUMENT IN *ON LIBERTY*

The vital centre of Mill's liberalism, as he expounds it in *On Liberty*, is not to be found in any of the consequential arguments he adduces there in support of liberal freedoms of thought, expression and association, but rather in a conception of human nature and self-development. The central argument of *On Liberty* is the claim that a liberal society is the only kind of society in which people confident of their own manifold possibilities but critical of their own powers and of each other, people who aspire to the status of autonomous agents and who cherish their own individuality, will consent to live. His conception of 'man as a progressive being' suggests to Mill the necessity of defining the sphere of legitimate social control in such a way as to promote the development of men as autonomous agents and he does this by proposing the famous *principle of liberty*. In fact this principle assumes various forms at different stages in his argument, but its main force is contained in the injunction that the liberty of the individual should be restricted by society or by the state only if his or her actions are (or may be) injurious to the interests of others.

It is important that present-day readers of *On Liberty* take note of two points about Mill's principle of liberty. First, though he carefully stresses that it states a necessary and not a sufficient condition of justified limitation of liberty (since costs of enforcement may make it wrong to limit liberty even where the interests of others are clearly damaged by a given kind of action), he also insists that the principle of liberty is violated in modern societies whenever individuals enjoy a traditional freedom to act in ways injurious to others. The example of a traditional right unjustifiable by the principle of liberty which he cites most frequently is that of unrestricted procreation, which is injurious both to the interests of the offspring of irresponsible parents and to the interests of all who compete with them for scarce jobs and resources. Mill would have had no objection in liberal principle to proposals for the institution of 'child licences' (though he might well have had doubts about their practicability), and he would certainly have been sympathetic to those who advocate population control – including even coercive measures – as part of a freedom-preserving policy for an already overcrowded world.[2]

Second, it is a clear implication of Mill's principle that, in laying down a necessary condition of legitimate limitation of liberty, it disallows an indefinitely large range of interferences with personal freedom, and he is at pains to draw his readers' attention to two classes of intervention which his principle prohibits. These are: restrictions of liberty designed to prevent individuals from causing harm to themselves; and restrictions designed to bring an individual into conformity with the received moral ideas of his community.

Importantly, Mill goes much further than most contemporary liberals in ruling out such paternalist restrictions on liberty as are involved in legal prohibitions of the sale of 'hard' drugs. Equally, there can be little doubt that he would adopt an uncompromising libertarian stand on questions of censorship and pornography, and would reject all legislation on sexual behaviour which has a moralistic rather than a straightforwardly harm-preventing rationale. Nor can it be doubted, finally, that he would have extended his support to the campaigns of those, like Dr Thomas Szasz, who wish to see the practice of the confinement and involuntary treatment of those judged mentally disordered discontinued or at least subject to far more stringent legal controls.[3] Whether or not contemporary liberals follow Mill in his intransigent opposition to state paternalism and legal moralism, they would be well advised if they were to consider carefully his objections to such policies.[4]

MILL'S RADICALISM

Though fashionable progressive opinion will find Mill's stand on the question of drug use and censorship congenial, it is worth noting that his no less sensible views on the proper organization of national education find little favour in such circles. His view that 'an education established and controlled by the state should only exist, if it exists at all, as one among competing experiments, carried on for the purpose of example and stimulus, to keep the others up to a certain standard of excellence',[5] despite the fact that it flows directly from his concern with the promotion of diversity and variety in all spheres of life, finds few echoes in contemporary political life outside the right wing of the Conservative Party and the far-left disciples of Ivan Illich, though for many years liberals have continued unnoticed to advocate voucher schemes as an alternative or a supplement to state education.[6] It is paradoxical that radicals who bemoan the fate of such schools as Risinghill have not grasped the simple truth that bold experiments are unlikely to flourish in a monopolistic state education system dominated by conservative bureaucracies and politically vulnerable local authorities. Mill's views on education reveal an important difference between his anti-collectivist radicalism, which sought always to assist the disadvantaged by widening their opportunity for free choice and self-reliance, and the Fabian paternalism by which it was supplanted, whose goal apparently is to make the poor dependent on an expansionist apparatus of social workers and benevolent planners.

This overall contrast between Mill's radicalism and that of twentieth-century political parties (to which I shall return shortly in another context) is worth remarking on in that it discloses one of the most important tendencies of his political thought, which is expressed in his constant search for methods which alleviate distress and strike at the roots of social injustice while restricting personal liberty to the minimum practicable extent. The relevance of his anti-collectivist approach has increased rather than diminished in the century and more since his death, for we know now that vast nationalized social services not only involve considerable loss of liberty, but often facilitate a net redistribution of income and resources from the poorer to the better-off sections of the community. Indeed, those who give up the most freedom under such schemes are the poor who get least in return.

Mill's whole approach to the social injustices of industrial society involves a critique of orthodox socialism which can be deeply instructive to radical reformers well over a century later. Presciently identifying the fate of revolutionary socialism, he warned that catastrophist strategies to socialism, since they presuppose the collapse into chaos of the existing social order, are bound to generate, not the benign classless anarchy of which their proponents dream, but rather a dictatorship, in all probability far more oppressive than the old regime, in which there will be little or no room left for individuality of any kind. He was no less perceptive about the dangers of reformist socialism of the statist or Fabian variety. If it is plainly mistaken to count Mill among the precursors of Fabianism, it is probably equally inaccurate, however, to suggest that he would be at home in the Selsdon Group;[7] for Mill developed a series of proposals for the alleviation of the central injustices of the industrial society that was emerging around him which have the most radical implications today.

It should be a commonplace by now that Mill was no inflexible adherent of *laissez-faire* – for that matter, none of the classical economists subscribed to *laissez-faire* principles without making important exceptions and qualifications to them – and he acknowledged the propriety of a wide range of governmental activities, many of the kind which have become taken for granted in the liberal democracies of the twentieth-century western European and English-speaking world. It is important to recognize, however, that his proposals for tackling the social problems of an industrial civilization go far beyond anything that merely suggests the kind of activities undertaken by the post-war welfare state.

The major targets of Mill's criticism of the arrangements of the emergent industrial society of his day were the maldistribution of property and the oppressive system of industrial organization. In the posthumous 'Chapters on Socialism', published in the *Fortnightly Review* in 1879, he declared that, in existing society, 'reward, instead of being proportional to the labour and abstinence of the individuals, is almost in an inverse ratio to it'. One of the primary causes of this inequitable distribution of rewards, according to Mill, was the concentration of fortunes facilitated through their uninterrupted accumulation across the generations, and his remedy for this, though much discussed in subsequent economic writings, seems as utopian today as it did when he proposed it in the first edition (in 1848) of his *Principles of Political Economy*. He advocated the institution, not of an estates duty, but of what we would nowadays call an accessions duty or an inheritance tax, to be levied on the recipient and not on the donor of the capital.

The merit of such a tax is that, unlike other arrangements, it need not transfer wealth from private individuals to the state, since it is eminently avoidable through the desirable expedient of dispersing one's wealth widely. Mill's support for a reform of inheritance taxation which would promote the diffusion of wealth, when taken in conjunction with his opposition to the progressive taxation of income, distinguishes his radical sense of social injustice sharply from that which animates most socialists. Though it prompted him to favour a redistribution of property and so of incomes in the context of the industrial society of his day, his radical conception of social justice has no specifically egalitarian orientation, condemning the inheritance of large fortunes rather on the grounds of its undeservedness and because huge concentrations of wealth may ultimately become inimical to liberty – whether they are held in governmental or in private hands. Equally, however, Mill's conception of social justice separates him from all those conservatives who are, at bottom, concerned with nothing more than the preservation of entrenched privilege. In the first edition of *Principles of Political Economy*, his advocacy of what amounts to a guaranteed annual income or social dividend for all confirms this contrast with conservative thought, and shows how close is his position to that of contemporary radicals in the same tradition.[8]

An inequitable distribution of property is, of course, closely related to that mode of capitalist industrial organization in which enterprises are owned and managed by owners of capital who stand in an authoritarian relationship with wage-earners. Throughout his life Mill was opposed to such a system of industrial organization. He opposed it because, in the first place, it institutionalized a permanent conflict of interests between owners of capital and wage-earners, and no system of productive association which rested on such a contradictory basis could be expected to be either stable or efficient. In the second place, the separation between wage-earners on the one hand and owners and managers on the other, deprived workers of any real opportunity for personal initiative. In so doing, it stultified their growth and prevented them becoming anything like the responsible, autonomous individuals that Mill had theorized about in *On Liberty*. His fundamental objection to the capitalist system of his day led him to take a lifelong interest in schemes for profit-sharing, industrial partnership, and producers' co-operation; but his boldest vision goes far beyond such proposals, and can best be described as a form of non-revolutionary, competitive syndicalism. As he put it:

The form of association . . . which, if mankind continues to improve, must be expected in the end to predominate, is not that which can exist between a capitalist as chief, and work-people without a voice in the management, but the association of the labourers themselves on terms of equality, collectively owning the capital with which they carry on their operations, and working under managers elected and removable by themselves.[9]

MILL'S POST-CAPITALIST SOCIETY

A number of points need making at once about the syndicalist or non-state socialist vision which is expressed in this passage. Crucially, Mill's vision of a post-capitalist society, unlike that of virtually all socialists, does not include the elimination of competition. Indeed, as far as he was concerned, no changes in the existing system of industrial organization would bring about a tolerable society which sought to suppress competition between enterprises and individuals, or which resulted in competition becoming less effective. If he is in any sense a socialist – and he certainly envisaged a social order which was no longer recognizably that of nineteenth-century England, and which differs at least as much from our own capitalist society – then his was decidedly a 'market socialism'. Unlike market socialism of the Yugoslav variety, however, Mill's vision of a post-capitalist society is not one in which the institution of private property in the means of production has been abrogated: there is no suggestion that the workers' shares in their enterprises will not be marketable, and there is every reason to think that he wanted to see an improvement in the capital market, with an entrepreneurial class of industrial pioneers having an acknowledged place even in the fully realized syndicalist society. Again, it should be noted that, despite his unorthodox sympathies with trade unionism, he envisaged no real place for trade unions in the society of the future; he looked forward to a time when the harmony of interests between all partners in production, facilitated by workers' ownership and self-management, would allow 'the true euthanasia of trade unionism'. In other words, his proposals for workers' participation in management were at the furthest remove from those contemplated by Western socialist theorists, which apparently envisage no more than the inclusion in management of faithful representatives of our reactionary trade union bureaucracies.

Perhaps the cardinal example of how Mill's thought catches up with our preoccupations in the last quarter of the twentieth century is to be found in his advocacy of the stationary-state economy. Like other classical economists, he accepted that economic growth could only be temporary in a world of scarce natural resources, in which population constantly pressed on land and food reserves. In contrast with all other economists in the classical tradition, however, he did not fear the arrival of a stationary economy, but rather welcomed it as an opportunity for a large-scale transformation in social values. It is true, of course, that a large part of his concern that society be reordered so as to allow a peaceful transition to a no-growth economy derives from his neo-Malthusian insistence on the finitude of the world's resources and the constant danger of overpopulation – an insistence which seems far less unreasonable now than it did twenty years ago. Yet the larger part of his advocacy of a stationary-state economy is not concerned with considerations of resource depletion but with the damaging effects on human character of the unremitting pursuit of possessions and with the destructive consequences for our natural environment of open-ended economic growth.

I suggest that it is a feature of Mill's radicalism – one which makes it especially relevant to contemporary radical reformers – that, unlike almost all forms of socialism, it is not based on the illusory prospect of a cornucopian abundance created by the magical fecundity of technology. At a time when such a viewpoint was almost unknown, Mill told his readers that:

It is only in the backward countries of the world that increased production is still an important object: in those most advanced, what is economically needed is a better distribution, of which one indispensable means is a stricter restraint on population.[10]

Again, he concludes the prophetic chapter of *Principles of Political Economy* on 'The stationary state' with the remark that 'a stationary condition of capital and population implies no stationary state of human improvement.'[11] Mill's summons to us to welcome a stationary-state economy has increased in relevance during a century in which the self-defeating and destructive aspects of indefinite economic growth have become one of our most central concerns. It is more than ever urgent that we heed it at a time when an unplanned curtailment of economic growth precipitated by a rise in the cost of energy has panicked many public figures into supporting a desperate search for new methods of sustaining the growth economy.

THE RELEVANCE OF MILL'S RADICAL LIBERALISM

My discussion of the relevance of Mill's thought to contemporary liberals should have illuminated some of the reasons why it is a mistake to regard him as a patron saint of a defunct creed. In at least three respects, I suggest that his radical liberalism still has much to offer those in search of a reasonable radicalism. His is a decentralist, anti-statist radicalism, which, unlike orthodox socialism, addresses itself to the problems involved in meeting the widely acknowledged need for political devolution and the diffusion of power and initiative within the great entrenched institutions of our society. It is a radicalism which, while calling for a massive redistribution of property and therefore of incomes, offers an alternative conception of social justice to that of a levelling-down egalitarianism – which, in practice, seems inexorably to result in either a stagnant and uniform society, or in a society where differentials in power and authority replace far more innocuous differentials in monetary reward. Moreover, it is a radicalism which is well prepared to meet the challenges posed by an end to economic growth in the world's developed (or overdeveloped) societies. Mill's political thought should be a central inspiration of those who seek to modify the institutions and policies of liberal societies while remaining faithful to the central ideals of the liberal tradition.

It would do no good to pretend that we can find in Mill's writings answers to all the major problems that confront us now – and, in any case, he would have deprecated any such attempt. He cannot tell us how we are to combat explosive inflation and ever increasing unemployment while preserving traditional liberal freedoms: we will look in vain in his works for illumination regarding the multiple crises of contemporary economic systems (both 'capitalist' and 'socialist'). In forging institutions to cope with unprecedented economic conditions, we need (as Keynes emphasized) new wisdom for a new age. It would be disloyal to the spirit of inquiry which Mill stood for, if we were to exempt from criticism any of the political or economic institutions which we have inherited from the great age of English liberalism. As he himself argued, radical reforms in our political institutions will be necessary if we are to realize the promise of democracy, while avoiding the danger of a democratic tyranny of the majority.[12] Though we must not expect from his writings a blueprint for the achievement of a liberal society in a world in many ways very different from his, it has been my argument that radicals will be unreasonable if they neglect his thought on some of the principal dilemmas that perplex us today. Mill always regarded his age as an age of transition: and our age is no less an age of transition. It would be a hopeful augury if the current decomposition of conventional political wisdom were to encourage liberals to re-examine his views on how this great transition should be conducted.

1976

3

Santayana's alternative

The thought of George Santayana has never had a wide influence.
Both the style and the substance of his philosophy go against the
current of twentieth-century sensibility and whatever echoes his philosophical writings had among his contemporaries have long since faded
into silence. Neglect of Santayana's work by professional philosophers and by educated opinion is unfortunate for many reasons. His
prose style – condensed, aphoristic and ornate at the same time –
is beautiful and unique in twentieth-century philosophical writing,
bearing comparison only with that of such earlier and very different
philosophical stylists as Montaigne and Hume. Again, though his
work never formed part of any recognized tradition or school,
Santayana's contributions to a range of philosophical disciplines –
the theory of knowledge and scepticism, metaphysics and ethics – still
contain something from which we can learn, if only we are ready to
read him with intellectual sympathy. His contributions to these subjects have been ignored, partly as a result of the vulgar academic
prejudice according to which anyone who can write exquisitely must
be a bellelettrist or prose poet rather than any sort of serious thinker,
and partly because the idiom of Santayana's writings consorts badly
with that of the analytic schools which have dominated Anglo-
American philosophy for most of our century. The chief reason for
neglect of his thought, however, probably lies in the circumstances of
his own life. It is in any case lamentable that his works are rarely
seriously studied nowadays, since we are thereby deprived of his
thoughts on society and government, which encompass one of the
most profound and incisive critiques of liberalism ever developed. It
is a symptom of the intellectual temper of our times that one of the

very few systematic studies of Santayana's philosophy to be published in recent years omits altogether any consideration of his political philosophy.[1] It is hard to resist the suspicion that Santayana's political thought is not only unknown to modern opinion, but (where it has even been heard of) deeply unfashionable and indeed thoroughly uncongenial. For this reason alone, it may well have much to teach us of the ironies and limitations of the ruling liberal worldview.

The circumstances of Santayana's life were uncommon, and are more than usually relevant to the understanding of his thought. Born in Spain in 1863 of Spanish parentage, he retained his Spanish nationality throughout his life and (though in fact he left Spain at the age of nine) always regarded himself as a Spaniard. He was nevertheless educated in the United States, wrote all his philosophical works and his poetry in English, and had his only long-term association with a university, as a student and later a professor, at Harvard. Santayana's intellectual temperament, aloof, ironical and poetic, had little in common with that which, then as now, dominated American culture, and he became increasingly disaffected with American life. His distance from, and even disdain for, American culture was evident to his colleagues at Harvard, and was reciprocated by his polar opposite there, William James, whose earnest, optimistic and sermonizing outlook was outraged by Santayana's detachment, and who expressed his condemnation of the style and substance of the Spaniard's thought famously when he called it 'the perfection of rottenness'. Santayana's colleagues were stupefied and outraged when in 1911 he acted upon his estrangement from American life and academic culture by resigning his professorship at Harvard and departing for ever for Europe, where he lived the life of an independent scholar, residing in hotels and eventually a convent, and remaining productive until the year of his death in 1952. There can be little doubt that his repudiation of the academic milieu in which philosophical inquiry had become professionalized and institutionalized, together with his indifference to the moralistic and world-improving sensibility which animated much in American thought and life during his lifetime, reinforced the neglect of his work engendered by its peculiarities of tone and content.

Immensely erudite though he was in the history of philosophy, Santayana appears to have been uninfluenced by any of the thinkers

he studied. In his later years, he tended to represent himself as a
spokesman for a human orthodoxy, as sceptical as it was naturalistic,
which had hitherto rarely found a voice, and then chiefly in poets,
such as Lucretius. His philosophical development is easily summarized. Aside from his doctoral dissertation on Lotze's philosophy, his
first significant publication was in aesthetic theory. *The Sense of
Beauty*, published in 1896,[2] contains many of the themes which
were to pervade his writings over the next half-century and more –
and, most particularly, an analysis of a spiritual value in naturalistic, bodily and partly sexual terms which at no point descends to
a crude reductionism. The distinctive Santayanian conjunction of a
sturdy Lucretian materialism about that which exists with a strong
affirmation of the spiritual reality of a realm of essences is already
manifest in this very early work, and is worked out in systematic
detail in his first major philosophical statement, *The Life of Reason*,[3]
published in five volumes in 1905–6. Santayana's metaphysical doctrine, a rather obscure and perhaps ultimately incoherent combination
of a materialist ontology with a pluralist theory of essences, was
further elaborated in the four volumes of his *Realms of Being*,[4] published between 1927 and 1942. In addition to these major treatises,
Santayana published many collections of essays, of which *Winds of
Doctrine* (1913)[5] and *Soliloquies in England and Later Soliloquies*
(1922)[6] are among the most notable. *Winds of Doctrine* contains
Santayana's coruscating and devastating assessment of the early philosophy of his friend Bertrand Russell, in which he comments on
Russell's belief – derived from G. E. Moore, and later abandoned by
Russell under the impact of Santayana's criticism – that there are
objective moral qualities in no way dependent upon the constitution
of human beings for their content, by observing that:

For the human system whisky is truly more intoxicating than coffee, and
the contrary opinion would be an error; but what a strange way of vindicat-
ing this real, though relative, distinction, to insist that whisky is more
intoxicating in itself, without reference to any animal; that it is pervaded,
as it were, by an inherent intoxication, and stands dead drunk in its bottle![7]

Santayana's *Soliloquies* are noteworthy in that they contain some
of his most penetrating analyses of the failings of liberalism, and of

the transformations of opinion wrought by the catastrophe of the First World War. The main themes of his political philosophy are scattered throughout these and other essays, but it receives a complete and magisterial statement in his *Dominations and Powers*, which appeared a year before he died.

What are the most essential elements in Santayana's political thought, and how do they bear on his critique of liberalism? We find the very kernel of his rejection of liberalism in his observation that:

this liberal ideal implies a certain view about the relations of man in the universe. It implies that the ultimate environment, divine or natural, is either chaotic in itself or undiscernible by human science, and that human nature, too, is either radically various or only determinable in a few essentials, round which individual variations play *ad libitum*. For this reason no normal religion, science, art or way of happiness can be prescribed. These remain always open, even in their foundations, for each man to arrange for himself. The more things are essentially unsettled and optional, the more liberty of this sort there may safely be in the world and the deeper it may run.[8]

Santayana here illuminates the central dogma of modern liberalism, unreflectively and stubbornly held – the dogma that human nature is a fiction, a chaos or an unknowable thing, so that it is not unreasonable for each generation to start life afresh, to try every experiment in living again and await what comes of it. The sceptical dogmatism of the modern liberal mind is at the furthest remove from the outlook of the ancients, for whom human nature was in most essential respects knowable and fixed, a stable matrix within which variations among individuals and peoples might safely occur. For the ancients, accordingly, liberty was not a fundamental right to indeterminacy, founded on chaos, but a very definite thing:

When ancient peoples defended what they called their liberty, the word stood for a plain and urgent interest of theirs: that their cities should not be destroyed, their territory pillaged, and they themselves sold into slavery. For the Greeks in particular liberty meant even more than this. Perhaps the deepest assumption of classical philosophy is that nature and the gods on the one hand and man on the other, both have a fixed character; that there is consequently a necessary piety, a true philosophy, a standard happiness, a normal art . . . When they [the Greeks] defended their liberty what they defended was not merely freedom to live. It was freedom to live well, to live as other nations did not, in the public experimental study of the world and of human nature. This liberty to discover and pursue a natural happiness, this liberty to grow wise and to live in friendship with the gods and with one another, was the liberty vindicated at Thermopylae by martyrdom and at Salamis by victory.[9]

Classical liberty, for Santayana, was the freedom of self-rule, in which civilized peoples pursued the arts of life in the assurance that knowledge of the human good was (within limits, like everything else) achievable. Liberal freedom, on the contrary, is the freedom of inordinacy, an hubristic compound of antinomian individualism with a sentimental humanism which the Greeks would have despised had they been decadent enough to be able to imagine it. The contrast between classical freedom and the freedom of liberal modernity is clear enough, but it should not lead us into misinterpreting Santayana's moral vision and political perspective. Santayana, like the Greeks, believed human nature to be a stable and knowable thing, with definite limits and a bounded range of variations. He differed radically from the Greeks – at least from the dogmatists among them, such as Aristotle – in his conception of the status and content of the human good. For Santayana, the human good was as various as the diverse kinds of human beings who achieved or failed to realize it. There is not one supreme good for all men – contemplation, say, as Aristotle would have it, or a life of work and prayer, as for Aquinas – nor is there a single form of collective life, such as that of the *polis*, in which human flourishing may occur. Instead there is a constrained but legitimate diversity of goods, individual and collective, and it is a tyrannous impulse in political philosophy (well exemplified in modern liberalism) to elevate any of them to the status of *summum bonum*. Just as the good life for an individual may be one of bourgeois productivity or aristocratic leisure, religious piety or the pleasures of the senses, so monarchy and republicanism, free enterprise or the feudalism of a traditional social order may be equally lawful facets of the human good. What the human good encompasses in any one time or place is a matter for study and deliberation, not legislation, and there is always a margin of contingency and caprice in it, which no theory can tame. What is definitely excluded by Santayana's moral outlook is not the partial relativity or indeed the limited subjectivity of the good, which he affirms, but instead its infinite variability, its unknowable openness to unheard-of novelty, its plasticity and malleability by human will and the utopian or reformist imagination.

What is excluded by Santayana's moral conception is, in short, *progress*. It is not that Santayana, in a spirit of misanthropic perversity, denies that human arrangements are ever improvable. Nor does he subscribe to radical relativism: he does not deny, but affirms, that there are better and worse forms of government, virtues and vices that are common to all men. He departs from the parochial dogmatism of the classic Greek moralists when, in the tradition of Democritus and Lucretius, he insists on a legitimate variety of mores and ways of life, but he nowhere endorses the heresy of liberal toleration – the heresy that there is nothing to choose between traditions and cultures. His rejection of progress has other and more reasonable grounds. In the first place, even when incontestable improvement takes place in human affairs, there is nothing inevitable about it; it occurs as a matter of chance or human will, and it is always reversible. As Santayana puts it:

Progress is often a fact: granted a definite end to be achieved, we may sometimes observe a continuous approach towards achieving it, as for instance towards cutting off a leg neatly when it has been smashed; and such progress is to be desired in all human arts. But *belief* in progress, like belief in fate or in the number three, is a sheer superstition, a mad notion that because some idea – here the idea of continuous change for the better – has been realized somewhere, that idea was a power which realized itself there fatally, and which must be secretly realizing itself everywhere else, even where the facts contradict it.[10]

The idea of a law of progress, or of an all but irresistible tendency to general improvement, is then merely a superstition, one of the tenets of the modernist pseudo-religion of humanism. Even if such a law or tendency existed and were demonstrable, the liberal faith in progress would for Santayana be pernicious. For it leads to a corrupt habit of mind in which things are valued, not for their present excellence or perfection, but instrumentally, as leading to something better; and it insinuates into thought and feeling a sort of historical theodicy, in which past evil is justified as a means to present or future good. The idea of progress embodies a kind of *time-worship* (to adopt an expression used by Wyndham Lewis) in which the particularities of our world are seen and valued, not in themselves, but for what they might perhaps become – thereby leaving us destitute of the sense of the present and, at the same time, of the perspective of eternity. The idea of progress has yet another radical fault. It supposes that there is a constant standard by which improvement may be measured, or at any rate a consecutive series of such evolving standards. Now it is true that human beings, like other animal species, have certain needs in common, and their lot is improved the better these needs are satisfied. But in the human species, if not in other species, the satisfaction of these basic needs evokes others, and changes the standards whereby future improvement may be measured. Nor is this self-transformation of mankind by the satisfaction of its needs a linear or one-dimensional process, since different individuals and peoples in different historical and cultural milieux suffer it differently. And its effects are not always beneficent in terms of human well-being:

It is perhaps only in transmissible arts that human progress can be maintained or recognized. But in developing themselves and developing human nature these arts shift their ground; and in proportion as the ground is shifted, and human nature itself is transformed, the criterion of progress ceases to be moral to become only physical, a question of increased complexity or bulk or power. We all feel at this time the moral ambiguity of mechanical progress. It seems to multiply opportunity, but it destroys the possibility of simple, rural or independent life. It lavishes information, but it abolishes mastery except in trivial or mechanical efficiency. We learn many languages, but degrade our own. Our philosophy is highly critical and thinks itself enlightened, but it is a Babel of mutually unintelligible artificial tongues.[11]

Whereas it pervades modern culture, especially in America (where it animates much that passes there for conservatism), the idea of progress is naturally most at home in liberalism. It is the central irony of modern liberalism that a political creed devoted to liberty (as it was with the classical liberals, with Tocqueville, Constant, Madison and the Scottish Enlightenment) should by way of the idea of progress come to subordinate liberty to the promotion of general welfare. 'The most earnest liberals', as Santayana observes, are quickest to feel the need of a new tyranny: they are the first to support vast schemes of world improvement, reckless of their concomitant effects on the liberty which an earlier generation of wiser liberals prized. 'They [the most earnest liberals]', he tells us, 'save liberal principles by saying that they applaud it [the new tyranny] only provisionally as a necessary means of freeing the people. But of freeing the people from what? From the consequences of freedom.'[12] Nothing in his analysis suggests that this metamorphosis in liberalism from a creed of liberty to a creed of progress through a new tyranny was avoidable, or is somehow (as latter-day classical liberals such as Hayek imagine) now reversible. Nor does he suppose the present regime of welfare-state or corporate-capitalist liberalism (as we would now call it) to be stable or enduring. 'They [the liberals] were no doubt right', he says, 'to be confident that the world was moving toward the destruction of traditional institutions, privileges and beliefs; but the first half of the twentieth century has already made evident that their own wealth, taste and intellectual liberty will dissolve in some strange barbarism that will think them a good riddance.'[13] The liberal age is, then, for Santayana most definitely a transitional one: its ruling conceptions of progress and liberty degraded, confused or incoherent, its benefits in the growth of wealth and knowledge doubtful and precarious, and the stability of the social order on which this expansion of human powers depended fragile. The question arises: by what, in his view, might liberalism be replaced?

Whatever he thought might supplant liberalism, Santayana was clear that it would not be an extension of liberalism in some other form: for, as he says, 'if any one political tendency kindled my wrath, it was precisely the tendency of industrial liberalism to level down all civilisations to a single cheap and dreary pattern.'[14] A post-liberal epoch, if one were to come about, and mankind not simply relapse into barbarism, would not be the anarchic utopia that has always been a temptation of liberalism, and which is naively theorized in the

writings of those ultra-liberals, the anarchists, such as Fourier and
Proudhon, and, in our own day, the epigones of libertarianism. If
anything, a post-liberal age would be the exact opposite of such a
play-filled utopia. It would, to start with, shed that spirit of individuality, virtually unknown among the Greeks and Romans, which is
the gift of Judaism and Christianity to our civilization. Santayana
perceives, what is concealed in modern culture, that liberalism and the
other political religions of our age are only the illegitimate offspring
of the Judeo-Christian tradition, repressed versions (in precisely the
Freudian sense) of the human need for transcendence and the sacred.
If, as the *philosophes* of the French Enlightenment hoped and projected, European culture were to abandon its Christian inheritance,
it would likely abandon its individualism along with it, and the result
would be far from that dreamt of by liberal theory:

Health and freedom ... if recovered against the lingering domination of
Christianity, may reserve some surprises to the modern mind. The modern
mind is liberal and romantic; but a state of society and a discipline of the
will inspired by pure reason would be neither romantic nor liberal. It would
be sternly organic, strictly and traditionally moral, military, and scientific.
The literary enemies of Christianity might soon find reason to pine for that
broad margin of liberty and folly by which Christianity, in merry Christian
times, was always surrounded. They could have played the fool and the wit
to better advantage under the shadow of the Church than in the social
barracks of the future; and a divided public allegiance, half religious and
half worldly, might have left more holes and cracks to peep through than
would the serried economy of reason.[15]

Santayana himself seemed hardly to regret the passing of that spirit
of individuality which Christian faith had nurtured and sheltered.
Without sharing the primitive fantasies of Enlightenment rationalism,
he inclined to welcome a sort of ideal paganism in which religions
would be candidly accepted as local varieties of poetry, and the
relativity of piety would become a commonplace. The political form
of this post-liberal epoch would be a universal empire. Himself
entirely a marginal man, through the prism of whose thought were
refracted many national cultures – Spanish, English and American,
among others – Santayana rightly abominated the tribalistic passions

associated with the modern nation-state. The form of economic and social life he commended, one simpler, more local and more frugal than that of liberal societies, was to be protected by the framework of a global peace. His political ideal, and his prescription for a post-liberal order, is an idealized version of the ancient polity, and is well characterized in an essay of 1934, 'Alternatives to Liberalism':

The ancients were reverent. They knew their frailty and that of all their works. They feared not only the obvious powers bringing flood, pestilence or war, but also the subtler furies that trouble the mind and utter mysterious oracles. With scrupulous ceremony they set a watchtower and granary and tiny temple on some gray rock above their ploughed fields and riverside pastures. The closed circle of their national economy, rustic and military, was always visible to the eye. From that little stronghold they might some day govern the world; but it would be with knowledge of themselves and of the world they governed, and they might gladly accept more laws than they imposed. They would think on the human scale . . . In such a case, holding truth by the hand, authority might become gentle and even holy.[16]

Santayana's conception of a post-liberal regime, which has great strengths as well as disabling weaknesses, has been criticized from a variety of standpoints, some more vulgar than others. It has been attacked as proto-Fascist, but this is surely a baseless criticism, with nothing to support it save that Santayana was living in Fascist Italy at the time he published 'Alternatives to Liberalism', and may have thought the Mussolini regime preferable to the realizable alternatives. The criticism of Santayana's post-liberal vision as proto-Fascist is indefensible, if only because there are unequivocal evidences in his writings of his repudiation of Fascist doctrine and practice. It is hard to interpret the following passage from *Dominations and Powers* as other than an explicit critique of the vulgar Nietzschean pretensions of the Fascist leaders:

Can it be that these *Realpolitiker* have forgotten the rudiments of morals, or have never heard of them? Are these supermen nothing but ill-bred little boys? . . . The oracular Zarathustra, become prime minister, will sit at his desk in goggles, ringing for one secretary after another . . . Poor superman!

As things get rather thick about him, will he regret the happy irresponsible days when, in the legend of a Borgia, he could publicly invite all his rival supermen to a feast, in order to have them poisoned at his table? Or will he remember how, distracted by the heat and nobly fearless, he drank the poisoned wine by himself, and perished instead most horribly? Ah, those bold romantic crimes were not really more satisfactory than the entanglements of this official slavery. Both are vanity. And in that case, what follows? It follows that these wild ambitions (though some lovely thing may be summoned by them before the mind) are themselves evil, at least in part; and that the misguided hero, like a Damocles or like a poor ghost-seeing and witch-hunting Macbeth, will lose his soul in gaining a sorry world, and his wishes, once attained, will horrify him. These are trite maxims, and elementary: but I am talking of children, to children: a pack of young simpletons led by some young scoundrel.[17]

The real criticisms of Santayana's vision lie elsewhere. There is in the first place a decidedly arcadian quality about his conception of a post-liberal order. It is not only post-liberal but also post-industrial. It is an obvious, but also a decisive objection to such a conception, that it is incompatible with the maintenance of the world's existing population. A less crowded world might well be a better one, our present population may indeed be unsustainable over the long run; but it is clear that it will be reduced only by a catastrophe in whose wake not only the industrialism Santayana despised, but also the possibility of a post-industrial order on the lines envisaged, would be effectively destroyed. There are also deep difficulties in his account of the imperial framework within which the local and rustic economies he prized would be sheltered. His idea of a liberal universal empire has many attractions. It acknowledges, what contemporary liberal thought cannot admit, that it is the empire, and not the nation-state, that is the most appropriate political order for the realization of the goals of individual liberty, the rule of law and peace among diverse communities. As Santayana, outlining the idea of a universal liberal empire, asks rhetorically:

Why not divorce moral societies from territorial or tribal units, so that membership in these moral societies, as in a free Church, should be voluntary, adopted only by adults with a full sense of their vocation for that special life, and relinquished, without any physical hindrance, as soon as that vocation flagged, or gave place to some other honest resolution?[18]

Again, he observes:

Under such a Roman peace, as we call it, a further development is possible. Not only may each nation, within its territory, preserve its language and laws and religion under the imperial insurance, but where different nations have intermingled, as often happens in great cities or in provinces vaguely open to any immigrant, each may preserve all its moral idiosyncrasy, its speech, dress and domestic life, side by side with the most alien races.[19]

Santayana's conception has the decisive merit of acknowledging the political form of empire to be that best suited to maintaining the condition of cultural pluralism – the variety of traditions and ways of life – advocated, but everywhere discouraged, by modern liberalism. There is nevertheless a vast unreality in his speculations on how this liberal universal empire might come about. He rejects the idea that it might be a *Pax Americana*, on the plausible ground that the very virtues of American culture – its evangelizing reformism and incorrigible optimism – ill fit the United States for an imperial role. More disputably, he rejects the British Empire (as it existed when he first wrote in 1934 what later became a chapter in *Dominations and Powers*)[20] as a model for a Roman peace on the ground that the British had a contemptuous indifference to the customs of their subjects that rendered them odious as rulers. (The observation may be correct, but the British attitude to their subjects had many points of affinity with that of the Romans to theirs – and it at least protected the British from the folly of a messianic liberalism.) Most absurdly, Santayana – not perhaps without a motive of perversity – suggests that 'Perhaps the Soviets might be better fitted than any other power to become the guardians of universal peace.' With the utmost naivety (or disingenuousness), he goes on:

In regard to tenure of land, and to the management of industry and communications, if the management were competent, a universal communism, backed by irresistible armed force, would be a wonderful boon to mankind ... The Soviets would ... have to renounce all control of education, religion, manners and arts. We are proletarians and unwilling Communists only in the absence of these things; in their presence, we all instantly become aristocrats. Everything except the mechanical skeleton of society . . . must be left to free associations, to inspiration founding traditions and traditions guiding inspiration. The local attachments of such culture are important, and a just universal government would not disturb them. Each nation or religion might occupy, as private property under the common law, its special precincts or tracts of lands; or it might live locally intermingled with other nations and religions; but each in its own home would be protected from annoyance, and free to worship its own gods with the homage of a complete life fashioned in their image.[21]

Here Santayana's hostility to liberal culture has led him radically astray. It was evident to any judicious observer by the mid-1930s, and certainly by the time *Dominations and Powers* was published, that the Soviet system was perhaps the most destructive of local traditions, and above all of religious practices, in human history, and everywhere implemented a revolutionary Communist messianism incomparably more tyrannous than any identified by his strictures against the United States. For this reason, if we were ever to fall under a *Pax Sovietica*, it would be the peace of universal impoverishment and barbarism, and not the just liberal empire of which Santayana dreamt.

In truth, Santayana was unable to give an account of any plausible alternative to liberal society. He comes very close to admitting this, when in 'Alternatives to Liberalism' he identifies liberal society as a transitional state, but cannot specify its successor:

liberalism presupposes very special conditions. It presupposes a traditional order from which the world is to be emancipated. It presupposes heroic reformers, defying that order, and armed with a complete innate morality and science of their own by which a new order is to be established. But when once the new order has been thoroughly destroyed, that kind of heroic reformer may well become obsolete. His children will have no grievances and perhaps no morality. Even the abundance of their independent sciences, without an ultimate authority to synthesize or interpret them, may become a source of bewilderment. Add interracial war and a breakdown in industry, and there may seem to be occasion for turning over a new leaf. As to what may be found, or may come to be written, on the next page, no political programme can give us any assurance.[22]

If this diagnoses sapiently the ills of the liberal condition, Santayana is here (confessedly) unable to offer us a panacea for them. His *critique of liberalism*, however, retains considerable value. He illuminated the chief danger to liberal society in liberalism itself – in a political religion of *man-worship* which had lost the humility, and indeed the scepticism, that informs the historic Western religions. With its incoherent doctrine of progress, its inordinate and antinomian individualism and its ultimate subordination of the claims of liberty to those of an imaginary general welfare, liberalism has at length become the enemy of the civil society it once sought to theorize. As Santayana puts it in his *apologia pro mente sua*:

My naturalism and humanism seemed to them [his liberal readers] to give *carte blanche* to revolution: and so they do, if the revolution represents a deeper understanding of human nature and human virtue than tradition does at that moment; but, if we make allowance for the inevitable symbolism and convention in human ideas, tradition must normally represent human nature and human virtue much better than impatience with tradition can do; especially when this impatience is founded on love of luxury, childishness, and the absence of any serious discipline of mind and heart. These are the perils that threaten naturalism and humanism in America.[23]

Santayana's political thought, despite his hopes for it, does not encapsulate any realistic account of a post-liberal order. What it most powerfully suggests is the necessity (if the historical inheritance of liberal society which is our patrimony is to be preserved and not squandered) of abandoning the Romantic culture of limitless hubris for a classical ethos of limitation and constraint. Political wisdom is the sad business of prescribing for ordinary mortals, not a recipe for adventures in infinite freedom. This humble view was not unknown to the early theorists of liberalism, but it has been repressed and obliterated by modern liberalism, with its hallucinatory perspectives of open-ended world improvement and global betterment. We conceive government aright, if we conceive it as Hobbes did, and as some of the early liberals did, as a shelter against the worst of evils, civil war and the reversion to nature. It is the limited government which we inherit as our tradition – now far gone in desuetude – which protects us against such misfortune, and which thereby allows the emergence of civil society as the artificial remedy for our natural imperfections. Santayana reminds us, in his remarkable essay on Freud, that:

The human spirit, when it awakes, finds itself in trouble; it is burdened, for no reason it can assign, with all sorts of anxieties about food, pressures, pricks, noises and pains. It is born, as another wise myth has it, in original sin. And the passions and ambitions of life, as they come on, only complicate this burden and make it heavier, without rendering it less incessant or gratuitous.[24]

Political wisdom lies in accepting this human lot, not in seeking to wish it away by vast projects of reform. We alleviate the human lot as best we can by repairing and renewing the traditional institutions we have inherited, where these are themselves founded on a sane awareness of the human condition. For us, this means returning to the minute particulars of the liberal inheritance of civil society that we are at present frittering away in crazed fads and fashionable experiments. Our danger is that, like an ageing debauchee who has grown used to drawing on his patrimony, we may not realize until it is too late that it has largely been consumed. It is such a condition of which Santayana wrote when he observed that:

we sometimes see the legislator posing as a Titan. Perhaps he has got wind of a proud philosophy that makes will the absolute in a nation or in mankind, recognising no divine hindrance in circumstances or in the private recesses of the heart. Destiny is expected to march according to plan. No science, virtue or religion is admitted beyond the prescriptions of the state ... Here is certainly an intoxicating adventure; but I am afraid a city so founded, if it could stand, would turn out to be the iron City of Dis. These heroes would have entombed themselves in hell, in scorn of their own nature; and they would have reason to pine for the liberal chaos from which their satanic system had saved them.[25]

The final insight of Santayana's critique of liberalism is not that liberal society is inherently a transitional state of things. It is that the nemesis of liberal society is its self-destruction by liberal ideology, by a frenzy of theorizing which is willing to lay waste the inherited institutions of a liberal order – limited government, private property, the rule of law – for the sake of an imagined improvement of the human condition. Santayana's insight – an insight he did not always himself grasp, captivated as he sometimes was by delusive visions of radical alternatives to liberal society – is that the preservation of the liberal inheritance has as its most necessary condition a comprehensive disenchantment with liberal theory. Unless we can shake off the hubristic illusions of liberalism, the spiralling decline in our civilization is unlikely to be arrested, and may well end in the collapse of liberal society itself.

1989

4

Oakeshott as a liberal

*What may now be meant by the word 'liberal' is anyone's
guess.*   Michael Oakeshott[1]

The claim that the conception of political life that animates the
thought of Michael Oakeshott, clearly one of the most original and
profound British political philosophers since Hume and certainly this
century's greatest conservative writer, is a liberal conception may
seem unacceptably paradoxical or even wilfully perverse. Yet it is far
from being novel. Commentators such as W. H. Greenleaf and Samuel
Brittan have seen in Oakeshott's thought deep affinities with the
intellectual tradition of classical liberalism; an entire paper (greatly
admired by Oakeshott himself)[2] has been devoted to interpreting
Oakeshott as a liberal theorist; and both of the two recent book-length
studies of Oakeshott's work[3] characterize his outlook on politics as
at least akin to that of a liberal. For all that, it still remains unclear
just what sort of liberal Oakeshott might have been, what it was that
he took from liberal thought and what he rejected, and how the
liberal element of his thought coheres with the rest.

It is not too hard to be clear about what Oakeshott rejected in
liberal thought. The liberal project of fixing, by way of a doctrine or
a theory, the proper scope and limits of the authority of government,
determinately once and for all, as it was attempted by Locke or Kant,
J. S. Mill or, in our own time, by Rawls and Nozick, Oakeshott
rejected as a prime example of rationalism in politics. From this point
of view, liberalism is (or was) merely a species of ideology – of
that rationalist abridgement of the contingencies and vicissitudes of

practice that aspires to be, but can never succeed in becoming, an authoritative, prescriptive guide for practice. The proper tasks and limits of government cannot be determined by reasoning from first principles (supposing there could be such things); they can be established, always provisionally and never indisputably, only by reasonings that are circumstantial and which invoke precedents, judgements and practices that are already present in current political life. Oakeshott's rejection of the rationalist (or fundamentalist) element in liberalism expresses one of his most profound insights – that political deliberation and political discourse are closer in their character to conversation than they are to any sort of demonstrative reasoning. For Oakeshott, as for Aristotle, political discourse is a form of practical reasoning, and in virtue of that character can never issue in, or rest upon, the certainty found (according to Aristotle, at any rate) in the theoretical disciplines. Political discourse, then, though it may contain passages of argument, is not an argument, but a conversation.

Oakeshott's repudiation of this aspect of liberalism – perhaps its most definitive or constitutive – has far-reaching implications for the current understanding (or confusion) we have of the relations of political philosophy with political practice, and it contains lessons which, if we could learn them, might at least temper the barbarism into which political life has long since fallen among us. The first lesson is that the hubristic project of doctrinal or fundamentalist liberalism – the project attempted by all the liberal thinkers mentioned earlier of fixing the boundaries of government action by some principle or doctrine, be it *laissez-faire*, a specification of allegedly natural (but patently conventional) rights, or a list of basic liberties derived (as in Rawls and Dworkin)[4] from a conception of justice rooted only in the fleeting local knowledge of the American academic nomenklatura – embodies a mistaken conception of philosophy itself. Whereas philosophy can clarify the presuppositions or postulates of practice, and thereby perhaps in some degree illuminate it, it can neither found practice nor govern it. For it is practice that is always primordial. Accordingly, if philosophical inquiry has any practical effects or benefits, they are oblique, indirect and prophylactic. (And, of course, philosophy need have no other goal than the pursuit of understanding.) Oakeshott's conception of philosophy radically undermines the liberal foundationalist project, which seeks to circumscribe the authority of government by a theory. It also serves to chasten the ambitions of philosophers, who seem always to have been astonished that political life could proceed without their constant supervision.

Oakeshott's conception of political life as a conversation may have a prophylactic role to play in respect of the barbarization of political discourse and practice that in our day is far gone. The tendency of much in recent thought and practice has been to try to assimilate political discourse to some other, supposedly superior mode, and thereby to deny to political life its autonomy. This decline is, perhaps, furthest gone in the United States, where in the context of a common culture whose resources are fast depleting every political question is now couched in legalist terms. The idea of politics as a conversation in which the collision of opinions is moderated and accommodated, in which what is sought is not truth but peace, has been almost entirely lost, and supplanted by a legalist paradigm in which all political claims and conflicts are modelled in the jargon of rights. In such a context, not only is civilized political discourse virtually extinguished, but the legal institutions into which it is transplanted are corrupted. The courts become arenas for political claims and interests, each of them inordinate and resistant to compromise, and political life elsewhere becomes little more than bargaining and logrolling. The result of the American assimilation of politics to law has, then, been the corruption of both. In the course of this development, the profound insights of the authors of *The Federalist Papers* into the limitation of government, not primarily by constitutional devices, but by the civic virtues of a free people that has in common a devotion to the culture and practice of liberty and which understands the ground of that practice to be the imperfectibility of our species, have been almost lost. In Europe, and in Britain, the virus of legalism has been less pervasive, but the presence of other ideologies more powerful. If socialism is everywhere on the wane, other ideologies are waxing – including ideological strands within conservative thought and practice, which ascribe to governments the objectives of restoring a lost moral consensus, of reviving a fragmented national integrity, or of promoting maximal wealth-creation. Here the autonomy of political life is compromised by its attempted assimilation to the modes of discourse of history, economics or industrial management. If we could recover the understanding of political discourse Oakeshott has theorized for us, that understanding might – far more than the institution of what Oakeshott, in the new edition of *Rationalism in Politics* published by Liberty Press of Indianapolis and edited by Timothy Fuller,[5] calls 'the absurd device of a Bill of Rights' – protect us from the inordinacies and invasiveness of the modern state.

What we have seen so far is that the rationalist projects of doctrinal liberalism, spawned by a false philosophy that pretends to govern rather than merely to struggle to understand practice, have had the effect of corroding our historical inheritance of civil society and of weakening traditional constraints on the activities of government. We have yet to see what Oakeshott retains of liberal thought. We find this, if I am not mistaken, in the understanding of civil life he develops in his conception of *civil association*, which may be taken to be the living kernel of liberalism, and the chief element in his thought in virtue of which it deserves the appellation 'liberal'. In his account of civil association, Oakeshott (as Wendell John Coats Jr shows in his admirable paper)[6] synthesizes a variety of seemingly disparate understandings, Aristotelian and Ciceronian, Roman and Norman, Lockean and Hegelian, to yield an account of that form of human association – emerging distinctively only in late medieval Europe, and never without opposition in any modern European state – in which people live together, not under the aegis of any common end or hierarchy of ends, but instead by their subscription to a body of non-instrumental rules, whereby they can (in all their variety and conflicting purposes) coexist in peace. Civil association has, from the first, had a rival in *enterprise association* – that mode of association constituted by shared adherence to a common objective, the mode of association animating an industrial corporation, say. What distinguishes a civil association from an enterprise association, most fundamentally, is that the former is purposeless in having no projects of its own, whereas the latter is constituted by its projects. For Oakeshott, this is to say that civil association is a form or mode of association that is non-instrumental and moral, whereas the latter's authority derives solely from the projects that animate it.

Oakeshott is clear that modern European states have always partaken of both modes of association. Rarely, if ever, has such a state been merely a guardian of civil association. As he observes: 'Modern history is littered not only with visions, in various idioms, of a state as a purposive association, but also with projects to impose this character upon a state.'[7] Like the minimum state of classical liberalism, civil association is an ideal type, or a limiting case, not found in the real world of human history. In historical fact, all modern European states have had elements – managerialist, mercantilist or corporatist – in virtue of which they have acquired the character of enterprise associations, and their role as custodians of civil association has accordingly been compromised. Indeed, it may be said of twentieth-century totalitarian states that they are nothing but enterprise associations, committed for that reason to the destruction of civil association. And one of the inheritances of liberal ideology, the idea of progress in history, has made it hard for any modern state not to claim for itself the role of an agent of world-betterment. Indeed civil association itself has been defended as a means to prosperity – a complete misunderstanding of it in Oakeshott's terms. One may say, in fact, that, though it has never been altogether silenced, the voice of civil association has in our century never been very loud: it has, most of the time, been shouted down by all those ideologies and movements that perceive the authority of the state only in its success in exploiting the earth's resources. It is this Baconian conception of the office of government that, in Oakeshott's view, pervades all contemporary conceptions of the state-as-enterprise-association, be they Fascist or Fabian, Marxist or Manchesterist in inspiration.

We can now see what Oakeshott's thought has in common with classical liberalism. For the classical liberal, the authority of the state did not depend on its contribution, if any, to economic growth, any more than it depended on the local cultural identity of its subjects. It depended on its being recognized, not in terms of desirable projects or particular cultural values, but in terms of law or justice – of *lex*. As Robert Grant has put it, in what is by far the most perceptive and illuminating account of Oakeshott's thought we possess, 'A *civitas* (or civil association) need not be culturally homogeneous (though doubtless a degree of homogeneity will help). The only homogeneity which counts, and which is essentially 'cultural', consists in a common disposition to value *lex* above one's local cultural identity.'[8] It is in his account of the authority of the office of rule as being formal or abstract in this fashion, then, not in his eloquent defence of individuality, that the most fundamental affinity between Oakeshott and classical liberalism is to be found. It shows him to have more in common with Kant, in the end, than with Burke or Hegel.

It may well be that it is precisely in its kinship with classical liberalism on the nature of the authority of the state that the Achilles heel of Oakeshott's political thought lies. Both assert that the authority of a modern state depends neither on its success in any substantive purpose nor on its relationship with the cultural identity of its subjects. Both claims are profoundly questionable. As to the former, less fundamentally important claim, it is a matter of brute historical fact that no government can, in any modern democratic state, long survive if it does not preside over sustained economic growth. For this reason, every modern government is inexorably drawn into the dreary business of aligning the economic with the electoral cycle: all are in some significant measure mercantilist or corporatist in practice. In short, all modern states are to a considerable degree enterprise associations. The project of effecting a radical disseveration of government from the conduct of economic life, which Oakeshott shared with the classical liberals, has in common with classical liberalism a quality otherwise entirely absent from Oakeshott's thought – namely, its utopian character. The project of denying to the modern state its character as, in significant part, an enterprise association, is hardly a conservative one; if it could be achieved, the transformation of political arrangements thereby wrought would be little short of revolutionary. This is, in effect, tacitly acknowledged by Oakeshott, when in his most overtly political essay, 'The Political Economy of Freedom',[9] he endorses the radical proposals advanced by the Chicago economist Henry Simons, in his *Economic Policy for a Free Society*.[10] More typically, the debacles of Thatcherism and Reaganism suggest that, for us, the enterprise-association state is an historical fate, which we may indeed strive to temper, but which we cannot hope to overcome.

The second claim – that the authority of a modern state does not depend on its subjects having a common cultural identity – is yet more questionable, and more importantly so. It is the claim, found in Kant and in much recent American constitutional theory, that the recognition of the state as embodying abstract or formal principles of law or justice is all that is needed for its authority. Recent history does little to support this claim. On the contrary, it may be observed that, insofar as a polity is held together by little else than allegiance to abstract principles or procedural rules, it will be fragmented and unstable, and its authority weak. The point may be made in another way. The idea that political authority could ever be solely or mainly formal or abstract arose in times when a common cultural identity could be taken for granted. For Kant as for the framers of the Declaration of Independence, that common cultural identity was that of European Christendom. Insofar as this cultural identity is depleted or fragmented, political authority will be attenuated. We may see this ominous development occurring in microcosm in Britain, where a minority of fundamentalist Muslims that is estranged from whatever remains of a common culture, and which rejects the tacit norms of toleration that allow a civil society to reproduce itself peacefully, has effectively curbed freedom of expression about Islam in Britain today. We may see the same sombre development occurring on a vast scale in the United States, which appears to be sliding inexorably away from being a civil society whose institutions express a common cultural inheritance to being an enfeebled polity whose institutions are captured by a host of warring minorities, having in common only the dwindling capital of an unquestioned legalism to sustain them. Oakeshott himself observes that:

the authority of an office of rule remains always a delicate matter of current belief. It must be able to survive a rainy day; it must be proof against disapproval and ridicule of the performances of the office and it cannot be bought with good works; it hangs like a drop of dew upon a blade of grass.[11]

For us, who live in an age of mass migrations and fundamentalist convulsions, and who are witness of the dependency of political allegiances on resurgent local cultural identities, ethnic and religious, in the post-Communist world, it is clear that the authority of a state that (however inevitably compromised by its engagements as an enterprise association) acts as a custodian of civil association is frailer even than Oakeshott perceived, and cannot long do without the support given it by a common culture.

It may be that what Oakeshott has taken from the liberal tradition about the authority of the state is not, finally, his most important borrowing from it. It is his conception of civil association, in which the historical European inheritance of civil society is cleansed of its theoretical accretions, such as notions of natural rights, *laissez-faire* and the minimum state, that is likely to be his most enduring gift to political philosophy, and it is one that can plausibly be termed liberal. In Oakeshott's writings on education,[12] again, one finds a conception of education that is liberal in the best sense of that term – a view of education, not as the inculcation of an orthodoxy, the acquisition of information or the transmission of useful skills, but as initiation into a cultural inheritance in the course of which we learn to become civilized conversants. If, in very unOakeshottian vein, we were to ask which element in his thought has most contemporary relevance, it would perhaps be his idea of a liberal education as an unchartered intellectual adventure, with no goal beyond its own inner *telos* – an idea which some of us may recognize in our pasts, but which is threatened now on every side, as much by managerial conservatism as by left-wing ideologues.

Of Oakeshott as a philosopher and as a man I have so far said nothing. As to his philosophy, ably and comprehensively expounded by Paul Franco[13] (himself a pupil of Timothy Fuller, America's best Oakeshott scholar), it is his pluralist affirmation of the diversity of modes of discourse and experience, of moralities as vernacular languages whose nature it is to be many and divergent, and of the miscellaneity of practice, which no theory can hope to capture, that embodies his most distinctive contribution to philosophy. It is only in the later Wittgenstein (whose thought, though influenced by Spengler, lacks the deep historical consciousness of Oakeshott's) that we find a comparable critique of traditional rationalism and contemporary Positivism. It is a comment on the current state of academic philosophy that Oakeshott's contribution to it has gone almost unnoticed.

If one had to express the spirit of Oakeshott's thought in a single phrase, one might say that it is *a critique of purposefulness*. The image of human life that Oakeshott conveys to us is not that of a problem to be solved or a situation to be mastered, it is the poetic (and religious) image of our being lost in a world in which our vocation is to play earnestly and to be earnest playfully, living without thought of any final destination. For those of us lucky enough to have known the man, Oakeshott's writings will always evoke the memory of his conversation, in which intellectual passion commingled with a fathomless gaiety, and the dry reasonings of philosophy became, as in the dialogues of Socrates, dialectical, and at last lyrical.

1992

5

Notes towards a definition of the political thought of Tlön

In his celebrated fiction, *Tlön, Uqbar, Orbis Tertius*, Jorge Luis Borges tells of the discovery of an encyclopaedia of an illusory world, *The First Encyclopaedia of Tlön*. The fantastic world of Tlön was, he tells us, congenitally Idealist in its philosophy. For the peoples of the planet of Tlön, as for Bishop Berkeley, to be is to be perceived; the world is not a manifold of objects in space, but a series of mental events. In such a world, causal connections are only associations of ideas, and the idea of a continuous universe that exists independently of our momentary states of consciousness is unknown except as a *jeu d'esprit* of metaphysical speculation. The doctrine of materialism has indeed been formulated, but as a paradox or a conceit; however ingenious the arguments in its favour, they do not convince the inhabitants of Tlön. It might be supposed that a world consisting only of successive and irreducible states of mind would be a world without science and philosophy; but this, Borges tells us, would be a mistake. The world of Tlön abounds in sciences, countless in number, as it does in metaphysical systems; all are treated as dialectical games, or branches of fantastic literature, from which is sought not conviction, but astonishment. It is to the description of this illusory world, its languages, religions, numismatics, 'its emperors and its oceans, its architecture and its playing cards', amounting to a complete history of an unknown planet, that *The First Encyclopaedia of Tlön* is devoted.

By an association of ideas that is natural and perhaps inevitable, Borges's elegant story suggests to the reader the idea of a *Companion to Contemporary Political Philosophy* whose subject matter is the political thought of a fictitious world, a world of human beings like ourselves, but having histories and conceptions of themselves very different from those surveyed in Robert Goodin and Philip Pettit's *Companion to Contemporary Political Philosophy*.[1] In this exercise in fantasy, the topics treated encompass nationality and monarchy, ethnicity and political theology; the systems of ideas include legitimism and theocracy, nationalism and Byzantinism. This alternative *Companion* devotes much space, also, to the political philosophy of contemporary Western liberalism. It gives coverage to the question why in the late twentieth century socialism existed as an intellectual movement only in the United States; to the heroic effort of the foremost contemporary theorist of justice at a transcendental deduction of the British Labour Party as it was in the 1950s; to the ingenious neo-Hegelian interpretation of history, which appears to have governed US foreign policy during the post-Communist period in which national or else ethnic allegiances were the only remaining sources of political legitimacy in much of the world, and which affirmed that ethnicity and nationality were spent political forces; to the powerful school of Anglo-American jurisprudence in which all political questions are resolved by appeal to the demands of a single fundamental right, the right to meaning; and cognate topics in contemporary liberal theory. At the same time the fictitious *Companion* does not confine itself to liberal theory, or indeed to Western thought. It treats also the neo-Confucian political ideas of the East Asian peoples, the varieties of Islamic political theory, and the ambiguities of Orthodoxy in recent Russian theorizing. If it deals only in passing with the idea of a secular civil society, focusing principally on the theoretical and political inheritances of Atatürkism, that is because it seeks to understand the thought of countries, such as India, whose emerging political cultures seem to confirm the editors' belief that secularism is in most parts of the world an ephemeral episode. In this imaginary *Companion*, then, Western liberal thought is not neglected; but it is treated as only one trend among many, and not that which has the greatest political resonance in the illusory world it surveys.

Goodin and Pettit's *Companion to Contemporary Political Philosophy* has a coverage and subject matter that are incommensurable with those of its fictitious rival. Nevertheless, particularly if its editors' statement of its intended coverage is taken as authoritative, it is itself best understood as belonging to a sub-genre in fantastic literature, by comparison with which the fictitious *Companion* seems a laboured exercise in realism. Their book is divided into three broad parts, with the first treating the contributions of different disciplines – analytical philosophy, sociology, law, economics and so on – to contemporary political philosophy, the second discussing the major ideologies that have figured in the subject, and the third consisting of shorter treatments of a variety of particular topics. In the introduction, the editors give their reasons for treating the ideologies chosen for discussion in the book's second part: 'In selecting the ideologies to be covered in the second part, we tried to identify those principled world-views that have a substantial impact in contemporary life as well as an impact on philosophical thinking.' They go on:

Nationalism – still less racism, sexism or ageism – does not figure, on the grounds that it hardly counts as a principled way of thinking about things ... Yet other ideologies – like theism, monarchism, fascism – are omitted on the grounds that, whatever impact they once had on public life, they would seem to play only a marginal role in the contemporary world.

These remarks imply that nationalism, easily the most powerful political phenomenon in the contemporary world, not only has no defence in principled thought, but never did; that the reflections of Hegel on the nation-state, and of Herder on national culture, do not count, and presumably never counted, as exercises in principled thought; and they invite the question, if only as a move in a dialectical game: by what standards are these theorists of nationality to be excluded from the canon of principled thinking?

The editors' observation that theism plays only a marginal role in the contemporary world will evoke in many readers – Salman Rushdie, perhaps, or the beleaguered secular intelligentsia of contemporary Egypt – astonishment rather than conviction, at least to begin with. For such readers, whether they be in Algeria or India, Turkey or Pakistan, the claim that theistic ideologies have little impact on contemporary public life may have an air of paradox, if not unreality: their societies may seem to them to be convulsed by a life-or-death struggle between secularism and theocracy. True, with regard to the many parts of their readers' world that are ravaged by conflicts between adherents of different religions – Bosnia, Lebanon,

Nagorno-Karabakh and unnumbered others – the editors might maintain that these countries are sundered by political conflicts whose causes are found not in the religious beliefs of the protagonists, but elsewhere. This hardly justifies the claim – which has an almost fantastic aspect, even in the context of a secular republic such as the United States – that the impact of theism on contemporary public life is marginal; and it leaves members of any contemporary society who believe their lives to be at risk solely because of their religious allegiances with an intriguing conundrum in the logic of social explanation.

Equally, the claim that Fascism has only a marginal role in the contemporary world may strike Jews, in France or Germany, say, whose synagogues have been daubed with swastikas, or Hungarian liberals who opposed the triumphal reburial of Admiral Horthy, as unconvincing. The editorial methodology which justifies sections in the book's second part on anarchism and feminism, but not on nationalism or Fascism, and in the third section supports briefer discussions of autonomy and democracy, but not of authority or of war, is the Tlönist methodology, according to which only that has reality which is at any particular time perceptible in academic discourse. It is this conventionalist methodology which explains the otherwise anomalous facts that the apocalyptic degradation of the natural and human environments in the former Soviet Union, about which there had long been a mass of evidence from émigré sources that lacked academic and therefore (from a conventionalist perspective) epistemic credentials, surfaced in academic discourse only when the Soviet *glasnost* had given it respectability, while the unreformability of the Soviet system, a commonplace among its subjects, was accepted as a possibility by the Western academic class only after it was informed by trusted nomenklaturist sources that the Soviet Union had, in fact, collapsed. And it is probably the Tlönist methodology of the Western academic class that accounts for the paucity in academic literatures of studies of another world-historical transformation, currently under way – the adoption in China of market institutions and the ongoing shift in economic and cultural initiative from Europe and North America to the peoples of East Asia and the Pacific Rim. This latter world-historical shift is as yet barely recognized in academic discourse, and certainly does not feature in Goodin and Pettit's *Companion*. In the life of the academic mind, the owl of Minerva seldom flies as early as dusk.

It must be stressed that the forty-one chapters of this indispensable book contain several that violate Tlönist canons of method by engaging with the real world of human history and experience rather than solely with passages in academic discourse. In the third section on special topics, Allen Buchanan contributes an exemplary section on secession and nationalism, in which the intellectual rigour of analytical philosophy is put to work in a masterly consideration of historical examples. Stephen Macedo gives a consideration of fundamentalism and toleration which is wholly admirable in its comprehensiveness, seriousness and in its historical sense of the multiplicity of challenges that presently confront the old-fashioned liberal ideal of toleration. Chandran Kukathas provides a critical survey of recent thought on liberty which focuses sharply and rightly on the central contributions of Berlin, Cohen, Steiner and Skinner to its philosophical and theoretical analysis while recurrently returning our thought to the institutional and political preconditions and implications of the diverse conceptions of liberty he discusses. John Dunn contributes a fascinating section on trust, which contains (among several other invaluable passages) a distinction between trust as a passion and as policy, an argument for the marginal political contribution, by comparison with economics, of academic philosophy and a critique of the hollowing-out of the political realm in recent theories of social justice. In the second section, Alan Ryan gives an account of liberalism, and Anthony Quinton of conservatism, which in their treatment of the historical contexts as well as the philosophical contents of these traditions are as nearly definitive as makes no matter. In the long first section on disciplinary contributions to contemporary political philosophy, Geoffrey Brennan discusses the contribution of economics with a degree of sensitivity to the limits of economic explanation that is surpassingly rare among practising economists, and Richard Tuck considers in a marvellously illuminating and balanced piece how the awareness of discontinuous conceptual change promoted by the 'new' history of ideas practised by Quentin Skinner, John Dunn and himself affects the way we theorize our institutions and political life. In these and some other contributions to Goodin and Pettit's *Companion* we see it in its aspect as a compendium of lively essays by first-rate practitioners, which are worth reading in their own right as exemplars of political philosophy when that seeks to reflect the real world of human history.

On the whole, however, the essays collected in this book are to be read as a mirror of the subject as we find it today and not of the world in which we live. It might be argued that Goodin and Pettit's *Companion* can hardly be faulted for being a mirror of the other books that are its subject matter. The questions remain why these other books are such poor mirrors of the world, and why Goodin and Pettit enhance the distorting properties of political thought as an academic subject in their choice of ideologies and topics for inclusion in their book. The answer is not to be found, as might be supposed, in their view of political philosophy as an inherently and centrally normative subject, and in a consequent neglect of feasibility constraints on the attainment of political ideals as these are found in the real world, since Goodin and Pettit need no reminding of the anti-utopian commonplace that politics is the art of the possible. Indeed Goodin makes the suggestion that the main constraint on achieving political ideals is not any one of the more familiar economic, sociological or psychological constraints, but rather the availability of political ideas themselves, a dearth of well-worked-out policy options, of 'technologies to solve ethical problems', and – giving us a clue to the origins of the distorting perspective of contemporary political philosophy – recommends that 'normative theorists ought to shift attention, at least for a while, from values to mechanisms for implementing them'.[2]

From these and other remarks it is apparent that for the editors of this *Companion*, as for the overwhelming majority of practising political philosophers today, there is no doubt as to what are the relevant political ideals; they are the liberal ideals of the European Enlightenment project. These are the ideals – of subjecting all human institutions to a rational criticism and of convergence on a universal civilization whose foundation is autonomous human reason – that are taken as unproblematic, even axiomatic, in virtually all recent Anglo-American political philosophy. Even when, as in communitarian theory, the liberal individualist fiction of the disembodied or unsituated human subject, which has a history only by accident, is criticized as a political residue of the Kantian noumenal self, it is only to advance another fiction, an idea of community – the noumenal community, let us call it – that has none of the particularistic allegiances of every human community that has ever existed. It is plain that Western political philosophers have yet to learn to view the liberal ideals of the Enlightenment project with Nietzsche's 'suspecting glance'. It has not occurred to them to ask what claim these ideals have on human beings, why the Western societies that are identified with them are plagued with anomie and nihilism, nor why they are increasingly repudiated by non-Occidental peoples.

Political philosophy, as it is reflected in the distorting mirror of this *Companion*, is the self-awareness of a Western academic class whose identity is defined by the ephemera of Western liberal opinion. A view of the world as seen through this broken looking-glass occludes perception both of the longer tradition of Western political thought that is not liberal in any sense and of the non-Western traditions that are being reasserted in many parts of the contemporary world. To say this is not to put in a plea for multiculturalism in political philosophy, since multiculturalism is, after all, a peculiarly, and indeed parochially, Western preoccupation. It is to comment on the oddity, at this point in human history, of an account of contemporary political philosophy that is so Europocentric in its perspective that Confucian ideas, which animate thought and practice in the extraordinary East Asian experiments, under way in Japan, in Singapore, in China and in Korea, of harnessing the dynamism of market institutions to the needs of stable and enduring communities, are not even mentioned in the index. Nor is it to deny liberalism its legitimate place in the Western intellectual tradition. The point is that the virtual hegemony in contemporary political philosophy, and in this *Companion* to it, of an unhistorical and culturally parochial species of liberal theory disables the understanding when it is confronted by the most powerful political forces of our age. The hegemony of liberal discourse and ideals to which this book attests leaves these forces – of ethnicity and nationalism, for example – in an intellectual limbo, akin to that of sexuality in Victorian times, from which they emerge intermittently as evidence of persisting human irrationality, to be discussed nervously in a strangulated Newspeak of difference and otherness, or else dismissed as barely intelligible departures from principled thought. To pass over in this way, as regrettable atavisms or lapses from theoretical coherence, the ruling forces of the age, does not augur well for contemporary political philosophy, or for liberalism.

Speaking of the heresy of materialism, according to which there is a world of things that persist independently of our consciousness of them, Borges tells us that 'The language of Tlön is by its nature resistant to this paradox; most people do not understand it.' In the Tlönist world, materialism can be only a feat of specious reasoning, or else a play on words, not a compelling view of things. Perhaps congenitally conventionalist, academic political philosophers will find hard to grasp the proposal that their books should aim to be mirrors of the world before they seek to change it, and will treat it as a mere paradox, even suspecting in it a motive of perversity or of irony. Evidently they cannot accept that a world in which their liberal ideals are constantly mocked does not secretly revere them.

Or it may be that the task of understanding the intractable conflicts of our world does not satisfy the passion for symmetry, the craving for any semblance of order, which finds expression in systems – structuralism, neo-conservatism, critical theory – that at once pacify the intelligence and gratify the moral appetites. If this is so, then perhaps academic political philosophy can be no more than an hermetic activity, whose product is a self-referential text in which the world is mentioned only in inconspicuous and misleading footnotes. It is a measure of how far political philosophy has approached that condition that all but the most perceptive reader of Goodin and Pettit's estimable and useful *Companion* could come from it in ignorance of the Holocaust, of the Gulag, and of every world-historical transformation of our age. Perhaps, given the condition of the subject, the political philosopher is best occupied in the modest exegesis of texts – like Mill's *Liberty*, say – whose charm is in their distance from our world, or any world we are likely to find ourselves in.

1993

6

Isaiah Berlin: the value of decency

Western political thinking between the end of the Second World War and the collapse of Communism was shaped by the experience of totalitarianism. The rise of National Socialism and Stalinism produced a sense of the fragility of liberal civilization that persisted after the Nazi regime had been destroyed and Soviet power contained. The question that troubled many was how liberal values could have collapsed so precipitately and completely in much of Europe, while Communist regimes that claimed to embody Enlightenment values repressed freedom on an unprecedented scale. It was clear that if the disasters of the twentieth century were not to be repeated, the intellectual roots of totalitarianism had to be uncovered and destroyed, even if this meant relinquishing some cherished Western beliefs.

Among those who took up this challenge Isaiah Berlin occupies a highly distinctive place. On both the right and the left there have been many who have dismissed Berlin as a thinker whose ideas are irretrievably dated, and in recent years it has become fashionable to question the idea that the twentieth century witnessed the rise of a new, totalitarian type of dictatorship. For his part Berlin never doubted the reality of totalitarianism. Given the background of his life he could hardly have done so. Born in Riga in 1909, he was part of the generation of European Jews that experienced the twentieth century at its most destructive and horrific. When he was six his family moved to Petrograd, where in 1917 he witnessed the liberal revolution in February and the Bolshevik seizure of power in November. In 1921 his family moved to England and he was educated at Oxford, where he obtained his first academic post. Apart from his years abroad during the Second World War he remained in Oxford for the rest of his life.

In 1941, after the German invasion of the Soviet Union, the Nazis murdered both his grandfathers and several other family members. During the Second World War, Berlin worked for the British government, first in New York and Washington and then for a time in Moscow. When in Russia, he came into contact with Anna Akhmatova and other members of the Russian intelligentsia who lived in an environment where intellectual and personal freedom had been almost wholly eclipsed. The events of these years had a formative influence on the work in political theory and the history of ideas he did after resuming his academic life in Oxford after the war. In conversation he used to observe that in its mass murders the twentieth century was the worst in history, and to an extent that has not been appreciated the view of liberty and ethical pluralism that he developed in the 1950s was an attempt to undermine the beliefs that helped engender the crimes of totalitarianism.

Those who argue that Berlin's thought was shaped by the history of the last century are not mistaken, but in dismissing it as dated they neglect the larger historical perspectives that informed it and miss its continuing power. Berlin posed a formidable challenge not only to totalitarian ideologies but also to recent varieties of liberalism. At times he seemed – to use a distinction he borrowed from the ancient Greek poet Archilochus to interpret Tolstoy in a celebrated lecture – more like the fox that knows many things than the hedgehog that knows one big thing. Both as a thinker and as a man he had many facets; he refused to tether himself to any simple formula for dealing with human affairs. Yet if there is a single idea that links together his surprisingly voluminous writings on Mill and Machiavelli, Herder and de Maistre, Vico and Herzen and many lesser-known thinkers, and which gives his defence of liberalism its distinctive character, it is his thesis of the plurality of values.

Berlin was never a very systematic thinker, and he nowhere stated his theory of value-pluralism in anything like complete or canonical form. Several versions of it are presented in his writings; but common to them is a consistent rejection of the idea – which he rightly viewed as being fundamental in the Western intellectual tradition – that all genuine human values must be combinable in a harmonious whole. In this view conflicts of values are symptoms of error that in principle can always be resolved: if human values seem to come into conflict that is only because our understanding of them is imperfect, or some of the contending values are spurious; and where such conflicts appear there is a single right answer that – if only they can find it – all reasonable people are bound to accept. In opposition to this view Berlin maintained that conflicts of values are real and inescapable, with some of them having no satisfactory solution. He advanced this view not as a form of scepticism but as a universal truth: conflicts of value go with being human. Inklings of this pluralist viewpoint can be detected in some of Berlin's pre-war writings on analytical philosophy, but it was only after the war that he stated it clearly and applied it to the pathologies of twentieth-century politics.

Political Ideas in the Romantic Age[1] is the longest text Isaiah Berlin ever produced. Written between 1950 and 1952, much revised, and then set aside and seemingly forgotten, it is described by Henry Hardy – the dedicated editor and literary trustee who in thirty years of scholarly labours has rescued so many of Berlin's surprisingly voluminous writings from undeserved oblivion – as the '*Grundrisse*, the ur-text or "torso", as Berlin called it, from which a great deal of his subsequent work derived'. Indispensable for anyone interested in the history of ideas and the development of liberal thought, it contains most of the central themes of Berlin's work, together with some of its recurring ambiguities. In a characteristic passage Berlin attacks the Enlightenment belief that a condition of society is in principle attainable in which all values that are truly important can be fully realized. In a wide range of Enlightenment thinkers, he writes,

we find the same common assumption: that the answers to all the great questions must of necessity agree with one another; for they must correspond with reality, and reality is a harmonious whole. If this were not so, there is chaos at the heart of things: which is unthinkable. Liberty, equality, property, knowledge, security, practical wisdom, purity of character, sincerity, kindness, rational self-love, all these ideals ... cannot (if they are truly desirable) conflict with one another; if they appear to do so it must be due to some misunderstanding of their properties. No truly good thing can ever be finally incompatible with any other; indeed they virtually entail one another: men cannot be wise unless they are free, or free unless they are just, happy and so forth.

Here we conspicuously abandon the voice of experience – which records very obvious conflicts of ultimate ideals – and encounter a doctrine that stems from older theological roots – from the belief that unless all the positive virtues are harmonious with one another, or at least not incompatible, the notion of the Perfect Entity – whether it be called nature or God or Ultimate Reality – is not conceivable.

This passage encapsulates Berlin's analysis of the intellectual roots of some of the major political disasters of the twentieth century: the role in the Enlightenment of a utopian ideal of social harmony; the derivation of this ideal from older metaphysical and religious beliefs that have a long history in Western thought; and the claim that in refusing to accept the testimony of experience, with its message of irresolvable conflict among human ideals, the Enlightenment propagated a monistic philosophy that opened the way to new forms of tyranny. Berlin's broad-brush picture leaves out Enlightenment thinkers such as David Hume who emphasize the limited role of reason and understates the extent to which Adam Smith and others acknowledged human imperfectibility. Even so Berlin was right in thinking that a major strand of Enlightenment thinking featured a belief in attainable harmony that had no basis in experience. The belief that conflicts of values can be left behind in a new type of society, to which many Enlightenment thinkers have subscribed, is not a product of observation or scientific inquiry; it is a relic of faith. These thinkers may have imagined that they embodied the voice of reason, but they were in fact believers in an idea of perfection inherited from religion.

In one facet of his work, Berlin, then, was a critic of the Enlightenment – but not an enemy. He does not belong among the thinkers of what he called the Counter-Enlightenment – thinkers such as J. G. Hamann and Joseph de Maistre, who were virulently hostile to the Enlightenment's core beliefs in freedom, equality and the value of rational inquiry. Berlin shared these Enlightenment beliefs; but he found in some of the most influential Enlightenment thinkers a monism he viewed as dangerously mistaken, and in this he was influenced by some of the Enlightenment's Romantic critics. In a seminal essay he praised the Romantic movement for having 'permanently shaken the faith in universal, objective truth in matters of conduct', and described the Enlightenment faith in future harmony as 'an ideal for which more human beings have, in our time, sacrificed themselves and others than, perhaps, for any other cause in human history'.[2]

It is a strong claim, and it is questionable whether it applies to all forms of twentieth-century totalitarianism. It was not any faith in human harmony that fuelled Nazi ideology. Nevertheless Berlin highlights an aspect of twentieth-century history that is often forgotten, or else stridently denied. The repression of liberty that took place in the countries in which Communist regimes were established cannot be adequately explained as a product of backwardness, or of errors in the application of Marxian theory. It was the result of a resolute attempt to realize an Enlightenment utopia – a condition of society in which no serious form of conflict any longer exists.[3]

While Berlin's analysis of the dangers of monism is acute and forceful, he never developed a fully convincing account of value-pluralism. He based his version of pluralism on a view of human nature, which is set out in a passage cited by Joshua Cherniss in his admirably lucid and well-balanced introduction:

Man is incapable of self-completion, and therefore never wholly predictable; fallible, a complex combination of opposites, some reconcilable, others incapable of being resolved or harmonised; unable to cease from his search for truth, happiness, novelty, freedom, but with no guarantee ... of being able to attain them.

Berlin presented this formulation as an account of the picture of human nature held by John Stuart Mill, but as with many of his interpretations of past thinkers it could just as well be a statement of his own view. Like Mill, Berlin was much influenced by the Romantic belief that humans do not owe their values to God or nature, but freely create them. Again like Mill he rejected the ultra-Romantic notion that humans invent themselves out of nothing and can be anything they choose to be. He also rejected the post-modern and

relativist view that human values are highly elastic cultural constructions. He insisted that basic human needs and potentialities do not
vary much across cultures and repeatedly affirmed the desirability of
something like a universal moral minimum. He was a convinced
exponent of universal human values, whose distinctive contribution
was to acknowledge that these values could be at odds with one
another. Unfortunately he never spelled out which values are truly
universal and which culturally specific, and this leaves his account
of value-pluralism and its relations with liberalism precarious and
unstable.

It is not always clear what Berlin means by 'values' – are they
fully fledged ideals of the good life, or anything that can be judged
desirable? Again, how are values defined and distinguished from one
another – should we use the methods of cultural anthropology to
identify them, or employ some kind of conceptual or linguistic analysis, as Berlin sometimes did? Yet again, how do we know when we
have reached a point at which conflicts of values are irreconcilable?
If we reasoned further, might we not increase our understanding and
resolve the conflict? Most seriously, it is unclear whether negative
liberty – which he sees as the central value of liberalism – belongs in
the category of values that are universally human. For Berlin negative
liberty meant the ability to act, or to express thoughts, without being
interfered with by others and especially the state. After all, as he
himself often noted, the ancient Greeks lacked the notion of a sphere
of life that ought to be protected from political interference, and it
was only in modern times that an ideal of negative liberty was formulated. If it is such a latecomer in the history of human values, why
should we value it so highly? How must we accord it such priority,
if – as Berlin maintained – it is only one value among many and often
clashes with others whose claims are no less valid?

2

Berlin came to prominence as a political theorist with his celebrated
lecture 'Two Concepts of Liberty', which he delivered in 1958 after
he took up the Chichele Chair of Social and Political Theory at

Oxford in 1957. One of the many absorbingly interesting features of *Political Ideas in the Romantic Age* is that it shows that Berlin's defence of negative liberty was closely linked with his attack on monism. In a long chapter entitled 'Two Concepts of Freedom: Romantic and Liberal', he sets out his view that Western political theory contains two conceptions of freedom, which are not different interpretations of a single idea but opposed political ideals. The distinction between these two conceptions is far from simple, but the core of his argument is that whereas negative liberty refers to matters in which individuals can act without interference from others, positive liberty involves acting in accordance with reason. This might be the reason of a collectivity, as in Rousseau's theory of the general will, or of each individual, as Spinoza believed. Either way, it was assumed that only one way of living could be fully rational.

Berlin rejected this assumption. Unlike many liberal thinkers today he did not view the value of negative freedom as coming from its contribution to personal autonomy, an ideal he viewed with suspicion.[4] In his view autonomy is only one human ideal among many and cannot be allowed to crowd out others to which many people are reasonably attached. A liberal society will surely contain people who cherish personal autonomy, understood as a condition in which their lives are governed by principles and goals which they have subjected to rational scrutiny; but it will have room for others – Romantic believers in personal spontaneity and followers of traditional religious practices, for example – who do not accept any such ideal. For Berlin the value of negative liberty is not that it promotes the best or most rational way of living – autonomous or otherwise. Rather, it enables many different ideals to flourish. It may sometimes be right to limit negative liberty in order to promote other ideals and values; but we should understand what we are doing. Liberty is one thing, the good life another.

In many of his writings Berlin tried to argue that a liberal ideal of freedom can be defended as a response to the truth of value-pluralism, and he has been followed in this effort by a number of recent writers.[5] The fact remains that the two views point in unmistakably different directions. Berlin's pluralism expressed a kind of Romantic universalism in which the diversity of cultures was celebrated as something intrinsically valuable instead of being seen – as in the Enlightenment – as a stage on the way to a single, all-embracing civilization. While this is a view that affirms universal values it does not support the universal claims of liberal societies. We may be able to reach agreement on universal values – a list of goods that are necessary to the well-being of all human beings and evils that obstruct any worthwhile human life, for example; but such a list does not provide a universal *morality* – a set of principles that guides us in settling conflicts among these values. Even if negative liberty were agreed to be a universal value it would come into conflict with other values that are also humanly universal. The claims of liberty may clash with those of security and equality; they can also compete with values of community and social cohesion. When this occurs, pluralism gives no reason for according freedom – negative or positive – any overall priority. Pluralism of the kind Berlin defended so eloquently is more potently subversive than he imagined, or wished. It undermines all universal moralities, including liberal moralities.

It may be that the true upshot of Berlin's pluralism is not liberalism but instead an ideal of basic decency. He always affirmed the necessity of a moral minimum in human affairs, and emphasized that upholding it should take precedence over remote and nebulous ideals. It is true that he gives no clear guidance to the content of such a minimum. When he talked of a 'common moral horizon' that applied to all of humankind, he often seemed to mean only that people with very different values can understand one another; but mutual intelligibility between divergent moral outlooks is not the same thing as having common values or agreeing on what should count as minimal moral decency. Still, Berlin could reasonably argue that some practices are so inimical to any human life worth living that their eradication should take priority over other goals. Slavery, genocide, religious and political persecution and torture are plausible examples of such practices, and are recognized as such in the international treaties that were agreed on after the Second World War. More generally, any practice that requires inflicting the universal evil of humiliation can reasonably be judged as indecent. A decent society may not protect the full panoply of liberal freedoms, but from a pluralist perspective it could be more humanly desirable than a predominantly liberal society in which some of the requirements of minimal decency are violated.[6]

An ideal of basic decency of this sort may seem a modest outcome of Berlin's thought, but when applied to politics at the start of the twenty-first century it has a sharp critical edge. There is today a school of 'hard' or 'muscular' liberals, often allied with neo-conservatives, who seek to promote democratic revolution in countries around the world by means that include military force. Some have been willing to accept the relaxation of the prohibition of torture that – despite the resistance of officials in many branches of American government – has been allowed during the Bush administration. These 'hard liberals' like to see themselves as defenders of Enlightenment values; but they represent another version of the utopian strand in Enlightenment thinking whose disastrous influence on twentieth-century politics Berlin illuminated. Neo-conservatives have been ready to use force on a large scale, and in some cases to condone torture, as means of promoting an ideal of global democracy. It is more than doubtful that democracy can be promoted in this way, but in any case democracy is not liberty, whether negative or positive, nor is it peace or the cessation of terrorism. These are distinct goods, and nothing ensures that in achieving one the others will also be achieved; indeed as one is realized others may become more distant. To think that all of these values can be realized together is a fantasy, which like the utopias of the last century can only end in debacle.

3

Berlin's thought is a call to realism and humility, which asks us to accept our inability to create a harmonious future. During the Cold War there were some who found this message dispiriting and un-heroic. In countries behind the Iron Curtain Karl Popper and Friedrich Hayek were read more widely than Berlin, and George Orwell was read more widely than anyone else, and it may be the relative simplicity of their moral vision that accounted for the popularity of these writers. In comparison with Hayek and Popper, Berlin seemed to leave too many moral issues negotiable, while his account of the intellectual origins of totalitarianism lacked the immediacy of Orwell's dark fables. Yet this view of Berlin was by no means universal in the Communist world, and particularly in Poland he found sympathetic readers.

One such reader was Beata Polanowska-Sygulska, a young political theorist and intellectual historian who wrote to Berlin in 1983 (when Poland was just emerging from a period of martial law) and maintained an active correspondence with him until a few months before he died in November 1997. *Unfinished Dialogue*[7] is a record of this exchange, containing not only Berlin's letters but also interviews he gave to Polish periodicals, transcripts of recorded conversations, and a number of articles by Polanowska-Sygulska in which she compares Berlin's view of freedom with that of other liberal thinkers and examines its contested relations with value-pluralism.

The resulting collection is of great value in preserving a record of Berlin's unique style of conversation – at once irrepressibly gossipy and richly learned, unfailingly generous and yet revealing an underlying steel when confronted with anything that smacked of moral insincerity or woolly thinking. As he put it in a characteristic remark:

I am optimistic enough to believe that there are certain basic human needs, wishes, values, and all I ask is for the breakdown of prison houses, if need be by decisive action, and for enough opportunity to be given for at any rate some of the central values to realize themselves at some but not too much cost to other ones. It's a very dreary piece of advice . . . But I cannot help thinking that if idle bloodshed is to be avoided, my dull solution is valid.

The book is no less valuable in bringing out what it was in Berlin's thought that had appeal in the harsh environment of Poland at that time. Unlike the liberal philosophies based on rights that have been dominant over the past generation, Berlin understood that vital human freedoms do not form a harmonious system; they can conflict with one another and when they do we must choose between them. At the same time he knew that there are situations in which freedom of any kind is lost. The evil of totalitarianism is not only that it fails to protect specific liberties but that it extinguishes the very possibility of freedom. It was his grasp of this truth that made

Berlin's thought an inspiration to Polanowska-Sygulska and others in Poland.

The exchanges between Berlin and the distinguished Polish scholar Andrzej Walicki[8] reveal another side of Berlin's pluralism. More than any other intellectual historian Walicki has worked to retrieve nineteenth-century Russian liberal thought from neglect, and many of the letters to him from Berlin that are reproduced in *Dialogue and Universalism* show Berlin's sympathy for this project. Walicki contributes a long prefatory essay, 'Isaiah Berlin as I Knew Him', which contains some of the most perceptive and intriguing observations on Berlin I have seen. He suggests that Berlin's way of thinking renewed the Russian liberalism of Ivan Turgenev's time, which feared a threat to freedom not only from authoritarian rule but also from revolutionary radicalism. The freedom that Russian liberals such as Turgenev and Alexander Herzen feared was in danger was above all spiritual freedom, which they saw as being threatened by any regime or movement that tried to apply a doctrine of historical necessity. Against the many Russian thinkers influenced by Hegel who believed that history was governed by universal laws to which one could only submit, Turgenev upheld the freedom of different societies to pursue different paths of development and of individuals to pursue, even in opposition to powerful historical forces, their own goals and values. Here Turgenev endorsed the celebrated dictum of Alexander Herzen, with whom he disagreed on many other matters: that history has no libretto. Human history is a realm of contingency and unpredictability, in which each generation faces conflicts that have no ideal solution. In the view of such Russian liberals the belief in a universal pattern of development with which every society must conform was not only a delusion; it was also a recipe for tyranny. Sacrificing present liberty for the sake of an imaginary future harmony was fanatical folly.

Much of Berlin's post-war work was an attack on ideas of historical inevitability that echoed these Russian liberal thinkers. As Walicki puts it, Berlin 'transplanted that specifically Russian understanding of liberalism onto British soil'. He did so not only because he was deeply attracted by it but also as a 'chosen stance'. Walicki suggests that Berlin's 'Russianness' was a 'conscious construct', and there is an element of truth in this. By identifying himself with Russian thought, particularly with the work of Herzen, Berlin was able to achieve a distance from the kind of philosophy that was prevalent in Oxford and much of the English-speaking world. In post-war analytical philosophy clarity was valued more than anything else. Intellectual respectability demanded a certain laborious dullness, and the notion that philosophy could express a vision of human life was anathema. As a result philosophy was often a display of technical virtuosity, and had nothing much to say about the great conflicts of the time. By speaking in the voice of the Russian thinkers he retrieved from neglect, Berlin was able to present a distinctive vision of human life and use it to interpret some of the defining experiences of the twentieth century.

Berlin often told the story of how talking with the British logician Henry M. Sheffer in Washington persuaded him that philosophy is not a progressive discipline in which knowledge could be accumulated. After spending a night in the darkness of an unpressurized bomber flying back to Britain, unable to sleep because of the need to take in oxygen regularly from a pipe, he decided to give up philosophy for the study of the history of ideas. It is a persuasive tale but it can hardly be the whole truth. In one of the conversations recorded in *Unfinished Dialogue*, where he retells the story, he remarks: 'Before the war I was an ordinary Oxford philosopher.' By switching disciplines he was able to throw off the constraints that went with that role. Yet he did not give up philosophy, but went on to practise it in another way.

Among the writers Berlin most admired was the Russian Jewish religious philosopher Lev Shestov. In a series of provocative and moving books and essays Shestov mocked the idea of unity that guided philosophers from Socrates onward. 'The idea of total unity', he wrote, 'is an absolutely false idea.'[9] In Shestov's view Western philosophy was captivated by an idea of rational necessity that undermined human liberty. At the same time it had distorted the biblical message – the message of Genesis and the book of Job, which was one of freedom from universal laws. Berlin was not a religious believer, and did not follow Shestov in his radical rejection of reason as a guide to life. But he was at one with him in refusing any belief in ultimate harmony. The belief in unity that has fuelled so many utopian dreams is an effort to reconcile the irreconcilable that ends in repression. Berlin suggests we renounce this venerable faith, and learn how to live with intractable conflict.

2006

7

George Soros and the open society

No single person has done more to promote the open society – a society in which free expression and political opposition are protected – over the past thirty years than George Soros. During the Communist era he used his Open Society Foundation to support greater freedom in the Soviet bloc and China. After the Communist system imploded his foundations acted to mitigate the impact of ethnic war in former Yugoslavia. Later they backed reform movements in Georgia and Ukraine, and Soros formed close relationships with the new leaders who emerged, such as President Mikhail Saakashvili of Georgia. This led Russian President Vladimir Putin to accuse him of orchestrating the 'colour revolutions'.

For many years his global network of foundations has helped people in many countries suffering from persecution – women, gays and lesbians, gypsies and others – to achieve a secure place in society. In the United States the Open Society Institute has contested current policies on illegal drug use, HIV/AIDS and health care during terminal illness. More recently it has addressed the 'resource curse' – the damaging effect of sudden oil wealth in developing countries. Soros has also taken a strong stand against US foreign policy, opposing the Iraq war and attacking the 'war on terror' as misconceived and counter-productive. Aiming to make the world safe from terrorism and at the same time to entrench American supremacy, the Bush administration has made the world more dangerously unstable while causing a steep decline in American power.

In *The Age of Fallibility*[1] – his most important book to date and a stark warning of the dangers facing open societies today – Soros attempts to explain this turn of events. Much of the book is a probing re-examination of the conceptual frame that underpins his activities both as an investor and as a philanthropist: but some of its most interesting passages have to do with his personal experiences of what he calls 'far-from-equilibrium situations' – conditions in which accepted rules of human behaviour are suspended or destroyed.

Such a situation came into being with the Nazi invasion of Hungary in 1944, when like other members of the country's Jewish population Soros and his family faced mortal danger. Soros survived owing to the foresight and courage of his father, Tivadar, who acted decisively to help the family and many others. 'It was his finest hour,' Soros writes.[2] Tivadar Soros, he adds, was mentally prepared for the collapse of normal life by his time in Siberia after having been taken prisoner by the Russians when serving as a volunteer in the Austro-Hungarian army in the First World War. He instilled in his fourteen-year-old son the fact that 'there are times when the normal rules do not apply, and if you obey the rules at those times you are liable to perish'. Soros describes this as 'the formative experience of my life', and there can be little doubt that it imbued in him a willingness to depart from established expectations and wipe the slate clean each day that has shaped his career as an investor. At the same time it implanted in him questions that have pursued him ever since. How could human beings be seized by irrationality as so many were in the Nazi period? What are the flaws in human reason that make such 'far-from-equilibrium situations' possible?

The range of social and political causes to which Soros has contributed is remarkably wide, but this is not simply a large-scale exercise in philanthropy of the sort that is now commonly practised by some among the seriously rich. Uniquely, Soros has used his wealth to promote a view of human knowledge and progress that confronts some of the central dilemmas of liberal thought at the present time. In managing his foundations – which he does with the active intensity he brought to his hedge funds – he has been guided by a version of Karl Popper's view of human knowledge. Mainstream Western philosophy has traditionally aimed to secure a foundation for knowledge that is beyond reasonable doubt, but according to Popper we should not seek any such foundation. In science, which Popper sees as the model for all branches of inquiry, false theories are eliminated so that better ones can be developed; but no theory can claim to contain the final truth. Rejecting any method of induction in which past experience is used as a guide to the future, Popper advocated a method of trial and error in which knowledge grows by a process of falsification. Our most rational beliefs are not those that are most strongly verified, but those that have best survived criticism and refutation.

This philosophy is often called 'fallibilism' – a term coined by the American pragmatist Charles Sanders Pierce, which has also been applied to describe John Stuart Mill's theory of knowledge. Popper's fallibilism is distinctive in rejecting induction, and many philosophers think that in leaving no reason for thinking that we can approach truth it may in the end be closer to scepticism. In contrast, for Popper an acceptance of fallibility facilitates the growth of knowledge and is also the defining feature of a progressive society. As he explained it in *The Open Society and its Enemies* (1945), an open society is one whose public policies are formulated and tested as scientific theories, with those that fail being revised or abandoned. Accepting their fallibility and employing trial and error, open societies can bring about a cumulative improvement of human life that parallels the growth of knowledge in science.

Soros has always acknowledged the vital importance to him of Popper's philosophy, but he is by no means an uncritical disciple. When it is applied to human affairs, he believes, Popper's theory of fallibility does not go far enough. Popper believed that the same methods could be used in natural science and in social inquiry; but we cannot study the human world in the way we study natural objects. Social objects are not like stars or stones, which exist independently of how humans think about them; social objects are partly created by human perceptions and beliefs, and when these perceptions and beliefs change, social objects change with them. This introduces an element of uncertainty into our view of the world that makes us even more prone to error than Popper believed: we can never have objective knowledge of society, if only because our shifting beliefs are continuously changing it.

Soros calls this relationship 'reflexivity', and argues that it undermines standard economic theories. Believers in *laissez-faire* – or market fundamentalists, as Soros sometimes calls them – claim that when left to their own devices markets tend to equilibrium. But as Soros rightly notes, this theory 'is just as much a perversion of supposedly scientific verities as Marxism-Leninism is'.[3] Since they are created and run by fallible human beings, markets have a built-in tendency to overshoot and collapse in recurrent cycles of boom and bust. It is not only that our prevailing economic theories may be mistaken. Rather, they are bound to give a distorted picture of social reality. For example, money is not something that can be measured unproblematically in the way physical processes can be. It is embodied in human practices, which may change when it is known that an attempt at measurement is being made. When we act on a theory about society we always risk altering the reality to which the theory refers. As a result of this fact – which Soros terms 'radical fallibility' – the condition of co-ordination postulated in economic models of equilibrium, which rests on an assumption of perfect knowledge, is not even a theoretical possibility.

Soros believes this insight into reflexivity has been vitally important in his investment career; but his extraordinary success, which includes remarkable financial results over long periods and developing the hedge-fund model of investment beyond anything that existed before, may owe more to his early experiences and his intuitive gifts than to his theoretical beliefs. That does not mean his insight may not, in essence, be sound.

In a well-known critique the Nobel Prize winner Robert Solow argued that Soros neglects well-established theories of disequilibrium while his account of the boom–bust process 'is not a theory at all'.[4] No doubt Solow is right that many economists have questioned equilibrium models – most obviously John Maynard Keynes, who identified a large-scale breakdown of equilibrium in his analysis of the Great Depression.[5] It is also true that Soros is not always consistent in his account of how reflexivity operates, referring sometimes to the paradoxes that arise when we try to predict our own behaviour, sometimes to the dynamic interactions that occur in public settings where others are influenced by what we do or say, and sometimes to self-reinforcing shifts of mood of the kind that have been studied in the psychology of crowds. When in *The Age of Fallibility* he illustrates the workings of reflexivity in financial markets he refers to all of these processes without clearly distinguishing them, and it would be clarifying if he could do so in future writings.

Even so, it seems to me Soros is right to think that the fact of reflexivity implies a basic limitation in our knowledge of the social world. Like other aspects of human life, economic activity is shaped by volatile beliefs. The goal of natural science is to develop theories that contain universal laws; but the social sciences deal with unique historical processes, and the shifts of human beliefs cannot be expressed in such laws. To object to Soros's account of reflexivity on the ground that it is not a consistent theory is to miss the central point, which is that theories of the kind that have been developed in natural science are not possible in the study of society.

Soros is not alone in thinking that the phenomenon of reflexivity limits the ambitions of the social sciences. Philosophers such as Ludwig Wittgenstein and Peter Winch have thought likewise, as have hermeneutic theorists such as Alfred Schutz and Charles Taylor and sociologists such as Anthony Giddens. All these thinkers accept that the project of a unified science – which was central in the Vienna School of Logical Positivism, and which, despite his hostility to that school, Popper shared – breaks down when it is applied to the human world. In also rejecting this project Soros has moved away from Popper's philosophy, but he continues to share Popper's belief that progress can be achieved in ethics and politics by using the methods of science. Like Popper he assumes that when public policies prove to be ineffective or disastrous the reason can only be that they embody mistaken hypotheses, whose errors can be corrected by criticism. This assumption is central to Popper's brand of rationalism, and it also shapes much of Soros's analysis of the failings of the Bush administration. The trouble is that the view of the world expressed in Bush's foreign policies may not be formed from beliefs that can be falsified.

In an earlier book, *The Bubble of American Supremacy* (2004), for example, Soros noted that the outlines of the Bush doctrine were set out in a 1997 mission statement of the neo-conservative Project for the New American Century.[6] Noting that at the close of the twentieth century the United States was the world's pre-eminent power, the signers proposed a number of policies aiming to entrench this position. Soros argued that as a result of these policies the United States entered:

far-from-equilibrium territory. I see a certain parallel between the pursuit of American supremacy and the boom–bust pattern that can be observed from time to time in the stock market. That bubble is now bursting.

In *The Age of Fallibility*, Soros goes further: 'In the years since 9/11, America's power and influence in the world have declined more than at any other time in its history.' The proximate cause of this change is the invasion of Iraq, which Soros describes as 'an ill-conceived and ill-executed adventure that would undermine the American supremacy that it was meant to underpin'. The goal of the Bush administration may have been to secure American primacy in a stable world order, but the upshot has been to create a situation in which 'the main obstacle to a stable and just world is the United States'.

In *The Bubble of American Supremacy* Soros argued that the Bush administration adhered to a far-reaching ideology. Market fundamentalism, religious fundamentalism and the neo-conservative doctrine of American supremacy came together to support a foreign policy that emphasized rivalry between states rather than the possibilities of international co-operation. In *The Age of Fallibility*, Soros modifies this view: 'The current regime has the support of disparate groups unified only by the desire for political power and influence.' He is right to accept that his original analysis was faulty. For much of the time since Iraq was invaded, the administration has been floundering, unable to mount a coherent response to the calamitous developments it has set in motion. It would be fanciful to suppose that it has been implementing any rationally defensible theory or strategy.

But that does not mean it lacks a definite view of the world. Though Soros notes 'the rise of religious fundamentalism which until recently stayed at the fringes of politics', he says little in *The Age of Fallibility* about the role of religion in the Bush administration. Yet it is here more than anywhere else that it has departed from its predecessors. Some of the most dangerous features of its approach to foreign policy betray the influence of beliefs deriving from Christian fundamentalism. Consider strategies for dealing with terrorism. Soros acknowledges fully that terrorist threats exist; but he suggests that the 'war on terror' embodies a mistaken metaphor. Successful counter-terrorist strategies have focused chiefly on security measures and political initiatives rather than conventional military operations. These strategies may include concentrated military action – as when Taliban bases were destroyed by America and its allies in Afghanistan – but campaigns of the kind that the US is fighting in Iraq tend to alienate the general population and boost terrorist recruitment. These facts are well understood by military and intelligence analysts in the United States and throughout the world. If the administration persists in its counter-productive policies the reason cannot be that it is unaware of their effects. No doubt intellectual inertia plays a part, but the administration's view of the world has a delusional quality that goes beyond such errors of judgement.

The 'war on terror' is not just a mistaken metaphor. It embodies a tendency to think of international conflict in theological terms that has long been present on the American right, which the increased power of evangelical Christianity has reinforced. A Homeland Security Planning Scenario document published in July 2004 describes the terrorist threat facing the United States as being perpetrated by the Universal Adversary – a description that is echoed in Bush's many references to a 'war against evil'.[7] Conservative evangelicals count heavily both in funding the Republican Party and as voters. There is not much doubt that they form the principal intended audience of Bush's apocalyptic rhetoric.[8] The Christian right's role in the Bush administration is not simply that of an ally that must be courted and appeased, however. There is a clear affinity in worldview. Millennialist beliefs shape the administration's thinking, in secular as well as overtly religious forms.

In his seminal study of late medieval millenarian movements,[9] Norman Cohn argued that the beliefs that animated these movements did not die out in modern times. They were reproduced in twentieth-century totalitarian ideologies. In different ways, Nazism and Communism claimed to be based on science but were actually vehicles for apocalyptic myths. Each believed a major rupture in history was imminent that would usher in a new world. Cohn's analysis of the political role of millenarian beliefs may be relevant today. Though they may present their views as based on social-scientific theories of modernization, neo-conservatives who believe that humankind is on the brink of an American-led 'global democratic revolution' in which tyranny will be overthrown for ever are voicing a chiliastic faith. They are engaging in prophecy, no less clearly than their allies among Christian evangelicals when they speak of Armageddon and the end-time. The belief that a catastrophic conflagration in the Middle East would inaugurate a new world order to which some on the Christian right subscribe is not an empirical hypothesis that can be revised on the basis of experience. For those who accept it, it is a revealed truth. Equally, no reverse will alter the belief of neo-conservatives that the world is destined to adopt an American version of democracy. Inasmuch as it is shaped by such millenarian beliefs the Bush administration's foreign policy is a faith-based mission rather than a rational engagement with the world.

Soros tries to account for the disastrous foreign policy record of the Bush administration since 11 September as the result of a series of errors, but he is plainly dissatisfied with this explanation. 'Who would have thought', he asks, that 'the oldest, most well-established, and most powerful open society in the world could pose a threat not only to the concept of open society at home but also to peace and stability in the world? Yet that is what has happened in the aftermath of the terrorist attack of 9/11.'

No doubt part of the answer is in the trauma induced by the terrorist attacks, which the administration exploited to stifle criticism of its policies. Yet this can hardly be the whole story. Soros tells us that he 'watched events unfold after 9/11 with a bias rooted in my adolescent experience of Nazism and communism. My conceptual framework was also based on that experience.' He is far from claiming that the United States is becoming a totalitarian regime – it remains 'a functioning democracy with an independent judiciary and the rule of law'. He suggests that there are some 'similarities in propaganda methods' between totalitarian propaganda and opinion management by the Bush administration, and refers to George Lakoff, whose work in cognitive science has enabled the manipulation of public opinion to be better understood.[10] But he remains bemused by the success with which the administration has been able to impose its interpretation of reality: 'How is that possible? It is almost as if people were clamoring to be deceived.'

The missing element here is the pivotal political role of millennialist religion. The attacks activated apocalyptic beliefs widely current in sections of the American population, which the Bush administration has been able to mobilize in support of its agenda. This was not simply cynical manipulation, for there seems little doubt that Bush shares these beliefs. Millenarian belief systems of the kind found on the Christian right are not explanatory theories that can be overturned by contrary evidence. They are myths, which serve a need for meaning rather than truth. The worldview of the Christian right embodies a view of history that is framed in eschatological concepts, according to which American power can be used to rid the world of evil. In theological terms the belief that human action can eradicate evil is decidedly heterodox. Judged by empirical standards it can only be termed irrational.

During much of the last century it seemed that the capture of power by irrational systems of belief could occur only in dictatorial regimes. Nazi Germany and the Stalinist Soviet Union were closed societies whose ruling ideologies could not be exposed to critical scrutiny. Given the success of liberal democracy in defeating its rivals and spreading throughout much of the world it was easy to assume that it has a built-in rationality that gives it an advantage over any kind of authoritarianism. Open societies were liberal democracies, almost by definition, and it seemed they would come into being wherever dictatorship had been overthrown.

Soros is clear that this was much too simple a view:

The collapse of a closed society does not automatically lead to an open society; it may lead to continuing collapse and disintegration that is followed by some kind of restoration or stabilization. Thus a simple dichotomy between open and closed society is inadequate . . . Open society [is] threatened from both directions: too much liberty, anarchy, and failed states on the one hand; dogmatic ideologies and authoritarian or totalitarian regimes of all kinds on the other.

In fact, Popper's taxonomy may need a more fundamental revision than Soros has yet realized. When closed societies collapse but fail to make the transition to openness the reason need not be that they languish in anarchy or suffer a return to dictatorship. It may be that they adopt an illiberal form of democracy. Along with the liberal democratic tradition that goes back to Locke and the English civil war there is a tradition, originating in the French Revolution and formulated theoretically by Rousseau, which understands democracy as the expression of popular will. The elective theocracy that is emerging in much of post-Saddam Iraq is a democratic polity in the latter sense, as is the current regime in Iran; so is the Hamas government in Palestine.

To be sure, these regimes often lack freedom of information and expression and legal limitations on government power, which are essential features of democracy in the liberal tradition. In these respects they are closed societies; but they are not dictatorships. It is often forgotten that democracy, defined chiefly by elections and the exercise of power in the name of the majority, can be as repressive of individual freedom and minority rights as dictatorship – sometimes more so.

To the extent that they repress intellectual freedom, authoritarian regimes necessarily depart from any ideal of the open society; but they may on occasion apply reason in the formulation of their policies more consistently and successfully than the most well-established liberal democracy. This is illustrated in the ongoing expansion of Russian power. With characteristic candour Soros declares himself 'astounded' by the re-emergence of Russia as a key player in the international system.

In part this is a side-effect of the global energy crisis, which he examines in an incisive chapter. Russia is able to assert itself in international affairs and disregard Western disapproval of its regressive internal policies because it commands vast reserves of natural resources – above all, oil and natural gas – that are urgently needed during the present period of accelerating globalization. Russia's revival as a major power is also, however, a product of the policies the Putin regime has pursued. Using European and international dependency on Russian energy supplies as a lever, Putin has skilfully advanced Russia's geopolitical interests. He has made mistakes – such as his heavy-handed intervention in Ukraine – but they have arisen from miscalculations rather than irrationality. Except with respect to the intractable problem of Chechnya, Russian policies have been highly effective in achieving their goals. Chinese foreign policy has followed a similarly pragmatic pattern, and if anything has been even more successful. While Russia and China are advancing, America has suffered an unprecedented loss of power and influence. No doubt the Bush administration has committed many avoidable mistakes; but its central folly has been to implement a faith-based foreign policy in which the identification and correction of errors play hardly any part.

Indeed, rather than recognizing and rectifying its errors the administration tends to compound them. It seems likely that some neo-conservatives in the administration would welcome an escalation of the current conflict in the Middle East to the point where US military action against Iran could appear justified. In part their concern is caused by the rise of Iran as the predominant power in the Gulf – a development furthered by the war in Iraq, which by destroying Saddam's secular despotism removed the chief counterweight to Iran's regional power and created the conditions for the emergence of an Islamist regime that is bound to be increasingly subject to the influence of Teheran.

American air strikes on Iran would reinforce the negative consequences of the war. They would have a highly destabilizing effect on global oil supplies, damaging the US and benefiting Russia. They would also increase the influence in the Gulf and throughout the Islamic world of the apocalyptic Shia tradition expressed by Iranian president Mahmoud Ahmadinejad, and embroil the US in an expanded and intensified regional conflict. The overall result would be to accelerate the decline of American hegemony that began with the invasion and occupation of Iraq. Less than twenty years after the Communist collapse, the rising powers in the international system are authoritarian regimes that will not tolerate open political opposition. Closed or semi-closed societies are proving more capable of framing and executing rational strategies than the world's premier open society, whose faith-based foreign policies have been consistently counter-productive. The 'new American century' could last less than a decade.

Soros's early experiences left him with a need to understand human behaviour in extreme circumstances, which led to his lifelong engagement with the ideas of Popper. Popper never doubted that the ills of society could be remedied by the use of reason, and despite his criticisms of Popper's philosophy Soros would like to agree. It is a belief – or hope – that has inspired him to promote intellectual and political pluralism throughout the world and it informs his admirable stand in opposing the follies of the Bush administration. Yet the searching self-criticism he undertakes in this book points in a different direction. If there cannot be a science of society, neither can society be expected to repeat the cumulative advance that has been achieved in science. The extreme situations that Soros experienced as a youth, and which in a different form he sees today, are not solely a result of fallibility – even of the radical kind he discusses in his account of reflexivity. They have a deeper source in irrational beliefs, which remain potent forces in politics. Over the long sweep of history, far-from-equilibrium situations are normal. Open societies can never be safe from the disorders of faith.

2006

PART TWO

The Euthanasia
of Conservatism

8

Hayek as a conservative

Is Hayek a conservative? Many conservatives will quickly deny that he can be anything of the kind. They will cite the famous Postscript to his *Constitution of Liberty*,[1] 'Why I am Not a Conservative', in which Hayek disavows the characteristically conservative project of using the power and authority of the state to protect endangered moral traditions and to shore up threatened social hierarchies, and argues instead for a version of the classical liberal view, that the primary task is the curbing of all such political power. Conservatives often invoke this and other evidence in support of a picture of Hayek as a doctrinaire defender of liberty, whose general outlook is little different from that of Nozick, or a partisan of *laissez-faire* such as Milton Friedman. It is a short step from radical libertarianism to an ideology which, while centred on the defence of the market economy, is neglectful of the moral tradition which makes a market economy possible. Hayek's conservative critics take this step on his behalf, and condemn him accordingly.

It is not hard to show that the standard conservative view of Hayek's thought is ill founded. His position is distinctive, to be sure. It embodies the best elements of classical liberalism and also suggests a criticism of many conventional conservative positions. At the same time it derives from some of the most profound insights of conservative philosophy, and puts them to work in an original and uncompromising fashion.

We must recall Hayek's birth and education in the last two decades of the Habsburg Empire, in whose defence he fought as an aircraftman, and remember that his formative intellectual influences were not those of English-speaking empiricist philosophy. Central among these influences were the philosophies of Immanuel Kant and Ernst Mach, variants of which dominated the intellectual life by which Hayek was surrounded in his youth. His thought also bears the imprint of the Viennese critics of language: of Karl Kraus, of the now almost forgotten Fritz Mauthner, and of Hayek's half-cousin, Ludwig Wittgenstein. The reflections of these men on the decay of intelligence wrought by the perversion of language have always inspired Hayek, and have played a part in many of his later writings. (His devastating analysis of the expression, 'social justice',[2] in which he illuminates its workings so as to make clear its lack of definite sense, may be best understood as continuing the Krausian tradition of resisting the modern idolatry of general words.)

Most importantly, though, Hayek's writings reflect his lifelong aspiration to come to terms with the debacle of the First World War, when the high civilization and the rule of law established in Habsburg Austria–Hungary gave way to chaos and barbarism. As a result of this weakness, Europe has been engulfed by vast movements dedicated to the repudiation of the European inheritance. Hayek's attempt to synthesize the deepest insights of conservatism with the best elements of classical liberalism merits our closest scrutiny, if only because the experience which inspired it – the experience of an apparently inexorable drift to dissolution and barbarism in all the central institutions of society – may not be so far from our own. His researches into the ultimate sources of the current malaise of civilized authority led him deeply into the theory of knowledge and into philosophical psychology: for it is Hayek's view that the impossible ambitions spawned by contemporary culture arise from a false understanding of the human mind itself.

The well-spring of all Hayek's work in social philosophy and in economic theory is, then, a conception of human knowledge. His theory of knowledge can be understood, in the first place, as a sceptical variant of Kantianism. For him, as for Kant, our knowledge is not based in incorrigibly known sensations,[3] and the empiricist attempt so to reconstruct it is forlorn. Our minds are no more passive receptacles for sensory data than they are mirrors for reflecting the necessities of the world: they are creative powers, imposing order on a primordial chaos by way of a built-in set of categories. Philosophy cannot hope to step outside these categories so as to attain a transcendental point of view, or to reach an Archimedean point of leverage from which to assess or reform human thought. For Hayek, as for Kant, philosophy is reflexive and critical rather than transcendental or constructive: it plots the limits of the human understanding but cannot hope to govern it.

Hayek's sceptical Kantianism has features, however, which take it far from anything that Kant could have accepted and which give to it a wholly distinctive turn. The organizing categories of the human mind are, for Hayek, neither immutable nor universal; rather they express evolutionary adaptations to a world that is in itself unknowable. His thought has here a real point of affinity with that of his friend Sir Karl Popper, who has long expounded a naturalistic and evolutionary theory, in which human knowledge is regarded as continuous with animal belief. More decisively, however, Hayek differs from Kant in denying that the governing principles of our minds are fully knowable to us. We will always be governed by rules of action and perception, which structure our experience and behaviour down to their last details, and some of which will necessarily elude our powers of critical inquiry. In recognizing these elements of our mental life – these 'meta-conscious rules' of action and perception, as he calls them[4] – Hayek identifies a limit to the powers of reason more severe than any Kant could have admitted. For if such rules exist, then (though we can at no point learn their content), we can be sure that critical thought itself is governed by them. Hence our own minds, no less than the external world, must in the end remain a domain of mystery for us, being governed by rules whose content we cannot discover.

Hayek is a Kantian, then, in denying that we can know things as they are in themselves, or can ever step out from the categories which govern our understanding. He goes further than Kant, in seeing the categories of our understanding as mutable and variable, and in some major degree unknowable to us. Most distinctive in Hayek's sceptical and Kantian theory of knowledge, however, is his insight that all our theoretical, propositional or explicit knowledge presupposes a vast background of tacit, practical and inarticulate knowledge. His insight here parallels those of Oakeshott, Ryle, Heidegger and Polanyi; like them he perceives that the kind of knowledge that can be embodied in theories is not only distinct from, but also at every point dependent upon, another sort of knowledge, embodied in habits and dispositions to act. Some of this practical knowledge is found in rules of action and perception imprinted in the nervous system and transmitted by genetic inheritance. But much of the most significant part of the practical knowledge expressed in our dealings with each other is passed on mimetically, in the cultural transmission of traditions or practices, some of which are bound to be inaccessible to critical inquiry. In all our relations with the social world we are informed and sustained by these elements of tacit knowledge, which we know to be pervasive in our thought and conduct, but whose content we can scarcely guess at.

In his own view, and surely rightly, Hayek's conception of the human mind as governed by rules, some of which must escape conscious scrutiny, has the largest consequences for social philosophy. For it entails the bankruptcy of the rationalist project, undertaken in different ways by Bacon, Descartes and Spinoza, of subjecting the mind to a systematic purge of tradition and prejudice. We can never know our own minds sufficiently to be able to govern them, since our explicit knowledge is only the visible surface of a vast fund of tacit knowing. Hence the rationalist ideal of the government of the mind by itself is delusive. How much more of a mirage, then, is the ideal of a society of minds that governs itself by the light of conscious reason. The myriad projects of modern rationalism – constructivist rationalism, as Hayek calls it – founder on the awkward fact that conscious reason is not the mother of order in the life of the mind, but rather its humble stepchild. All of the modern radical movements – liberalism after the younger Mill as much as Marxism – are, for Hayek, attempts to achieve the impossible. For they seek to translate tacit knowledge into explicit theory and to govern social life by doctrine. But only tacit knowledge can engender government, and tacit knowledge may be lost by its translation into overt, propositional form. Hayek is here developing, in its political implications, a version of the thesis of the primacy of practice in the constitution of human knowledge. The thesis has a distinguished pedigree in the writings of a number of contemporary philosophers, of whom Oakeshott, Wittgenstein and Heidegger are perhaps the most notable.

The thesis of the primacy of practice leads Hayek to refine the argument that rational resource-allocation under socialism is impossible – an argument which Hayek inherited from his colleague L. von Mises. In his disputes with socialist economists, Mises had contended that, in the absence of market-pricing of all factors of production, chaos in calculation was bound to ensue, and could be avoided only be relying on world capitalist markets and domestic black markets. (Saul Kripke has noted[5] an interesting analogy between this argument of Mises's and Wittgenstein's arguments against the possibility of a private language – an analogy I can only remark upon, but not pursue here.) Hayek sees, as his colleague Mises did not, that the knowledge which is yielded by market-pricing cannot be collected by a central authority or programmed into a mechanical device, not just because it is too complex, nor yet because it is knowledge of a fleeting reality (though this is closer to the nub of the matter), but rather because it is knowledge given to us only in use. It is knowledge stored in habits and in practice, displayed in entrepreneurial flair and preserved in the countless conventions of business life. Unhampered markets transmit this knowledge, which is otherwise irretrievable, dispersed in millions of people. One may almost say that, for Hayek, this practical knowledge achieves a full social realization *only* when market-pricing is not interfered with. For – like much traditional knowledge – it is holistic, a property of the entire society, and not the private possession of any of its separate elements or members.

Hayek's case against socialist planning, and in favour of the unhampered market, rests upon these considerations rather than upon any Lockean theory of property rights, or upon a fanaticism for *laissez-faire*. The impossibility of socialism, and of successful intervention in the economy, is an *epistemological* impossibility (as well as a moral impossibility). His differences with Keynes, for example, are imperfectly understood if one does not grasp that the Keynesian macroeconomic manager must claim knowledge which Hayek insists is available to no one. The Keynesian planner may indeed achieve temporary successes, by exploiting money illusion and manipulating business confidence, but this is bound to be a short-lived victory. Such Keynesian policies work only insofar as they are contrary to established expectations which they cannot help eroding. Moreover, they take no account of the inevitable discoordination of relative prices and incomes. Governments can do next to nothing to remedy these consequences, since it is given to no one to know what is the correct relative price structure. Hayek nowhere suggests that market failure is an apodictic impossibility; but he is surely on firm ground in arguing that it is in the unhampered operation of the market process itself that we have the best assurance of economic co-ordination.

Socialism and interventionism, then, are but long shadows cast by a false philosophy of mind. The order we find in society, no less than that which prevails in our own minds and bodies, is an undesigned order, and not a product of rational planning. The dominant super-stition of the Age of Reason is the belief that vital social institutions – the law, language and morality, as well as the market – must be or can become products of conscious contrivance and control, if they are effectively to serve human purposes. This modern superstition results from an anthropomorphic transposition of mentalistic cate-gories to the life of society. Hayek's criticism echoes a distinguished line of anti-rationalist thinkers, of whom Pascal is perhaps the closest to him, in his celebrated distinction between *l'esprit de géométrie* and *l'esprit de finesse*. It is because the rational principles of social life are immanent in its practices that we cannot trust our reason in its speculative projections for reform.

This is why, especially in his later writings, Hayek attaches so great an importance to the spontaneous development of the law in the institution of an independent judiciary. He goes so far as to see, in the contemporary recourse to legislation, a major threat to liberty and to social stability. There is, indeed, an important analogy between Hayek's arguments for the impossibility of comprehensive economic planning and his criticism of a legal system that is dominated – as all now are – by statute. Just as no economic plan can approach the sensitivity and subtlety of the market process in integrating men's plans and achieving co-ordination in the use of resources, so statutory legislation cannot match the sensitivity of the common law in responding to and adjudicating the concrete problems of man's social existence. But the common law, which relies on the doctrine of prece-dent, cannot survive without a strong, independent and decentralized judiciary.

It is not that Hayek supposes that a modern state can altogether forswear legislation,[6] any more than it can wholly dispense with economic policy; but in both cases the balance needs to be redressed, in favour of spontaneous order, whether that of the market or that of the judicial process. The two issues of economic planning and the rule of law are therefore inseparably connected for Hayek. He sees clearly that the rise of the administrative state, together with the prevalence of grandiose projects for redistribution and social welfare, pose a major threat to the rule of law, and therefore to individual liberty. A government which seeks to regulate prices and incomes is bound to transfer large powers to administrative authorities. In the nature of things these authorities will exercise a terrifying discretion over the lives and fortunes of the citizens. Such authorities may clothe their arbitrariness in an ideology of social justice, or they may attempt to revive the doctrine of the Just Wage. But their decisions cannot be contained within the rule of law, for they crucially depend upon a claim to knowledge which no one possesses – a claim which, in the nature of things, cannot be adjudicated.

Aside, then, from the fact that policies of intervention in the market and in the provision of social goods tend to expand as their failures are recognized, such policies necessarily involve a transfer of authority over our lives to administrators effectively unconstrained by law, and often uninhibited by common moral sentiments. Hayek's criticism of the ambitions of the administrative and welfare states should be less implausible in conservative circles than it was when his *Road to Serfdom*[7] appeared. We can see now the accuracy of his prediction that the expansionist state will be captured by movements and professions whose outlook and interests are deeply at odds with the preservation of established ways of life.

What in turn may conservatives learn from Hayek's thought? His chief importance, I think, is that he has freed classical liberalism from the burden of an hubristic rationalism. He has thereby produced a defence of liberty which aims to reconcile the modern sense of individuality with the claims of tradition. He shows that we are bound to rely primarily on inherited traditions of thought and conduct in all our dealings with each other. The inarticulate character of the great submerged part of our knowledge means that we always know far more than we can ever say. It also means, crucially, that the rational criticism of social life must come to a stop when it reaches the tacit component of our practices.

There is an uncomfortable lesson here for conservatives, since Hayek's diagnosis condemns the attempt to retard or reverse the flood of social change, no less than it undermines the reformer's desire to remodel society, according to some more 'rational' plan. Hayek would heartily endorse Wittgenstein's remark, that trying to salvage damaged traditions by wilful effort is like trying with one's bare hands to repair a broken spider's web. The most we can do is to remove those artificial impediments to the vitality of our traditions which have been imposed by the state. And with its policies in education and housing, the state has surely been a far greater destroyer of traditions and communities than has the market.

Hayek's chief lesson for conservatives, then, is that it is a delusion to think that conservative values can be protected by a successful capture of the expansionist state. The damage done to social life by an invasive state is integral to its existence, and conservative governments are better occupied during their tenure of office in whittling down the state and in restoring initiative to the people, than in the futile enterprise of trying to convert the state's bureaucracies to a conservative view of things.

This is not to say that Hayek's thought is not open to legitimate conservative criticism. At times he seems to subscribe to a doctrine of historical progress which, though it was accepted by such conservatives as Burke and Hegel, cannot be endorsed by any twentieth-century conservative. Here I think we must turn to Michael Oakeshott's writings[8] for the insight that human history is not to be construed as a single evolutionary process, but rather as a series of distinct adventures in civilization. Although Hayek is perhaps right to see the conquest of the world by European individuality as an historical fate, which it is idle to wish away, he may be too ready to see this as a stage in a global progressive development. There is a faint echo in his writings, which a conservative would wish could not be heard, of the historical theodicy of the Enlightenment. This theodicy is an indefensible and indeed pernicious part of the inheritance of classical liberalism, which in most other respects we are wise to cherish.

Finally, Hayek's thought poses a dilemma for conservatives which few of them have yet come to recognize. The dilemma is found in his perception, especially in his later writings, that the modern development of age-old European moral and intellectual traditions has produced an outlook that is deeply destructive of civilized institutions. The peculiarly modernist outlook – a combination, I should say, of homeless moral passion with rationalist fantasy – is now so pervasive as to have acquired deep roots in popular sentiment and a secure place in virtually all the disciplines of thought. It results in what Hayek calls 'unviable moralities'[9] – systems of moral thought and sentiment incapable of sustaining any stable social order; in the bizarre intellectual constructs of contemporary sociology; and even, as in architecture, in a corruption of the practical arts. Taken together, these developments create a climate of culture which is profoundly hostile, not only to its traditional inheritance, but even to its own continued existence. We confront the phenomenon of a culture permeated throughout by a hatred of its own identity, and by a sense of its purely provisional character. This culture is not without sources in our most ancient religious and moral traditions – for example, in Platonic rationalism and in Christian moral hope.[10] In his writings on Mandeville, Hayek has made clear that the defence of the market economy may demand a far from conservative revision of ordinary morality.[11] His latest thoughts on the phenomenon of intellectual and moral inversion[12] suggest that he has illuminated what is, from a conservative viewpoint, an even greater problem: since much of contemporary culture is possessed by a death-wish brought on by pathological developments in some of our oldest traditions, a modern conservative must also be a moral and intellectual radical.

1983

9

A conservative disposition

INTRODUCTION

It is said . . . that conservatism in politics is the appropriate counterpart of a generally conservative disposition in respect of human conduct: to be reformist in business, in morals or in religion and to be conservative in politics is represented as being inconsistent. It is said that the conservative in politics is so by holding certain religious beliefs; a belief, for example, in a natural law to be gathered from human experience, and in a providential order reflecting a divine purpose in nature and in human history to which it is the duty of mankind to conform and departure from which spells injustice and calamity. Further, it is said that a disposition to be conservative in politics reflects what is called an 'organic' theory of human society, that it is tied up with a belief in the absolute value of human personality, and with a belief in the primordial propensity of human beings to sin. And the conservatism of an Englishman has even been connected with Royalism and Anglicanism.

Now setting aside the minor complaints one might be moved to make about this account of the situation, it seems to me to suffer from one large defect. It is true that many of these beliefs have been held by people disposed to be conservative in political activity, and it may be true that these people have also believed their disposition to be in some way confirmed by them, or even to be founded upon them; but, as I understand it, a disposition to be conserva-

132

tive in politics does not entail either that we should hold these beliefs to be true or even that we should suppose them to be true. Indeed, I do not think it is necessarily connected with any particular beliefs about the universe, about the world in general or about human conduct in general. What it is tied to is certain beliefs about the activity of governing and the instruments of government, and it is in terms of beliefs on these topics, and not on others, that it can be made to appear intelligible. And, to state my view briefly before elaborating it, what makes a conservative disposition in politics intelligible is nothing to do with a natural law or a providential order, nothing to do with morals or religion; it is the observation of our current manner of living combined with the belief (which from our point of view needs to be regarded as no more than an hypothesis) that governing is a specific and limited activity, namely the provision and custody of general rules of conduct, which are understood, not as plans for imposing substantive activities, but as instruments enabling people to pursue the activities of their own choice with the minimum frustration, and therefore something which it is appropriate to be conservative about. Michael Oakeshott[1]

The common belief that there cannot be such a thing as a conservative political philosophy expresses a prejudice of rationalism which conservatives are not obliged to share. It embodies the primitive view that any political philosophy worth its salt must be articulated in a system of precepts that is universal in application, grounded in immutable principles and capable of resolving any significant political dilemma. Whatever else it may be, a conservative political philosophy cannot be that. A central element of the conservative outlook is found in the sceptical denial that a political philosophy of that universal and rationalist sort can be anything other than an illusion. From this standpoint of scepticism, however, it does not follow that conservatism in politics cannot be given a coherent articulation, intelligible and acceptable to most who think of themselves as conservatives, and having a claim on the consideration of reasonable people who are not themselves conservatives.

As it has been articulated in the British tradition, in the writings of Hume and Oakeshott, Burke, Disraeli and Salisbury, Churchill and Thatcher, the most fundamental tenet of the conservative outlook on politics is the limited character of the role of government. For a conservative in the British tradition, political life is not a project of world improvement, or the reconstitution of human institutions on the pattern of any ideal model, but instead something much humbler. The office of government is to palliate the natural and unavoidable evils of human life, and to refrain from adding to them. Any government animated by a conservative outlook takes for granted the imperfectibility of human affairs. The political predicament of our species is not that of a creature of infinite possibilities that have throughout its history been inexplicably shackled. We are not, each of us, as our liberal culture encourages us to imagine, a limitless reservoir of possibilities, for whom the past is an irrelevance and the future an empty horizon. We are finite, mortal selves, burdened by the evils of our history and the miseries natural to the human condition, who achieve excellence and a measure of well-being only insofar as we accept the disciplines of civilization. Conservatives acknowledge the imperfectibility of human life, not in virtue of subscribing to any metaphysical speculation, but as a result of ordinary experience and common observation. These were summarized by Thomas Hobbes, who, if he is not perhaps a conservative, nevertheless has an assured place in the Tory pantheon, when he famously observes that:

It is true, that certain living creatures, as Bees, and Ants, live sociably one with another, (which are therefore by *Aristotle* numbred amongst Politicall creatures;) and yet have no other direction, than their particular judgements and appetites; nor speech, whereby one of them can signifie to another, what he thinks expedient for the common benefit: and therefore some man may perhaps desire to know, why Man-kind cannot do the same. To which I answer,

First, that men are continually in competition for Honour and Dignity, which these creatures are not; and consequently amongst men there ariseth on that ground, Envy and Hatred, and finally Warre; but amongst these not so.

Secondly, that amongst these creatures, the Common good differeth not from the Private; and being by nature enclined to their private, they procure thereby the common benefit. But man, whose Joy consisteth in comparing himselfe with other men, can relish nothing but what is eminent.

Thirdly, that these creatures having not (as man) the use of reason, do not see, nor think they see any fault, in the administration of their common businesse: whereas amongst men, there are very many, that thinke themselves wiser, and abler to govern the Publique, better than the rest; and these strive to reforme and innovate, one this way, another that way; and thereby bring it into Distraction and Civill warre.

Fourthly, that these creatures, though they have some use of voice, in making knowne to one another their desires, and other affections; yet they want that art of words, by which some men can represent to others, that which is Good, in the likenesse of Evill; and Evill, in the likenesse of Good; and augment, or diminish the apparent greatnesse of Good and Evill; discontenting men, and troubling their Peace and their pleasure.

Fifthly, irrationall creatures cannot distinguish betweene *Injury and Dammage*; and therefore as long as they be at ease, they are not offended with their fellowes: whereas Man is then most troublesome, when he is most at ease: for then it is that he loves to shew his Wisdome, and controule the Actions of them that governe the Common-wealth.

Lastly, the agreement of these creatures is Naturall; that of men, is by Covenant only, which is Artificiall: and therefore it is no wonder if there be somwhat else required (besides Covenant) to make their Agreement constant and lasting; which is a Common Power, to keep them in awe, and to direct their actions to the Common Benefit.[2]

On this Hobbesian view, politics is a way of coping with the hazards that come from the unalterable defects of the human animal. Accordingly, the primary task of a conservative government is not the pursuit of indefinite betterment, but the staving off of ever present evils. It is, first and foremost, in the avoidance of civil strife, in the prevention or containment of war, in the mitigation of the arbitrariness of power through the institution of a rule of law, and in the provision of a sound currency that the achievements of a conservative government are properly to be measured.

Because conservatives deny the evanescence of imperfection, they reject the Procrustean politics of the utopian blueprint. They are rightly suspicious, moreover, not only of politics as the pursuit of perfection but also of the idea of history as a narrative of progress, with ourselves as its *telos*. As I understand it, the conservative outlook – at least as it is found within the European intellectual tradition of which British conservatism is an integral part – is deeply at odds with that sentimental religion of humanity, with its ruling superstitions of progress and of convergence on a universal civilization, which is the secular creed of our times and which has largely succeeded in supplanting the traditional Western faiths. The growth of scientific knowledge, together with increased virtuosity in its applications, have given us conveniences – anaesthetic dentistry and flush lavatories are examples – whose place in the scheme of things is not to be despised. Scientific and technological advance has not, and cannot, diminish the realm of mystery and tragedy in which it is our lot to dwell.

This is to say that a conservative may be an agnostic, even an atheist, but never a humanist. By contrast with classical liberals and with American neo-conservatives, British Tories have not swallowed the canard that human life is open to indefinite improvement by judicious use of critical reason. For them, human reason is a weak reed, on which they must rely in daily life and in the formation of policies, but in which it is folly to have faith. Conservatives in the British and European traditions have been spared the hubris of those who make a religion of world-improvement. This is to say that, though they are committed to reform of institutions and practices that fail to serve human needs, they aim to do good in minute particulars, not in grand schemes. It is not that conservatives cannot be reformers, even at times radical reformers. Rather, the costs and advantages of reform need always to be weighed in detail, radical reform should go with the grain of the national character and tradition rather than against it, and conservatives should view with the deepest suspicion proposals for radical reform that are inspired by hubristic ideology rather than by evident necessity. Unlike the classical liberal worldview that has, regrettably, formed much of the thought of the New Right, conservatism is not a secular faith, a historical theodicy that aims to displace traditional faiths. On the contrary, conservatives seek to return religion to its proper sphere, and to divest political questions of the almost transcendent importance that they have acquired (by a return to public life of a religious sensibility that secular rationalism has subjected to an almost Freudian repression) in modern times. For this reason, conservatives are always friendly to the religious life in its proper sphere. At the same time, it is a cardinal point of my argument that people in Britain live in a culture that is in large part post-Christian and even post-religious, and in which a sceptical and secular conservatism is therefore appropriate. This is not at all to deny that Christianity is an enduring and precious part of British cultural inheritance, nor that the institution of an established Church has considerable advantages as an element in the unfixed and unwritten constitution. It is merely to observe the fateful fact that secularization is in Britain far advanced and likely to be irreversible, so that the culture and traditions that bind people together cannot any longer be distinctively Christian or informed by any shared transcendental faith.

For a conservative, however, the waning of religious faith is not to be welcomed, even if it is conceived to be inevitable, because of the belief that:

> Civilisation is hooped together, brought
> Under a rule, under the semblance of peace
> By manifold illusion; but man's life is thought
> And he, despite his terror, cannot cease
> Ravening through century after century
> Ravening, raging and uprooting that
>   he may come
> Into the desolation of reality.[3]

One of the tasks of conservative statecraft is to mitigate, so far as it can, the desolation of reality that overtakes human beings in a post-religious age that has grown too wise to swallow the shallow illusions of the Enlightenment. In this task, conservatives acknowledge that human beings may well have flourished better in ages, such as that of medieval Christendom, which had at the bottom of them an unquestioned transcendental faith. It will be one of my contentions in this chapter, at the same time, that sound conservative policy cannot be nostalgist in inspiration: once the cake of custom is broken, we must do our best with what is left. It cannot be baked anew. In practice, this means a policy which aims to infuse an irreducibly pluralist and self-critical society with the conservative virtues of coherence, self-confidence and stability. Nor should policy be informed by the triumphalist belief that government can secure the conditions for the successful pursuit of happiness. For a conservative in the sceptical tradition of Hobbes, Hume and Oakeshott, happiness is a matter of chance, and its pursuit is a profitless enterprise. People are better employed in struggling to reconcile themselves to their circumstances, on the whole, than in striving to alter them. The task of government is to bolster those institutions and forms of life which, if they cannot confer happiness, nevertheless enable the natural sorrows of human life to be endured in a meaningful and dignified fashion. In this respect, the British conservative tradition – and its Tory element in particular – has little in common with the Whiggish spirit which animates American neo-conservatism and libertarianism. It resembles far more the Augustinian vision that inspired the Founding Fathers.

It follows from what has so far been said that, though conservative government is limited government, it has nothing in common with the minimalist, *laissez-faire*, night-watchman state advocated by libertarian doctrinaires such as Herbert Spencer and Robert Nozick. A limited government has tasks that go well beyond keeping the peace – the vital Hobbesian task of staving off the nemesis of anarchy and civil strife in which commodious living is an impossibility. It has also a responsibility to tend fragile and precious traditions, to protect and shelter the vulnerable and defenceless, to enhance and enlarge opportunities for the disadvantaged, to promote the conservation and renewal of the natural and human environment and to assist in the renewal of civil society and the reproduction of the common culture without which pluralism and diversity become enmity and division. My argument in this chapter will be, therefore, firstly, that the role of government is other and larger than that specified in the libertarian dogmas of contemporary neo-liberalism. Contrary to neo-liberalism, a conservative government has good reason to concern itself with the well-being and virtue of its subjects, since if these are not promoted liberal civil society will decay and loyalty to the liberal state will tend to wane. Conservatives must therefore resist the pressure for the political disestablishment of morality that is the common coinage of liberalism in both its libertarian and its revisionist egalitarian varieties. But, secondly, this legitimate concern for the moral foundations of civil society cannot justify policies of social engineering aiming to revive a lost (and doubtless partly imaginary) moral solidarity among people. The project of restoring an organic national community, as currently advocated most perceptively by Roger Scruton,[4] is a distraction from serious policy-making in a society that is irreversibly pluralist, even if it has merit as an antidote to the lifeless abstractions of liberal doctrine. People today are not Victorians, nor even the folk portrayed by Ealing Studios, and serious policy must address them in all their intractable idiosyncrasy.

In the third section of this essay, I will consider the kinds of policy that seem appropriate for a conservative government in the present historical circumstance. The upshot of my reflections will be that the free-market economy, which contemporary conservatives rightly see as the engine whereby a modern civil society reproduces itself, is not something free standing, primordial or self-moving. It rests upon the foundations of a common culture of liberty and has as its supports the institutions of a strong state that tempers its excesses and shelters those – the very old, the disabled, the chronically sick, the educationally disadvantaged, for example – who may be without the resources, or skills, to prosper in it. Whereas the institutions of the free market are indispensable conditions at once of liberty and prosperity in Britain and similar countries today, it is prudent to be sceptical of the radical libertarian ideology with which in recent political discourse they have come to be associated. The legitimacy of the free market in the political realm depends not only on its uninterrupted delivery of economic growth – something that, we are now reminded, cannot be always guaranteed – but also, and more importantly, on its being contained and sustained by the common allegiances nurtured by traditional Toryism, and tempered by a liberal social policy that is in harmony with the spirit of the age. Only in this way can conservative individualism have a political future.

THE LIMITS OF LIBERALISM

The argument that government should not concern itself with the virtue and well-being of its subjects, but only protect them from each other, is given a classic statement by J. S. Mill in his *On Liberty*.[5] There he makes a case for the view that individual liberty may rightly be restrained only when its exercise threatens harm to others. It follows that the coercive authority of law may never be invoked to protect people from themselves, or to promote the virtues. Mill's is a classic statement of the argument for the legal disestablishment of morality, which has found many echoes in later liberal theorists such as Hart, Dworkin and Rawls.

It is an argument that no conservative, and certainly no conservative individualist, can accept. The idea that one person may harm him or herself without affecting others, that there is a sphere of self-regarding conduct which deserves absolute immunity from legal and social intervention, neglects the interdependency of human beings that is a central ingredient in any view of society that can be reasonably called conservative. We are not, in truth, Mill's sovereign selves, parading our individuality before an indifferent world: we are born in families, encumbered without our consent by obligations we cannot by voluntary choice renounce. If we harm ourselves, we harm those who care for us or who depend upon us. Government has a legitimate interest in protecting us from self-harm, if only because there are few such harms that are not also harms to others. Government may rightly concern itself, also, with the quality of the lives its subjects lead. Lives that are dominated by avoidable addictions, for example, are poorer than they need be; they result in the atrophy of the powers of choice on which responsibility depends; they are not examples of human flourishing. In the idiom of modern moral philosophy, government – and certainly conservative government – has good reason to undertake policies of paternalism and moralism, where these can expect a decent measure of success, and do not impose unreasonable burdens on the law. Conservatives have no reason to seek to privatize the good life.

In enacting policies that express concern for the virtue and well-being of the citizenry, and which do not merely protect people from one another, conservative governments accept (what is suppressed in liberal theory) that human individuality is not a natural fact but a cultural achievement, won with difficulty and easily lost. The matrix of human individuality is a cultural environment in which people are formed as choosers with responsibility for their actions. The formation of individual character cannot itself be a direct concern of government – it is rather the task of intermediary institutions, families, churches and voluntary associations. Nevertheless, government has an indefeasible obligation to tend and nurture those intermediary institutions. The society that a conservative individualist envisages is not one in which the solitary individual confronts the minimum state. Such a purely Hobbesian polity would likely command neither the allegiance nor the affection of its subjects. The limited government favoured by conservative individualists is one with a strong commitment to the intermediary institutions in which individuals are formed and in which for the most part their lives find meaning.

A society held together solely by the impersonal nexus of market exchanges, as envisaged by Hayek[6] (whose insights into the failings of central planning have now been vindicated by events in the countries of the former Soviet bloc) and other neo-liberal thinkers, is at best a mirage, at worst a prescription for a return to the state of nature. Nor can any human society hope to approximate the Areopagitic and Socratic ideals of Mill or Popper[7] – the ideal of an open society of rational inquirers, united only in the activity of mutual criticism. It is more than doubtful whether such a society would be tolerable, even if it were achievable. For most people, the meaning of their lives is a local affair, and the examined life may turn out to be hardly worth living. Liberal ideologues, in the nescience of their rationalist conceit, suppose that they can answer the question posed by the greatest twentieth-century Tory poet: what are days for? These ideologues have still to learn that, when local knowledge is squandered in incessant self-criticism, people realize that:

> solving that question
> Brings the priest and the doctor
> In their long coats
> Running over the fields.[8]

Conservative individualists recognize that, before anything else, even before freedom, human beings need a home, a nest of institutions and a way of life they feel to be their own. Among conservatives, the practices of market exchange and of rational argument are familiar ingredients in, and even necessary conditions of, their way of life. They are not the whole of the way of life that they inherit, and they cannot hope to flourish, or in the end to survive, if the common culture of liberty and responsibility that supports and animates them is eroded in the pursuit of the mirage of the sovereign individual of liberal ideology.

What follows for policy from these reflections? In the first place, contrary to Mill's antinomian individualism, policies of legal prohibition may sometimes be justified in respect of activities that strike at the roots of individual responsibility and the common values that support civil society. Where, as in Britain, the legal prohibition of very addictive and highly dangerous drugs has been reasonably successful, there is every reason to resist libertarian demands for drug legalization. It is only where, as is plausibly the case in the United States, the war against drugs is unwinnable and its costs insupportable that the conservative individualist will endorse decriminalization. Again, the conservative individualist will find unproblematic the proscription of pornography which involves violence or the exploitation of children or animals, though he or she may well have serious reservations about the large discretionary powers of the apparatus of censorship set up to control the video industry in Britain. The conservative individualist, unlike the Millian individualist, can have no objection to policies of legal prohibition of these sorts, where other measures are demonstrably ineffectual, and the activities proscribed pose a real threat to the values that sustain a liberal civil society.

It is in social policy, however, that the errors of unrestrained neo-liberalism are most egregious. Consider policy on poverty. There has been a tendency in neo-liberal thought to seek a technical fix for poverty in the appealing device of a universal negative income tax. Such policies neglect the heterogeneity of modern poverty, and suppress the distinctive causes of its most disturbing variant, the poverty of the underclass. It has been the great achievement of Milton

Friedman to show that, at least over the longer run and in the last resort, inflation is always and everywhere a monetary phenomenon. Contrary to Friedman and his disciples, however, the poverty of the modern underclass is nowhere primarily a monetary phenomenon. It is instead a cultural phenomenon, caused by family breakdown, the depletion of human skills across the generations and the emergence of a dependency culture. No policy in regard to this species of poverty could be worse devised than the negative income tax, which supplements low incomes regardless of their causes, and thereby abrogates responsibility in the recipients. It also distracts the attention of policy-makers from those varieties of modern poverty which *are* occasioned primarily by lack of money: the poverty of the old who were prevented by inflation and confiscatory taxation from making provision for themselves, of the disabled, of the sick and of those whom catastrophe has struck.

There is a deeper lesson in the neo-liberal error about poverty. It is that social policy cannot be value-free or non-judgemental, and cannot be neutral with regard to the institutions that undergird the market economy. If, as is manifestly the case, much underclass poverty is a product of family breakdown, then policy must address the conditions of family stability – a large question that encompasses not only welfare benefits but also tax policy and divorce law. In all of these areas, sensible policy cannot and should not avoid giving legal recognition to specific forms of family life. The model animating policy ought never to be that of a society of strangers, bound together by a limitless diversity of contractual agreements. The concern which animates policy should instead be that of repairing and renewing, sustaining and supporting those inherited intermediary institutions which experience has shown are best capable of nurturing the responsible individuals who make up a free society. In framing policies to this end, it is necessary to beware, above all, the fixation on particular measures that has bedevilled neo-liberal thought. No policy is without costs and hazards, all necessitate trade-offs between legitimate interests and values, and none is a panacea. Schemes for targeting welfare benefits and other forms of selective provision have the cost of a cumbersome administrative apparatus and the hazard of generating disincentives for self-provision. In some instances – child benefit and basic pensions, perhaps – universal benefits *may* be the least undesirable forms of income support.

Voucher schemes, also, have important costs and dangers. Like all species of government provision of income, they are liable to inflation by the operation of political competition in the democratic market place: they have in this respect no advantage over direct provision of services by government. In some areas, such as schooling (where they may on balance offer the best solution to current problems), they carry with them the risk of blurring the distinction between the public and the private sectors, and effecting a covert socialization of the latter in which it loses its present independence.

Again, in many countries, such as France, where (despite recent difficulties) state provision of schooling has been accompanied by the maintenance of traditional standards, experimenting with privatization or a voucher scheme would be to disregard the deeper conservative wisdom expressed in the question, 'Why mend that which is not yet broken?' (This deeper conservative wisdom may be especially relevant to the post-Communist societies, whose schooling systems – once free of Communist deformation – are in general more traditionalist in character than Western schools and for that reason superior in performance. In such a context, privatization – which in Britain and the United States is a counsel of despair about state schools – would be an absurd measure.) In many other areas, voucher schemes are simply unworkable, or else indefensible. Whereas voucher schemes may have a valuable role in community care for the elderly and the disabled, they have little or no place in other areas of medical care, where people may be uninsurable and the resources they need not easily measurable.

Further, even where a voucher-based insurance scheme in medical care is feasible, experience shows that it issues in a ruinous inflation of medical costs. Is there any British conservative who wishes to import into the United Kingdom the pernicious American system, in which nearly forty million people lack any entitlement to medical care, and even the middle classes are bankrupted by catastrophic illness? For all of its imperfections, the National Health Service – preferably in its unreformed version – has a vital place in the common life in Britain as a provider of decent, basic medical care that is available to all, which any future Conservative government is bound to safeguard.[9] In these and some other areas of policy, it is reasonable to accept that direct provision by government may be the only viable option.

Voucher schemes have indeed a signal virtue – that of combining governmental provision with the market allocation of services. They are not for that reason perfect, costless or without hazards, and they are not a magic wand that will spirit away all ills. A conservative policy aiming to support the intermediary institutions, the common culture and the values that animate a free society, and to protect those in it who would otherwise be bereft of care, is bound to be pluralist in the measures it adopts. Certainly, no conservative policy-maker can afford the doctrinaire attachment to specific measures (such as the voucher and the negative income tax) that has been evident in much recent neo-liberal thought.

The spirit of conservative individualism can be seen to be far removed from the antinomian self-assertion that infuses *On Liberty* and which informs the more radical varieties of contemporary libertarianism. In the antinomian perspective, conventions are restraints on individuality, institutions (when they are recognized at all) are artefacts of agreements, traditions are burdens and habits symptoms of debility. Conservatives recognize, by contrast, that where conventions have fallen into desuetude and the authority of the past is denied, only a Hobbesian sovereign can keep the peace. It is an infallible sign of a genuinely free society, however, that in normal times peace is the mark of common life, and the powers of the Hobbesian sovereign are deployed chiefly against the outlaw – the terrorist or the criminal who has chosen to step outside of the circle of law and civility. This is to say that the transmission of freedom and individuality across the generations demands more than a framework of common rules. It presupposes a common culture – a shared culture of liberty and responsibility.

THE LIMITS OF COMMUNITY AND DIVERSITY IN A COMMON CULTURE: NOTES TOWARDS THE DEFINITION OF A LIBERAL CIVIL SOCIETY

The individualism that is favoured by a conservative is, therefore, to be distinguished sharply from that sponsored by liberalism and libertarianism. In their different ways, these latter forms of individualism embody a romantic cult of self-assertion that is alien to the Tory sensibility and the British conservative tradition. Liberal individualism, in its political manifestations, impoverishes British culture by delegitimating its traditions and conventions by representing them all as constraints upon individual liberty, thereby obscuring their true role as necessary conditions of individuality and civil life. For conservatives, by contrast, the individualism that is prized is inherited as the patrimony of a common culture, which government may rightly act to reinforce.

At the same time, the historical circumstance of Britons today is not that of guardians of a common culture which they receive as a seamless garment. In society there is a prodigious diversity of histories, ethnicities, styles of life and views of the world. Since time immemorial, England itself has been an individualist culture,[10] whose individualism has owed much to its Christian heritage. For several centuries, the United Kingdom has been a composite state, encompassing four nations. In recent decades, this inherited diversity of national traditions has been enriched by large-scale immigration from Commonwealth countries – an immigration which has introduced into national life powerful currents of non-Christian religious belief and practice. Further developments in cultural diversity in Britain are to be expected as a result of the increasingly deep integration in a widening European community that encompasses many of the post-Communist states. These aspects of the current circumstances make cultural diversity a brute historical fact with which any serious conservative outlook is bound to reckon.

The task of latter-day conservative government is not only to accept but to welcome this enhanced diversity, while seeking to buttress and undergird it with the rudiments of a common culture. Since the present historical circumstance is no longer that of a culture unified by a single religion, however fragmented, and since Britain has never in recent centuries been in a situation in which political allegiance and nationality are coextensive, the project of restoring an organic national community in Britain is vain, chimerical and perhaps harmful – if indeed such a community ever existed there. Like Spain, Britain is an artefact of the institution of monarchy, an institution which has the inestimable advantage that political allegiance is not dependent on nationality or ethnicity. Because Britain is a constitutional monarchy, not a national republic, and because of its imperial history, the country is in a better position than most to absorb the new elements of cultural diversity that recent decades have brought. The pursuit of a vision of nationhood that has no purchase on historical traditions can, for Britain, be only an aberration, a distraction from the task of sustaining the bonds which are shared and which in fact can hold people together.

Because of British history and institutions, political and national allegiance for people in Britain today cannot be founded in ethnicity. It may, and should, invoke a shared sense of Britishness, where this means a sense of fair play, of equality before the law, and a spirit of toleration and compromise on matters about which people have deep differences. For people in Britain today, allegiance cannot express a deep community of shared values, since the communitarian ambition – the ambition of making political loyalty coterminous with membership of a single moral community – could not be more inappropriate. People are not, in the jargon of recent philosophy, 'radically situated selves',[11] persons whose identities are defined by membership of a single, all-inclusive community. They are members of many and sometimes conflicting communities: they are (in Fulke Greville's phrase) 'suckled on the milk of many nurses'. With such a plural inheritance, people cannot reasonably expect that political and national allegiance will express a deep culture of common values. It is to be hoped, nevertheless, that people have in common enough respect for the ruling ideas of a civil society – ideas of toleration, of responsibility and of equality under the rule of law – for diversity in society to be fruitful rather than an occasion for division.

What does all this mean for policy? In the first place, it suggests the wisdom of law having a minor, and often a merely regulatory role, in matters about which people deeply disagree. Consider, in this regard, the liberal reforms of the 1960s, in which homosexuality was legalized, divorce and censorship relaxed, capital punishment abolished and abortion made freer. It is significant that, for all the charges of authoritarian moralism levelled against it, the Thatcher government (like its conservative predecessors and successor) has never sought to reverse these liberal reforms. In this it has, surely, been right. If there is a consensus on morality among conservatives, it is a liberal consensus that, where the interests of children are not concerned, adults may live as they choose, subject only to the law of the land as it applies to all. This is not to say that existing law may not profit from specific reforms, since, as recent proposals for the reform of the law on divorce suggest, the current legal environment may accord freedom to adults at the expense of the interests of dependent children. On the whole, however, the liberal reforms of the 1960s ought to be accepted by conservatives, partly because they express an actually existing consensus on values. They are to be commended to conservative individualists, I suggest, because they also embody the good old liberal ideal of toleration – an ideal that has lately been occluded by obscurantist discourse about the rights of minority groups and cultures. It is in the nature of conservative thought and practice that it preserves its identity by absorbing other traditions, and in this case it does so by appropriating an old-fashioned liberal idea that has now entered deeply into common life.

Or consider policy towards the family. Here the principal danger to be avoided is that of revivalism – of attempting to restore a pattern of family life that economic change has radically altered, and whose legitimacy is no longer self-evident. 'Like prices in a free market', we are reminded by the greatest conservative thinker of our time, 'habits of moral conduct show no revolutionary changes because they are never at rest.'[12] Policy cannot sensibly be modelled on a form of family life which was common half a century ago, and which has now become that of, very nearly, a minority. It may, as I shall argue later, concern itself with irresponsibility in procreation and with the deleterious effects of unchosen single-parenthood. It cannot seek to impose any single pattern on the varieties of family life in society today. Some women choose the role of wife and mother for much or even all of their lives; many seek to combine motherhood with career; most, perhaps, alternate between work at home and work in the wider economy. Conservative government must be even-handed, and respect each of these choices. It makes itself absurd if, Canute-like, it seeks to stem the tide of social and moral change that floods inexorably from changes in the economy and in general outlook. Conservative policy cannot emulate the spurious liberal ideal of neutrality in respect of all forms of family life that meet some minimal requirement of rights-protection, since it recognizes that there are forms of family life – particularly that of involuntary single-parenthood – which are injurious to children and to those who have to care for them. It must nevertheless respect and seek to sustain the legitimate diversity of forms of family life that spring from the responsible decisions that people make.

The question of the proper conservative policy towards the family suggests broader questions about education and about multi-culturalism. The starting-point of reflection must be that, in present society, no one can flourish who does not possess the basic skills of numeracy and literacy in the English language. The bottom line of governmental responsibility for schooling is not in providing insti-tutions which are successful in inculcating these skills, but rather in defining and enforcing a national framework of assessment and achievement in respect of them. Whereas opinions may legitimately differ as to the best mode of provision, the duty of government to set and inspect national standards in schooling is beyond reasonable doubt. It may be true that, when British culture was far more homo-geneous in its traditions and ways of life, curricular choice could be safely left to the tacit understandings of headteachers and staff. With the advent of mass immigration and other species of cultural diversity, a national curriculum, or something like it, is a manifest necessity. Current proposals are far from being the best that can be conceived in that, as Sheila Lawlor has shown,[13] they give insufficient priority to a core curriculum comprising English, mathematics and science. It is the inculcation of such skills of numeracy, literacy (in the English language) and scientific thinking that is the proper aim of any national curriculum.

There are clear implications for the issue of multiculturalism in this conclusion. Cultural minorities, such as the British Muslims, have an undeniable entitlement to government funding for their schools, if only on grounds of equity given the current practice in regard to Catholics and Jews. Along with every other school, however, a Muslim school ought to receive such subsidy only if it conforms to a streamlined national curriculum by teaching the basic skills to all of its pupils, both male and female. In Britain, it is taken for granted (even if the realities often fail to match this expectation) that opportunities for men and women, whether as children at school or later in life, be the same. The form of life that is inherited today, with all of its many variations, confers upon men and women the same responsibilities and opportunities. With regard to schooling, it follows from this that conservative governments cannot endorse, by subsidy or otherwise, schools that deny this equality of opportunity to the sexes. This is but one of the important limits on cultural diversity that any government which is committed to the protection of civil society is bound to impose.

It expresses a deeper and less fashionable truth. Cultural minorities, whether indigenous or immigrant in origin, cannot expect public subsidy for aspects of their ways of life which flout the central norms of liberal civil society. They are entitled to protection from forms of discrimination which deny them full participation in the common life. They cannot justifiably claim privileges or immunities of the sort enshrined in policies of affirmative action and of group rights, which effectively shield them from the healthy pressures of the larger society. Although it is to be hoped that cultural minorities in Britain will retain many aspects of their traditions, including traditions of hard work and family stability in which many recent immigrants excel over the indigenous population, civil peace in the kingdom depends on their integration into the civil society that enables them to live in freedom. The lessons of states which have allowed unrestricted immigration of incompatible minorities or which have inherited profound ethnic divisions, are sobering and indeed ominous for liberals who indulge the dangerous fantasy that civil peace can be maintained solely by obedience to common rules. History and the news of the day suggest otherwise: that pluralism must be bounded by the norms and the common culture of civil society. Pluralism must have such limits, or else Beirut will be the likely fate.

The American experience, in which the courts (now virtually the only effective agents of policy-making in America) have been hijacked by ethnic and other special interests, illustrates vividly the dangers of pluralist societies that only legalism holds together. It intimates the hard truth that a multiracial society, if it is to be peaceful and free, cannot also be radically multicultural. In particular, entry into civil society in Britain presupposes subscription to its norms, among which toleration, voluntary association and equality before the law are uppermost in importance. It must be made plain by any conservative government that cultural diversity cannot mean the subordination of women in state-funded schools, or (as in the Rushdie case) toleration of threats which endanger freedom of expression. The common culture to which people aspire is that culture of liberty which animates a civil society. This common culture may be reinforced by laws and policies which resist pluralism when pluralism threatens the norms of civil society itself. A civil society such as in Britain is entitled to assert its identity against those – be they recent immigrants or long-established indigenous groups – who challenge its central, defining practices of toleration and compromise. It is, indeed, these practices that set the limit to pluralism in Britain today.

The pursuit of a delusive organic community distracts from the humbler but indispensable task of filling out that thinner common culture of respect for civil society that presently enables people to coexist in peace. Building up that common culture, in turn, effectively enfranchises all people as active citizens in a polity to which everyone can profess allegiance. A conservative policy, rightly conceived, is not one which seeks to renew old traditions by deliberate contrivance; it is one which nurtures the common traditions that are currently shared, while respecting the variety of practices whereby they are held in common.

CONSERVATIVE INDIVIDUALISM, THE FREE MARKET AND THE COMMON LIFE

The preceding reflections may be regarded as offering provisional answers to the question, 'What must be true for the free market to be possible?' The market, we have concluded, is not a self-sustaining order, but presupposes as its matrix a network of intermediary institutions animated by a culture of liberty. The political legitimacy of the free market depends on these institutions being in good repair and, where necessary, on their being tended and nurtured by government. The duties of government in according to the free market a political legitimacy that assists its reproduction across the generations go well beyond according intermediary institutions the space and resources they need. Conservative government has the responsibility of protecting and renewing the public environment without which the lifestyle of market individualism is squalid and impoverished. Conservative individualists, unlike their liberal and libertarian counterparts, recognize that the capacity for unfettered choice has little value when it must be exercised in a public space that – like many American cities – is filthy, desolate and dangerous. The exercise of free choice has most value when it occurs in a public space that is rich in options and amenities, and its value dwindles as that public space wanes. Free choice is worth little indeed if the life in which it issues is nasty, brutish and short, because the environment in which it is exercised approximates a state of nature. We do not want to walk the path of privatization if Detroit is at the end of it.

Everything suggests that it is possible to go further in extending the reach of the free market, if at the same time measures are devised to renew the physical and institutional environment that confers legitimacy on it. It is not my brief here to consider specific policies – a task in any case beyond my competence – but rather it is to explore the kinds of policies suggested by these concerns. In regard to poverty, I have already cautioned against the disastrously misconceived neoliberal panacea of the universal negative income tax, which is objectionable both in effecting a further socialization of income and in lumping together very different sorts of poverty. Without attempting to specify policy in any detail, what is most needed at present is a division within policy between measures which enable the vulnerable and defenceless who cannot expect to return to the economy as self-reliant producers nevertheless to live dignified and meaningful lives, and measures which assist and encourage the underclass of the families unemployed across several generations to reintegrate in the wider society. Policy in the first area – in respect of the mentally and physically disabled, the chronically sick and the old and frail – has under all recent governments been distinguished by its niggardliness, by a lack of the sense of human solidarity, and by want of compassion. The shelving of the Griffiths Report,[14] the prospect of under-funding when it is at length implemented, and the low levels of benefits for those who care for dependants at home are aspects of policy in recent years which compound the neglect of community care for the most vulnerable and which are surely unacceptable to any humane conservatism, and certainly to any Tory. The evidence suggests that, in this area, the best policy is one which confers vouchers for community care on those who need it (or their guardians) – a measure which would widen choice for the consumer of such care and thereby avoid the paternalism of the otherwise admirable Griffiths Report (with its excessive reliance on bureaucratic assessment of individual needs). Voucher schemes in these areas will work, and work well, if and only if they are fully adequate to the needs of those concerned. Community care under conservative government should embody the values that its name suggests and should demonstrate the commitment of government to its most defenceless citizens.

Policy regarding the underclass confronts difficult dilemmas which cannot be explored here. What is clear is that, in regard to the able-bodied, public assistance generates obligations, and the goal of such assistance should not be lifelong pauperdom but speedy recovery of independence where this has been lost, and the inculcation of the skills of self-reliance where these are lacking. Training vouchers for the unemployed are one step in this direction. In general, a greater commitment of resources to the reskilling of the unemployed, together with a willingness to reduce or withdraw benefit if retraining for genuine employment is not accepted, or to replace it by workfare, are elements of a workable policy aiming to reintegrate the underclass. Since, as we have seen, family breakdown appears to be a vital element in the creation of the underclass, recent measures introduced in Britain 'aiming to enforce paternal obligations on delinquent fathers of one-parent families', though not without their own difficulties, are essential ingredients in any policy agenda on reinforcing family responsibility. On the thorny and intractable issue of family benefit, there must be little that is new that can now usefully be said. What is clear is that the neo-liberal knee-jerk response of abolishing it altogether, and replacing it by a means-tested benefit, is to be rejected because of the costs and disincentives of targeting. At the same time, the existing benefit is massively wasteful and plainly inequitable. The proposal of David Willetts MP that child benefit be restricted to the first five years but substantially increased (and also made taxable) seems one that is eminently worthy of consideration, especially if (in order to guarantee even-handedness) it is combined with further aid (such as tax-deductibility for child care) for those mothers who choose to work during their children's early years. In none of these areas of policy are there measures that avoid the necessity of trade-offs among conflicting values. There is in policy-making not only a scarcity of resources but also a moral scarcity (profoundly illuminated in Isaiah Berlin's most recent collection of essays)[15] that is endemic. It is important in tax and welfare policy to respect these trade-offs where they occur, and not make a fetish of the 'neutrality of the level playing field'.

With regard to education, it has already been argued that government has an indefeasible duty to equip children with the skills of numeracy and literacy without which they cannot hope to prosper in society. It is nevertheless important to beware of the danger that education becomes wholly or primarily vocational in purpose and content. In primary and secondary schools, the goal must be to initiate children into the history and principles of the civil society they will enter as adults, and to this end there is a case for courses in civic or political education. In higher education, the danger is that universities come to be regarded by government as little more than auxiliaries of economic policy. In education policy, as elsewhere, it ought to be a central maxim of conservative government that autonomous institutions have their own, internal ends and purposes and are not mere instruments of the ephemeral goals of the government of the day.

So far neglected here is an area of policy that is likely to loom ever larger in the years to come – that of the environment, natural and humanly constructed, in which we have to live. It must surely be clear that people in Britain do not want their cities to follow the American example and become places where people work furtively and in fear and then flee. The goal is, or ought to be, to renew cities in the British and European tradition as public spaces in which individuals and autonomous institutions live out their lives – and this cannot be done without significant injections of public money. Revitalizing the cities will entail a reconsideration of the role of the private motor car in relation to public transport – a reassessment that will in any case soon be forced upon us by mounting evidence of its environmental hazards. The point will soon be reached when the dominant policy objective of post-war British governments (that of aligning the electoral and economic cycles so as to achieve re-election through uninterrupted economic growth) will be replaced by a new imperative in which the quality of life dominates, even though it cannot altogether supplant, the pursuit of economic growth. It will be wise to pursue, so far as possible, market solutions to the problems of the environment – road pricing for urban traffic congestion and a suitable tax regime for polluters. However, it will be foolish to suppose that market solutions alone will solve the environmental problems that now loom up as the chief threats to the quality of our lives and to those of our children. A Green agenda should come as a natural one for Tories, for whom the past is a patrimony not to be wantonly squandered; and in any case environmental policy is too important to be left to the Greens. The emerging Green agenda within British conservatism shows, more clearly than anywhere else, that a flourishing individualism cannot be envisaged save in the context of rich forms of common life which government has a positive responsibility to protect.

CONCLUSION

For over a decade, the policy agenda of British conservatism has been dominated by the goal of freeing up the market and according the market economy its rightful legitimacy. This policy orientation has had some impressive results and has produced a shift in the stance of government in regard to the market that is probably irreversible. There can be no return to the collusive corporatism of the 1960s and 1970s, with its legacy of stagnation and backwardness. Nor is the agenda of marketization yet exhausted. There is much further to go in extending market institutions into hitherto sacrosanct areas, in reducing taxation, inflation and government expenditure, and in privatizing industries and services. There is a strong case for introducing market choice in many social and welfare services. In all of these areas, the achievements of the past decade will provide a sound base.

Yet it is, in all likelihood, only a reassertion of the traditional Tory concern for compassion and community in one nation that can hope to preserve the free market which the last decade of conservative government has achieved. Conservative policy which neglects or seems to neglect the needy and the vulnerable, or which is so committed to market freedoms that the human and natural environment in which markets operate is left to its own devices, will provoke a revulsion in which traditional Tory concerns for the health of the community are captured by egalitarians and collectivists. Accordingly, if this danger is to be averted, conservative policy presently needs a significant shift in orientation from concern with the market economy to concern with its social and cultural preconditions. Vital as the market is as an expression of individual freedom, it is only one dimension of society in which individuals make choices and exercise responsibility. People also live in families and belong to churches and other voluntary associations in which market exchange is inappropriate or peripheral. It is this cultural and institutional matrix of the market that conservative policy must now address. It must not be forgetten that, like any other human institution, the market is imperfect (and imperfectible). As the subtlest and least-known critic of economic theory in our time has said of the idea of equilibrium in economics, 'It is an arresting triumph of the formal imagination. Beauty, clarity and unity are achieved by a set of axioms as economical as those of classical physical dynamics.' But, he asks, 'Can the real flux of history, personal and public, be approximately understood in terms of this conception? The contrast is such that we have difficulty in achieving any mental collation of the two ideas. Macbeth's despair expresses more nearly the impact of the torrent of events.'[16] These wise words should caution us against attributing to the market a perfection we have learnt not to ascribe to government. They should encourage us to recognize that, in certain areas of policy, exclusive reliance on market forces is a recipe for failure. We need only look to Germany and Japan for lessons in how, without resort to dubious corporatist strategies, market allocation may be supplemented – in science policy, for example – by the constructive engagement of government.

For a conservative, political life is a perpetual choice among necessary evils. Being an individualist, the conservative will have good reason to seek to devolve from government all those activities that are better done in markets, and so he will make a choice between the imperfections of markets and those of governments, in the hope that the resultant mixture will best promote freedom and community. On the view presented here, however, the conservative individualist will never concede hegemony to the institutions of the market. The market is made for humans, not humans for the market. The conservative individualist will deny that there can be long-term economic benefit in restricting free trade, for example, but will at the same time acknowledge that there may be reasons of military strategy, of the preservation of the common culture or the protection of the environment, which may defeat the ideal of unrestricted free trade. Even if, as with monetary policy, there may be good reasons for removing elements of the market from the political process – reasons that may support the institution of an independent central bank that is insulated from the democratic process and guided by clear policy objectives rather than by discretionary authority – conservatives must in general wish to preserve the primacy of the political order over the realm of the market.

Let us not suppose that an individualist form of life is the only one in which the human good can be realized. The lessons of history, and the present example of Japan, teach otherwise. However, for us individualism is a historical fate, which we may temper but cannot hope to overcome. The task of conservative policy is to tend the culture and institutions that are the matrix of individualism, so as to ensure that the individualist form of life does not so deplete its moral and cultural capital that it becomes (as Schumpeter feared it would)[17] a self-limiting episode. There is surely benefit to be gained from a study of that school of Tory pessimism, best exemplified in the writings of Lord Salisbury,[18] that viewed with foreboding the prospects in the longer term of freedom and excellence under a regime of democratic capitalism. At the same time much can be learned from Salisbury's great contemporary, Disraeli, who saw that conservative values could be preserved if their benefits were extended to ordinary people, and an obligation of concern for the poor accepted by those who had made a success of wealth creation. Indeed, one may safely predict that, unless these older Tory traditions are revived, the enterprise culture that has been so ardently fostered will turn out to be a shallow and an ephemeral affair. It is not, however, primarily in the revival of an older, patrician Toryism that can be rested any hope that conservative values will survive and prosper in the generations to come. That happy outcome will come about only if conservative governments are perceived to be committed to extending the advantages of freedom and independence to all. The measures introduced recently in Britain to foster a savings culture (by exempting small savings from taxation) are an admirable example of the judicious use of government to promote conservative values and secure loyalty to them among ordinary people. It is in extending the culture of choice and opportunity to the widest degree that the real prospects of conservatism, in Britain and elsewhere, are found. In the view presented here, the danger of market liberalism consuming itself is greatest if policy is allowed to be formed on the tacit supposition that the cultural preconditions of the market can safely be left to look after themselves.

For any conservative in the sceptical British tradition – a tradition which is shared with much of the rest of Europe, and which is exemplified in the writings of Montaigne and Charron, Savigny and Eotvos among others – there is in any case an incongruity in putting one's faith in any one remedy. It is a basic conviction, after all, that the human lot is imperfectible. The task of conservative government is primarily to concern itself with those cultural continuities to which the market is bound to be indifferent, but upon which its strength finally depends. The market is only as strong as the culture that underpins it – a culture of responsibility and choice-making that we must transmit to our children and they to theirs. Conservatism is not, like socialism or liberalism, a one-generation philosophy, but rather the opposite. For this reason it is necessary to repudiate firmly the neo-liberal metaphor of society as a contract, in which market exchange is primordial. If society is a contract, it is only in Edmund Burke's sense – a contract between the living, the dead and those that are yet unborn.

The Conservative Party in Britain, like conservative parties else-where, can never be solely or exclusively the party of capitalism – though it has no reason at all to be ashamed of its association with the desire of people to improve their standard of living and quality of life. Any conservative government, in Britain or elsewhere, must express not only the individual freedoms embodied in market capitalism but also the cultural identities that are renewed across the generations.

It is the most fundamental insight of conservatism, after all, that persons' identities cannot be matters of choice, but are conferred upon them by their unchosen histories, so that what is most essential about them is, in the end, what is most accidental.[19] The conservative vision is that people will come to value the privileges of choice all the more when they see how much in their lives must always remain unchosen.

The danger of the neo-liberalism that has lately come to dominate conservative thinking is the danger of utopianism – the belief or hope that the predicament in which people find themselves, in which goods are not always combinable and sometimes depend upon evils, and in which the elimination of one evil often discloses another, can some-how be transcended. This was the danger inherent in the domination of conservative thought by the ideology of the New Right – the dangerous delusion that contemporary problems could be conjured away, in their entirety and presumably for ever, by the resurrection of the theorizings of the Manchester School of *laissez-faire* liberalism. At its deepest, this once-dominant strand in conservative thought expressed the thoroughly unconservative conviction that the crookednesses of practice could once and for all be straightened out by the application of a correct theory. The conservative politics of imperfection[20] amounts to a rejection of this seductive, dangerous and delusive view. It is for this reason that, for a conservative government, a sceptical turn of mind is indispensable. Above all, conservatives must recall the dangers of ideology, and the limits of theory: philosophy, if it is good, can do little more than effect prophylaxis against the virus of ideology, and then return us to the vicissitudes of practice; theories, at their best, can only remind us how little we know. It is this sceptical spirit that should inform the policies devised by conservatives, and which the greatest conservative philosopher of all evinced,[21] when he wrote:

there are in England, in particular, many honest gentlemen, who being always employed in their domestic affairs, or amusing themselves in common recreations, have carried their thoughts very little beyond those objects, which are every day exposed to their senses. And indeed, of such as these I pretend not to make philosophers, nor do I expect them to be associates in these researches or auditors of these discoveries. They do well to keep themselves in their present situation; and instead of refining them into philosophers, I wish we could communicate to our founders of systems, a share of this gross earthy mixture, as an ingredient, which they commonly stand much in need of, and which would serve to temper those fiery particles, of which they are composed.[22]

1991

10

The strange death of Tory England

The self-destruction of British conservatism by New Right ideology and policies is best interpreted as an exemplification of a central neo-liberal theme – the importance of unintended consequences in social, economic and political life. The radical free-market policies implemented in Britain since 1979 have had as one of their principal effects an unravelling of the coalitions of economic interests and the social hierarchies on which pre-Thatcher conservatism depended. In sweeping away the post-war settlement which all major parties endorsed for a generation, Thatcherism demolished the social and economic base on which conservatism in Britain stood, and created several of the necessary conditions for a prolonged period of Labour hegemony. The medium-term effect of neo-liberal Conservative policy in Britain has been to destroy ethos in institutions such as the Civil Service and the National Health Service by remodelling them on contractualist and managerialist lines. In addition to squandering a large part of Britain's patrimony of civilized institutions, this neo-liberal project of refashioning social life on a primitive model of market exchange has speeded the delegitimation of established institutions such as the monarchy and the Church. Further, by stripping democratic local government in Britain of most of its powers and building up the unaccountable institutions of the Quango State – the apparatus of committees appointed by central government to oversee the operation of the newly marketized public services, which is now larger in manpower and in the resources it allocates than democratic local government in Britain – the Conservatives have marginalized their own local party organizations and thereby contributed to the steep and swift decline of the Conservative Party itself. Indeed, the catastrophic performance of the Conservatives in the local council elections of May 1995, in which they suffered their worst electoral rout since the start of the century, suggests that the neo-liberal project of permanent institutional revolution in Britain may well count its political vehicle, the Conservative Party, among its casualties. It is difficult to see how in any near future the Conservatives can recover from the unintended consequences of a neo-liberal project that has hollowed out legitimacy from many British institutions and fractured and dislocated their party machine. Even if, in the normal fortunes of political life in Britain, the Conservative Party is somehow able to renew itself, it will be in a form that cannot presently be foreseen. As for Tory England – that rich network of interlocking interests, social deferences and inherited institutions that Tory statecraft has successfully protected and reproduced for over a century by its skilful adaptation to democratic institutions in Britain – it is now as good as dead.

The self-undermining effect of neo-liberal policy in Britain has been even more cruelly ironic than this brief narrative reveals. Thatcher's principal insight was to perceive that there was, in Britain in 1979, an economic constituency for union-bashing, budget-cutting, low-tax policies – a constituency whose very existence was denied by the patrician Tory 'Wets', but which she made politically visible and electorally decisive from the early 1980s onwards. The irony is that it is this group that – aside from the various constituencies of the poor which it has become fashionable to lump together under the American category of the underclass – has lost most in the 1990s. For, in a development that verged on an inevitability, the deregulated labour markets engineered by Thatcherism in the 1980s undermined in the 1990s the job security of the upwardly mobile social group – Essex man and woman – which contained Thatcherism's most electorally significant beneficiaries. The deregulation of financial institutions that in the late 1980s flooded the economy with easy money and caused asset values to float to unsustainable heights, at the same time spawned new financial instruments – personal pensions and endowment mortgages – that spelt loss or ruin for millions of households. (An index of the magnitude of the side-effects of financial deregulation in Britain is the fact that during the first five years of the 1990s over 300,000 homes have been repossessed – an eviction on a scale that is unparalleled in Britain since the Highland enclosures of the 1740s.) The very economic constituency that gained most from early Thatcherism has been most savaged by its longer-term effects. At the same time, the Quango State built up in the wake of the Thatcherite attack on democratic local government and the Majorite policy of marketizing public services and intermediary institutions has facilitated the growth of a new class of Tory nomenklaturists, managing vast resources without any form of effective democratic accountability. In its last phase, in one of its crowning ironies, the neo-liberal project in Britain, which began as a response to failing corporatist institutions, has given rise to new economic institutions, which may be termed the institutions of *market corporatism*. These institutions are not only themselves democratically unaccountable; they cannot for long be politically legitimated through democratic institutions. The neo-liberal corporate state, in Britain as in any other democratic country, is inherently politically unstable.

Neo-liberalism in Britain, for these and many other reasons, has proved a self-limiting project. Yet, contrary to those on the left – by far the majority – who saw it as a blip on the screen of history, it has transformed irreversibly the social and institutional landscape of Britain, and thereby the terms of political trade. If it has signally failed as the Gramscian project of securing the legitimacy of unfettered market institutions in Britain it was undoubtedly originally conceived to be – if it has failed so completely, in fact, as to destroy for the foreseeable future the electoral prospects of the Conservative Party – neo-liberal conservatism nevertheless has one achievement, unintended and doubtless still uncomprehended by its authors, to its credit – the destruction of Tory England. In the longer perspective of history this role as a brutal and unconscious agent of modernization – including the modernization, and so the return to electability, of the Labour Party – may prove to be Thatcherism's sole historic justification. The cost of this modernization, however, has been not only the near-destruction of much of Britain's institutional inheritance, but also the obliteration of that humane post-war liberal conservatism – embodied in such figures as Butler, Boyle, Macleod and Macmillan – in which Tory paternalist and communitarian traditions were adapted to the conditions of a late modern industrial society.

Any understanding of the history of the neo-liberal project in Britain must begin with the fact that the dissolution of the post-war settlement was under way well before Thatcher's coming to power in 1979.[1] Unlike corporatist institutions in Germany and Austria, which acted as pace-makers for wealth-creation and guarantors of social peace, British corporatism in the 1960s and 1970s had produced economic stagnation, industrial and social conflict and a fiscal crisis of the state which triggered the intervention of the IMF. The key neo-liberal policy framework of fiscal conservatism and its conse- quence, the retreat from macroeconomic management having full employment as its objective, were accordingly in place in Britain when Margaret Thatcher came to power. The neo-liberal project – the project of reining back the activities of the state, extending the scope of market institutions to the limits of political possibility and securing for unfettered markets an unchallengeable legitimacy in the public culture – was formulated and adopted by the Conservatives during the years between Thatcher's succession to the leadership of the party in 1975 and the Conservative victory in 1979 – the same years in which fiscal conservatism was imposed by the IMF on the Callaghan Labour government (1974–9). It is worth recalling that the earlier Conservative government of Edward Heath (1970–74) had attained power with something akin to a neo-liberal agenda, and that it had come to nothing. The Heath government was elected on a programme of reversing the post-war trend to overextended government in Britain, but it had abandoned this programme long before it suffered electoral defeat in February 1974 as a result of its confrontation with the miners. It was, however, the defeat of the Heath government by the miners which most shaped the early stages of Thatcherite policy.

The first phase of the neo-liberal project, as it was conceived and implemented in the early 1980s, was not an attack on the welfare state, nor the marketization of major social institutions, but instead the abandonment of full employment as an objective of public policy and the development of a stable framework of public finance – both policies which had the effect of diminishing the power of organized labour in Britain, and both of them expressing the anti-corporatist orientation of early Thatcherism. Thatcherite policy in the early 1980s was in considerable measure reactive in seeking to break up the triangular relations of collusion between employers, unions and government that had sustained the bankrupt British corporatism of the 1970s. That it soon became proactive in attempting to reshape British society and public culture according to the crude abstractions of economic liberalism is to be accounted for by Thatcher's first and most fateful act of privatization – the privatization of policy-making whereby it was removed from the control of the Civil Service and contracted out to right-wing think-tanks.

The New Right thought which these think-tanks – above all, the Institute of Economic Affairs – had incubated during a long sojourn, throughout the 1950s and 1960s, in the political wilderness at the margins of British public culture, was neither monolithic nor even particularly coherent. It contained a diversity of intellectual trends, of which Chicago economics, Virginia Public Choice theory, and elements of Austrian economics derived from the work of Hayek were the most prominent. Nevertheless, it is true of all of the think-tanks – even the Centre for Policy Studies, set up by Keith Joseph and Margaret Thatcher in 1975 as an explicitly Conservative foundation – that their intellectual inspiration was not any kind of conservatism, as that had been traditionally understood in Britain and in other European countries, but classical liberalism. The most distinctive features of New Right ideology in Britain in the 1970s and 1980s – its use of an abstract and rationalistic conception of *Homo economicus*, its doctrinaire pursuit of a general theory of minimal government, its individualist and legalist conception of contractual relationships as the basis of economic and social order and its utopian preoccupation with constitutional devices – are all symptomatic of its roots in nineteenth- or even eighteenth-century classical liberalism, and of the influence upon it of classical liberalism's twentieth-century followers. No British or other European conservative thinker has ever supposed that the principle of consumer sovereignty, together with institutions designed to prevent the capture of government by producer interests and a constitution protecting individual rights, could frame an adequate political philosophy; yet this thin gruel of economism and legalism was all that the political thought of the New Right had to offer. By contrast, the historicism and cultural relativism of British and European conservative thought, the criticisms of commercial society mounted not only by Disraeli but by Adam Smith and Adam Ferguson, by Carlyle and Ruskin, are noteworthy for their complete absence in New Right political thought. The sharp critique of the Enlightenment developed by many conservative thinkers, even Burke, is similarly lacking.[2] The pervasive influences on New Right thought in Britain in the 1970s and 1980s – by contrast with the United States, where, except in certain varieties of doctrinally libertarian thought, populist and even fundamentalist influences were never altogether absent – were those of classical liberal rationalism, as that has been revised in our time by such thinkers as Popper and Hayek.[3]

New Right thought in Britain, then, was distanced or detached from the larger tradition of European conservative philosophy of which British conservative thought has always been a part. Its distance from its own intellectual and political tradition was enhanced by a further influence – that of the American right. It is useful to recall that the British New Right achieved its ephemeral hegemony in public discourse during the Cold War, had its political expression in the most unequivocally (and uncritically) pro-American prime minister of the post-war period, and coincided with the combination in Reaganite America of a strongly anti-Communist foreign policy with an intensely market-oriented domestic policy. This shared historical context made it all the easier for American rightist thought – the thought, that is to say, of neo-conservatives and libertarians of various sorts – to exercise an influence over British conservatism that was decidedly anomalous in terms both of its European intellectual inheritance and of Britain's underlying public culture. The weakness, or virtual absence, in the United States of anything comparable with European conservatism, the near-ubiquity in American intellectual culture of individualist, universalist and Enlightenment themes – the fact, in other words, that in the United States conservative thought is merely an indigenously American variation on classical liberal themes of limited government, individualism and economic progress – made the kinship of the British New Right with the American right a matter of elective affinity and not merely of historical accident.

This kinship between the classical liberal thought of the British New Right – whose hegemony in the 1980s was in the longer and larger history of British conservative thought highly incongruous –

and the indigenous American tradition of individualism and universalism was strengthened by the opposition of most on the neo-liberal right in Britain to European federalism.[4] For many on the New Right in Britain, and certainly for Thatcher, Britain's cultural affinities lay with the United States rather than with the nations of Europe. Thatcher may have had differences with Reagan, over the voodoo economics of self-financing tax cuts and the Panglossian claim that the Strategic Defence Initiative could exorcize the spectre of nuclear war. Yet there is no doubt that she harboured the Churchillian fantasy of a transatlantic Anglo-Saxon civilization. Their ties reinforced by conservative hegemony in both countries, Britain and the United States would not only renew the 'special relationship' but also follow parallel paths of economic and (presumably) social development, with Britain emulating American individualist market capitalism. In this Thatcher not only misread Britain's strategic situation, which was that of a European power, but misjudged British public culture, which differs from that of the United States in all the most crucially important respects. In Britain, market capitalism has never enjoyed unqualified political legitimacy, being challenged by a powerful socialist culture and accepted by Tories prior to Thatcher only with deep reservations; religion is weak and society substantially post-Christian; and the Enlightenment faith in world-improvement is lacking, or qualified – as all ideological claims are qualified – by an enduring scepticism. More decisively, perhaps, for the fate of the neo-liberal project, Britain remains a far less individualist society than the United States, with attitudes to geographical and occupational mobility, for example, being uniformly far more negative; and the relationship of the British people to the British state remains one of wary trust rather than of suspicion or enmity. It was ignorance of, or perhaps refusal to accept, these profound divergences between British and American culture and political life which made the interventions in British public discourse of such American ideologues and publicists as Charles Murray and Michael Novak predictably marginal. If Thatcher's project was that of the Americanization of Britain, these enduring features of British culture – which attest to its greater and deeper affinities with the cultures of continental Europe – foredoomed it to failure.

The remaking of the Conservative Party in the image of the Republican right, which progressed throughout the 1980s with the systematic marginalization of those Tories (such as Chris Patten) who saw its future in convergence with European Christian democratic parties, cut the Conservatives loose from their moorings in British and European culture and in the history of their own party. At the same time, the long march through British institutions begun by Thatcher and continued by John Major's government has emptied them of much of their ethos and legitimacy, while the pulverizing force of labour market deregulation, which had been applied to the unions in the 1980s, has been applied to the professional middle classes in the 1990s. The result has been a cataclysmic collapse of Tory support in Scotland and Wales, with the Conservatives there trailing as the third or fourth party. In the Tory heartland of England the permanent revolution of marketization sponsored by neo-liberal Conservative policy has confounded expectations and enhanced economic insecurity among the Conservatives' core supporters, producing a collapse of support on a similar scale.[5] As of May 1995 the Tories did not control a single metropolitan town council and only one county council. The Tories are paying the price of attaching their fortunes to an economic philosophy which recognizes only the human interest in increased income and consumer choice and fails to perceive the weightier interest people have in limiting the personal economic risk to which they are subject. In forgetting the truism of conservative philosophy that most human beings are risk-averse creatures, the Tories have condemned themselves to replicating the fortunes of the Western-inspired economic liberals of the post-Communist countries, who have been swept from office by social democratic parties which grasp this elementary truth.

In political terms, the strategic situation of the Conservatives is that the most they can hope for in the foreseeable future is to turn impending catastrophe into mere defeat. Either outcome spells displacement for the Tory nomenklatura which mans the institutions of the Quango State, and its members, along with sitting Tory MPs, will use every means at their disposal to limit the spell in opposition which they cannot now avert. Within the British conservative intelligentsia it is not uncommon to find a period of opposition welcomed as a respite from power and an occasion for reflective thought. It is difficult to know, however, what supports the confidence of Conservative thinkers in Britain that the leisure of opposition will allow them to develop the intellectual resources to address the profound changes in British society that Conservative policies have engendered or reinforced. For it is now wholly unclear what, if anything, British conservatism can realistically or coherently set itself to conserve. The hollowing out of the legitimacy of traditional institutions by economic and cultural changes which neo-liberalism has accelerated makes a restorationist or revivalist policy orientation a hopeless dead end – as the farcical flirtation of the Major government with a 'back-to-basics' rhetoric of family values showed vividly. The halcyon England of the 1950s conjured up by Major's nostalgist rhetoric, insofar as it has any semblance of historical reality, was an artefact of the Labour-led post-war settlement which the Conservatives have destroyed. Even if it were desirable to recreate it – which is more than doubtful – it is now irretrievable. An American-style stance of cultural fundamentalism has attractions for many British conservative thinkers, nonetheless, because it enables them to avoid confronting the central contradiction in their thought and policy – the contradiction between endorsing the permanent revolution of the global market and the preservation of stable forms of family and community life. If, as is manifestly the case, the effect of unfettered global market institutions is to overthrow settled communities everywhere, to undermine the stability of families by imposing on their members the imperative of unceasing mobility and to dissolve traditional practices and institutions in a flood of novelty, neo-liberal conservatives are compelled to ascribe these changes to factors other than unchecked market forces. The explanation is then sought in antinomian or relativistic doctrines supposedly propagated in schools and universities, in the legacy of 1960s libertarianism, in media bias or similarly absurd conjectures. The social – and for that matter economic – failures of market fundamentalism are patched up, or at least obscured, by recourse to the atavistic fantasies of cultural fundamentalism. Only by invoking a conspiratorial elite of liberal intellectuals can the conservative intelligentsia explain to itself why – after seventeen years of neo-liberal hegemony – the ordinary people it claims to speak for in

Britain show every sign of consigning to electoral oblivion the party whose policies they continue to support.

The political collapse of the New Right in Britain has many causes, including ones that are highly contingent, such as the adoption of the poll tax (which was one of the occasions of the Tory coup that toppled Thatcher) and the ignorance and hubris which led ephemeral neo-liberal ideologues to proclaim in the 1980s that 'Labour will never rule again.' It is still too early to attempt a balanced and comprehensive historical assessment of the conflicts of interest and personality, the errors in policy and the complex interactions of closed ideology and human folly with political power which have brought the neo-liberal experiment in Britain to a close. It is not too early to elicit a couple of lessons from its whimpering debacle. The first is that the pretensions of the New Right to an intellectual hegemony in political discourse were always spurious. The neo-liberal project exercised a transitory *political* hegemony in Britain which it owed to an unrepeatable confluence of fortunate circumstances – the bankruptcy of Labourist corporatism, the disintegration of Soviet institutions, the decline of European social democracy and the trend to economic globalization which weakened organized labour. It contributed nothing significant to conservative political thought. Indeed, its policies have only speeded the obsolescence of conservative thought by illuminating its helplessness before the dominant economic forces of the age.

The second lesson is that there remains, in Britain at least, no historical space for coherent conservative thought. The historical possibility of serious intellectual conservatism has been closed off by the policies of the last decade and a half. To be sure, if history is any guide, the Conservative Party will somehow renew itself, in the normal fortunes of political life in a two-party system; but Tory England, which it existed to conserve, is already no more than a historical memory. Conservative thought, in this new historical circumstance, is likely to be a mixture of fashionable techno-utopianism – such as the proposition, recently seriously advanced, that the virtual communities of the Internet can replace the local communities that free markets have desolated – and opportunistic fundamentalism. This is not a form of thought from which enlightenment or guidance can reasonably be expected. The enduring human needs which conservative philosophy once acknowledged are not now addressed by conservatives, partly because meeting them entails radical and – for today's conservatives – unwelcome changes in current economic institutions. Meeting these human needs – for deep and strong forms of common life, fulfilling work and a rich public environment – demands re-embedding the market processes which neo-liberal policy has emancipated from any kind of political control or accountability in the cultures and communities they exist to serve. And this is a project, little short of revolutionary in its implications, that no form of conservative thought today is willing to contemplate.

1995

11

Tony Blair, neo-con

I only know what I believe.   Tony Blair[1]

Neo-conservatism is not the most recent variety of conservatism. It is a new type of politics that can emerge at any point on the political spectrum. In Britain, neo-conservatism's political vehicle was not the Conservative Party but the new party that Blair created when he seized the Labour leadership.

The single most important fact in Blair's rise to power was Thatcher's new settlement. Both in economic and political terms it was an established fact, but while this was an index of Thatcher's achievement it was also a source of weakness for the Conservatives. Thatcher often declared that she aimed to destroy socialism in Britain. She never paused to consider what would be the effect on her party if she succeeded. For much of the twentieth century the Conservatives acted as a brake on collectivism. The Conservative Party existed to oppose not just socialism but also – and more relevantly – any further advance towards social democracy. By dismantling the Labour settlement Thatcher removed the chief reason for the existence of the Conservative Party. Without a clearly defined enemy it lacked an identity. Labour had never been a doctrinaire socialist party – as Labour Prime Minister Harold Wilson remarked, it had always owed more to Methodism than to Marx – but by identifying New Labour with the market, Blair was able to deprive the Conservatives of the threat that had defined them for generations. As a result they were mired in confusion for nearly a decade.

While Blair's embrace of neo-liberal economic policies was a strategic decision, it soon acquired an ideological rationale. More conventional in his thinking about domestic issues than most politicians and having an even shorter historical memory, Blair embraced without question the neo-liberal belief that only one economic system can deliver prosperity in a late modern context. Modernization became the Blairite mantra, and for Blair it meant something precise: the reorganization of society around the imperatives of the free market. When he was still in opposition he attracted support from disillusioned Conservatives by representing himself as a One Nation Tory – a progressive conservative who accepted the central role of the market but also understood the importance of social cohesion. Once in power it was clear that Blair came not to bury Thatcher but to continue her work.

Blair's One Nation Toryism was like his fabled Third Way, a political marketing tool. The Third Way originated in Bill Clinton's practice of 'triangulation' – a tactic invented in the mid-1990s by Clinton's adviser Dick Morris, which involved Clinton setting himself up as a more pragmatic alternative to both parties in Congress. Adopting the same tactic Blair attacked his own party as much as the Conservatives. His successful campaign to remove Clause Four (which mandated common ownership of the means of production) from the Labour constitution in 1995 was a symbolic act rather than a policy shift. At the same time it was a marker for larger challenges to Labour's social democratic inheritance. Blair carried on the agenda of privatization that had developed from Thatcher's original programme into core areas of the state such as sections of the justice system and prison service, and inserted market mechanisms into the NHS and the schooling system.

In these respects Blair did no more than consolidate Thatcherism. He did not change British society in the way Thatcher had. His chief impact has been on his own party. New Labour was constructed to bury the past and in this if in nothing else it succeeded. It began as a coup masterminded by a handful of people – Tony Blair, Gordon Brown, Peter Mandelson, Alistair Campbell, Philip Gould and others – who aimed to rebuild the party as an instrument for securing power. New Labour was a purpose-built construction with few links to the political tradition that preceded it. If it displayed any continuity with the past it was with the Social Democratic Party that had split from Labour in the 1980s, but unlike the Social Democrats New Labour grasped that issues of strategy and organization are more important than questions of policy. New Labour's first priority was to restructure the party as a centralized institution. Power had to be concentrated before anything else could be done. New Labour always had a Leninist aspect, but it was a Leninism that focused on reshaping the image of the party. If New Labour was 'modern' in its acceptance of the free market it was 'post-modern' in its conviction that power is exercised by changing the way society is perceived.

Blair's most prominent talents were his skill in using the techniques of public relations and his sensitivity to the public mood. These traits have led some observers to the view that he is an opportunist with no underlying convictions. It is true there has never been anything like a Blairite ideology, but that does not mean Blair has no beliefs. His career in politics is testimony to the power of neo-conservative ideas, which guided his most fateful decisions. He was a neo-liberal by default, but a neo-conservative by conviction.[2]

Neo-conservatism diverges from neo-liberalism at crucial points, and it is specifically neo-conservative beliefs that shaped Blair's view of the world. Unlike neo-liberals, neo-conservatives do not aim to return to an imaginary era of minimum government. They perceive that the social effects of free markets are not all benign and look to government to promote the virtues the free market neglects. Blair has always been a strong advocate of 'law and order', and made this a theme when he served as shadow home secretary under Labour leader John Smith. In part this was a strategic move to wrest the territory from the Conservatives, but it also matched his instincts. Neo-conservatives may not always be admirers of Victorian values – some (including Blair) have seen themselves as having liberal views on personal morality – but they reject the view that the state can be morally neutral. Government must act to promote the good life, which involves accepting the need for discipline and punishment. It also means promoting religion. Unlike neo-liberals, who are usually secular in outlook, neo-conservatives view religion as a vital source of social cohesion – a view expressed in Blair's support for faith schools.

Above all, neo-conservatives are unwilling to rely on social evolution. Commonly more intelligent than neo-liberals, they understand that while capitalism is a revolutionary force that overturns established social structures and topples regimes this does not happen by itself – state power and sometimes military force are needed to expedite the process. In its enthusiasm for revolutionary change, neo-conservatism has more in common with Jacobinism and Leninism than with neo-liberalism or traditional conservatism. The common view of Blair as a crypto-Tory could not be more mistaken. There is no trace in him of the scepticism about progress voiced by Tories such as Disraeli. Nor is he simply another neo-liberal prophet of the free market. He is an American neo-conservative and has been throughout most of his political life.

It is in international relations that neo-conservatism shaped Blair most deeply. Whatever he may have wished his inheritance to be – British entry into the single European currency, perhaps – he will be remembered for taking the UK into a ruinous war. His part in the Iraq war destroyed him as a politician, and he cannot have wanted this result. It would be a mistake to imagine that he was as committed at the beginning of this ill-conceived venture as he later came to be; he made errors of judgement at every stage. At the same time his support for the war expressed his most basic beliefs.

From one point of view it was a misjudged exercise in *realpolitik*. Like other British prime ministers Blair feared the consequence of opposing US policies and was prey to the conceit that by being America's unswerving ally Britain could help shape its behaviour in the international system. Anthony Eden's attempt to topple the Egyptian President Nasser and reassert British control of the Suez Canal in 1956 destroyed his political career and underlined the risks of any British leader opposing American power. Later prime ministers successfully distanced themselves from American policies – most notably Harold Wilson, who wisely declined to send troops to support the Americans in Vietnam – but Blair was insistent that Britain must give the US full support. He feared the impact on the international system if the US acted alone and saw an opportunity for Britain to 'punch above its weight' by acting as the bridge between America and Europe.

In fact, the war left the transatlantic divide wider than at any time since the Second World War, with British opinion alienated from the US, and Britain at the same time more at odds with Europe even than in Thatcher's time. But it was not only a misguided attempt at higher strategy, and there can be no doubt that Bush's decision to overthrow Saddam chimed with Blair's convictions. Saddam was a tyrant who represented a stage in human history whose time had passed. A new international order was under construction with America in the lead, and Blair wanted to be at the forefront of this project. As John Kampfner has written, 'Blair was not dragged into war with Iraq. He was at ease with himself and his own beliefs.'[3]

What were those beliefs? In a span of six years Blair took Britain into war five times. He sanctioned air strikes against Saddam Hussein in 1998, the Kosovo war in 1999, British military intervention in Sierra Leone in 2000, the war in Afghanistan in 2002 and Iraq in 2003. He dispatched further contingents of British troops to Afghanistan in 2006 when US forces were run down in the country. There is a strong strand of continuity in these decisions. Blair believes in the power of force to ensure the triumph of the good. From this point of view the attack on Iraq was a continuation of policies in the Balkans and Afghanistan. In each case war was justified as a form of humanitarian intervention. This may have had some force in the Balkans and Sierra Leone. It was dubious in Afghanistan and duplicitous in Iraq.

Blair justified these military involvements in terms of a 'doctrine of international community', which he presented in a speech at the Economic Club in Chicago in 1999. His new doctrine rested on the belief that state sovereignty could no longer survive in an interdependent world:

We are witnessing the beginnings of a new doctrine of international community. By this I mean the explicit recognition that today more than ever before we are mutually dependent, that national interest is to a significant extent governed by international collaboration and that we need a clear and coherent debate as to the direction the doctrine takes us in each field of international endeavour. Just as within domestic politics, the notion of community – the belief that partnership and cooperation are essential to advance self-interest – is coming into its own; so it needs to find its own international echo.[4]

Blair's speech reflects the unreal intellectual climate of the time. In the 1990s it was fashionable to maintain that the world had moved into a 'post-Westphalian' era – so called after the Treaty of Westphalia of 1648, which is often seen as marking the point at which the modern state was recognized in law. This system had ended in the post-Cold War period, it was believed: state sovereignty was no longer at the centre of the international system, which was governed by global institutions. In fact the sovereign state was as strong as it had ever been, and its seeming decline was a by-product of the interval after the end of the Cold War in which the US seemed able to act without restraint from other powers. The interval was destined to be brief. China and India were emerging as great powers whose interests diverge at important points but which are at one in rejecting any system based on American hegemony. In the 1990s as in the past several great powers were interacting in a mix of rivalry and co-operation. In many ways this was a re-run of the late nineteenth century with different players.

The idea that the sovereign state is on the way out was nonsense, but it served Blair well. In the first place it matched his view of the world in which human development is seen as a series of stages, each better than the last. This is a Whiggish variant of the belief in providence to which he subscribed as part of his Christian worldview. It would be unwise to take too seriously his claim to have been inspired by the Quaker philosopher John Macmurray (1891–1976) – a Christian communitarian thinker who developed from the British Idealist tradition and argued for a positive understanding of freedom as a part of the common good. To a greater extent than most politicians, Blair's view of the world was formed by the conventional beliefs of the day. He never doubted that globalization was creating a worldwide market economy that must eventually be complemented by global democracy. When he talked of the necessity for continuing 'economic reform' – as he often did – he took for granted this meant further privatization and the injection of market mechanisms into public services. The incessant 'modernization' he demanded was, in effect, an ossified version of the ideas of the late 1980s. Like Thatcher – with whom he has very little else in common – Blair lacked scepticism. For him the clichés of the hour have always been eternal verities.

As with George W. Bush, however, there is no reason to doubt the reality of Blair's faith. Like Bush, Blair thinks of international relations in terms derived from theology. To be sure this is not the theology of Augustine or Aquinas. It failed to persuade Pope John Paul II when Blair had an audience with him in late February 2003. Medieval Christian thinkers developed a rigorous theory of the conditions that must be satisfied before a war can be considered just, and the pontiff rightly believed they had not been met. The audience must have pained Blair, but it failed to shake his sense of rectitude. It was enough that he felt he was right. The scrupulous casuistry of medieval thinkers regarding the consequences of human action was of no interest. Good intentions are what matter and they are bound in the end to prevail. And yet these same 'good intentions' were promoted through ill-conceived and ideologically motivated policies, whose distance from any prudent assessment of facts he seemed unable to perceive.

The idea that the international system was moving towards global governance expanded the traditional purposes of war. The 'international community' could take military action whenever it was morally right to do so. Not only 'rogue states' that threatened the international system by developing weapons of mass destruction but also states that violated the human rights of their citizens should be the target of armed force. The aim was not just to neutralize threats – even pre-emptively. It was to improve the human condition. War was no longer a last resort against the worst evils but an instrument of human progress. In his speech in Chicago, Blair acknowledged that military action should be taken only when diplomacy had failed, and then only if it had a reasonable prospect of achieving its goals. Nevertheless he dismissed the views of those – many of them in the professional military in the UK and the US – who demanded that an exit strategy be identified before military intervention could be seriously contemplated. For Blair their caution smacked of defeatism. 'Success is the only exit strategy I am prepared to consider,' he declared.[5] Later speeches show him accepting that military force alone cannot bring about the radical transformation in the international system to which he is committed. Addressing the World Affairs Council in Los Angeles in August 2006 he declared that the struggle against terrorism 'is one about values'. He was reticent in specifying what these values might be; but whatever they were, he had no doubt they spearheaded human advance: 'Our values are worth struggling for. They represent humanity's progress throughout the ages and at each point we have had to fight for them and defend them. As a new age beckons, it is time to fight for them again.'[6] Blair returned to the subject in January 2007, when he opined: 'Terrorism destroys progress. Terrorism can't be defeated by military means alone. But it can't be defeated without it.'[7]

Lying behind Blair's view of international relations is a view of America. Along with his fellow neo-conservatives in Washington he regards America as the paradigm of a modern society. Propelled by the momentum of history, it is invincible. In giving his backing to the Bush administration in Iraq, he was able to believe that he was aiding the cause of human progress while having the consoling sense of being on the side of the big battalions. His faith in American invincibility was misguided. America's defeat by the Iraqi insurgency was in no way unexpected. The French were driven from Algeria despite prosecuting the war with extreme ruthlessness and being backed by over a million French settlers. In conditions more like those that American forces faced in Iraq, the Soviets had also been driven from Afghanistan. The lesson of asymmetric warfare – where the militarily weak use unorthodox tactics against the seemingly overwhelmingly strong – is that the weak have the winning hand.

If Blair failed to heed these lessons, the reason was partly ignorance. A politician who had unusual intuitive gifts in divining the British public mood, he lacked the knowledge necessary to make well-founded judgements in international contexts. His record of success in domestic politics was based on banishing the past. He was led into the Iraq debacle by the belief that history was on his side. Actually he knew very little history, and what he did know he refused to accept when it undercut his hopes. History was significant only as a record of human advance. To turn to it to chasten current ambitions was unthinkable, even immoral. Like Bush, Blair viewed history as the unfolding of a providential design, and a feature of their view is that the design is visible to the faithful. Others may be blind to the unfolding pattern, and in that case they may have to be guided. In

Augustinian terms this is unacceptable, for only God can know the design of history. Here Blair has been the modern man he claims to be: for him a sense of subjective certainty is all that is needed for an action to be right. If deception is needed to realize the providential design it cannot be truly deceitful.

Blair's complicity in deception in the run-up to war has led to him being seen as mendacious. This is a misreading. It is not so much that he is economical with the truth as that he lacks the normal understanding of it. For him truth is whatever serves the cause, and when he engages in what is commonly judged to be deception he is only anticipating the new world that he is helping to bring about. His silences serve the same higher purpose. He has remained silent regarding the abuses that occurred at Abu Ghraib and he has dismissed well-sourced reports that American planes have used British airports to implement the policy of 'special rendition' in which terrorist suspects are kidnapped and transported to countries where they can be tortured. His stance on these issues must by ordinary standards be judged to be thoroughly dishonest, but it is clear he believes ordinary standards do not apply to him. Deception is justified if it advances human progress – and then it is not deception. Blair's untruths are not true lies. They are prophetic glimpses of the future course of history, and they carry the hazards of all such revelations.

During Blair's decade in office British government changed in character. All administrations aim to present a positive image of themselves, and some have departed from truth in the process. Where Blair was unique was in viewing the shaping of public opinion as government's overriding purpose. The result was that whereas in the past lies were an intermittent feature of government, under his leadership they became integral to its functioning.[8] Writing about the role of lying in Soviet politics, the French political thinker Raymond Aron observed:

In the exact, strict sense of the word, he who consciously says the opposite of the truth is lying: Lenin's companions were lying when they confessed to crimes they had not committed, and Soviet propaganda was lying when it sang of the happiness of the people during the days of collectivization . . .

On the other hand, when the Bolsheviks, the Communists, call the Soviet

Union *socialist*, must we say that they are lying? ... if they recognize the difference between what socialism is today and what it will be when it conforms to its essence, then they are not, in the strictest sense, lying, but rather substituting for reality [something that can be described as] 'pseudo reality': the meaning that they give something in terms of a future they imagine as conforming to the ideology. Despite everything, Sovietism becomes a step along the road to socialism, and hence a step toward the salvation of mankind.[9]

If there is an historical precedent for Blair's methodical disregard for truth it is in the Soviet era, when a generation of Western Communists represented the USSR as a stage on the way to universal democracy. Believing they were serving an invincible cause, these fellow travellers were ready to 'lie for the truth' by portraying the Soviet system not as it was in fact but as it would inevitably – so they believed – become. It was absurd to describe the Soviet Union as a democracy. It is no less absurd to suggest that Iraq is an emerging liberal democracy and to refer to the country as the place in which the war against global terrorism is being won. In factual terms Iraq is a failed state, and insofar as there is anything like democracy it is working to produce Iranian-style theocracy. In the same way, facts tell us that the US-led invasion has turned the country into a training ground for terrorists. Blair did more than conceal these facts. He constructed a pseudo-reality that aimed to shape the way we think. As in the Soviet case, the pseudo-reality failed to withstand the test of history.

2007

12

Margaret Thatcher and the euthanasia of conservatism

The end of history? The beginning of nonsense!
Margaret Thatcher on Francis Fukuyama[1]

Margaret Thatcher did not start as a revolutionary, and there was little that was utopian in the cast of mind she brought to her first government. 'Thatcherism' is a term coined by the left that gives her policies an ideological flavour they did not always possess. Her early programme was a demanding yet realistic agenda whose most important requirements she implemented. Judged in terms of her original aims, Thatcher was a successful reforming prime minister – one of several in a long British tradition. She began as a leader like de Gaulle, focusing on national issues. By the time she was toppled she had come to see the policies she had implemented in Britain as a model for a global programme.

Thatcher became a neo-liberal only towards the end of the 1980s, but the origins of the neo-liberal period in Britain were in the economic crisis of the 1970s. Neo-liberalism refers to a body of thought that claims to return to liberal values in their original form – which, neo-liberals believe, requires strictly limited government and an unfettered free market. Despite its claim to scientific rationality, neo-liberalism is rooted in a teleological interpretation of history as a process with a preordained destination, and in this as in other respects it has a close affinity with Marxism. Just as Marxists underestimate the importance of historical accidents in the establishment of the Communist regime in Russia, neo-liberals overlook the role of chance in the rise of Margaret Thatcher.

Thatcher became leader of the Conservative Party at a time when the post-war settlement in Britain was ceasing to be viable. Her central task was to dismantle it and set up a new framework for the British economy. Labour governments had tried to do this and failed. Thatcher succeeded because she approached the job with a winning mix of ruthlessness and caution. The result was a far-reaching change in British life that created a society different from any she envisioned or desired.

It is a truism of politics that policies often have consequences different from those that are expected. In Thatcher's case the discrepancy was exceptional. She was bent on destroying socialism in Britain, so that – in the words of a crass slogan that circulated among the right-wing think-tanks in the 1980s – 'Labour will never rule again.' Instead she brought the Conservative Party to the brink of collapse and destroyed conservatism as a political project in Britain. As she thrust market forces into every corner of British life with the aim of 'rolling back the frontiers of the state', the state grew ever stronger. Just as constructing the free market in early Victorian England required a large-scale exercise of state power, so did restoring a partial version of it towards the end of the twentieth century. Victorian *laissez-faire* was engineered by a series of parliamentary acts that enclosed what had up to that time been common land, creating private property where none had existed before – a process that involved mass coercion. It was a change that could be brought about only by highly centralized government, and the same was true of Thatcher's programme. The unavoidable result of attempting to reinvent the free market was a highly invasive state.[2]

The price of Thatcher's success was a society in many ways the opposite of the one she wanted. Her goal of unshackling the free market was achievable, and to a measurable degree it was realized; but her belief that she could free up the market while shrinking the state was utopian, and so was her aim of reinstating bourgeois values. Utopia is a projection into the future of a model of society that cannot be realized, but it need not be a society that has never existed. It may be a society that once did exist – if not in exactly the form in which it is fondly remembered – but which history has since passed by. In a television interview in January 1983 Thatcher declared her admiration for Victorian values and her belief that they could be revived. Actually, the country of Thatcher's nostalgic dreams was more like the Britain of the 1950s, but the idea that unleashing market forces could re-create this lost idyll was strikingly paradoxical. The conservative Britain of the 1950s was a by-product of Labour collectivism. Thatcher tore up the foundations of the country to which she dreamt of returning. Already semi-defunct when she came to power in 1979, it had vanished from memory when she left in 1990. In attempting to restore the past she erased its last traces.

Thatcher propagated an individualist ethos of personal responsibility, but in the type of society that is needed to service the free market old-fashioned virtues of saving and planning for the future are no longer profitable. A makeshift lifestyle is well suited to the incessant mobility of latter-day capitalism. Chronic debt has proved to be a mark of prudence, and a readiness to gamble is more useful than diligent application to the job in hand. Though an earlier generation of social theorists anticipated that as capitalism developed it would foster *embourgeoisement* – the spread of a middle-class ethos throughout society – it has done the opposite. Most of the population belong in a new proletariat, with high levels of income but nothing resembling a long-term career. The deliquescence of bourgeois society has come about not through the abolition of capitalism but as a result of capitalism operating without restraint.

Neo-liberals see the advance of the free market as an unstoppable historical process, which no human agency promoted and none can prevent. Yet it was Thatcher who advanced it in Britain and it is only in retrospect that her rise to power looks inevitable. The accidental quality of her ascendancy can be seen in the people and events, many now forgotten, that made it possible. If Tory Prime Minister Edward Heath had not called a general election on the issue of who governed the country and in so doing lost the support of much of his party; if the party chairman and old-style grandee Willie Whitelaw had not been loyal to Heath and refused to stand as leader; if the volatile member of parliament and right-wing ideologue Keith Joseph had not given a public lecture in which he seemed to favour eugenic policies aimed at discouraging the poor from having children and thereby disqualified himself from standing for leadership of the party;

if former party chairman Edward du Cann had not abruptly with-drawn from the leadership race; if Thatcher's campaign for the leader-ship had not been skilfully orchestrated by Airey Neave, the MP, wartime escaper and connoisseur of special operations who was later assassinated by the Irish National Liberation Army (INLA) – if any of these circumstances had been different Thatcher would very likely not have become leader of the Conservative Party. Again, if the Labour Prime Minister James Callaghan had not delayed calling a general election until 1979 when the government was deeply unpopu-lar, or if Thatcher had not been advised on public relations by the advertising firm led by Charles and Maurice Saatchi, which produced the killer campaign slogan 'Labour isn't working' – then she might well not have become prime minister.

Thatcher's coming to power turned on the fall of a leaf. Once in office her agenda was imposed by history. British politics was shaped by memories of industrial conflict and government defeat. The three-day week, which Prime Minister Edward Heath introduced in re-sponse to industrial unrest in December 1973, the miners' strike that ejected him from power in the spring of 1974, the winter of discontent that paralysed the Labour administration in 1978–9, when refuse disposal, petrol supplies and for a time the burial of corpses were disrupted by strike action – these events, symbolic at once of national decline and the chronic weakness of government, shaped Thatcher's political outlook and her initial policies more than any ideology.

The agenda of Thatcher's first government contained few of the policies that later became neo-liberal orthodoxy. The general election manifesto of April 1979 did not mention privatization, a term that came into use only in the 1980s. One state-owned corporation (the National Freight Company) was earmarked for selling off and a commitment made to start selling off council houses, but there was no talk of bringing market mechanisms into public services. There was a promise to end the closed shop and restrict industrial picketing, but this went with a commitment to consult the trade unions on public-sector pay claims. Remarkably in view of Thatcher's later policies, the German system of wage-determination was singled out for praise. Looked at from the perspective of her reputation for scorning consensus this was an incongruously moderate document.

Yet the effect of her early policies was to bury the post-war settlement and with it British social democracy.

A major influence in shaping Thatcher's early agenda was Sir John Hoskyns, a businessman who by 1978 had become the chief strategist in her private office. In the autumn of 1977 Hoskyns presented Thatcher with a paper, 'Stepping Stones', which set the objectives with which she came to power.[3] The paper was a diagnosis of the forces underlying the current British malaise and recommended curbing union power, controlling inflation and securing balanced budgets. An archetypal early Thatcherite, Hoskyns displayed the characteristics of that breed, well summarized by Hugo Young: 'a fierce pessimism about the past, millennialist optimism about the future and a belief in the business imperative as the sole agent of economic recovery'.[4] These attitudes marked Thatcher off from the other leading politicians of her party and the rest of the British political class at that time. From the start she displayed some of the qualities of a missionary; but in the early days she did not aim to save the world, only Britain.

Post-war policy in Britain was based on the belief that steady economic growth could be promoted by a combination of deficit financing and lax monetary policy. Whether John Maynard Keynes would have endorsed the mix may be open to question, but a generation of politicians, civil servants and academic economists viewed this 'Keynesian' combination as an infallible recipe for economic growth. Yet by the 1970s growth was faltering and unemployment and inflation were rising, while industry was locked into a series of destructive wage disputes. On the wilder fringes of the right there was talk of something like a Communist state coming to power. There was never any danger of this happening – the risk in the 1970s was that Britain would become a country more like Argentina than anywhere in the Soviet bloc. Still, the crisis was real. The old ways had stopped working.

Margaret Thatcher was not the first leading British politician to accept that the post-war settlement was no longer viable. It was Denis Healey, the Chancellor of the Exchequer in James Callaghan's Labour government, who thrust this fact into the centre of British politics. Throughout the mid-1970s Healey tried to persuade his party that the post-war settlement no longer worked, but Labour's strong links with the trade unions and the opposition of much of its membership thwarted the shift in policy he wanted. Thatcher also faced entrenched opposition. Her overriding priority was to alter the system of collective wage bargaining that governed much of British industry. This meant a showdown with the trade unions, and after the miners' strike of 1984–5 their power was broken. Henceforth the economy would grow within a new framework that ensured low inflation and a flexible labour market. The social costs of putting this framework in place were high, involving a period in which unemployment rose steeply and a long-term increase in economic inequality, but in political terms it was a resounding success. Thatcher's vision of the kind of government and society that would come about when something like the free market had been reinvented was chimerical and utopian; but the deregulation of market forces she engineered formed the basis of a new settlement that was sufficiently productive to be generally accepted, and is likely to remain in force until history renders it irrelevant.[5]

Thatcher's successful challenge to the British consensus did not satisfy her ambitions. Like de Gaulle she had come to see herself as embodying the nation. Unlike the General, she launched a wide-ranging assault on national institutions. She regarded local government with particular scorn, and prompted by the right-wing think-tanks she adopted the poll tax, a flat-rate local levy that was deeply unpopular. The poll tax sowed deep doubts about Thatcher's leadership in her own party and among the public, but her hostility to Europe may have been a more significant factor in the coup that brought about her downfall in 1990. It was the irrational extremity of her European policy that led Geoffrey Howe to resign as deputy prime minister and triggered a leadership challenge from Michael Heseltine. It was hostility to Heseltine's pro-European stance that led the Thatcherite wing of the party to mount the all-out effort to prevent him succeeding as leader, which resulted in the election of John Major. It was Major's attempt to mend relations with Europe that led to his joining the European Exchange Rate Mechanism at the wrong rate – a decision that rebounded when sterling was ejected from the mechanism on 'Black Wednesday' in September 1992. Major's government never recovered, civil war broke out among Conservatives on Europe, and the Conservative Party became an ungovernable rabble.

Thatcher's successors struggled for nearly a decade to understand what made their party unelectable. Clearly a number of decisions and events had contributed to this result, including the coup that toppled Thatcher in 1990. But Conservative unpopularity had deeper causes, and it was only when David Cameron became leader that the party was forced to accept that the obstacle to electoral success was conservatism itself. Post-Thatcher Britain is a less cohesive society than the one she inherited, but it is also more tolerant – unbothered about 'family values', no longer pervasively homophobic, less deeply racist and (though markedly more unequal) not so fixated on issues of class. While he relegated Thatcher to the history books Cameron accepted the society she had, contrary to her intentions, helped create. By burying Thatcher while embracing post-Thatcher Britain he made his party once again a contender for power.

2007

PART THREE

From Post-Communism to Deglobalization

13

The system of ruins

As it has been disclosed to us in twentieth-century political history, the fate of Marxism is to be the first worldview in human history that is genuinely self-refuting. To be sure, all systems of general ideas about man and society have unintended consequences when they are given practical effect, and it is a commonplace that the distance between doctrine and practice is nowhere wider or harder to bridge than in political life. Further, it is a familiar theme in political thought that social institutions may over the long run have a self-destroying tendency insofar as they cannot help breeding expectations they must fail to satisfy.

None of these traditional themes succeeds in capturing the thoroughly paradoxical role of Marxian ideas in contemporary political life. The distinctive achievement of Marxism, peculiarly ironical in a system of ideas committed *au fond* to the unity of theory with practice, is that its most spectacular victories in the real world have afforded the most devastating criticisms of its fundamental tenets. Accordingly, in installing in Russia and in much of Asia new economic and political institutions to which nothing in the old orders corresponded, the Communist regimes have exhibited unequivocally that radical autonomy of general ideas in the political realm which their official doctrine, no less than classical Marxism, tirelessly denies. The stupendous successes of Communism in the real world have given a practical self-refutation of the Marxian system, since in every case the actual result of a revolutionary socialist victory has been to flout the aspirations of the revolutionaries as it demonstrates once again the impossibility of Communism as Marx conceived it.

The self-refutation in practice of Marxism over the past half-century

GRAY'S ANATOMY

was not unanticipated in the theoretical writings of Marx's critics. In a rare moment of realistic insight, the great Russian anarchist, Bakunin, predicted that the outcome of a Marxian socialist revolution would be a form of dictatorship more repressive and more exploitative than the bourgeois political order it replaced. In a far more systematic fashion, Böhm-Bawerk in his *Karl Marx and the Close of his System* (1896)[1] dissected the errors of Marx's economic theory and showed how they debilitated his account of market capitalism, while Böhm-Bawerk's successors in the Austrian School of Economics, L. von Mises and F. A. von Hayek, developed in the 1920s and 1930s powerful theoretical arguments explaining the failures in resource-allocation of socialist systems. Apocalyptic though it has been, the history of Marxism in practice over the past half-century has served only to give concrete historical exemplification to criticisms of Marx's ideas that were developed during his lifetime and in the first fifty years after his death.

The ruin of Marx's system by the events of the past half-century has in no way inhibited the production of Marxian theoretical literature in Western societies. Throughout the past hundred years, Marxian ideas have served in capitalist societies as weapons in the armoury of cultural criticism, as tools in projects for revisionary history, and as postulates for sociological research. In fulfilling this role of promoting self-criticism within Western society, Marxian thinkers have been compelled to refine the central notions of Marx's system beyond anything he could have recognized or endorsed, and in so doing they have often obfuscated important questions in the interpretation of his writings. It is one of the few hopeful features of the flurry of activity surrounding the anniversary of his death that a handful of books has appeared that give Marx's life and work the benefit of a detached and scrupulous historical analysis. In this connection, the *Dictionary of Marxist Thought*[2] edited by Tom Bottomore is an invaluable aid in identifying the key terms in Marx's own work and distinguishing their force in Marx from the uses made of them by later writers. Bottomore's *Dictionary* is usefully complemented by Gérard Bekerman's *Marx and Engels: A Conceptual Concordance*,[3] in which the crucial ideas of the two writers are illustrated by quotations from their writings, carefully chosen by Bekerman and skilfully translated by Terrell

Carver. These works of reference will prove indispensable to anyone who wishes to form a reasoned judgement about the currently fashionable thesis that it was Engels who made of Marx's subtle and eclectic thought a crude and mechanical system.

A very different, but equally valuable service is performed by David Felix's *Marx as Politician*.[4] Felix's method is unique in Marxian scholarship inasmuch as he develops his incisive criticism of Marx's theories through the medium of a demystifying political biography. His strategy is to deconstruct Marx's chief theoretical claims by illuminating their force as acts in his struggles for political power over the emergent working-class movements of nineteenth-century Europe and their rivalrous leaders. Nowhere in Felix's elegantly and acidulously written book does he suggest that understanding Marx's theories in this way, as aspects of his political practice, by itself devalues their claims to truth, but he shows convincingly that we can best account for the manifest incoherences of Marx's system by viewing it as a makeshift, constantly reworked according to the political necessities of the moment. Again, without ever replicating the vulgarities of psychohistory, Felix gives a psychological gloss to his political reading of Marx's theoretical activity by displaying its roots in an ungovernably assertive and domineering personality. Marx's virulent contempt for ethical socialism, his rigid posture of opposition to all existing social orders and his cynical dismissal of the claims of small nations and vanquished classes are given a compelling interpretation by reference to his anomic and obsessional fascination with power. Felix's final assessment of Marx's political vision grasps firmly a truth that has been stubbornly resisted by all of his conventional biographers when he writes, ' "Nazi" was the simplified acronym for National Socialist German Workers Party. It was an accurate name for the party Marx would like to have led in Germany in 1848–9, nationalistic, socialistic, and as anti-Semitic as tactically useful.'

The many affinities between Marx's political vision and the ideas and movements of the radical right which Felix identifies are profoundly explored in Ernst Nolte's important collection of essays, *Marxism, Fascism, Cold War*.[5] Since his seminal study, *Three Faces of Fascism*,[6] Nolte has been widely misread as a theorist of Fascism who conceives it in Marxian terms as the radical anti-socialist response to capitalist crisis and who seeks the elimination of the liberal category of totalitarianism in the explanation of both Communism and Fascism. The discursive and wide-ranging essays assembled in this volume should lay to rest any such interpretation of Nolte's work, which is distinctive in representing contemporary Marxist practice as having authentic origins in Marxian doctrine and instructive in perceiving the structural similarities of Marxian and Fascist contestations of bourgeois society. Thus in identifying, in his brief essay on 'The Conservative Features of Marxism',[7] the character of Marxism (understood here to mean the doctrines held in common by Marx and Engels) as a critique of modernity, Nolte helps us towards an explanation of the encrusted cultural conservatism of all actual Communist regimes that is more adequate than any to be found in the strained apologetics of Western Marxian writers. The enmity of Communist governments to all the most radical expressions of the modern spirit – in art and philosophy as well as lifestyle and popular culture – is correctly perceived as emanating directly from the anti-individualist animus which pervades the thought of Marx and Engels alike. The repression in Communist states of all modernist movements is not, then, an aberration or even an unintended consequence of Marx's doctrine, but simply an expression of its original intent. In its application to the Fascist phenomenon, Nolte's analysis is conclusive in linking the Rousseauesque primitivism of Marx's fantasy of ending the social division of labour with the Fascist rebellion against commercial society. As Nolte drily observes:

Fascism can be directly compared with Marxism of the Soviet nature only in its radical form, in respect of its inner solidarity and its appeal to comrades of like mind in all countries; Italian Fascism, in its phase as a development dictatorship, and more than ever the Croatian Ustase and the Romanian Iron Guard were in fact, on the contrary, more like many of today's 'national liberation movements' than like late National Socialism ... there is nothing more grotesque than a 'theory of Fascism' which denounces capitalism with much sincere indignation as the root of Fascism, at the same time overlooking that the theory identifies itself with conditions which show all the formal characteristics of Fascism. It is not astonishing that the liberal capitalist system produces Fascism under certain circumstances, but it is astonishing that in the great majority of cases Fascism has not succeeded in gaining power in spite of certain circumstances. The explanation can only lie in the fact that this social system with its peculiar lack of conception, its deep-rooted divergencies, its inborn tendency to self-criticism, its separation of economic, political and spiritual power obviously offers strong resistance to a transformation to Fascist solidarity, and is aware that the deliverance which is promised would at the same time be loss of self. Thus capitalism is indeed the soil of Fascism, but the plant only grows to imposing strength if an exorbitant dose of Marxist fertilizer is added to the soil.[8]

The most important essay in Nolte's collection deals not with the question of Fascism, however, but with errors in the historical interpretation of early industrial capitalism which have been widely disseminated by Marxian writers. Along with radical Tories such as Oastler, Sadler, Southey and Disraeli, Marx and Engels associated the industrial revolution with the pauperization of the masses and the devastation of their traditional ways of life. By comparison with the factory system as it developed under *laissez-faire* capitalism, pre-industrial life was pictured in almost arcadian terms of satisfying work, harmonious community and a reasonable sufficiency of material goods. Nolte is assiduously specific in documenting how Marx and Engels and the reactionary and Romantic critics of industrialism and the factory system neglected the filth, squalor and waste of human life endemic in pre-industrial society. In this Nolte's analysis parallels that of a number of contemporary economic historians, among whom the most distinguished is R. M. Hartwell, whose researches have gone far to establish that the Marxian immiseration thesis is as false in respect of early industrialism as it is of our own capitalist economies. An explosion of population involving a massive decline in infant mortality rates, increasing consumption of commodities hitherto regarded as luxuries, and many other empirical factors point to the early industrial period in England as one of much enhanced popular living standards.

At the same time, Nolte is careful to specify the background of this explosion in living standards in several centuries of European and, above all, English political and cultural development, which preceded it. Noting that 'European society is, from its beginnings in the early middle ages onward, the society of a functioning or dynamic pluralism whose several relatively autonomous powers, such as royalty and the aristocracy, the state and the church, and also the individual states restrict each other, and yet they remain even in sharpest struggle, related to each other and subject to mutual influence,' Nolte inverts the historical materialist thesis of the primacy of technological and economic factors in accounting for social and political changes and explains the technological development of early industrialism as a variable dependent upon pluralist legal and political institutions. In so doing he is concerned to stress particularly the importance of the English example, wherein the industrial revolution was the culmination of several centuries of agrarian development on a market model. His account of the background and conditions of the industrial revolution in England converges at several points with that given by Alan Macfarlane in his fascinating *Origins of English Individualism*,[9] and it would be encouraging to suppose that Nolte's book will do something to subvert the legend, which the writings of Karl Polanyi and C. B. Macpherson have made a central element in academic folklore, that the seventeenth and eighteenth centuries in England encompassed a radical transition from communitarian to individualist forms of social life.

The upshot of Nolte's analysis is that European capitalism is a historical singularity, in no way the necessary or inevitable outcome of human social development taken as a whole. It was as a lucky chance, the unlikely outcome of a serendipitous conjunction of events, that market processes were able to spread in the early Middle Ages and thus to lay down the necessary conditions for the emergence of large-scale capitalist production. This conclusion goes against one of the central tenets of Marx's thought, and allows us to pinpoint one of its most disastrous errors. For all his insistence on the particularities of specific cultures and on the unevenness of economic development in different nations, Marx (and Engels after him, albeit with fewer saving reservations) subscribed to a belief in something like a law of the increasing development over human history of productive forces. He asserted this not just as a brute historical fact nor yet as a mere trend, but as the unifying principle of human history. It is such a principle, something midway between the statement of a trend and the enunciation of a law, that G. A. Cohen terms the Development Thesis in his *Karl Marx's Theory of History: A Defence*.[10] It is one of the most noteworthy features of Cohen's book, which sets standards of competence and rigour in argument which have been matched by few twentieth-century Marxian thinkers and which non-Marxian philosophers would do well to try to emulate, that his defence of the Development Thesis is feeble and admittedly unsuccessful. In the end Cohen is driven to invoke in its support a starkly Benthamite, and for that reason wholly unMarxian, conception of man as an economizer of his efforts.

This move has to confront, however, the inconvenient fact that the systematic and continuous expansion of productive forces over many centuries appears to have occurred within capitalist Europe and its offshoots and nowhere else. Explaining the singularity of capitalist development generates a most fundamental criticism of the Marxian scheme of historical interpretation. For, contrary to Cohen's attempted reconstruction of historical materialism in Darwinian functionalist form, a mechanism for filtering out inefficient productive arrangements exists *only within the capitalist mode of production*. Within a capitalist market economy, there is a powerful incentive for enterprises to innovate technologically, and to adopt innovations pioneered by others, since firms which persist in using less efficient technologies will lose markets, reap dwindling profits and eventually fail. Nothing akin to this selective mechanism of market competition existed to filter out inefficient technologies in the Asiatic mode of production, and it has no replica in existing socialist command economies. Cohen's defence of the Development Thesis is bound to fail because it attempts to account for the replacement of one productive mode by another by invoking a mechanism which features internally in only a single mode of production, market capitalism.

Cohen's argument has the virtue of confronting a central difficulty in Marxian historical materialism which most Marxian writers prefer to pass over. Thus the problem is mentioned by Alex Callinicos neither in his propagandist tract, *The Revolutionary Ideas of Karl Marx*,[11] nor in his more reflective and self-critical *Marxism and Philosophy*.[12] None of the writers in David McLellan's *Marx: The First*

Hundred Years[13] takes it up, even when (as in the essays by Raymond Williams, Ernest Mandel and Roy Edgley) their contributions focus more or less directly on problems and applications of historical materialism. This omission is striking and lamentable, but eminently understandable, since any recognition of the inadequacy of the Marxian scheme of historical development is bound to undermine the viability of Marxian socialism itself. If we acknowledge, as did Marx, the essentially unconservative character of capitalist enterprise, we will find it incongruous that he and his followers imagine that the prodigious virtuosity of capitalism can be retained while its central mechanism, market competition, is abolished. There is, in fact, no reason to think that the productive achievements of capitalism will even be maintained, still less surpassed, once market mechanisms for allocating resources are removed. It is this insight which explains the vast chaos and colossal malinvestments which are typical of all existing socialist command economies. In Marx's own writings, in accordance with his refusal to engage in utopian speculations, no proposal is ever advanced for the co-ordination of economic activity in socialist or Communist societies: it is simply assumed, with the utmost naivety, that an acceptable allocation of resources to particular uses will emerge spontaneously, without the need for markets or pricing, from the collaborative discussions of socialist citizens. It was indeed to this gigantic evasion that Lenin referred obliquely, when he confessed that the principal task of the Bolsheviks in the USSR was the construction of state capitalism. Aside from the fact that it entails inexorably a concentration of power in bureaucratic institutions which Marx always sought to avoid, but which was realized fully in the Stalinist period, Lenin's project of a state capitalist regime was bound to founder on the absence within it of the central capitalist institution for resource allocation.

In the event, the Soviet experience amply confirmed the predictions of those economists of the Austrian School, particularly Mises and Hayek, who argued for the impossibility of rational resource allocation under socialist institutions. In the Soviet Union, working-class living standards after over sixty years of state capitalist construction are probably lower than in Brazil, while elsewhere, in Hungary and in China, only the expedient of reintroducing capitalist institutions is allowing wealth to grow and incomes to rise. These developments exemplify in concrete historical contexts the theoretical insights with which the Austrian economists prevailed over their socialist opponents in the great debates of the inter-war years. Yet, despite their intellectual victory, the Austrian arguments have been ignored by generations of economists and their relevance to the Soviet experience has been expounded in depth only by Paul Craig Roberts in his vital and neglected book *Alienation and the Soviet Economy*.[14] It is entirely characteristic that in his contribution to the McLellan collection, Mandel, after showing an awareness of the calculation debate that distinguishes him from the bulk of his professional colleagues, should demonstrate his inability to grasp the nature of the problem at issue when he remarks innocently of Mises's argument that it has 'in the meantime been taken care of by the computer'. As it has turned out, history has forced back on to the intellectual agenda a debate which the intelligentsia for several generations consigned to the memory hole.

The ruin of Marxism both as a scheme of historical interpretation and as a theory of economic organization has evoked a variety of responses among contemporary Marxian writers. The great majority has tried to prevent the destruction of the doctrine by intractable facts through the elaboration of protective *ad hoc* hypotheses. Accordingly, an effort has been made to explain the catastrophic impact of Marxism in Russia by seeking out continuities between the political culture and institutions of Tsarism and those of the Soviet power, with the underlying insinuation that in Russia an enlightened Western European creed of democracy and freedom was corrupted by contact with tyrannous native traditions. Its culturally racist features aside, this argument misrepresents Tsarism, which for the last sixty years of its history was an open, progressive authoritarian system, far less inhumane or repressive of individual liberty than the great majority of member states in today's United Nations, and evolving in a context of extraordinary economic growth and brilliant cultural achievement. The real Russian tragedy was the reverse of that imputed by the conventional and complacent view in that the blossoming civic traditions of Tsarism were in 1917 barbarized and destroyed by the incursion of a totalitarian ideology of Western European origins.

On a more general level, this sort of protective manoeuvre within Marxism must be criticized on the Popperian ground that it has the effect of transforming what was in Marx's hands a living and corrigible body of thought into an intellectual deadweight of reinforced dogmatism. Thus every contribution to the Norman Fischer volume on *Continuity and Change in Marxism*[15] (with the partial exception of a cryptic and suggestive piece by Kostas Axelos) reveals an abandonment of the empirical content of Marx's thought in favour of a reassertion of its Hegelian essentialist metaphysics. This metamorphosis of Marxism from a body of empirical social theory and of historical interpretation into a self-enclosed metaphysical system is most evident in the Frankfurt School, but despite all protestations to the contrary it characterizes Althusser's Cartesian reconstruction of Marx's thought as well as Marcuse's Heideggerian variations on Marxian and Hegelian themes.

In fairness it must be said that the multiple ironies involved in this retreat to metaphysical inquiry from a system of thought which at its height promised an end to philosophy have not gone unnoticed by all Marxian thinkers. The tension between the metaphysical turn in recent Marxism and the anti-philosophical bent of Marx's own mature thought is at the heart of Callinicos's *Marxism and Philosophy* and it motivates Susan Easton's search for affinities and convergences in *Humanist Marxism and Wittgensteinian Social Philosophy*.[16] Easton's intriguing project of linking up a form of Marxism in which human activity and not historical law is central, with the Wittgensteinian conception of knowledge as embodied in social practices, does not face its hardest difficulty in the biographical fact that Wittgenstein's own political views were conservative, not to say reactionary, and were never seen by him to conflict in any way with his developed philosophical outlook. The most serious difficulty for this kind of Marxian theorizing is its irresistible tendency to slip into an Idealist constructivism about the social world of precisely the sort that Marx repudiated in his attacks on Hegel and on Stirner. The metaphysical turn of humanist Marxism is sure to be a dead end because it begins by shedding the realist commitments which Marx himself rightly thought to be most distinctive of his view of social life.

In their retreat from empirical theorizing to essentialist metaphysics, the Hegelian Marxists forgo one of Marx's most ambitious projects: the development of a comprehensive theory of ideology. Any theory of ideology, and above all a Marxian theory, incorporates a distinction between appearance and reality in society which the Idealist implication of humanist Marxism tends to occlude. Further, the abandonment of the claim to scientific realism in Marx's thought suggests an obvious question about the ideological character of humanist Marxism itself. This is a question that haunts Jorge Larrain's meandering and inconclusive discussions in *Marxism and Ideology*,[17] but which is posed decisively at several points in Jean Cohen's *Class and Civil Society: The Limits of Marxian Critical Theory*.[18] Cohen's is a luminously intelligent investigation of the limitations of Marxian class theory which takes seriously the criticism of socialist and Marxist thought as itself having the mystifying and repressive functions of an ideology. She considers in this context not only the theory of Konrad and Szelenyi, which echoes the predictions of the late-nineteenth-century Polish anarchist, Waclas Machajski, in representing Marxism in the Soviet bloc as the instrument of a novel form of domination, but also Western theorists of the new class such as Irving Kristol and Alvin Gouldner.

Cohen's own attitude to Szelenyi's class analysis of the Eastern-bloc societies – of which a most useful exposition is given by Szelenyi himself in his contribution to M. Burawoy and Theda Skocpol's *Marxist Inquiries*[19] – is not free from ambiguity. She recognizes the truth in Szelenyi's and Konrad's claims regarding the existence of an exploitative social stratum which has arisen in the Communist regimes via its control of education and of access to information, but she goes on to criticize their approach as flawed because it adopts a strategy of analysis whose limitations are those of Marx's class theory. The opposite situation seems to me to be the true one: the theory of the new class in its control of education and of access to information cannot be stated in Marxist terms, but she goes on to criticize their approach with Marxian class theory. That the new class is not a Marxian class is a criticism of the theory of Szelenyi and Konrad only insofar as they see themselves as completing Marxian social theory rather than abandoning it whenever new forms of injustice and exploitation elude its grasp.

The general relevance of the theory of the new class is that it encourages us to look at the ideological function of socialist thought itself. In so doing we harness the critical intent which motivated Marx's analyses of the classical economists to examine Marxian and other socialist systems of ideas as vehicles for the protection and promotion of the interests of specific social groups. Essential to the theory of ideology, after all, is not only the identification of a distance between reality and appearance in society, but the demonstration that this distance is functional in enabling some social interest to prevail over some other. Ideology, in short, facilitates domination and exploitation as ongoing social relationships. Not only in its manifestations in the Soviet bloc, but also in Western societies, socialist thought invites ideological analysis as an instrument in the social struggle among competing groups for access to state power and thereby to the resources the modern interventionist state commands. Whereas a theory of the ideological functions of the socialist system promises much in the illumination of the chronic legitimation crisis of the Communist regimes and of the conflicts in our own societies, the project of developing fully such a theory is one that even independent critical thinkers of the stature of Jean Cohen seem to retreat from.

The undefended assumption that socialist goals stand in need of no ideological demystification, even if socialist regimes sometimes do, is an outstanding feature of Barry Smart's able exploration of the relations of Foucault's thought with Marxism,[20] and the inherent progressiveness of the socialist ideal figures as a presupposition of analysis, inhibiting fundamental criticism, equally in George G. Brenkert's *Marx's Ethics of Freedom*.[21] It seems that the stance of radical criticism does not extend, so far as these writers are concerned, to the socialist conventional wisdom of the Western academic class.

A re-emergence of Marxism as a progressive research programme in social theory may be predicated upon several rather exacting conditions. A new Marxism worthy of serious critical attention would have to confront the Austrian thesis that market competition and bureaucratic command structures are together the mutually exhaustive means of resource allocation in complex industrial societies, with command economies having ineradicable tendencies to vast waste and malinvestment. It would have to consider the possibility that the economic chaos and political repression characteristic of all socialist command economies are not mere aberrations, but structurally inseparable results of such economies. It would, above all, need to confront the repressed possibility that the Gulag represents an unavoidable phase in socialist construction rather than a contingent incident in Soviet (and Chinese) experience. In order to face these hard questions, a new Marxism would demand a purer and more self-critical method of thought than any variety of Marxism has so far achieved. It would need to engage directly with the moral theory of justice and exploitation and to abandon the forlorn pretence that it can deploy some special, dialectical logic to circumvent contradictions within its own theories. The central concern of such a new Marxism – to link normative exploitation theory with empirical class analysis – is in fact the subject matter of a powerful new school of Analytical Marxism, led by such figures as G. A. Cohen, Jon Elster and John Roemer, with whose works the future of Marxism, if it has any, must henceforth be associated.

It is hard to imagine that the version of Marxian theory which looks like being developed by these thinkers will do more than generate a few scattered insights which are easily absorbed into normal social science. Once the spurious claim to esoteric insight and omnicompetent method is given up, Marxian thought confronts the same intractable difficulties in the theory of justice and in the philosophy of social science which have bedevilled non-Marxian thought, and it has little that is special of its own to offer. The attraction of Marxism to the Western intelligentsia was, in any case, never that of an analytically superior theoretical system in social science. It was rather the appeal of a historical theodicy, in which Judeo-Christian moral hopes were to be realized without the need for a transcendental commitment which reason could not sanction. In the Communist societies where Marxism has been institutionalized as the official ideology, its mythopoeic elements have not indeed been especially prominent. For all the paraphernalia of the Lenin cult, Marxist ideology has functioned there in Hobbesian fashion, as an instrument of political discipline, and has had no role in spiritual life. If anything, the inability of Communist Marxism to function as a comprehensive view of the world has added a new twist to the history of its practical self-refutation, as when the

Soviet Buryat Mongols appropriated the official legend of the Paris communards and prayed to their spirits, which had come to rest in the home of the Buryats' traditional objects of worship under Lake Baikal. Yet the irony of Marxism's self-effacement in the Soviet Union is unlikely to be altogether evaded in the liberal intellectual cultures of the West, even if it does not take the beautiful form of a Shamanistic metamorphosis of Marxist piety. Western analytical Marxism will flourish and expand just insofar as it possesses those mythic elements in Marx's thought that it is committed to shedding.

At the same time, eliminating the mythic content of Marxism will rob it of its distinctive power and speed its recuperation by bourgeois social science. The final dilemma of Western Marxism is that, unless it represses in the interests of criticism and objective knowledge the mythopoeic impulse which explains its appeal over the past century, it can only present to the rest of us the spectacle of an esoteric and barely intelligible cult, whose devotees pass their time picking reverently among the shards and smithereens of a broken altar.

1983

14

Cultural origins of
Soviet Communism

What are the cultural origins of Soviet Communism? In order to answer this question we must ask another: what are the intellectual antecedents of Marxism? Leszek Kolakowski[1] has located one source of Marxism in the Greek, and especially the neo-Platonic preoccupation with the contingency of human existence, which was transmitted to Marx via Hegel. In this account, Marxism is a secularized version of the mystical soteriology of Greek Platonism in which a return to the unalienated human essence replaces reabsorption in the Absolute as the form of salvation and release from contingency. Kolakowski's analysis neglects or underestimates the contribution of Christian traditions to the intellectual and moral formation of Marxism. For it was Christianity, with its conception of human history as a moral drama, which allowed the Platonistic soteriology to be transformed into an historical theodicy. This is the insight captured by Eric Voegelin in his interpretation of modern political religions as gnostic immanentizations of Christian eschatology. As Voegelin puts it:

The characterisation of modern political mass movements as neopagan, which has a certain vogue, is misleading because it sacrifices the historically unique nature of modern movements to a superficial resemblance. Modern redivinisation has its origins rather in Christianity itself, deriving from components that were suppressed as heretical by the universal church.[2]

The same point is made by Michael Polanyi:

Had the whole of Europe been at the time of the same mind as Italy, Renaissance Humanism might have established freedom of thought everywhere, simply by default of opposition. Europe might have returned to – or if you like relapsed into – a liberalism resembling that of pre-Christian antiquity. Whatever may have followed after that, our present disasters would not have occurred.[3]

On this interpretation, Marxism is a Christian-historicist gloss on a Greek-rationalist doctrine of salvation. It should be noted here, however, that contrary to the conventional academic wisdom, Western Christianity is far more implicated in the generation of Marxism than Eastern Christianity. For Western Christianity imbibed the elements of Aristotelian rationalism as transmitted via Aquinas into the medieval world, together with the humanist values of the Renaissance and the secularizing impact of the Reformation, that had little impact on Russian Orthodoxy. For Orthodoxy, with the exception of a few iconoclastic thinkers (such as the early Berdyaev),[4] Marxism represented the incursion of a Western ideology into Russian Christianity – and one which, furthermore, had emerged in the West partly because of the decadence of Western Christianity. This is not to deny that, as Alain Besançon has shown,[5] Soviet Communism has some sources in an alienated Russian intelligentsia – a point emphasized by Solzhenitsyn[6] and prophetically made by Dostoyevsky.[7] It is to question the common Western belief that Soviet Communism was ever sustained by elements in Russian religious life – against which it has waged a perpetual war.

It is from its expression of the central tenets of the European Enlightenment, however, that Marxism, and its embodiment in Soviet Communism, derives its essential appeal to Western intellectual opinion. It is here that the Jacobin lineage of Leninism and the character of the French Revolution as the first precursor of twentieth-century experiments in social engineering via the mass liquidation of entire social groups need to be noted. The recent revisionist historiography[8] of the French Revolution has noted its terrorist nature, in particular the fact that, whereas at the time the Bastille was stormed it contained fewer than ten inmates, by the time the Terror had run its course around half a million Frenchmen were incarcerated for political reasons, many of whom would perish in jail. We know that Lenin was himself much influenced by the Jacobin precedent as an early experiment in what J. L. Talmon has well called 'totalitarian democracy'.[9] There seems to be good reason, then, to see a clear historical linkage between the two revolutions, as to their goals, their strategies and the types of institutions they produced.

It is in the common origins in the secular faith of the Enlightenment that the affinity of the two revolutions is most plainly seen. The ideas of a self-consciously planned society and of a universal civilization grounded in scientific knowledge are central elements of that religion of humanity that is expressed in both Marxism and liberalism. They express, in a distinctively modernist fashion, values and beliefs – rationalistic and optimistic – derived both from the Greco-Roman classical tradition and the Judeo-Christian traditions that are coeval with Western civilization. It is in this truth that the central paradoxes of totalitarianism are to be found: the paradoxes of its enmity to the civilization that gave it birth and the paradox that, though Marxism-Leninism is a modernist ideology, Soviet totalitarianism is at war with the most fundamental institutions of the modern world as it has thus far developed. We may justly judge that Theodore von Laue exaggerates greatly when he avows that 'it was the West which, by the model of its superior power, has shaped the Soviet dictatorship. Soviet totalitarianism was basically no more than the caricature echo of Western state and society, the best copy feasible under Russian conditions.'[10] Laue's extreme overstatement, like the claim that Western societies have totalitarian aspects, nevertheless expresses a grain of truth – the truth in the claim that totalitarian ideology has its roots in Western tradition, and totalitarian regimes are episodes in the global process of Westernization, aberrant and distorted not by the traditional societies which they destroy but by elements within the Western tradition itself.

Western opinion's blind spot in regard to the nature of Soviet Communism is congenital and incorrigible. It expresses an integral part of the Western worldview. One may even say, without too much exaggeration, that (just as totalitarianism is only the shadow of modern civil society) so Soviet Communism is only the shadow cast by the European Enlightenment. A realistic perception of Soviet enmity to Western civil societies presupposes an insight into the defects or limitations of Western traditions of which the animating ideology of the Soviet regime is an authentic development. Nothing supports the hope that Western opinion is capable of the self-criticism such an insight requires. If it comes to pass, the fall of Soviet totalitarianism is most likely to occur as an incident in the decline of the occidental cultures that gave it birth, as they are shaken by the Malthusian, ethnic and fundamentalist conflicts which – far more than any European ideology – seem set to dominate the coming century.[11]

1989

15

Western Marxism:
a fictionalist deconstruction

The visits that Wittgenstein made to the Soviet Union in the late 1930s must be among the least researched episodes in his life. Most of his biographers mention the visit he made in 1935, and a few refer to a later visit in 1939. None tells us anything of substance about what he did there, and, in particular, none of them gives any clue to how his experiences in the USSR might have influenced his philosophical development. We learn that during his first visit Wittgenstein was offered a chair in philosophy at the University of Kazan (where Tolstoy had studied) and that for a while he considered seriously the possibility of settling in the Soviet Union. We learn nothing, or little, of his intellectual contacts in the Soviet Union. It is only very recently, in fact, that we have come to know of the most formative of his intellectual encounters in the Soviet Union, which occurred in his conversations in 1935 and 1939 with the neglected Hungarian Marxist thinker, L. Revai.[1]

Since Revai's life and work remain little known in the West, it is worth sketching their main outlines. Born in Budapest in 1881, the first son of a well-established banking family, Revai made a minor mark on Central European intellectual life in the first decade of this century as a literary theorist. His work at that time (now virtually unobtainable and nearly forgotten) was derivative and unoriginal, being an eclectic weaving together of a variety of currently fashionable themes. It reveals nothing of the intellectual radicalism which distinguishes his mature theorizing and amounts to a highly conventional application of Kantian and Schopenhauerian conceptions to familiar questions in the theory of culture. In the 1920s Revai published hardly at all. He had joined the Communist Party shortly after its foundation in 1918, abandoning the romantic syndicalism of his youth for a Leninism he was never to renounce, and seems to have occupied himself for a decade or more in political and organizational work. Little is known, even now, of his thought during this period. We know that in 1933 he left Hungary for the USSR, and stayed there until 1945. From the present volume we learn, for the first time, that in 1936 he was incarcerated in a labour camp, from which (as one of the very few to have returned from internment at that time) he was released in 1938. It is only with the present volume, above all, that we learn that on several occasions in 1935 and 1939 Revai met Wittgenstein, and engaged with him in conversations which left a lasting mark on the philosopher's later thinking.

Revai's life after the war was uneventful. He pursued his oblique and elusive career in Hungary as a translator and occasional anonymous contributor to Budapest cultural reviews. Scarcely known in his own country or elsewhere, seeming to have acquired few, if any, disciples or followers, he published nothing under his own name (except for a brief statement of neutrality during the disturbances of 1956). He died in 1973. Throughout nearly thirty years of obscurity in his native land, ignored by the authorities and without even the dubious privileges of a dissident intellectual, Revai worked patiently and indefatigably on his master-project – the development of a Marxist theory of language.

Revai's life-work was never completed. The six essays collected in *The Word as Deed: Studies in the Labour Theory of Meaning* are only fragments, embodying all that remains of a massive project, and constituting the literary remains of a thinker whose input on the development of Western thought has thus far been entirely esoteric. It is, indeed, only owing to the resourcefulness of the collection's two editors that Revai's work has been rescued from oblivion and its bearing on Wittgenstein's philosophy revealed. In an extended biographical foreword to the collection, Olsen and Kahn piece together an account of Revai's life and thought from the evidences of the papers recovered (through the intervention of his sole disciple) from his modest apartment in Budapest. They are able to tell for the first time how Revai, having by then emerged from a stay in the Gulag, spoke with Wittgenstein about the conception of language as an incident in human labour which he had begun developing in the 1920s in Hungary, and which his experiences in the camps had crystallized into a more definite doctrine. In the camps, Revai told Wittgenstein, the complex grammar of civil society was dissipated, and speech returned to its more primordial function as an integrating mechanism in the human transformation of physical energy. It was in the camps, where the forces of production were developed in transparent social relations without the mediation of mystifying ideological structures, that the adverbial labyrinth of language was deconstructed into the aboriginal rudiments of imperatival speech. Revai's discovery in the camps was of an *Ursprache*, made up of speech-acts whose sense was exhausted in their uses in the ongoing *praxis* of labour. It was this discovery which Wittgenstein exploited, when in the *Investigations*[2] he experimented with the possibilities of a language consisting only of words connected with a single activity.

The philosophical concept of meaning has its place in a primitive idea of the way language functions. But one can also say that it is the idea of a language more primitive than ours. Let us imagine a language ... The language is meant to serve for communication between a builder A and assistant B. A is building with building-stones: there are blocks and pillars, slabs and beams. B has to pass the stones, and in the order in which A needs them. For this purpose they use a language consisting of the words 'block', 'pillar', 'slab', 'beam'. A calls them out; B brings the stone which he has learnt to bring at such-and-such a call. Conceive this as a complete primitive language.

In Wittgenstein's work, the manifest political content of Revai's discovery is lost, sublated and recuperated in a reactionary and unhistorical reification of ordinary usage. For Revai, by contrast, the *Ursprache* of the camps was the problematic from which he was to develop his first formulations of a materialist theory of meaning. And the discourse of the camps had in Revai's thought another significance, elaborated fully by him only much later, as a dialectical prefigurement of the speech community of Communist society, in which words are only shadows cast reflexively by the self-consciousness of deeds.

In part, no doubt, because the exercise of dating Revai's writings remains speculative and conjectural, the collection is organized in conceptual rather than chronological fashion. It is in the first three essays that we find Revai's chief theses on meaning, use and labour set out in programmatic terms. His most radical thesis concerns the place of the most primitive unit of meaning, the *ergoneme*, in the constitution of the act of labour. Revai's insight here – an insight that he probably communicated to his colleagues at the Marx–Engels Institute in Moscow, and which may have been a factor in his subsequent incarceration – was that the decisive step to the human species from its animal forebears cannot consist, as Engels supposed, in the development of tools. If man is a tool-using animal, he is defined (and defines himself) by the exercise of the most distinctively human tool of all, that of language. What is only *work* in animals – the expenditure of energy through the manipulation of matter – becomes *labour* in humans, since it is from the first saturated with a semantic superstructure. This is the dialectical counterpoint of Goethe's bourgeois-humanist dictum, *Im Anfang war die Tat* (In the Beginning was the Deed). Revai insisted that, whereas speech is a moment in the constitution of the act of labour (and language itself the shadow of speech), labour itself is the most primitive of all speech-acts. Without the *ergoneme*, which is the reflexive self-recognition of deeds, we have, not labour, but only work. But the most primitive unit of meaning is not theorized, for Revai, after the fashion of bourgeois-semantic atomism as an element from which complex structures of meaning are constituted piecemeal. Rather, the *ergoneme* is found only in the holistic semantic structures which arise along with the social relations of labour. It is, for this and other reasons, a radical error to model language-use on the reified metaphor of *the speaker*. To do so is to consecrate the fetish, central to the *bourgeois-Robinsonnade* of Western linguistic theory, of the autonomous language-user, and to suppress recognition of speakers as social ensembles of *ergonemes*. It may be said that Revai's entire project was a project of transcending the subjectivist-Idealist problematic of *the speaker*. As he puts it himself, magisterially: 'It is not speakers who labour, but labour that speaks.'

For Revai, accordingly, the primitive unit of meaning, the *ergoneme*, is a necessary constituent of the act of labour itself. Further

– and it is in the collection's second essay that he develops his critique of the ideological construction of *the speaker* – units of meaning are always distributed over complex semantic structures, which themselves mirror constellations of labour power. It is within these structures that we must situate the activity of speech. If we do this, we find, once again, not the speaker, but the speech-community – the historically specific construction of labour powers. It is here that Revai makes one of his boldest moves, and identifies speech-communities with classes. The radical intent of such a move in the USSR in the late 1930s should be obvious, and stands in need of no elaboration. The third and fourth essays treat of the political economy of meaning. Among the topics addressed are the unity of speech and act in pre-class societies, the primitive accumulation of meaning, surplus meaning and the expropriation of meaning, the sequestration and enclosure of meaning in early industrial capitalism, the estrangement of word from meaning in advanced capitalist orders, and related topics.

In the last two essays, Revai brings his theorizing to bear on theoretical controversies being conducted in the USSR from the late 1930s onwards. We learn from the editors that his thoughts were stirred in the late 1940s and early 1950s by the debates surrounding the contributions made by N. Y. Marr to linguistic theory. Stalin, we recall, had criticized Marr not only because of his attempts to develop a theory of the class-specificity of languages, but also because, in separating language from thought, he had lapsed into Idealism. Revai's paper bears the marks of his earlier thought, but it appears to have been occasioned by Stalin's response to the contributions of D. Belkin and S. Furer to the debate on Marr's linguistics. Stalin criticizes Belkin and Furer for failing to appreciate the distinctively human character of language-use, and so for neglecting to distinguish language-use from the signs and gestures of animals. Observing that:

linguistics treats of normal people possessing a language, and not of anomalous deaf mutes who lack a language, [Stalin asks:] How do matters stand with the deaf mutes? Does their thought function, do ideas originate? Yes, their thought functions, ideas do originate. It is clear that since the deaf mutes lack a language, their ideas cannot originate on the basis of language material ... The ideas of deaf mutes originate and can exist only on the basis of the images, perceptions and conceptions formed in practice about the objects of the exterior world and their relations among themselves, thanks to the senses of sight, touch, taste and smell. Outside of these images, perceptions and conceptions, thought is empty, devoid of any content whatever, i.e. it does not exist.[3]

Revai's commentary on this debate, never published in his lifetime, has as its problematic the thesis of the semantic constitution of the labour-act and (as its dialectical counterpart) the thesis of the construction of meaning by labour power. From this problematic he derives his further thesis that the question of the place of language in the 'superstructure' or 'base' of social relations is, and cannot avoid being, wrongly posed – a position he shared with Stalin. Much of the fifth essay is addressed to this question. It is in the last of the essays, however, that Revai reveals his political intent, when he comments, cryptically and suggestively, on *the epoch of silence*. The society of deaf mutes, he argues, is the society of Western capitalism in its final stages, in which language has been replaced by gestures, and labour evacuated of its meaning-content. The 'empty chatter' of capitalist verbosity, insofar as it expresses at no point the semantic content of labour, embodies *the silence of the proletariat* as its dialectical condition. The silence of the period of socialist construction, by contrast, is fecund with labour content. Revai does not try to suppress reflection on the organization by administrative measures of speech and language in the Stalin period, nor does he aim to pass judgement on it, after the fashion of bourgeois moralists. He sees the Stalin period, instead, as one in which the necessary publicity of meaning was, for the first time, given concrete historical realization. The fiction of the speaker, together with the Idealist shibboleths of subjectivity and private language-use, were during this period subjected to a decisive critique on the terrain of *praxis*. The socialist administration of language-use, then, is an historically necessary phase in the elimination of the problematic of the subject. In theorizing it in this fashion, Revai gestures in his last essay to the practice of speech in Communist society. There, he maintains, the interiority of thought is transcended, and speech utters itself in a dialogic context in which it is realized as the semantic form of the community of labourers. It is superfluous to comment on the remarkable affinities between Revai's conception of Communist discourse and that developed later by Habermas.

In addition to an extended biographical foreword, the collection is distinguished by a long analytical postscript, in which the editors consider how Revai's theorizing is to be assessed and developed. It must be said at once that their own perspective is very different from Revai's, whose classical labour theory of meaning they repudiate explicitly. Nor should this be surprising, since one of them, G. Olsen, had already in his important *Sense and Reference in Marxian Semantics*,[4] abandoned many of the central tenets of an orthodox Marxian account of meaning. By contrast with Revai, Kahn and Olsen are methodological nominalists, whose project is that of generating the complex semantic structures of Marxian linguistic theory from individual speech-acts. They invoke here work by another linguistic theorist of their school, P. Reimer,[5] who aims to reconstruct classical Marxian meaning theory, without postulating the *ergoneme*, solely on the basis of constellations of speech-acts. Most innovatively, drawing heavily on work of Kahn's, they advance a reformulation of the orthodox Marxian theory of surplus meaning, in which the exploitative extraction of meaning from workers is analysed and explained in terms of the thesis that the meaning-content of each labour-act is retained by the labourer only on condition that that of every other be subject to expropriation. 'Each may speak, but all are silent' – so Kahn summarizes a long chain of subtle reasonings whereby the silence of the proletariat is reaffirmed in the new Marxist theorizing. In the final section of the analytical postscript, Kahn and Olsen present competing accounts of the relations between labour power and semantic structure, with Olsen arguing against Kahn that the attribution to semantic structure of an inherent development tendency is an illicit global generalization from the historically specific semantic structures of the capitalist mode of production. In so developing rival theoretical paradigms within a shared problematic, Olsen and Kahn give further evidence, if such were needed, of the progressive character of the research programme on which they are engaged.

In Kahn and Olsen's postscript to this invaluable collection, the central insights of Marxist thought are preserved by the appropriation of the most powerful techniques of bourgeois thought. Until now, Revai's work had only an occult impact on Western thought by way of its influence on the greatest of twentieth-century philosophers. Given the creative development to which his thought is subject in Olsen and Kahn's postscript to this volume, it will be extraordinary if his work does not come to exercise a commanding authority over the most advanced sections of the Western academic class.

1989

16

The end of history, again?

It is a truism that socialism is dead, and an irony that it survives most robustly as a doctrine not in Paris, where it has suffered a fate worse than falsification by becoming thoroughly unfashionable, nor in London, where it has been abandoned by the Labour Party, but in the universities of capitalist America, as the ideology of the American academic nomenklatura. But socialism is most obviously, and most irreversibly, defunct as an ideology in the Communist bloc. There, *glasnost* has surpassed the wildest hopes of Western anti-Communists in discrediting the institutions of central planning and brilliantly illuminating the intractable problems of the Soviet system.

But what does the collapse of socialism as a political faith portend for the future of political life and thought? In a provocative and well-received article, 'The End of History',[1] Francis Fukuyama announces in a quietly apocalyptic voice that the failure of socialism means 'an unabashed victory of economic and political liberalism [and he promises] the end point of mankind's ideological evolution and the universalization of Western liberal democracy as the final form of human government'. The prophecy that human history is about to end and a new historical epoch about to begin is of course a recurrent one in the history of Western thought. It is probably an unintended irony that Fukuyama's article should stand as a contribution to the project of a secular theodicy first undertaken by the *philosophes* of the French Enlightenment, but most notably and energetically pursued in the Marxian system of thought which he correctly perceives to be now in a terminal decline. But it is in any case difficult to understand the basis for his confidence about the historic role of liberal democracy in bringing history to a successful close. His confidence cannot be a reflection of the state of liberal political philosophy, since that is manifestly parlous. In my recent book, *Liberalisms: Essays in Political Philosophy*,[2] and particularly in its Postscript, 'After Liberalism', I have argued that despite its overwhelming dominance in Anglo-American philosophy, liberalism has never succeeded in showing that liberal democratic institutions are uniquely necessary to justice and the human good. In all its varieties – utilitarian, contractarian or as a theory of rights – liberal political philosophy has failed to establish its fundamental thesis: that liberal democracy is the only form of human government that can be sanctioned by reason and morality. It therefore fails to give rational support to the political religion of the contemporary intelligentsia, which combines the sentimental cult of humanity with a sectarian passion for political reform.

The consequent debacle of liberal political philosophy is not something we have any reason to lament. For liberals are committed to the heroic enterprise of denying a very obvious truth – the truth that there is a legitimate variety of forms of government under which human beings have flourished and may still hope to prosper. Who can doubt that human beings flourished under the feudal institutions of medieval Christendom? Or under the monarchical government of Elizabethan England? It is in virtue of its repression of this evident truth that liberal discourse has acquired its stridency and intolerance – indeed, its almost obsessional character. In seeking to construct a liberal ideology, liberal theorists are attempting what even they must sometimes see to be impossible. They are struggling to confer the imprimatur of universal authority on the local practices they have inherited. The absurdity of this project has, indeed, been tacitly recognized by one of this century's subtler liberal thinkers, John Rawls, when in his later work he revealed that he aims only to give a coherent philosophical statement of the character and premises of a particular historical tradition – the (American?) tradition of constitutional democracy.

If Fukuyama's confident expectation of the End cannot be explained by the state of liberal philosophy, from what does it derive? It is the expression, most likely, not of a political philosophy, but of a philosophy of history, one dominated by the notion that liberal democracy is history's *telos*, other modes of government being recognized only as progressions towards, or aberrations from, that end.

The grain of truth in this interpretation of history is that it is only through the development of civil society – a society in which most institutions, though protected by law, are independent of the state – that a modern civilization can reproduce itself. Without those institutions – for example, private property and contractual liberty under the rule of law – modern societies invariably undergo a descent into poverty and barbarism. Civil society is the matrix of the market economy, which both history and theory show to be the precondition of prosperity and liberty in the modern world. This is a truth that even the Soviet leadership may now be learning, after having waged for over seventy years an incessant war on all the civil societies that have come within its sphere of domination. It is one that the Iranian fundamentalists are beginning to accept, however grudgingly, as they retreat from the position that a modern state can be governed exclusively through the precepts of the Islamic *sharyah*. And it is a truth that will become painfully clear to the aged Stalinists of Communist China, when they are forced by circumstances to perceive the economic ruin that flows from trying to confine an emergent civil society in a newly resewn totalitarian straitjacket.

To say that no modern state can renew itself with a decent degree of prosperity unless it contains the institutions of a civil society is, however, very far from allowing that liberal democracy is 'the final form of human government'. Civil societies come in many shapes and forms and thrive under a variety of regimes. The authoritarian civil societies of East Asia – South Korea, Taiwan and Singapore – have combined an extraordinary record of economic success with the protection of most individual liberties under the rule of law without adopting all the elements of liberal democracy.

Or consider the case of Japan, which Fukuyama's mentor, the Hegelian scholar Alexandre Kojève, rightly recognized as the key exception to the trend of global homogenization. To be sure, Japan has become a consumerist culture, and its political institutions are liberal democratic. Yet the crucial decades of modernization in Japan occurred in the late nineteenth and early twentieth centuries; modernization was generated internally and was not imposed from outside; and, uniquely, the Japanese succeeded in grafting on to the unbroken stem of a traditional culture the institutions of a modern civil society. As a result, Japan has in the last two decades emerged as a global economic superpower, and must willy-nilly (whether it wishes to do so or not) become a superpower *tout court* in the coming century. This has been achieved without any deep commitment to the constitution imposed upon Japan at the end of the Second World War, and certainly without the support of the ideas and values that are supposed to undergird market institutions in the West, such as individualism, universalism, natural rights, Judeo-Christianity or the idea of progress.

The East Asian examples show that Western achievements can be reproduced, and for that matter surpassed, without any acceptance of 'the Western idea' of which Fukuyama speaks when he refers to 'the triumph of the West'. The ongoing disintegration of Communism on the Soviet model gives his argument no better support. The avowed aim of the twin Soviet reform policies of *perestroika* and *glasnost* is to break the totalitarian mould and reconstitute a civil society. Even if it is successful, however, the Soviet reform policy is unlikely to result in a triumph of Western liberalism. To attempt to foretell the future cost of Gorbachev's reform policy is idle. Already, however, *glasnost* has to its credit a considerable achievement. It has revealed for all time the ruins of the totalitarian project initiated by Lenin in 1917. This is the project, intimated in Lenin's horrible saying, 'We must be engineers of souls,' of destroying the traditional identities of the human beings within its power and reconstructing them as specimens of the new socialist humanity. Prosecuted relentlessly and without mercy for over two generations in an incessant war against religion, the family and nationality, this totalitarian project has been shown by *glasnost* to have been a stupendous failure. As they emerge from the shadows of totalitarianism, the peoples of the Soviet Union reveal themselves, not as specimens of socialist (or liberal) humanity, but as Ukrainians or Balts, Catholics or Muslims, bearing traditional identities in no way compromised by decades of totalitarian indoctrination. The forms of national and religious life that are reasserting themselves in the Soviet Union give the lie to the totalitarian idea (echoed by innumerable Western liberals) that human beings can be remodelled according to the dictates of rationalist ideology. If anything, the traditional identities of the peoples of the Soviet Union may be healthier than those in many Western nations, where subtler forms of indoctrination have had a more corrosive effect in rendering traditional forms of life decadent.

It is precisely because the revelations of *glasnost* give the lie to the totalitarian project of reshaping human nature that they also confound Fukuyama's account. If the newly self-assertive peoples of the Soviet bloc are not specimens of *Homo sovieticus*, neither do their political beliefs have anything in common with the rationalist and egalitarian liberalism which has dominated American life for fifty years. They are defined, and define themselves, not primarily as buyers and sellers in markets, nor as abstract bearers of rights and entitlements, but in terms of their membership in a nation or a church. They may share a common longing for emancipation from the Soviet system, but that is all they share. Each of the subject peoples in the Soviet bloc harbours particular claims, territorial or otherwise in character, which sets it in conflict with the rest. It is for this reason that the waning of the Soviet system is bound to be accompanied by a waxing of ethnic and nationalist conflicts – just the sort of stuff history has always been made of. These conflicts are, in part, undoubtedly a legacy of Stalinism, since it was Stalin who ruthlessly dislocated entire peoples and relocated them without regard to their history or traditions. But these conflicts also embody age-old enmities and loyalties, which are now coming back to the surface after decades of totalitarian suppression. What we are witnessing in the Soviet Union is not, then, the end of history, but instead its resumption – and on decidedly traditional lines.

All the evidence suggests that we are now moving back into an epoch that is classically historical, and not forward into the empty, hallucinatory post-historical era projected in Fukuyama's article. Ours is an era in which political ideology, liberal as much as Marxist, has a rapidly dwindling leverage on events, and more ancient, more primordial forces, nationalist and religious, fundamentalist and soon, perhaps, Malthusian, are contesting with each other. In retrospect, it may well appear that it was the static, polarized period of ideology, the period between the end of the First World War and the present, that was the aberration.

If the Soviet Union does indeed fall apart, that beneficent catastrophe will not inaugurate a new era of post-historical harmony, but instead a return to the classical terrain of history, a terrain of great-power rivalries, secret diplomacies and irredentist claims and wars. The vision of perpetual peace among liberal states, which has haunted Western thought at least since it was given systematic formulation by Immanuel Kant, will soon be seen for what it always was – a mirage that serves only to distract us from the real business of statesmanship in a permanently intractable and anarchic world.

Fukuyama's brilliant and thoughtful argument is a symptom of the hegemonic power of liberalism in American thought. So ubiquitously pervasive are liberal ideas and assumptions in American intellectual life, and such is their constraining power over public discourse, that it sometimes seems barely possible to formulate a thought that is not liberal, let alone to express it freely. The domination of the American mind by liberal ideology has fostered blind spots in American perception of the real world that have been immensely disabling for policy.

The fetish of open government, as symbolized in the Freedom of Information Act, congressional oversight and the respectability given to leaking, prevents the United States from ever again engaging in any major covert operation. The domination of public life by the power of the invasive media calls into serious question the capacity of the United States to wage any war larger, more protracted or with significantly heavier casualties, than the invasion of Grenada. Liberal egalitarianism in education, coupled with absurd and counter-productive affirmative-action programmes, has resulted in a deskilling of America that is awesome in magnitude. (Consider that, whereas at age six Japanese and American children have roughly similar mathematical abilities, at age eighteen the average Japanese child has the mathematical competence of the top 1 per cent of American children.)

In many other areas, liberal ideology has in America proved itself to be the enemy rather than the friend of civil society. In its expression in radical feminism and in affirmative-action policy liberalism has sanctioned the invasion of privacy, the curtailment of freedom of association and the erosion of contractual liberty. Because of the ravages wreaked on civil society by liberal ideology America already has a more bureaucratized and regulated, less tolerant, more divided and more statist society than virtually any other modern democracy, squandering the historical patrimony of civil society on which American pre-eminence in the world rested. Liberal ideology guarantees blindness to the dangers that liberalism has itself brought about. In sum, the danger for America is that, confronted with comparative and soon, perhaps, absolute economic decline, an uncontrollable crime epidemic and weak or paralysed political institutions, it will drift further and further into isolation and disorder. At the worst, America faces a metamorphosis into a sort of proto-Brazil, with the status of an ineffectual regional power rather than a global superpower.

In general, all speculations about the future are riddled with hazards. Michael Oakeshott, the English conservative philosopher, has written that we know as much about where history is leading us as we do about future fashions in hats. There are, perhaps, only two things of which one may be reasonably sure. The first is that the days of liberalism are numbered. Especially as it governs policy in the United States, liberalism is ill-equipped to deal with the new dilemmas of a world in which ancient allegiances and enmities are reviving on a large scale.

We know this much at least: history will not end with the passing of liberalism, any more than with the collapse of Communism. The second thing we know for sure is that we have no reason whatever to expect that our future will be markedly different from our past. As we have known it, human history is a succession of contingencies, catastrophes and occasional lapses into peace and civilization. If this is the case, there is at least one misfortune that we will surely be spared – the melancholy and boredom that is evoked by the prospect of the end of history.

1989

17

What globalization is not

Capitalism, while economically stable, and even gaining in stability, creates, by rationalizing the human mind, a mentality and a style of life incompatible with its own fundamental conditions, motives and social institutions.

Joseph Schumpeter, 'The Instability of Capitalism'[1]

'Globalization' can mean many things. On the one hand, it is the worldwide spread of modern technologies of industrial production and communication of all kinds across frontiers – in trade, capital, production and information. This increase in movement across frontiers is itself a consequence of the spread to hitherto pre-modern societies of new technologies. To say that we live in an era of globalization is to say that nearly every society is now industrialized or embarked on industrialization.

Globalization also implies that nearly all economies are networked with other economies throughout the world. There are a few countries, such as North Korea, which seek to cut their economies off from the rest of the world. They have succeeded in maintaining independence from world markets – but at great cost, both economic and human. Globalization is an historical process. It does not require that economic life throughout the world be equally and intensively integrated. As a seminal study of the subject has put it, 'Globalization is not a singular condition, a linear process or a final end-point of social change.'[2]

Nor is globalization an end-state towards which all economies are converging. A universal state of equal integration in worldwide economic activity is precisely what globalization *is not*. On the contrary, the increased interconnection of economic activity throughout the world accentuates uneven development between different countries. It exaggerates the dependency of 'peripheral' developing states such as Mexico on investment from economies nearer the 'centre', such as the United States. Though one consequence of a more globalized economy is to overturn or weaken some hierarchical economic relationships between states – between Western countries and China, for example – at the same time it strengthens some existing hierarchical relations and creates new ones.

Nor does the claim that we are undergoing a rapid advance in the further globalization of economic life necessarily mean that *every* aspect of economic activity in any one society is becoming significantly more sensitive to economic activity throughout the world. However far globalization proceeds, it will always be true that some dimensions of a society's economic life are not affected by world markets, though these may shift over time.

The emergence of world market prices for some commodities is only the beginning of globalization. There are few societies today in which much of life is not interwoven with economic activities in distant parts of the world. Yet throughout the nineteenth century, and for much of the twentieth century, global markets left most societies virtually untouched. Most of those traditional societies have now disappeared, or else they have been drawn irresistibly into the network of global market relationships.

In China, until the past few decades, hundreds of millions of people lived in peasant communities whose relations with world markets were slight and intermittent. Having survived forced collectivization and the Cultural Revolution, these communities are now breaking up as the forced introduction of markets compels poor peasants to seek subsistence in cities or distant regions of China. Market reforms in India are challenging traditions of marriage and caste which had survived almost unchanged for forty years following the end of the British Raj. At the same time, these changes are provoking radical Hindu movements which contest the belief that modernization in India must mean further Westernization. In the former Soviet Union, marketization is succeeding, where Communism failed, in imposing a kind of modernity – even if it is only the modernity of poverty and cultural fragmentation – on social life. Socialist and traditional societies that in the past stood outside the world market can do so no longer.

Yet in another sense, globalization is shorthand for the cultural changes that follow when societies become linked with, and in varying measures dependent upon, world markets. The advent of modern information and communication technologies has meant that cultural lives are far more deeply influenced than ever before.

Brands for many consumer goods are no longer country-specific but global. Companies produce identical products for worldwide distribution. The popular cultures of virtually all societies are inundated by a common stock of images. The countries of the European Union share the images they all absorb from Hollywood movies more than they do any aspect of each other's cultures. The same is true of East Asia.

Behind all these 'meanings' of globalization is a single underlying idea, which can be called *delocalization*: the uprooting of activities and relationships from local origins and cultures. It means the displacement of activities that until recently were local into networks of relationships whose reach is distant or worldwide. Anthony Giddens sums this up: 'Globalization can . . . be defined as the intensification of worldwide social relations which link distant realities in such a way that local happenings are shaped by events occurring many miles away and vice versa.'[3]

Thus, domestic prices – of consumer goods, financial assets such as stocks and bonds, even labour – are less and less governed by local and national conditions; they all fluctuate along with global market prices. Multinational corporations break up the chain of production of their products and locate the links in different countries around the world, depending on which appears at any time to be the most advantageous to them. The products sold by multinationals are identified less and less with any single country and increasingly with a world brand or with the company itself; the same images are recognized – in advertising and entertainment – in many countries. Globalization means lifting social activities out of local knowledge and placing them in networks in which they are conditioned by, and condition, worldwide events.

Globalization is often equated with a trend towards homogeneity. That, again, is just what globalization is *not*. Global markets in which capital and production moves freely across frontiers work precisely because of the *differences* between localities, nations and regions. Had wages, skills, infrastructure and political risks been the same throughout the world, the growth of world markets would not have occurred. There would not be profits to be made by investing and manufacturing worldwide if conditions were similar everywhere. Global markets thrive on differences between economies. That is one reason why the trend to globalization has such an irresistible momentum.

If highly mobile, quicksilver capital avoids a given region or country because it lacks infrastructure, a skilled workforce or political stability – as private investment capital has avoided Central and West Africa over the past few decades – those parts of the world will grow poorer, and their differences from areas that are attractive sites for productive capital will be exaggerated. If new technologies spread from the Western countries in which they originated to East Asia, they will not carry with them the economic cultures – the varieties of capitalism – that produced them. On the contrary, they will fertilize and strengthen the indigenous economic cultures of those regions. When new technologies enter economies from which in the past they were shut out, or which lacked market institutions that could exploit them effectively, they will interact with indigenous cultures to generate types of capitalism that have hitherto not existed anywhere.

Consider China. The entry into world markets of mainland China does not mean that Chinese economic life will come to resemble that of any other industrialized country. It is already very different from the capitalism that has grown up in post-Communist Russia, in which family relationships are much less central. Chinese capitalism resembles most closely that practised by the Chinese diaspora throughout the world. But it has many distinctive and peculiar features arising from the turbulent and terrible history of the nation over the past two generations.

In China, as in all other societies, the life of markets expresses the larger and deeper culture of which markets are only the visible tip. The place that relationships of trust have in families and markets in different societies in itself guarantees that their economic cultures – the size of firms, the concentration or diffusion of holdings of capital, and so on – will vary considerably.

Since, in China, trust does not extend easily beyond family members, businesses are unlikely to take the form they have assumed in Japan, where relationships of trust that reach well beyond the network of kin are common. A fully capitalist market economy in mainland China would be as different from Japanese as from Western capitalism. It would probably contain many flourishing small family businesses and few large companies of the sorts that are common in Japan. It would not rest upon, or necessarily produce, a middle class of the kind that has long existed in Japan. In fact, this kind of capitalism does indeed seem to be emerging as a consequence of rapid market reforms in several regions of China.

It has many precursors in the Chinese diaspora. As Micklethwaite and Wooldridge have noted:

the entrepreneurial 'bamboo network' of family businesses created by the overseas Chinese is not just another interesting variant but a fully-fledged alternative model – and one which looks increasingly powerful . . . In the Philippines, the overseas Chinese make up only one per cent of the country's population but control over half of the stock market. In Indonesia, the equivalent proportions are 4 per cent and 75 per cent, in Malaysia 32 per cent and 60 per cent . . . by 1996 the 51 million overseas Chinese controlled an economy worth $700 billion – roughly the same size as the 1.2 billion mainlanders.[4]

The growth of global markets does not mean, either, that American business culture will be copied throughout the world. The American belief that corporations are above all else vehicles of shareholder profits is not shared in most other types of capitalism.

In Germany, the interests of many other 'stakeholders' in addition to the shareholders are represented on boards of companies. It is inconceivable that any large enterprise would withdraw from its indigenous labour market as suddenly and comprehensively as American companies did when relocating from California to Mexico. A global market framed to reflect American business practice will undermine social markets built on the post-war German model; but it will not turn German capitalism into a variation of American market individualism. Instead it will result in a transmutation of capitalism in both Germany and America.

No economic culture anywhere in the world can resist the changes forced on it by the existence of global markets. In every case, including the United States itself, the result will be to engender novel types of capitalism. Global markets impose a forced modernization on economies everywhere; they do not create replicas of old business cultures. New capitalisms are created, and old ones destroyed.

Nor does the spread of global communications produce anything resembling convergence among cultures. The American worldview that is purveyed through CNN – according to which, contrary to appearances and all underlying realities, American values are universal and American institutions the solution for the world's most intractable problems – is an ephemeral artefact of America's present lead in communications technologies. It is not a signpost on the road to a universal civilization. Media companies which vary their product to suit different cultures, such as MTV, may expect to remain global. If CNN remains fixed in its Americocentric worldview, it is likely soon to be no more than one national media company among many others.

By enabling practitioners of different cultures who are geographically scattered to interact through new communications media, globalization acts to express and to deepen cultural differences. The South Asian populations that are scattered across European countries reinforce their cultural ties when they watch satellite television channels that broadcast in their languages and embody their history and values. The Kurds exiled in European countries preserve their common culture through a Kurdish television channel.

The universal proliferation of similar images is a surface effect of global communications media. They break up common cultures and replace them with traces and fragments. Yet modern communications media can also – as in Japan, Singapore, Malaysia and China – enable cultures to assert their identity and differences from Western late modernity and from each other.

Economies *may* become more integrated with one another – as those of Japan and the United States have in recent decades – without significantly converging in the way they do business. Despite much increased levels of trade between the two countries, the corporate culture of Japanese companies remains very different from that of any American company. No Japanese company has had a downsizing or delayering on the scale that has become routine in nearly all key American corporations. These differences between American and Japanese companies reflect divergences between their parent cultures that show no signs of narrowing.

GLOBALIZATION BEFORE 1914, AND TODAY

The world before 1914 resembled a global market. There were few borders that mattered. Money, goods and people flowed freely. The technological foundations of the nineteenth-century global market had been laid in the submarine intercontinental telegraph cables and steamships of the second half of the century. From then on the world's ports were linked together and world prices for many commodities came into being. Again, by the latter part of the nineteenth century (roughly from 1878 to 1914) an international financial system came into existence which limited the economic autonomy of national governments. In that *belle époque* sovereign nation-states were as effectively constrained in the economic policies which they could pursue by the Gold Standard that was then in operation as they are now by the mobility of capital. In all these ways we can recognize in the pre-1914 world a precursor of today's global market.

Yet it is a fundamental mistake to conclude that we have returned to the international economy of the nineteenth century. All the magnitudes of economic globalization today – the speed, size and interconnections of the movements of goods and information across the globe – are enormously greater than any that have existed in any previous period of history. Consider a few of these magnitudes. During the post-war period world trade has grown twelve-fold. At the same time, output has grown only five-fold. In nearly all countries, imports and exports constitute a far larger proportion of economic activity than in the past. One academic assessment estimates that trade links between a fixed sample of sixty-eight countries have grown from

64 per cent in 1950 to 95 per cent in 1990.[5] Even in the vast American market in which purely internal trade is common for small companies, a fifth of firms having less than 500 staff exported goods or services in 1994, and that proportion is rising.[6]

There can be little doubt that, at least since the 1980s, the ratio of world trade to gross domestic product has exceeded that occurring at any time in the open international economy which existed before the First World War.[7] There has been a vast and unprecedented expansion in the volume of trade.

There is now a world market in capital as never before, and strong evidence that investors in many countries are diversifying their holdings of both equities and bonds globally and that, as a consequence, returns on capital have tended to converge in the 1980s and 1990s.[8] This is a trend far more advanced in regard to government bonds than it is in respect of equities, but it is unmistakable.[9] Increasingly, interest rates in all countries are being set by worldwide conditions, not by circumstances or policies in any one country. Private investment flows from advanced industrial countries to newly industrialized countries grew twenty-fold in the years from 1970 to 1992.[10]

Most significantly, perhaps, transactions in foreign exchange markets have now reached the astonishing sum of around $1.2 trillion a day – over fifty times the level of world trade. Around 95 per cent of these transactions are speculative in nature, many using complex new derivative financial instruments based on futures and options.[11] According to Michel Albert, 'the *daily* volume of transactions on the foreign exchange markets of the world totals some $900 billions – equal to France's *annual* GDP and some $200 million more than the total foreign currency reserves of the world's central banks.'[12]

This *virtual* financial economy has a terrible potential for disrupting the underlying *real* economy, as seen in the collapse in 1995 of Barings, Britain's oldest bank. Together with the accelerating development of global capital markets on which it stands, the virtual economy is a phenomenon unknown in the world's economic history. Nothing like it existed pre-1914.

The growth and power of multinational corporations is enormous and also unprecedented. Multinationals now account for about a third of world output and two-thirds of world trade. Most significantly, around a quarter of world trade occurs *within* multinational corporations.[13] In 1993, according to a United Nations survey, the combined output of multinationals was around $5.5 trillion – roughly as much as that of the United States as a whole.[14]

It is true that companies which trade and invest internationally also existed centuries ago – the Hudson Bay Company and the East India Company are examples. In that broad sense multinationals began life with European colonialism. But the role of multinationals in the world today is on a completely different scale. They are able to divide the process of production into discrete operations and locate them in different countries throughout the world. They are less dependent than ever before on national conditions. They can choose the countries whose labour markets, tax and regulatory regimes and infrastructures they find most congenial. The promise of direct inward investment, and the threat of its withdrawal, have significant leverage on the policy options of national governments. Companies can now limit the politics of states. There are few historical precedents for this kind of private power.

This is not to say that multinationals are homeless transnational institutions which move across borders without cost and express no particular national business culture. They are often companies which retain strong roots in their original economies and cultures. In a systematic and comprehensive survey Ruigrok and van Tulder concluded that few, if any, of the world's biggest companies are fully global. Even companies such as British Aerospace, most of whose business is done abroad, keep most of their assets at home.[15] Hirst and Thompson note that multinational companies 'typically have about two thirds of their assets in their home region country, and sell about the same proportion of their goods and services in their home region/country'.[16]

Again, very few multinationals are genuinely cross-cultural organizations. One of the rare examples is ABB, a Swiss–Swedish corporation which consists of 1,300 separate companies.[17] ABB may well be more truly cross-cultural than any other corporation: in this it may be unique. Nearly all multinationals express and embody a single-parent national culture. This is true especially of American firms.

It is fashionable to see multinational corporations as constituting a kind of invisible government supplanting many of the functions of nation-states. In reality they are often weak and amorphous organizations. They display the loss of authority and the erosion of common values that afflicts practically all late modern social institutions. The global market is not spawning corporations which assume the past functions of sovereign states. Rather, it has weakened and hollowed out both institutions.

SCEPTICISM ABOUT GLOBALIZATION

There is an influential body of opinion which denies that today's trends signify anything really new. It argues that, because the historical movement we call globalization began several centuries ago and because by most measurements the global openness of the international economy was high in the pre-1914 liberal economic order, late twentieth-century globalization is not a new phenomenon. There is truth and error in this revisionist view. It is a useful corrective for a utopian view of globalization advanced by some business thinkers. Kenichi Ohmae gives a canonical statement of what might be called the McKinsey worldview – the view of things propagated by American business schools – when he writes: 'with the ending of the Cold War, the long familiar pattern of alliances and oppositions among industrialized nations has fractured beyond repair. Less visibly, but arguably far more important, the modern nation-state itself – that artifact of the eighteenth and nineteenth centuries – has begun to crumble.'[18] In criticizing such theorists of hyper-globalization revisionists make a contribution to understanding the present; but they are attacking a straw man.

No one except a few utopians in the business community expects the world to become a true single market, in which nation-states have withered away and have been supplanted by homeless multinational corporations. Such an expectation is a chimera of the corporate imagination. Its role is to support the illusion of an inevitable world-wide free market.

Sceptics about globalization are right to point to the ideological role of these fantasies. They reinforce the belief that national governments nowadays have no real options. As Hirst and Thompson put it, 'Globalization is a myth suitable for a world without illusions, but it is also one that robs us of hope ... for it is held that Western social democracy and socialism of the Soviet bloc are both finished. One can only call the political impact of "globalization" the pathology of over-diminished expectations.'[19]

Yet Hirst and Thompson's scepticism about globalization itself serves a political purpose. By arguing that today's world market is not unprecedented they are able to defend as still viable political responses to globalization – such as European social democracy – that belong in the past.

They argue that:

the international economy was in many ways more open in the pre-1914 period than it has been at any time since ... International trade and capital flows, both between the rapidly industrializing economies themselves and between these and their various colonial territories, were more important relative to GDP levels before the First World War than they are today ... Thus the present period is by no means unprecedented.[20]

This view neglects some of the most decisive contrasts between the pre-1914 international economy and today's global market.

As the British political theorist David Held and his colleagues have noted,

Measured in constant prices the classical Gold Standard ratios (of trade as a proportion of GDP) had been surpassed by the 1970s and ratios are now significantly higher ... Further, much of postwar GDP growth has been in non-tradable services, particularly public services ... Tariff levels (as well as transport costs) have been lower than classical Gold Standard levels since the 1970s, thus indicating that markets are now more open.

They conclude: 'A global trading system emerged at the end of the nineteenth century, but it was less extensive than today and was often less enmeshed with national markets and production.'[21] This seems a reasonable assessment.

A key difference between the international economy now and as it was before 1914 is that power and influence are flowing away from the Western powers. The terms of world trade, the functioning of the financial system via the Gold Standard, and every other significant aspect of the pre-1914 economy were imposed and maintained by European states.

It is true that trade has grown mainly between the Western industrialized countries – if, absurdly, in 'the West' we include Japan. Yet the pattern of trade today is very different from what it was. As David Held et al. observe:

Trade has continued to grow relative to income, and has continued to be concentrated between industrialized countries, in contrast to the classical Gold Standard era when exchange of products between developed and developing countries accounted for half or more of total trade ... intra-industry trade led to relative growth in industries with scale economies and technological dynamism, whilst rising income levels increased demand for variety so that demand for imported differentiated products rose, largely between industrialized countries ... This ... has significantly increased the import content of manufactured goods in developed countries, except Japan.

What is more, newly industrializing countries can no longer be considered an homogeneous bloc. Incomes and wages in some of them – South Korea, Taiwan, Singapore – are actually higher than in the deskilled countries of the industrialized West, such as Britain. The balance of advantage, which in the pre-1914 era was fixed in favour of the European countries, is now shifting away from Western countries in many areas of economic activity.

If the pre-1914 open economy was an artefact of European control over the territories and economies of nearly every other society in the world, the global market whose chaotic infancy we have witnessed is based on no such hegemony. Which Western power can now claim plausibly to exercise significant leverage over China? Not even the United States now exercises over China anything like the influence that was commonplace for the imperial powers in the pre-1914 period.

In this, the period of advancing globalization in which we live is genuinely unprecedented. It is indeed partly because it contains no hegemonic power akin to Britain before 1914 or the United States after the Second World War that the stability in times of crisis of the global market today cannot be taken for granted. If there is a recent historical analogy for our world since 1989, it is not the world before 1914. It may be the volatile inter-war period after 1919.

The world economy today shows many features which, on Hirst and Thompson's own account, bring it closer to a disorderly globalized market than to the comparatively orderly international market that existed before 1914. They capture accurately aspects of today's realities when they tell us that 'The international system becomes autonomized and socially disembedded, as markets become truly global. Domestic policies, whether of private corporations or public regulators, now have routinely to take account of the predominantly international determinants of their sphere of operations.'[22]

Sovereign states today do not confront the predictable disciplines of a quasi-automatic Gold Standard. They are constrained instead by the risks and uncertainties, the perceptions and reactions of global markets. The policy options open to nation-states in the 1990s are not delivered to them as a menu with fixed prices. The governments of sovereign states do not know in advance how markets will react. There are few, if any, rules of monetary or fiscal rectitude whose violation will result in predictable penalties. At the margin, no doubt, policies that are ultra-risky in terms of inflation or government debt, say, will be punished by watchful bond markets; but the scale of severity of such market responses cannot be known in advance. National governments in the 1990s are flying blind.

The view of globalization advanced by academic sceptics such as Hirst and Thompson underestimates the novelty of late twentieth-century conditions. Today's world economy is inherently less stable and more anarchic than the liberal international economic order which collapsed in 1914. Like the hyperglobalizers, whose utopian fantasies they effectively criticize, globalization sceptics are trading in illusions. They cannot accept that globalization has made the world economy today radically different from any international economy that has existed in the past; that would spell death to their hopes of a revamped social democracy. They are right in their belief that a more radically globalized world is less governable – such a world economy makes their vision of 'continental Keynesianism' unworkable.[23] In truth a much less governable world is the inevitable result of the forces that have been at work over the past two decades.

HYPERGLOBALIZATION: A CORPORATE UTOPIA

A rival school of thought recognizes the novelty of the global market. It holds that global markets have rendered nation-states practically irrelevant. It envisions the global economy as inhabited by powerless nation-states and homeless corporations. As the powers of sovereign states wither, those of multinational corporations wax. As national cultures become little more than consumer preferences, so companies become ever more cosmopolitan in their corporate cultures.

The writers of this school represent as inevitable what is, in fact, a highly unlikely outcome of the current drive to create a global free market. It conflates the end-state favoured by that project with the actual development of economic globalization. It represents an historical transformation that has no end-state, and which is subverting American capitalism as well as its rivals, as a process leading to universal acceptance of American free markets.

'Hyperglobalization' theories – as these views have been termed by Held and his colleagues[24] – represent global markets as embodying something akin to perfect competition. In this illusive vision, transnational corporations can move freely and costlessly around the world to maximize their profits. Cultural differences have lost any political leverage on governments and corporations. As in the perfectly competitive markets of economic theory, the participants in this model of the global economy – sovereign states and multinational corporations, for example – are presumed to have all the information relevant to their decisions.

In reality they are navigating in a fog of risks and uncertainties whose hazards they can only surmise. A borderless world ruled by homeless transnationals is a corporate utopia, not a description of any present or future reality.

Kenichi Ohmae subscribes to this utopian view:

For more than a decade, some of us have been talking about the progressive globalization of markets for consumer goods like Levi's jeans, Nike athletic shoes and Hermès scarves – a process, driven by global exposure to the same information, the same cultural icons, and the same advertisements ... Today, however, the process of convergence goes faster and deeper. It reaches well beyond taste to much more fundamental dimensions of worldview, mind-set, and even thought-process.

He concludes that this market-driven convergence of cultures renders the institution of the nation-state marginal in economic life: 'in a borderless economy, the nation-focused maps we typically use to make sense of economic activity are woefully misleading. We must ... face up at last to the awkward and uncomfortable truth: the old cartography no longer works. It has become no more than an illusion.'[25]

Similarly, Nicholas Negroponte declares that 'Like a mothball, which goes from solid to gas directly, I expect the nation-state to evaporate ... Without question, the role of the nation-state will change dramatically and there will be no more room for nationalism than there is for smallpox.'[26] Bryan and Farrell write: 'Increasingly, millions of global investors, operating out of their own economic self-interest, are determining interest rates, exchange rates, and the allocation of capital, irrespective of the wishes or political objectives of national political leaders.'[27] Robert Reich speaks of 'the coming irrelevance of corporate nationality' and counsels that 'as corporations of all nations are transformed into global webs, the important question – from the standpoint of national wealth – is *not* which citizens own what, but which citizens learn how to do what, so that they are capable of adding more value to the world economy and therefore increasing their own potential worth.'[28] John Naisbitt asserts: 'We are moving toward a world of 1,000 countries ... The nation-state is dead. Not because nation-states were subsumed by super-states, but because they are breaking up to smaller, more efficient parts – just like big companies.'[29]

Neither states nor markets are orderly institutions of the kinds such a model envisages. There are few genuinely transnational corporations of the kind of which Ohmae and other business utopians speak. Most multinational companies retain strong roots in particular countries and business cultures. Ownership, executive boards, management styles and corporate cultures remain thoroughly national. The American companies which most nearly approximate Ohmae's model do so because they exemplify local American values and an indigenous business culture, not because they are global.

The few companies in the world that consistently behave with regard to their indigenous economy as rootless multinationals do so not because of properties they share with other international corporations. They do so because their corporate culture is governed by American corporate values in which profits override social costs and national allegiances.

According to one extended study, only around forty large firms world-wide generate at least half their assets abroad, while fewer than twenty maintain as much as half their production facilities abroad.[30] Moreover, as Hirst and Thompson have noted, key functions of firms, such as research and development, remain under tight domestic control: 'Japanese companies appear to have been reluctant to locate core functions like R&D or high value-added parts of the production process abroad.' They conclude: 'national companies with an international scope of operations currently and for the foreseeable future seem more likely than the true TNCs.'[31]

The model of hyperglobalization errs badly in writing off sovereign states as marginal institutions. For multinationals, sovereign states are not marginal actors in the world economy whose policies are easily circumvented. They are key players whose power is well worth courting. The leverage of sovereign states over business may actually be greater in some respects today than it has been in the past.

Corporations today do not have the protected relationships with governments that some enjoyed in the heyday of imperialism. If it is true that corporations can shop around the world for the tax and regulatory regime they want, it is also true that political risks have increased in many parts of the world. Where states are fragile it is harder to regulate mobile production and capital; but it is also harder for business to stitch up enduring corporatist relationships with governments. That is a limitation on the power of both states and corporations.

Today's competition between states for investment by multinational corporations allows them to exercise a leverage they did not possess in a more hierarchical world order. At the same time such competition limits the freedom of action of sovereign states. The leverage that states can exercise over corporations must be exercised in a global environment in which most of the competitive pressures that affect them work to limit the control of governments over their economies within a narrow margin.

Sovereign states remain the key arena of influence-seeking by corporations. Multinationals exercise influence over the policies of sovereign states as well as exercising their ingenuity in eluding their jurisdiction. This is the typical interaction of sovereign states and business in the late twentieth century.

There can be little doubt that NAFTA (the North American Free Trade Association between the United States, Mexico and Canada) prevailed over domestic political opposition in the United States largely because of the well-concerted lobbying activities of large American corporations.

Hyperglobalization theorists, like their sceptical critics, mistake today's world economy for a return to an earlier condition of orderliness. The reality of the late twentieth-century world market is that it is ungovernable by either sovereign states or multinational corporations.

GLOBALIZATION AND DISORDERED CAPITALISM

Both sets of theorists – the sceptics and the boosters – advance an unreal picture of the new global environment in which states must act. Sovereign states do not, as they did in the late nineteenth century, inhabit a familiar international environment that constrains their choices in predictable ways. They find themselves in an unfamiliar environment in which the behaviour of global market forces is decreasingly predictable or controllable. They are constrained not by institutions and conventions of international governance but by the risks and uncertainties that accompany an international market that tends to anarchy.

That multinational corporations expend considerable resources influencing the policies of governments contributes to the view that the sovereign state is not redundant. In most parts of the world, state institutions are a strategically decisive territory on which competition between corporations is waged.

Neither of the two main schools of thought have perceived that the emergence of a global economy is a decisive moment in the development of a late modern species of disordered, anarchic capitalism.[32] Capitalism today is very different from the earlier phases of economic development on which Karl Marx and Max Weber modelled their accounts of capitalism – and also from the stable, managed capitalisms of the post-war era.

The industrial working class has declined in size and economic significance. This has come about as manufacturing industries have shrunk and late modern economies become more comprehensively post-industrial. There has been a substantial shift from Taylorist forms of work organization – mass manufacturing through factory-based wage-labour – to flexible labour markets. In these new labour markets the classical capitalist institutions of wage-labour and job-holding are restricted to a dwindling proportion of the population.

Much of the workforce now lacks even the economic security that went with wage-labour. It exists in the world of part-time and contract work and portfolio employment in which there is no stable relationship with a single identifiable employer. Along with these changes has gone a collapse of national collective wage-bargaining and greatly diminished leverage of trade unions in the productive process.

The economic basis of political parties has weakened. At the same time the leverage of single-issue pressure groups has been enhanced. The political ideologies that organized political life in the post-war period are obsolete. This transformation has been accentuated by the emergence of a new economic consensus. In this new orthodoxy the role of national governments in overseeing their domestic economies through policies of macroeconomic management has been reduced or marginalized. The central economic task of government is that of devising and implementing microeconomic policies, promoting yet greater flexibility in labour and production.

The corrosion of bourgeois life through increased job insecurity is at the heart of disordered capitalism. Today the social organization of work is in a nearly continuous flux. It mutates incessantly under the impact of technological innovation and deregulated market competition.

The effect of the new information technologies is not merely an increased scarcity of many kinds of less skilled or knowledge-intensive work. It is the wholesale disappearance of entire occupations. For much of the population traditional bourgeois institutions such as career structures and vocations no longer exist.

The result is a reproletarianization of much of the industrial working class and the debourgeoisification of what remains of the former middle classes. The free market seems set to achieve what socialism was never able to accomplish – a euthanasia of bourgeois life.

The imperatives of flexibility and mobility imposed by deregulated labour markets put particular strain on traditional modes of family life. How can families meet for meals when both parents work on shifts? What becomes of families when the job market pulls parents apart?

There has been a hollowing out of the business corporation as a social institution. The growth of contracting out of labour tends to reduce the permanent workforce of late modern companies to a small cadre. A limiting case of this development may be Microsoft, a global company which dominates markets in several new technologies but whose actual core workforce is in the low thousands.

In limiting cases, companies are becoming vehicles for bill collection and profit distribution, their few remaining employees often having a stake in its capital. Whole strata of former middle-management employees have been dispensed with in corporate downsizings which have an immediate beneficial impact on profit statements. Businesses everywhere, but especially in the English-speaking countries, are unloading the social costs of their remaining employees. They are doing this by transferring responsibility for pension provision, for example, back to them as individuals.

The weakening of companies as social institutions goes in tandem with the further commodification of work. Labour has become something that is sold in pieces to corporations. Businesses have shed many of the responsibilities that rendered the world of work humanly tolerable in the past. Some are not far from being virtual institutions.

The inherent instability of anarchic global markets has been enhanced by the growth of an enormous, highly leveraged virtual economy in which currencies are traded for short-term profits. There is no stable framework for the governance of the international monetary system. Since the breakdown of the post-war Bretton Woods arrangement for international monetary co-operation between 1971 and 1973 there have been no agreements enforcing fixed exchange rates. Thus, the international monetary regime today is an anarchy of floating currencies. There are recurrent overshoots in the value of particular currencies and intermittent spasms of co-ordinated policy-making among the major powers (such as the Plaza Accords of 1985) in order to avert a breakdown of the system. Fluctuations in exchange rates can have such a profound destabilizing effect on economic activity that the present world monetary regime has been termed a system of 'casino capitalism'.[33]

We have seen a large shift from manufacturing and the provision of services as the central economic activities to the trading of financial assets. Financial engineering, not production, has become the most profitable activity.

These effects of disordered capitalism can be seen in societies as different as Italy, Sweden and Australia. Least advanced in Germany and Japan, they are most powerfully developed in the Anglo-Saxon economies. The United States, Britain, Australia and New Zealand stand out as standard-bearers of the new species of capitalism.

But the belief that capitalism everywhere will lead to similar disorder is a basic error. The ability to trade globally and rapidly tends to project these features of disorganized capitalism into every country; but how they impact on social and economic life varies deeply and widely.

In countries such as Spain, in which the extended family remains strong, the underclass of workless households that is so depressing a feature of Anglo-Saxon societies hardly exists. This is despite the fact that in Spain, to a greater degree even than in the other economies of continental Europe, unemployment has reached very high levels in recent times. This can partly be attributed to the fact that policy over the past two decades has not been dominated in continental Europe by objectives such as deregulation of the labour market. But this is unlikely to be the whole, or even the chief, reason for the persistence of such differences.

None of the countries of continental Europe has ever had an age of *laissez-faire*; market institutions have not achieved the independence from constraint by other social institutions that characterizes the Anglo-Saxon free market. No European society has the long and deep experience of individualist forms of family life and property ownership that distinguishes England, the United States and other Anglo-Saxon societies.

In every country, the new and more volatile strain of capitalism is transforming economic life. The impact of anarchic global markets on the economic cultures of continental Europe institutionalizes high levels of structural unemployment. In these societies the principal source of social division is unequal access to work.

In the United States, a highly deregulated labour market, together with a roll-back in welfare provision and an experiment in mass incarceration that has left over a million Americans behind bars, may succeed in keeping unemployment rates low. The principal source of social division in America is less likely to be lack of access to work as such but inequalities of income and wealth, together with inequalities in health, education, security from crime and the types of work that are accessible to different sectors of the population.

The indigenous Chinese capitalism that is emerging in China is not based around the large corporations that have developed in Anglo-Saxon capitalism. Apart from state enterprises, Chinese firms are small and family-owned. The disorders of capitalism in China are not the hollowing out of corporations or the fragmentation of families but a lack of solidarity between different sections of society and a pervasive degradation of the environment. Russian capitalism exhibits similar disorders.

These differences arise from long-term historical divergences in cultures and economic institutions – together with their continuing reflections in the different public policies of nation-states. The impact of disordered capitalism is to limit the autonomy of national governments. It is certainly not to suppress differences between them.

ANARCHIC CAPITALISM AND
THE STATE

Nation-states must now act in a world in which all options are uncertain. It is not as though they have before them a list of choices with price tags attached to them. National governments find themselves in environments not merely of risk but of radical uncertainty. In economic theory, risk means a situation in which the costs of various actions can be known with reasonable probability, while uncertainty is a situation in which such probabilities cannot be known. Many of the policies which governments know they can pursue do not have consequences to which probabilities can be attached.

Worse, governments often cannot know whether the response of world markets to their policies will be merely to make them costly or to render them completely unworkable. Governments are in a situation in which even the span of options that is available to them is uncertain. This continuing radical uncertainty is the most disabling constraint on the power of sovereign states.

The reduction in the leverage of sovereign states is a symptom of a broader trend, in which the powers gathered by the institutions of the state in early modern times are becoming dispersed or weakened. Even the power to make and conclude wars by having an effective monopoly of armed force, which has defined the sovereign state since its inception, no longer belongs to it unequivocally. Whatever the horrors of war in the nineteenth century it had limited goals and could be terminated by the states that waged it. That was the kind of war classically theorized by Clausewitz.

Since the Second World War Clausewitzian war between the agents of sovereign states has been partly supplanted by wars between irregular armies, tribal and ethnic groups, and political organizations such as the Palestine Liberation Organization (PLO) and the Irish Republican Army (IRA).[34] As the control of war has slipped in some measure from sovereign states the world has not thereby become more peaceful; it has become less governable and yet more unsafe.

Multinational companies have not gained the power and authority which sovereign states have lost and are as exposed to the vagaries of late modern societies as governments. Global corporations are not free agents that can defy public opinion without risk or cost. They are buffeted by shifts in the public cultures of the states in which they operate. Shell, a huge oil corporation, was deflected from use of an offshore platform at Brent Spar by a Greenpeace campaign that skilfully orchestrated media coverage. Shell proved as vulnerable a target for single-issue political action as any weak contemporary democratic state.

This does not mean that corporations will ever, as a matter of consistent policy, willingly bear the social and environmental costs of their activities. In a global free market they cannot. In addition to the unceasing pressures of global competition, multinational companies must now confront sporadic bursts of media attention which may deflect them from the single-minded pursuit of short-term profit.

Thus, in late modern contexts, power has leaked away from both states and corporations. Both institutions are mutating and evanescing, as global markets and new technologies transform the cultures from which each borrows its legitimacy and identity.

Sovereign states today act in an environment so transformed by market forces that no institution – not even the largest transnational corporation or sovereign state – can master it. In this environment the most unmanageable forces spring from a torrent of technological innovations. It is the combination of this unceasing stream of new technologies, unfettered market competition and weak or fractured social institutions that produces the global economy of our times.

As management gurus never cease reminding us, nation-states and multinational corporations can survive and prosper today only by using new technologies to achieve a competitive edge over their rivals. What most of them fail to note is that competitive advantage is inherently fleeting in the anarchic environment of disorganized global capitalism. In the late twentieth century there is no shelter – for corporations or for governments – from the global gale of creative destruction.

The decisive advantage that a multinational company achieves over its rivals comes finally from its capacity to generate new technologies and to deploy them effectively and profitably. In turn, this depends to a considerable extent on the ways in which companies enable knowledge to be conserved and generated. In the late modern competitive environment, business organizations which do not capture and exploit new knowledge, which waste the stock of tacit understandings among their employees or discourage them from acquiring new knowledge, will soon go under.

The global economy deskills people and organizations. It does so by making the environments in which they live and work unrecognizable to them. It thereby renders their stock of local and tacit knowledge less and less serviceable to them. A major problem that has not been solved by business organizations – except partially in Japanese companies[35] – is that of combining the institutional continuity needed, if the local knowledge of employees is to be harnessed, with the capacity for organizational innovation required to make the most of new technologies.

Sovereign states are not going to become obsolete. They will remain decisive mediating structures which multinational corporations compete to control. This pivotal role of sovereign states makes nonsense of the claims of hyperglobalists, business utopians and populists who maintain that multinationals have supplanted sovereign states as the real rulers of the world. It explains why global markets seek leverage over states and why they cannot ignore them. It illuminates the narrow margin in which governments can act to help their citizens control economic risk. This protective function of states is likely to expand, as citizens demand shelter from the anarchy of global capitalism.

Sovereign states have yet another function – seizing control of the natural resources that are necessary for economic growth. In Central and East Asia, the struggle for the control of oil is a source of diplomatic rivalries as much today as it was in the nineteenth century. It could well be a cause of war. As scarcities of natural resources increase, sovereign states are being drawn into military competition for the necessities of existence.[36]

The waning of American power means the emergence of a truly multipolar world. In such a world competition among sovereign states will be more, not less, pervasive and intense.

1998

18

The world is round

I

The belief that a process of globalization is under way which is bringing about a fundamental change in human affairs is not new. Marx and Engels expressed it in 1848, when they wrote in a justly celebrated passage in *The Communist Manifesto*:

All that is solid melts into air, all that is holy is profaned, and man is at last compelled to face with his sober senses his real conditions of life and his relations with his kind. The need of a constantly expanding market for its products chases the bourgeoisie over the whole surface of the globe. It must nestle everywhere, settle everywhere, establish connections everywhere. The bourgeoisie has through its exploitation of the world market given a cosmopolitan character to production and consumption in every country ... It compels all nations, on pain of extinction, to adopt the bourgeois mode of production; it compels them to introduce what it calls civilisation into their midst, i.e., to become bourgeois themselves. In one word, it creates a world after its own image.

Marx and Engels had no doubt that they were witnessing the emergence of a global market – a worldwide system of production and consumption that disregarded national and cultural boundaries. They welcomed this development, not only for the increasing wealth it produced but also because they believed it enabled humanity to overcome the divisions of the past. In the global market place nationalism and religion were destined to be dwindling forces. There would be many convulsions – wars, revolutions and counter-revolutions – before the Communist order was securely established; but when global capitalism had completed its work a new era in the life of humankind would begin.

The centrally planned economies that were constructed to embody Marx's vision of Communism have nearly all been swept away, and the mass political movements that Marxism once inspired are no more. Yet Marx's view of globalization lives on, and nowhere more vigorously than in the writings of Thomas Friedman. Like Marx, Friedman believes that globalization is in the end compatible with only one economic system; and like Marx he believes that this system enables humanity to leave war, tyranny and poverty behind. To his credit he recognizes the parallels between his view and that of Marx. He cites an illuminating conversation at Harvard in which the communitarian political theorist Michael Sandel alerted him to the fact that the process of global 'flattening' he examines in his new book[1] was first identified by Marx, quoting at length from *The Communist Manifesto* – including the passage cited above – and praising Marx for his prescience. This acknowledgement of the parallels between his view of globalization and Marx's theory of history is welcome and useful.

Friedman has emerged as the most powerful contemporary publicist of neo-liberal ideas. Neo-liberals have a wide variety of views on political and social matters, ranging from the highly conservative standpoint of Friedrich Hayek to the more rigorously libertarian position of Milton Friedman; but they are at one in seeing the free market as the fountainhead of human freedom. Though in some of his writings he shows a concern for the casualties of deregulated markets, Thomas Friedman is a passionate missionary for this neo-liberal faith. In his view the free market brings with it most of the ingredients that make for a free and humanly fulfilling society, and he has propagated this creed indefatigably in his books and in columns in the *New York Times*.

Friedman's views have been highly influential, shaping the thinking of presidents and informing American policy on a number of issues, and it may be instructive to note the matters in which he shares Marx's blind spots. Because they were on opposite sides of the Cold War it is often assumed that neo-liberalism and Marxism are fundamentally antagonistic systems of ideas. In fact they belong to the same style of thinking, and share many of the same disabling limitations. For Marxists and neo-liberals alike it is technological advance that fuels economic development, and economic forces that shape society. Politics and culture are secondary phenomena, sometimes capable of retarding human progress; but in the last analysis they cannot prevail against advancing technology and growing productivity.

Friedman is unequivocal in endorsing this reductive philosophy. He writes that he is often asked if he is a technological determinist, and with the innocent enthusiasm that is a redeeming feature of his prose style he declares resoundingly: 'This is a legitimate question, so let me try to answer it directly: *I am a technological determinist! Guilty as charged.*' (The italics are Friedman's.)

Technological determinism may contain a kernel of truth but it suggests a misleadingly simple view of history. This is well illustrated in Friedman's account of the demise of the Soviet Union. Acknowledging that there '*was* no single cause', he goes on:

To some degree the termites just ate away at the foundations of the Soviet Union, which were already weakened by the system's own internal contradictions and inefficiencies; to some degree the Reagan administration's military buildup in Europe forced the Kremlin to bankrupt itself paying for warheads; and to some degree Mikhail Gorbachev's hapless efforts to reform something that was unreformable brought communism to an end. But if I had to point to one factor as first among equals, it was the information revolution that began in the early to mid-1980s. Totalitarian systems depend on a monopoly of information and force, and too much information started to slip through the Iron Curtain, thanks to the spread of fax machines, telephones, and other modern tools of communication.

What is striking in this otherwise unexceptionable list is what it leaves out. There is no mention of the role of Solidarity and the Catholic Church in making Poland the first post-Communist country, or of the powerful independence movements that developed in the Baltic nations during the 1980s. Even more strikingly, there is no mention of the war in Afghanistan. By any account strategic defeat at the hands of Western-armed Islamist forces in that country (including some that formed the organization which was later to become al-Qaeda) was a defining moment in the decline of Soviet power. If

Friedman ignores these events, it may be because they attest to the persistent power of religion and nationalism – forces that in his simple, deterministic worldview should be withering away.

It is an irony of history that a view of the world falsified by the Communist collapse should have been adopted, in some of its most misleading aspects, by the victors in the Cold War. Neo-liberals, such as Friedman, have reproduced the weakest features of Marx's thought – its consistent underestimation of nationalist and religious movements and its unidirectional view of history. They have failed to absorb Marx's insights into the anarchic and self-destructive qualities of capitalism. Marx viewed the unfettered market as a revolutionary force, and understood that its expansion throughout the world was bound to be disruptive and violent. As capitalism spreads, it turns society upside down, destroying entire industries, ways of life and regimes. This can hardly be expected to be a peaceful process, and in fact it has been accompanied by major conflicts and social upheavals. The expansion of European capitalism in the nineteenth century involved the Opium Wars, genocide in the Belgian Congo, the Great Game in Central Asia and many other forms of imperial conquest and rivalry. The seeming triumph of global capitalism at the end of the twentieth century followed two world wars, the Cold War and savage neo-colonial conflicts.

Over the past two hundred years, the spread of capitalism and industrialization has gone hand in hand with war and revolution. It is a fact that would not have surprised Marx. Why do Friedman and other neo-liberals believe things will be any different in the twenty-first century? Part of the answer lies in an ambiguity in the idea of globalization. In current discussion two different notions are commonly conflated: the belief that we are living in a period of rapid and continuous technological innovation, which has the effect of linking up events and activities throughout the world more widely and quickly than before; and the belief that this process is leading to a single worldwide economic system. The first is an empirical proposition and plainly true, the second a groundless ideological assertion. Like Marx, Friedman elides the two.

2

In *The World is Flat*, Friedman tells us that globalization has three phases: the first from 1492 to around 1800, in which countries and governments opened up trade with the New World and which was driven by military expansion and the amount of horse power and wind power countries could employ; the second from 1800 to 2000, in which global integration was driven by multinational companies, steam engines and railways; and the third, in which individuals are the driving force and the defining technology is a worldwide fibre-optic network. In each of these phases, he tells us, technology is the driving force: globalization is a by-product of technological development. Here Friedman deviates from the standard view among contemporary economists, who see globalization largely as the result of policies of deregulation. Here he is closer to Marx – and to the realities of history.

In any longer perspective what we are witnessing today is only the most recent phase of worldwide industrialization. In the nineteenth century the world was shrunk by the advent of the telegraph; today it is shrinking again as a consequence of the Internet. Contrary to Friedman, however, the increasing facility of communication does not signify a quantum shift in human affairs. The uses of petroleum and electricity changed human life more deeply than any of the new information technologies have done. Even so, they did not end war and tyranny and usher in a new era of peace and plenty. Like other technological innovations, they were used for a variety of purposes, and became part of the normal conflicts of history.

It is necessary to distinguish between globalization – the ongoing process of worldwide industrialization – and the various economic systems in which this process has occurred. Globalization did not stop when Lenin came to power in Russia. It went on – actively accelerated by Stalin's policies of agricultural collectivization. Nor was globalization in any way slowed by the dirigiste regimes that developed in Asia – first in Japan in the Meiji era and later in the militarist period, then after the Second World War in Korea and Taiwan. All these regimes were vehicles through which globalization continued its advance. Worldwide industrialization continued when the liberal international economic order fell apart after the First World War, and it will carry on if the global economic regime that was established after the fall of Communism falls apart in its turn.

There is no systematic connection between globalization and the free market. It is no more essentially friendly to liberal capitalism than to central planning or East Asian dirigisme. Driven by technological changes that occur in many regimes, the process of globalization is more powerful than any of them. This is a truth that Friedman – as an avowed technological determinist – should accept readily enough. If he does not, it is because it shows how baseless are the utopian hopes he attaches to a process that abounds in conflicts and contradictions. Globalization makes the world smaller. It may also make it – or sections of it – richer. It does not make it more peaceful, or more liberal. Least of all does it make it flat.

Friedman's by now famous discovery of the world's flatness came to him when he was talking to Nandan Nilekani, CEO of one of India's leading new high-technology companies, Infosys Technologies, at its campus in Bangalore. The Indian entrepreneur remarked to Friedman: 'Tom, the playing field is being levelled.' The observation is commonplace, but it hit Friedman with the force of a revelation. 'What Nandan is saying, I thought, is that the playing field is being flattened . . . Flattened? Flattened? My God, he's telling me the world is flat!' Five hundred years ago, Columbus 'returned safely to prove definitively that the world was round'. As a matter of fact it was not Columbus who provided the proof but the Portuguese navigator Ferdinand Magellan, whose ship circled the globe in a three-year voyage from 1519 to 1522. Regardless, Friedman sees himself as a latter-day Columbus who has discovered that the world is no longer round: 'I scribbled four words down in my notebook: "The world is flat."'

The metaphor of a flat world is worked relentlessly throughout this overlong book, but it is not its incessant repetition that is most troublesome. It is Friedman's failure to recognize that in many ways, some of them not difficult to observe, the world is becoming distinctly less flat. While he acknowledges the existence of an 'unflat' world composed of people without access to the benefits of new technology, he never connects the growth of this netherworld of the relatively poor with the advance of globalization. At times his failure to connect is almost comic. Recalling his visit to the Infosys headquarters in Bangalore, he writes:

The Infosys campus is reached by a pockmarked road, with sacred cows, horse-drawn carts, and motorized rickshaws all jostling alongside our vans. Once you enter the gates of Infosys, though, you are in a different world. A massive resort-size swimming pool nests amid boulders and manicured lawns, adjacent to a huge putting green. There are multiple restaurants and a fabulous health club.

Friedman notes in passing that the Infosys campus has its own power supply. He does not ask why this is necessary, or comment on the widening difference in standards of life in the region that it represents. Yet it is only by decoupling itself from its local environment that Infosys is able to compete effectively in global markets. Infosys demonstrates that globalization does have the effect of levelling some inequalities in world markets, but the success of the company has been achieved by using services and infrastructure that the society around it lacks.

As it levels some inequalities, globalization raises others. Friedman tells us that he is in favour of what he calls 'compassionate flatism', which seems to mean a range of centrist or social democratic policies designed to enhance job mobility while preserving economic security, such as portable personal pensions. In an American setting these may be useful proposals, and it is strange that in the countries that have been most exposed to the disruptive effects of globalization Friedman appears to favour neo-liberal policies of the most conventional kind. He describes the fall of the Berlin Wall as a 'world-flattening event', and cites Russia as one of the countries that has most benefited from the new flat world.

There can be no doubt that the Soviet collapse represented an advance for human freedom. Yet since then Russia has suffered rising levels of absolute poverty and large increases in inequality of wealth, and it seems clear that the economic 'shock therapy' administered on Western advice just after the Communist collapse contributed to these developments. Price decontrol wiped out small family savings, and by limiting the benefits of privatizing government industries to a small number of insiders produced a marked concentration of wealth. As a result, large parts of the Russian population have been excluded from the benefits of the global market. Other policies could likely have avoided or mitigated this outcome.[2]

In view of the Soviet inheritance, the process of transition was bound to be prolonged and difficult. Attempting it in the space of a few years was folly, and shock therapy resulted in the impoverishment of many millions of people. It also fuelled a backlash against the West. Socioeconomic change on the scale that occurred in post-Communist Russia tends to produce a political aftershock, and the emergence of Vladimir Putin can be seen as an unintended consequence of Western-sponsored free-market policies. In some contexts free-market policies continue, but Putin has reasserted political control of the economy as a whole, reined in the political activities of the oligarchs and demonstrated a degree of independence from Western influences. As a result his quasi-authoritarian regime seems to possess a popular legitimacy that Yeltsin's lacked, and there is no discernible prospect of Western-style 'democratic capitalism'.

Globalization has no inherent tendency to promote the free market or liberal democracy. Neither does it augur an end to nationalism or great-power rivalries. Describing a long conversation with the CEO of a small Indian game company in Bangalore, Friedman recounts the entrepreneur concluding: 'India is going to be a superpower and we are going to rule.' Friedman replies: 'Rule whom?' His response suggests that the present phase of globalization is tending to make imbalances of power between states irrelevant. In fact what it is doing is creating new great powers, and this is one of the reasons it has been embraced in China and India.

Neo-liberals interpret globalization as being driven by a search for greater productivity, and view nationalism as a kind of cultural backwardness that acts mainly to slow this process. Yet the economic takeoff in both England and the US occurred against the background of a strong sense of nationality, and nationalist resistance to Western power was a powerful stimulus of economic development in Meiji Japan.

Nationalism fuelled the rapid growth of capitalism in the nineteenth and early twentieth centuries,[3] and is doing the same in China and India at the present time. In both countries globalization is being embraced not only because of the prosperity it makes possible, but also for the opportunity it creates to challenge Western hegemony. As China and India become great powers they will demand recognition of their distinctive cultures and values, and international institutions will have to be reshaped to reflect the legitimacy of a variety of economic and political models. At that point the universal claims of the United States and other Western nations will be fundamentally challenged, and the global balance of power will shift.

3

In *The Lexus and the Olive Tree* (1999), Friedman focused on the tension between the 'Lexus' forces of global economic integration and the 'Olive Tree' forces of cultural identity, and in *The World is Flat* he tells us that after 11 September he spent much of his time travelling in the Arab and Muslim worlds and lost track of globalization. Actually it was not globalization he lost sight of but rather the forces of identity that shape it. He writes that the nation-state is 'the biggest source of friction' in global markets. In fact nationalist resistance to globalization is more prominent in advanced countries such as France, Holland and the US than in emerging economies. Friedman himself expresses concern about the impact of outsourcing on American employment, and there has been a steady drift towards greater protectionism in the Bush administration's trade policies. American nationalism may already be acting as a brake on globalization. In the fast-industrializing countries of Asia, nationalism is one of globalization's driving forces.

Rising nationalism is part of the process of globalization, and so too are intensifying geopolitical rivalries. Just as it did when the Great Game was played out in the decades leading up to the First World War, ongoing industrialization is setting off a scramble for natural resources. The US, Russia, China, India, Japan and the countries of the European Union are all of them involved in attempts to secure energy supplies, and their field of competition ranges from Central

Asia through the Persian Gulf to Africa and parts of Latin America. The coming century could be marked by recurrent resource wars, as the great powers struggle for control of the planet's hydrocarbons.[4]

Moreover, worldwide industrialization appears to be coming up against serious environmental limits. An increasing number of expert observers believe global oil reserves may be peaking,[5] and there is a consensus among climate scientists that the worldwide shift to an energy-intensive industrial lifestyle is contributing to global warming. If these fears are well founded the next phase of globalization could encompass upheavals as large as any in the twentieth century.

It would be wrong to suggest that Friedman is oblivious of these risks. In an interesting aside, he writes:

Islamo-Leninism, in many ways, emerged from the same historical context as the European radical ideologies of the nineteenth and twentieth centuries. Fascism and Marxism-Leninism grew out of the rapid industrialization and modernization of Germany and Central Europe, where communities living in tightly bonded villages and extended families suddenly got shattered.

Again, Friedman recognizes that many of the innovations of the current phase of globalization are reproduced in al-Qaeda. In the past two decades some of the most advanced global corporations have ceased to be top-heavy bureaucracies, and become streamlined networks of entrepreneurs and venture capitalists. Al-Qaeda has emulated this change, operating as a network of autonomous cells rather than the highly centralized organizations of revolutionary parties in the past. Perhaps most interestingly, Friedman acknowledges that America's dependency on imported oil exposes it to attack, and urges American energy independence:

If President Bush made energy independence his moon shot, in one fell swoop he would dry up revenue for terrorism, force Iran, Russia, Venezuela, and Saudi Arabia on the path of reform – which they will never do with $50-a-barrel oil – strengthen the dollar, and improve his own standing in Europe by doing something huge to reduce global warming.

Friedman's advocacy of American energy independence illustrates the error of a unidirectional view of history. Energy autarchy may be an appealing policy, but it signifies a retreat from globalization. *The*

Lexus and the Olive Tree trumpeted the arrival of a harmoniously integrated world. Since then the US has suffered terrorist attack and become mired in an intractable insurgency in Iraq. Against this background the prospect of severing one of the crucial supply chains that link the US with the world is beginning to look extremely tempting. As he has done in previous books Friedman has expressed a powerful larger mood, and in this respect *The World is Flat* may prove a prescient guide to future American policy.

Yet while greater energy independence may be an American national interest the notion that it would force recalcitrant countries on to a path of neo-liberal reform is wishful thinking. A large drop in the oil price would surely destabilize the rentier economies of the Gulf and Central Asia, from Saudi Arabia to Turkmenistan, and in some countries could lead to the establishment of democratic rule. However, in a number of cases the chief beneficiary would likely be fundamentalism. Does Friedman really believe that democracy in Saudi Arabia would produce a liberal, pro-Western regime? In this and other countries, American energy independence could well further the advance of radical Islam.

As it has done in the past, globalization is throwing up dilemmas that have no satisfactory solution. That does not mean they cannot be more or less intelligently managed, but what is needed is the opposite of the utopian imagination. In a curious twist, the utopian mind has migrated from left to right, and from the academy to the airport bookshop. In the nineteenth century it was political activists and radical social theorists such as Marx who held out the promise that new technology was creating a new world. Today some business gurus have a similar message. There are many books announcing a global economic transformation and suggesting that governments can be re-engineered to adapt to it in much the same way as corporations. *The World is Flat* is an outstanding example of this genre.

Unfortunately the problems of globalization are more intractable than those of corporate life. States cannot be phased out like bankrupt firms, and large shifts in wealth and power tend to be fiercely contested. Globalization is a revolutionary change, but it is also a continuation of the conflicts of the past. In some important respects it is levelling the playing field, as Friedman's Indian interlocutor noted, and to that extent it is a force for human advance. At the same time it is inflaming nationalist and religious passions and triggering a struggle for natural resources. In Friedman's sub-Marxian, neo-liberal worldview these conflicts are recognized only as forms of friction – grit in the workings of an unstoppable machine. In truth they are integral to the process itself, whose future course cannot be known. We would be better off accepting this fact, and doing what we can to cope with it.

2005

PART FOUR

Enlightenment and Terror

19

The original modernizers

The distribution of the forces of tradition, entrenched over thousands of years of history, cannot be grasped in any quantifiable way.   Leszek Kolakowski[1]

The history of ideas obeys a law of irony. Ideas have consequences, but rarely those their authors expect or desire, and never only those. Quite often they are the opposite.

The Positivists are the original prophets of modernity. Through their influence on Marx, they stand behind the twentieth century's Communist regimes. At the same time, by their formative impact on economics, they inspired the utopian social engineers who constructed the global free market in the aftermath of the collapse of Communist central planning.

The Positivist catechism had three main tenets. First, history is driven by the power of science; growing knowledge and new technology are the ultimate determinants of change in human society. Second, science will enable natural scarcity to be overcome; once that has been achieved, the immemorial evils of poverty and war will be banished for ever. Third, progress in science and progress in ethics and politics go together; as scientific knowledge advances and becomes more systematically organized, human values will increasingly converge.

This Positivist creed animated Marx's ideal of Communism. It informed the 'theories of modernization' that were developed after the Second World War. It guides the architects of the global free market today.

The founder of Positivism was Count Henri de Saint-Simon (1760–1825).[2] Saint-Simon used to instruct his valet to waken him each morning with the words 'Remember, monsieur le comte, that you have great things to do.' Perhaps as a result, he had an eventful life. At the age of seventeen he was commissioned into the army and served with the French forces in the American War of Independence. Later in his military career he was taken prisoner and interned in Jamaica, after which he conceived the first of many grandiose schemes – a plan for a canal linking the Atlantic and the Pacific through Lake Nicaragua, which he unsuccessfully submitted to the Viceroy of Mexico. He amassed a fortune during the French Revolution by buying up houses vacated by noblemen who had emigrated or been guillotined. For a time he seems to have served as an agent of the British Foreign Office.

In later years Saint-Simon fell on hard times. Falsely accused of instigating an assassination, he spent some years in a private hospital for the insane. The daily reminders of his greatness given him by his manservant did not enable Saint-Simon to achieve the success to which he aspired. In his last years it was only the support that he received from his devoted servant that kept him from starvation.

Saint-Simon was an adventurer. He was also the first modern socialist. He analysed society into distinct classes, each with a different relationship to the means of production, and attacked market capitalism as anarchic, wasteful and chronically unstable. His critique of capitalism was hugely influential. But more influential still was his vision of the future of humanity, which at the close of the twentieth century re-emerged in the utopian project of a universal free market.

According to Saint-Simon, actually existing societies are chaotic and divided; but that is because they have not absorbed the findings of science. Progress in society is a by-product of progress in science. As knowledge advances, so does humanity.

Every society must pass through a series of definite stages. Each must move from a religious view of the world to a metaphysical outlook, and from that to the positive – or scientific – stage. In each of these three stages, human knowledge becomes more definite and – a vitally important point for the Positivists – more systematically organized. In the end, when all societies have passed through these stages, ethics will become a science, no less objective in its results than physics or chemistry. At this point, the moral and political conflicts of the past will disappear.

Where there is no conflict there is no need for power. As Marx put it in a phrase he borrowed from Saint-Simon, the government of men will be replaced by the administration of things. Marx knew little of the work of Comte, whom he read only in the late 1860s and then dismissed; but the influence on him of Saint-Simon was profound. With the growth of knowledge and the continuing expansion of production, Saint-Simon believed, the state will wither away. Marx followed Saint-Simon in this conviction, which became the core of his conception of Communism.

The Positivists did not aim merely to revolutionize society. Their aim was to found a new religion. Saint-Simon believed the 'positive doctrine' would become the basis for a new 'church' when all scientists united to form a permanent 'clergy'.[3] He envisaged an assembly of 'the twenty-one elect of humanity' to be called the Council of Newton. Newton's idea of universal gravitation was 'the basis of the new scientific system'. It should also be the basis of 'the new religious system'.[4] In Saint-Simon's new religion, however, it was not gravity that replaced the Deity. That place was filled by humanity. Saint-Simon's last work was the *Nouveau Christianisme* (1825) – a new version of Christianity in which the human species became the Supreme Being.

The practical transformation of Positivism into a religion began not long after Saint-Simon's death, when – as one historian of the movement puts it – 'The Saint-Simonians transformed themselves into a religious cult'.[5] Soon the Positivist cult acquired all the paraphernalia of the Church – hymns, altars, priests in their vestments and its own calendar, with the months named after Archimedes, Gutenberg, Descartes and other rationalist saints.

Auguste Comte (1798–1857), the most influential of the Positivist savants, completed the transformation of Positivism into a religion. The son of a local government official, Comte began his career by entering the Ecole Polytechnique in Paris in 1814 on the basis of a brilliant performance in the national entrance examination. It has been said of the young *polytechniciens* of this period that they believed that 'one could create a religion in the same way as one learned at the Ecole to build a bridge.'[6] Comte's approach to the design of a new religion was decidedly more emotional than rational, but like his peers in the Ecole Polytechnique he had an almost unlimited faith in the power of social engineering.

Comte began by ridiculing the cult that had grown up around Saint-Simon. Once Saint-Simon's protégé, he broke with him acrimoniously; thereafter he acknowledged no intellectual debt to the older man. Yet he took up Saint-Simon's idea that Positivism should become a religion and promoted it with a passion that verged on madness.

The development of Comte's system of ideas cannot be understood outside the context of his private life. Like his relationship with Saint-Simon, Comte's first marriage in 1822 ended in acrimony. His wife had nursed him through the first of many mental collapses, keeping him at home when a psychiatrist had declared him incurably deranged, and submitting to a bizarre Christian marriage ceremony (demanded by Comte's mother, who objected to their common-law union) in which Comte – by then suffering from paranoia – signed himself Brutus Napoleon Comte.

In an eerie rerun of Saint-Simon's career, Comte's mental instability recurred throughout his life. It was displayed in his relationship with Mme Clothilde de Vaux, a gifted and attractive married woman abandoned by her husband. Comte's affair with Clothilde was never consummated. She died tragically after a struggle with illness (probably tuberculosis). Comte was once again driven to the brink of insanity.

The motif of all Comte's later work and the inspiration of his new religion is well summarized by Manuel: 'After Clothilde's death Comte's whole life became devoted to a religious worship of her image.'[7] In a number of works written after her death, Comte scandalized his rationalist disciples by declaring love to be the moving force of humanity. They were further dismayed when he went on to nominate Clothilde as the Virgin Mother of the Church of Humanity and ordained that her grave be a place of pilgrimage.

There was method in Comte's madness. Taking the Catholic Church as his model, he devised a minute system of daily observances for followers of the new religion. In his *Système de Politique Positive* (1852–4), he laid down that the pious Positivist should pray three times a day for a total of two hours, once to each of his household goddesses, his mother, wife and daughter. He was to cross himself by tapping his head with his finger three times at the points where – according to the science of phrenology – the impulses of benevolence, order and progress were situated. There were nine Positivist sacraments, beginning with Presentation, an equivalent to baptism in which the infant was to be given two patron saints, and ending with the Sacrament of Incorporation. When he died, the good Positivist's remains would be deposited in the sacred wood surrounding each Positivist temple. At that point his memory would be incorporated into the Supreme Being. These observances were to be regulated by the Grand Pontiff of Humanity, who was to reside in Paris. In his will, Comte appointed thirteen executors, who were to preserve his lodgings as the permanent headquarters of the Religion of Humanity.

Comte specified the duties and organization of the Positivist clergy as follows:

During the seven years which elapse before he is full priest, every vicar must teach all the seven encyclopaedic sciences, and exercise his powers of preaching. After that he becomes a true priest ... Every philosophical presbytery has seven priests and three vicars. Their residences may be changed by the High Priest ... The number of these priestly colleges will be two thousand for the whole Western world. This gives a functionary for every six thousand inhabitants, or one hundred thousand for the whole earth.

With unwitting humour, Comte wrote: 'The rate may appear too low; but it is really adequate for all the services required.'[8]

The Positivists approached the construction of the new religion with an obsessive concern for detail. New forms of clothing were invented. Waistcoats were designed with the buttons on the back, so that they could be put on and taken off only with the assistance of other people. The aim was to promote altruism and co-operation. Sadly, the result was to provoke raids from the police, who – taking Saint-Simon's talk of 'the rehabilitation of the flesh' literally – suspected his disciples of taking part in orgies.

The Positivist religion – 'Catholicism minus Christianity', as T. H. Huxley called it – was eminently ridiculous. It was also extremely influential. Temples of Humanity sprang up not only in Paris but also in London, where a chapel was founded in Lamb's Conduit Street, and in Liverpool. The Positivist Church was notably successful in Latin America. In Brazil, where Comte's slogan 'Order and Progress' is part of the national flag, there are active Positivist temples to this day. In France, Comtean ideas of rule by a technocratic elite had a lasting influence in the Ecole Polytechnique. Through his deep impact on John Stuart Mill, with whom he maintained a long correspondence, Comte was instrumental in identifying liberalism with secular humanism – or, as Mill and Comte termed it, the Religion of Humanity.[9]

With all its absurdities, the Religion of Humanity is the prototype of the secular religions of the twentieth century. Marxism and neo-liberalism embody its central tenet: with the growth of scientific knowledge, mankind can rid itself of the immemorial evils of human life – war, tyranny and scarcity.

Saint-Simon and Comte inherited this Enlightenment faith from the Marquis de Condorcet (1743–94). Condorcet was the author of a celebrated essay on the progress of the human mind in which he asserted the perfectibility of human nature. Will not the growth of knowledge demonstrate, he asks, that 'the moral goodness of man is susceptible of indefinite improvement, and that nature links together truth, happiness and virtue by an indissoluble chain?'[10] Condorcet died in prison after being arrested by the revolutionary government of Robespierre.

Saint-Simon and Condorcet may well have met; but in any case Saint-Simon, and later Comte, imbibed from Condorcet the most fundamental beliefs of the Religion of Humanity: the advance of science is not an accident; it is a result of the nature of the human mind, which is inherently progressive. Allied with mankind's innate goodness, science can transform the human condition.

With Condorcet, Saint-Simon and Comte believed that the progress that humanity has achieved in government and society is an inevitable result of the progress of the human mind. History is only the development of human intelligence, itself inevitable, in which the truths discovered by science are used to transform society. There is a law of progress in human affairs, from which the future of the species can be predicted. Saint-Simon wrote: 'the progress of the human mind has reached the point where the most important reasoning on politics can and must be deduced directly from the knowledge acquired in the high sciences and the physical sciences. It is my aim to imprint a positive character on politics.'[11]

Saint-Simon and Comte looked forward to a 'positive' politics, in which science would be used to emancipate mankind. That is not to say they were liberals. Like Marx, they believed the advance of science made liberal individualism redundant. Unlike Marx, they viewed the Middle Ages with sympathy. As a result, they sought out alliances with conservative thinkers.

Comte asserted that history oscillated between 'critical' periods such as his own time and 'organic' periods. To be sure, he never imagined that society could return to the past. As an Enlightenment thinker, he was committed to the idea that humanity could someday live better than it had ever done in the past; but as an admirer of organic societies he incorporated elements from the past into his vision of the future. Partly for this reason, Positivist thought has had a recurring appeal for the European right, surfacing in the 1930s on the intellectual fringes of Fascism.

Both Saint-Simon and Comte were attracted by the ideas of Joseph de Maistre. An ultra-orthodox Catholic, de Maistre was a lifelong enemy of the Enlightenment. It may be hard to see what the leading savants of Positivism could have in common with such a relentlessly reactionary thinker. Yet, Saint-Simon surmised, the future of mankind may lie in a fusion of de Maistre and Voltaire.

The chief appeal of Positivism to the right came from the conviction of Saint-Simon and Comte that a science of society must be based solidly on the truths of physiology. Saint-Simon always emphasized that physiology is central and fundamental in any 'science of man'. Comte aimed to develop what he called a 'social physics', a physiologically based social science with which – he declared – 'the philosophical system of the moderns will be in fact complete.'[12] In that it gave a patina of intellectual authority to a belief in basically different human types, the idea that social science should be grounded in physiology had obvious attractions to the European right.

It would be absurd to hold Saint-Simon and Comte responsible for developments of their ideas of which they could know nothing; but there is a clear line of thought linking pseudo-science such as phrenology with the political ideas of the far right in Europe in the twentieth century. Comte's use of phrenology has already been noted. Later in the nineteenth century, phrenology was to feature in the 'criminal anthropology' developed by the Italian jurist Cesare Lombroso (1835–1909). Positivist ideas shaped Lombroso's thinking in a number of ways. In his view, there is an innate disposition to criminal behaviour, and it can be detected by the study of physiology and physiognomy. Favouring a judicial system in which experts played a leading role, he proposed using the techniques of 'anthropometry'. These involved measuring facial and cranial features, along with height and other physical characteristics, as a means of identifying criminals and 'criminal types'. Lombroso's anthropometric methods were used in the Italian judicial system and in many other countries right up to the Second World War.

Phrenology was also used to develop racial theories. In the 1860s, the founder of the British Anthropological Institute, John Beddoe, developed an 'Index of Nigrescence' based on cranial characteristics, which he used to support the claim that the Irish were 'Africanoid'. In the twentieth century, 'craniometric' techniques were used by the Nazis to distinguish 'Aryans' from 'non-Aryans'.

On left and right, the appeal of Positivism came from its claim to possess the authority of science. Nearly always, the appeal to science went with the rejection of liberalism. Yet this protean doctrine resurfaced at the end of the twentieth century among those who aimed to make a narrow version of liberal values universal.

If Positivism is the chief source of the twentieth century's most powerful secular religions it is partly through its impact on the social sciences. For Positivists, modernity is the transformation of the world by the use of scientific knowledge. For Comte, the science in question was sociology – of a highly speculative sort. For ideologues of the free market, it is economics – a no less speculative discipline. But whatever the science, its conclusions are supposed to apply everywhere.

In Positivist methodology, social science is no different from natural science. The model for both is mathematics. Nothing can be known unless it can be quantified. Applying this view, Comte invented sociology – a term he coined; but the idea that mathematics is the ideal form of human knowledge proved most powerful in economics, where it helped spawn the idea of a global free market.

Without realizing it – for few of them know anything of the history of thought, least of all in their own subject – the majority of economists have inherited their way of thinking from the Positivists. Working their way into the discipline via Logical Positivism, Saint-Simonian and Comtean ideas have become the standard methodology of economics.

Saint-Simon and Comte envisaged a unified science in which all of human knowledge would be reduced to a single set of laws. For Saint-Simon, the evolution of the human mind would not be complete until the whole of knowledge was shown to obey a single law. He wrote that, in the twelfth and last stage in the development of the human intelligence: 'The general system of our knowledge will be reorganized on the basis of the belief that the universe is ruled by a single immutable law. All the systems of application, such as the systems of religion, politics, morals and civil law, will be placed in harmony with the new system of knowledge.'[13] In much the same spirit, Comte wrote: 'the first characteristic of the positive philosophy is that it regards all phenomena as subjected to invariable natural laws. Our business is . . . to pursue an accurate discovery of these laws, with a view to reducing them to the smallest possible number.'[14]

The project of a unified science means that the social sciences are no different in their methods from the natural sciences. Both seek to discover natural laws. The only genuine knowledge is that which comes from scientific inquiry; and every science – including the social sciences – aspires to the generality and certainty of the laws of mathematics. For, as Comte declared, 'mathematics must . . . hold the first place in the hierarchy of the sciences.'[15]

The idea that the study of society should form part of a single unified science came into economics from the Vienna Circle – a group of scientists and philosophers that met in Vienna from 1907 onwards. After the appointment to a professorship at the University of Vienna of the philosopher Moritz Schlick in 1922, the Vienna Circle achieved considerable success as the disseminator of Logical Positivism.

The Vienna Circle sprang partly from the philosophy of Ernst Mach (1838–1916), a physicist and expert in ballistics who was hugely influential in Vienna at the turn of the century. Like Comte, Mach held that religion and metaphysics belonged in a primitive phase of the mind. Science alone gave knowledge of the world. In Mach's view, scientific knowledge was a construction from human sensations. A synthesis of Comte and Mach, the Vienna Circle viewed science as a combination of the necessary truths of logic and mathematics with data gleaned from the senses.

The core of Logical Positivism was the development of a scientific worldview. Going further than Saint-Simon and Comte, the Logical Positivists declared that only the verifiable propositions of science have meaning: strictly speaking, religion, metaphysics and morality are nonsense. In philosophy, in the writings of the early Wittgenstein, this doctrine reappeared as a mystical theory of the limits of language. In social science, it boosted the aspirations of economics to be a rigorous discipline on a par with physics and mathematics.

With the rise of Nazism, the Vienna Circle was scattered, many of its members fleeing to the United States. As a clearly defined movement in philosophy, Logical Positivism ceased to exist by the 1940s. Yet it had a formative impact on economics, shaping the views of Milton Friedman and many others.

None of the classical economists believed that mathematics should be the model for social science. For Adam Smith and Adam Ferguson, economics was grounded in history. It was bound up inextricably with the rise and decline of nations and the struggle for power between different social groups. For Smith and Ferguson, economic life can be understood only by examining these historical developments. In a different way, the same is true of Marx. Since the rise of Positivism in the social sciences this tradition has practically disappeared.

The decoupling of economics from history has led to a pervasive unrealism in the discipline. The classical economists knew that the laws of the market are only distillations from human behaviour. As such, they have the limitations of all types of historical knowledge. History demonstrates a good deal of regularity in human behaviour. It also shows enough variety to make the search for universal laws a vain enterprise. It is doubtful if the various forms of social studies contain a single law on a par with those of the physical sciences. Yet in recent times the 'laws of economics' have been invoked to support the idea that one style of behaviour – the 'free market' variety found intermittently over the past few centuries in a handful of countries – should be the model for economic life everywhere.

Economic theory cannot show that the free market is the best type of economic system. The idea that free markets are the most efficient mode of economic life is one of the intellectual pillars of the campaign for a global free market; but there are many ways of defining efficiency, none of them value-free. For the Positivists, the efficiency of an economy was measured in terms of its productivity. Certainly the free market is highly productive. But as Saint-Simon and Comte understood very well, that does not mean it is humanly fulfilling.

The idea that the free market should be universal makes sense only if you accept a certain philosophy of history. Under the impact of Logical Positivism, economics has developed into a thoroughly unhistorical discipline. At the same time, it has imbibed a philosophy of history that derives from Saint-Simon and Comte.

According to Positivism, science is the motor of historical change. New technology drives out inefficient modes of production and engenders new forms of social life. This process is at work throughout history. Its end-point is a world unified by a single economic system. The ultimate result of scientific knowledge is a universal civilization, governed by a secular, 'terrestrial' morality.

For Saint-Simon and Comte, technology meant railways and canals. For Lenin it meant electricity. For neo-liberals it means the Internet. The message is the same. Technology – the practical application of scientific knowledge – produces a convergence in values. This is the central modern myth, which the Positivists propagated and everyone today accepts as fact.

In some ways, the Positivists were wiser than their twentieth-century disciples. The idea that maximal productivity is the goal of economic life is one of the most pervasive – and pernicious – inheritances of Positivism; but it is an idea to which Saint-Simon and Comte did not hold consistently. They knew that humans are not just economic animals. As the growth of knowledge accelerates, they believed, the maintenance of social ties becomes ever more necessary.

At their best, Saint-Simon and Comte were not dogmatists. They knew that human life is extremely complicated – so much so that what is good in one society may be bad in another. Like Voltaire, they understood that in the real world of human history the best regime is not everywhere the same. In practice, if not in theory, the Positivists accepted that there is more than one way of being modern.

The architects of the global free market lack this wise political relativism. For them, only irrationality stands in the way of the best regime becoming universal. Nevertheless, the world they imagine they are building is unmistakably that envisaged by the Positivists. In a famous passage at the close of his *General Theory* (1936), Keynes wrote:

the ideas of economists and political philosophers, both when they are right and when they are wrong, are more powerful than is commonly believed. Indeed, the world is ruled by little else. Practical men, who believe themselves to be exempt from any intellectual influences, are usually the slaves of some defunct economist. Madmen in authority, who hear voices in the air, are distilling the frenzy of some academic scribbler of a few years back.[16]

Keynes was writing at a time when public policy was governed by outdated economic theories. Today it is ruled by a defunct religion. To link exotic figures such as Saint-Simon and Comte with the vapid bureaucrats of the International Monetary Fund may seem fanciful, but the idea of modernization to which the IMF adheres is a Positivist inheritance. The social engineers who labour to install free markets in every last corner of the globe see themselves as scientific rationalists, but they are actually disciples of a forgotten cult.

2003

20

The Jacobins of Washington

Around two hundred years ago, the great French reactionary thinker Joseph de Maistre wrote of 'the profound imbecility of those poor men who imagine that nations can be constituted with ink'. De Maistre, one of the fiercest critics of the Enlightenment, was targeting the radical *philosophes*, who believed that liberal republics could be established throughout the world. Against this sunny view, de Maistre insisted that nations are made from human suffering, as different cultures and traditions clash in unending historical conflict.

In de Maistre's day, it was the French Jacobins who believed that democracy could be spread throughout the world by fiat; today it is American neo-conservatives. There are many differences between the two, some of them profound: the sense of mission that animates the Bush administration owes as much to Christian fundamentalism as it does to Enlightenment universalism. Yet American neo-conservatives are at one with the French Jacobins on the most essential, and most dangerously misguided, point. Both are convinced that democratic government can be made universal, and in pretty short order.

To be sure, they also know that more than ink is required to realize this noble ideal. The Jacobins understood very well that blood would also have to be spilt. Equally, the neo-conservative intellectuals who are calling the shots at the White House accept that terror will be necessary; but, like their Jacobin predecessors, they believe it will be just and merciful, a brief pang before the advent of a new world. A think-tank warrior such as Richard Perle may think of himself as a realist, but the cold frenzy with which he urges war reminds one more of Robespierre than of Metternich. Like their Jacobin predecessors, Perle and his neo-conservative confrères believe they can rewrite history and bring humanity to unprecedented freedom and harmony.

We have seen the awful consequences in Iraq: the people of that unhappy country, much as they hate Saddam Hussein, have not embraced the American invaders in quite the way that Washington hoped. And the rest of us are compelled to face an uncomfortable truth: that though many may wish for the sudden collapse of Saddam's regime, a swift and decisive American victory, even if it comes about, can only embolden the Bush administration in its revolutionary new policies. Flushed with victory, the neo-conservatives would be ready to embark on a project of reconfiguring global politics as far-reaching as any attempted in the twentieth century, exporting US-style democracy to the Middle East and thereby guaranteeing America's global hegemony.

The hawks now fully in charge of Washington policy spurn multinational institutions and scorn the traditional arts of diplomacy. They have turned their backs on the policies of deterrence and containment that preserved the world from disaster in the Cold War. Instead, applying the new doctrine of preventive war, they are determined to eradicate threats to American power wherever they perceive them; but their objectives go far beyond simply defending the US from attack. They aim to entrench American global hegemony against any potential challenge. In their view, this demands more than disabling 'rogue states' (such as Saddam's Iraq) and putting friendly regimes in place. It requires reshaping post-war Iraq and much of the rest of the Middle East in an American image. After Iraq, Iran and Syria are in line for regime change. The entire region is to be reshaped to reflect American values.

This fantastical scheme will be tested to destruction in post-war Iraq. Current US pronouncements on rebuilding the country change from one day to the next and need not be taken too seriously, but it is clear that the Bush administration means to govern Iraq itself, with the UK serving, as ever, as its obedient junior partner, and the UN and the EU playing only a peripheral role. With transnational institutions marginalized, the Americans will face a major problem in legitimating their occupation of Iraq in the Arab world and, for that matter, the world as a whole.

Perhaps with this in mind, they talk of holding democratic elections in the country within a year. They say they want Iraq to be a self-governing nation; but Iraq is not and has never been a nation-state. Under Saddam, it has evolved into an extremely repressive regime in which power and privilege are concentrated in a single clan and its hangers-on; but it remains a multinational state, in some ways not unlike the former Yugoslavia. 'The Iraqi people' does not exist. The country comprises several distinct ethnic and religious groupings, which have been at one another's throats for many years. Along with some elements in the fractious Iraqi opposition, the Americans talk of a federal Iraq in which these groups will live peacefully together. But history shows that such constructions are extremely fragile. Democracy, above all the federal variety, requires trust, but trust is a commodity in desperately short supply in communities divided by historical memories of savage conflict.

As events in the Balkans have shown, when an authoritarian multinational state collapses, the result is not federalism. It is war and ethnic cleansing. The threat that Turkish forces will move into zones claimed by the Kurds is just the first sign of the bloody fragmentation that may lie in store for Iraq. To think that democracy can be established under such conditions is not just far-fetched, it is imbecilic.

From one angle, then, the Bush administration's project in Iraq is an exercise in the most radical utopianism. From another, it is pure geopolitics. Public statements show that the hawks in the White House and among the Pentagon's civilian leadership see the war as part of a grand strategy to shore up American hegemony, not just in the Middle East but throughout the world. This is where Iraq's oil comes in: not so much as a secure source of supply for America's profligate energy users, but as a lever against potential challenges to US supremacy. Remember the first Gulf war. That war was fought – rightly, as I still think – to stop Saddam gaining control of the oil supplies of Kuwait and Saudi Arabia, and so acquiring a stranglehold over the global economy. The second Gulf war is being fought to enable the US – and only the US – to seize the same prize. Controlling Iraq's oil will not only allow the US to loosen its ties with Saudi Arabia and break the power of OPEC. It will give the US a powerful weapon against states that it regards as strategic rivals – above all, China. Over the next decade or so, as industrialization gathers speed,

China will become heavily dependent on oil supplies from the Gulf. So, still, will much of the rest of the world. If the Americans succeed in Iraq, they will have achieved what Saddam sought in vain a dozen years ago, an unchallengeable hold over the global economy.

The mismatch between the Bush administration's schemes for post-war Iraq and its geopolitical goals is clear enough. What is less clear is how this disconnection will be resolved. There is a widespread view in Europe, Asia and parts of the Middle East that, when the US discovers how difficult it is to govern post-war Iraq, it will do what it always does in such circumstances: pack up and leave others to police the ruins.

Ruling post-war Iraq will be even more demanding than ruling Afghanistan. It will involve more than rebuilding its infrastructure, a vast enterprise that the US, with its ballooning budget deficits and sagging economy, cannot sustain. It requires a willingness to accept casualties.

Will American voters be ready to pay, in higher taxes and a steady flow of body bags, the price of the Bush administration's grand strategy? If not, it is hard to see how the US can remain in Iraq for the long haul. Yet its retreat would amount to a devastating defeat, even in the aftermath of an overwhelming military victory. American power would be damaged beyond repair.

America's war in Iraq is the brainchild of neo-conservative intellectuals who despise the traditional diplomacy of the State Department and the seasoned caution of the professional soldiers at the Pentagon. Like the Jacobins in the late eighteenth century and Lenin's Bolsheviks in the early twentieth, the American neo-conservatives are revolutionary intellectuals with a very hazy view of the world in which most of humanity actually lives.

They do not grasp the depth and intensity of the hatred with which American power is viewed in the Middle East. They have closed their ears to the derision with which America is discussed in much of Europe and Asia, in sharp contrast to the wide admiration it enjoyed in the wake of 11 September. They have shut out of their minds awkward questions about how counter-terrorist strategies can be effective when some of the countries that know most about the threat, notably France, may in future be less ready to co-operate with the

US. They appear unaware of the mounting risks of trade war that go with the threat of American economic sanctions against European countries such as France and Germany. With all their talk of weapons of mass destruction, they seem oblivious to the accelerating proliferation produced by their own rejection of arms control agreements. They are animated by the faith that American firepower can protect America from attack; but America's superiority in high-tech weaponry cannot protect it against the sort of asymmetric warfare practised by Osama bin Laden.

This is an alarming state of affairs, but it is not surprising. It is a natural result of the bizarre worldview of the neo-conservatives who have taken America into Iraq. An exotic mix of Dr Strangelove and Dr Billy Graham, they believe that once the war is won they can convert the Middle East to US-style democracy. As Joseph de Maistre knew, such attempts to rewrite history always end in tears. The dark forebodings of that sage of old Europe may have missed the gains in human well-being that were being achieved even as he lived; but they were borne out by the murderous history of the twentieth century. It looks like they will be vindicated again.

2003

21

Torture: a modest proposal

A new phase in the evolution of liberal values is under way in the United States. America's most celebrated defender of civil liberties has initiated a new debate on torture. The context of Professor Alan Dershowitz's argument is American, but its meaning, like that of all true liberal principles, is universal. The force of his argument promises to transform liberal institutions throughout the world.

Using impeccable scholarship and the most rigorous logic, the distinguished Harvard legal scholar has demonstrated that nothing in the US Constitution forbids the use of torture. In interviews with the American media, Dershowitz has noted that while the Fifth Amendment prohibits self-incrimination, that means only that statements elicited by torture cannot be used as evidence against the person who has been tortured. It does not prohibit torture itself. Neither does the Eighth Amendment, since the ban on 'cruel and unusual punishments' applies only after an individual has been convicted. The belief that torture is unconstitutional in America may be widespread, but it is a fallacy, the product of rudimentary errors in legal reasoning.

Torture is permitted by the American Constitution, but it remains legally unregulated. To fill this gap, Dershowitz advocates the introduction of 'torture warrants'. Just as the FBI applies to the courts for search warrants, so it should be able to apply for torture warrants. At present, there is nothing in the law that explicitly authorizes the use of torture to extract information from terrorists. If it is used, as it often is, it is used extra-legally. As Dershowitz has pointed out, this is a highly unsatisfactory state of affairs. The rule of law is a core liberal value. It cannot be compromised in the fight against terrorism.

Torture, therefore, must cease to be something practised beyond the law; it must become part of normal judicial procedure.

If liberal thinkers in the past have shied away from rigorous thinking about torture, it is because they have been unduly influenced by history. Enlightenment thinkers such as Montesquieu and Voltaire campaigned indefatigably against judicial torture, and viewed its abolition as a vital step in human progress. In their own time, no doubt, they were right. These partisans of liberty were locked in conflict with the entrenched tyrannies of Europe's *ancien régime*. In attacking judicial torture, they were aligning themselves with the cause of progress and humanity.

The present situation is quite different. In the despotic, reactionary states against which Montesquieu and Voltaire struggled, torture was used to bolster arbitrary power. Now the liberal civilization of which they dreamt actually exists – in the United States of America. Today torture is used to defend free societies from attack by their enemies. Many liberals, especially in Europe, seem unable to grasp this elementary distinction. Mired in the past, they are blind to the emerging new regime of universal rights.

Where European thinkers have allowed recourse to torture at all, they have allowed it only in extreme situations. For Hobbes, justice was a set of conventions that societies adopted in order to achieve what he called 'commodious living', a peaceful, civilized existence. When order breaks down, in this view, the conventions of justice lapse. If a radiological bomb has been planted on the London Underground, torture may be the only way of disarming the device in time and thereby saving hundreds of thousands of lives. No government can avoid recourse to torture in such circumstances. Human beings turn to the state for security. If the state fails to provide it, it will be overthrown.

The trouble with this view of torture is that it remains stuck in the blood-soaked history of old Europe. It assumes that any act of torture leaves an indelible moral stain, even when the alternative, the destruction of many innocent lives, is unthinkable. It reduces torture to a desperate expedient whose rightful place, if it has one, is in darkened cellars. Seeing the struggle against terrorism in this way only weakens our resolve. Rather than wallowing in pessimism, we need to view the reintroduction of judicial torture as the next step in human progress.

Bringing torture out of the cellar into the clear light of day will require a far-reaching modernization of the law, but before that can be achieved we need a parallel reform in our thinking about human rights. Fortunately, we can draw on the most advanced thinking in contemporary liberal philosophy, the theory of justice elaborated by the late John Rawls. The eminent Harvard philosopher seems not to have grasped the full implications of his theory; but one of its central features is the insight that basic liberties cannot conflict. For European thinkers such as Hobbes and John Stuart Mill, one liberty collides with another; and the same freedom exercised by one person can conflict with that of another. Freedom of expression clashes with freedom from hate speech; one person's freedom of association (in a whites-only club, for example) is another's wrongful discrimination. Hobbes and Mill saw these as conflicts that we cannot hope to resolve completely; the best we can do is to strive for a compromise in which the competing claims are balanced against one another.

American liberal philosophers have rejected this messy and uninspiring view. They have shown that all our liberties belong in a single, unified system. When they are properly 'contoured' – that is, defined so that they cannot collide with one another – human rights need never conflict. Thus, when freedom of speech clashes with freedom from hate speech, it is denied that the latter is a genuine freedom.

The relevance of this insight to the question of torture should be self-evident. The belief that torture is always wrong is a prejudice inherited from an obsolete philosophy. We need to shed the belief that human rights are violated when a terrorist is tortured. As Rawls and others have shown, basic freedoms must form a coherent whole. Self-evidently, there can be no right to attack basic human rights. Therefore, once the proper legal procedures are in place, torturing terrorists cannot violate their rights. In fact, in a truly liberal society, terrorists have an inalienable right to be tortured.

This is what demonstrates the moral superiority of liberal societies over others, past and present. Other societies have degraded terrorists by subjecting them to lawless and unaccountable power. In the new world that is taking shape, terrorists, although they themselves degrade human rights by practising terrorism, will be afforded the full dignity of due legal process, even while being tortured. We can look forward to a time when this right will be available universally.

It is clear that the new regime of human rights that is emerging will not be confined to the United States. The US will not rest until other states have also adopted it. Developing a modern, liberal regime for the practice of torture will require reform of international treaties. The UN Declaration of Universal Human Rights embodies the discredited view that torture is inherently incompatible with respect for human rights. Along with other international treaties, it needs modernization. Securing agreement on the changes that are required may seem a daunting task. Our experience during the Iraq crisis suggests it is not impossible, however. Using its formidable resources, the US has persuaded a number of refractory states of the wisdom of launching a pre-emptive attack to dislodge the rights-violating regime of Saddam Hussein. It can surely be relied upon to secure a similar agreement around reform of the international law on torture.

There is a deeper reason for believing that the new regime of rights will be universal. Dershowitz's contention that torture is not forbidden by the US Constitution may look like a purely local argument; but that is to disregard the universal validity of the principles on which the Constitution is founded. Human rights are not just cultural or legal constructions, as fashionable Western relativists are fond of claiming. They are universal values. To deny the benefits of the new regime of rights to other cultures is to patronize them in a way that is reminiscent of the colonial era. If the new regime on torture is good enough for the US, who can say that it is not good for everyone?

In practice, there will be countries that resist the new order and refuse to reintroduce torture. Such rogue states are nothing new. Those that choose to defy the emerging consensus, however, must accept that they thereby place their legitimacy in question. States that refuse to modernize their laws on torture cannot expect the protection afforded them in the past by old-fashioned notions of sovereignty. They must expect increasing pressure to conform to global norms. If, despite all attempts at persuasion, they persist in opposing the international community, they will face action to enforce regime change.

No one will deny that the reintroduction of torture into the legal process will present some tricky problems. At present, torture is normally contracted out to less developed countries; but sending terrorists to friendly dictatorships for interrogation is hypocritical, and possibly inefficient. Surely it is far better that we do the job ourselves. If we do, however, we will need a trained body of interrogators, backed up by a staff of doctors, psychiatrists and other specialists. A new breed of lawyer will have to deal with the cases that are bound to arise when people suffer injury or death under interrogation. We shall need expert social workers, trained to help the families of subjects under interrogation. Universities in particular must show they are capable of delivering the skills that will be required.

It would be wrong to forget the needs of the interrogators themselves. In the past, torturers were shunned as outcasts, a tacit admission that they acted as the servants of tyrants. If we are to put interrogators to work in defence of liberal values, their role in the community must receive proper recognition. They will require intensive counselling to overcome the inevitable traumas that this difficult work involves. They must be enabled to see themselves as dedicated workers in the cause of progress. Psychotherapy must be available to help them avoid the negative self-image from which some torturers have suffered in the past. Unlike torturers who violated human rights at the behest of tyrants, interrogators who apply their skills to terrorists today are in the vanguard of human progress. In effect, they are practitioners of a new profession. Those who enter it must feel that society values them.

Changing the law on torture may seem to be only one more item on the agenda of modernization, part of the ongoing process of law reform in which archaic notions about double jeopardy and trial by jury have already been swept away. Still, the problems posed by changing our policies on torture are undoubtedly more challenging than those we have confronted and overcome in other areas of reform. Especially in Europe, the reforms that are so urgently needed run up against an ingrained conservatism that treats inherited patterns of thought as sacrosanct. It is almost as if Europeans no longer believe in progress.

We need nothing less than a fundamental advance in moral thinking. Liberals have often stressed that we must question the values we inherit from the past. The debate initiated by Alan Dershowitz shows that, in America at least, they are not afraid to apply this lesson. The world's finest liberal thinkers are applying themselves to the design of a modern regime of judicial torture. At a time when civilization is under daily threat, there can be no more hopeful sign.

2003

22

A modest defence of
George W. Bush

The intensifying war in Iraq looks like being a watershed in modern history. Critics of the war have focused on the suffering it has involved, and pointed to a number of errors that have been made in the course of the country's ongoing reconstruction. The suffering and mistakes are real enough, but they should not be allowed to conceal the much larger change of which the war is a part. Liberal societies are evolving rapidly to a higher stage of development, in which many of the traditions of the past are obsolete.

Under the aegis of the world's most advanced liberal state, torture and collective punishment have once again become normal practice in the conduct of war. To some this may seem anomalous, even contradictory. In reality it is the inner logic of liberal values applied in a time of unprecedented transformation. Liberalism is a universal creed, and the crusade for freedom cannot be fettered by archaic legal procedures. Treaties such as the Geneva Convention may have served the cause of freedom in the past, but today they are obstacles to liberal values. A global revolution is in progress in which such quaint relics have no place.

There are many signs that the new American administration has grasped this truth. In Europe the Bush White House is frequently caricatured as an ultra-reactionary cabal, but this only shows that Europeans are mired in the past. It requires only a little impartial observation – unclouded by the anti-Americanism that is so prevalent in Europe – to see that it is in fact an administration dominated by ultra-liberals. By no stretch of the imagination can the neo-conservatives who are the intellectual and moral backbone of the administration be called reactionaries, or indeed conservatives. As they have always made clear, they are radical progressives dedicated to a worldwide democratic revolution in which the freedoms enjoyed by Americans become the entitlement of all. This and nothing else is Mr Bush's mission.

Over the coming four years we can expect to see its commitment to universal freedom continued and extended. In Iraq the liberation of Fallujah will be repeated in other cities, and America will take the fight for freedom to another level by using the 'Salvador option'. The reform of antiquated legal and penal practices that have been pioneered in Guantanamo will be taken further. Serious consideration will be given to applying the policies of pre-emptive attack and regime change to Iran, and perhaps Syria. In these and other areas the Bush administration will be acting as the vanguard of human freedom, and it will receive the unswerving support of all those – such as Mr Blair – who understand that it is doing no more than apply core liberal values in the turbulent conditions of our time.

Despite the evidence of the Bush administration's actions there will be those who quibble with the idea that it is dedicated to liberal ideals. In order to dispel this confusion, let us consider the nature of liberalism, and what – if applied consistently – it means in practice. Take regime change. For true liberals sovereign states can only be accidents of history, with no claim to our allegiance. Human rights know no borders. Only individuals have rights, and when states violate them they can be invaded and overthrown. A new state can then be established, which respects its citizens as autonomous individuals.

As we all know, things are not always so straightforward. When we are liberating human beings from oppressive regimes we must reckon with the deadweight of history. Many, perhaps even most, human beings display an irrational attachment to their actually existing identity, and it cannot be taken for granted that they will automatically welcome the freedom that is offered them after regime change. They may fail to perceive their culture as oppressive, and be tempted to resist the advance of liberal values. If regime change is really to work in these circumstances the entire society must be rebuilt. However, in order for that to be possible it must first be destroyed.

It is this insight that underpins the initiative that is presently being implemented in Fallujah. There are those who say that the destruction of Fallujah is an act of collective punishment for the murder of four American contractors last April. From a narrow legal point of view this may be correct, but 'flattening Fallujah' – as the initiative has come to be described by US forces – has a larger significance. It is an early trial of the top-to-bottom reconstruction of Iraqi society that will be required if liberal values are to prevail in the country and the new regime is to survive.

According to media reports, US sources have indicated that Fallujah's 250,000 inhabitants will return to the devastated city only slowly. This is in order for them to be biometrically catalogued – fingerprinted and retina-scanned – and given an ID card which they will be required to display at all times. With these cards in view they will be free to move to a number of authorized destinations. Access in and out of the city will be controlled by well-fortified checkpoints, with authority to use deadly force if any of the city's residents violate the conditions under which they have been permitted to return. Private motor vehicles will be forbidden. With these policies in place, the entire population can be subject to continuous surveillance.

From an historical standpoint this may seem no more than another variation on the 'secure hamlet' programmes that were used by the British in Malaya and the Americans in Vietnam, with limited success – particularly in Vietnam. But looking to the future it can be seen as a necessary first step in a programme of social reconstruction in which Iraqis are being prepared for life as autonomous individuals. A modern liberal society cannot function if people are locked into networks of family and clan, and acquire their beliefs and values from authoritarian religious leaders. If there is to be anything resembling personal autonomy in the new Iraq these traditional structures must be dissolved. It is not enough to raze buildings and empty cities. The underlying framework of society must be deconstructed, and reconstituted on a liberal model. This is the experiment under way in Fallujah, which will surely be extended to Mosul, Ramadi and other cities.

It is an ambitious undertaking, with no guarantee of success. For those who are not used to it freedom can come as a shock, and in Iraq the shock of freedom has been considerable. A certain amount of disorder has resulted, and except in the Kurdish zones (where there are no American forces) the forces of fundamentalism and terrorism seem temporarily to have been strengthened. Further military action will undoubtedly be required, including intensive bombing to soften up rebel-held cities and the deployment of hit squads to eliminate insurgents on the model of the action taken by the Reagan administration in El Salvador some twenty years ago.

Still, further military action by America's forces in Iraq – however intensive – cannot be expected to eradicate the insurgency entirely. The problem of terrorism is global, and it demands a global solution. It is in order to tackle this problem that Mr Bush is extending the far-reaching reforms of penal and judicial practice implemented during the first administration. It has been announced that US authorities are planning to use the facility they have established at Guantanamo for the permanent detention without charge or trial of some of its inmates. Under these new arrangements, detainees will be housed in humane conditions that permit activity and socialization during what is expected to be lifelong confinement. The first Bush administration's directives allowing the use of modern interrogation techniques will not be altered – and rightly so. As I noted in a *New Statesman* essay some time ago ('A modest proposal', 17 February 2003), the common belief that torture is always contrary to liberal values has no rational basis. No one has the right to attack basic human rights – and terrorism is above all an attack on human rights. No human rights are violated when a terrorist is tortured.

The American authorities – closely followed, as ever, by the British – have understood this basic truth, and are setting up a permanent legal framework in which torture can be regulated. In a hearing of the Senate Judicial Committee last week, President Bush's nominee for the post of Attorney General, Alberto R. Gonzales, strongly defended his record as legal counsel in the first Bush administration. In a memorandum to the President in 2002, Gonzales had announced the 'new paradigm' that 'renders obsolete Geneva's strict limitations on questioning enemy prisoners and renders quaint some of its provisions'. Questioned by members of the Committee the presidential nominee held to this view, and went on to suggest that the US should consider renegotiating such treaties.

Whether or not the US formally reneges on the Geneva Convention, torture has been re-established in the legal process – not only in America but also in Britain, where courts may now accept evidence obtained by its use. These reforms will surely prevent many abuses. The administrative confusion that prevailed at Abu Ghraib, which allowed a number of embarrassing incidents to be widely publicized, is unlikely to recur.

It is no accident that torture has been reintroduced by the world's pre-eminent liberal state. To be sure, torture is used in many regimes – not only those inspired by liberal ideals. It is routinely employed in tyrannies and the ramshackle failed states that litter the globe; but only in liberal states is it part of a crusade for human rights. Liberalism is a project of universal emancipation, and torture will be necessary as long as the spread of liberal values is resisted. When the Bush administration authorizes the use of torture it does so in the cause of human progress.

It is this that explains why there has been so little resistance to its reintroduction. The reform of legal procedure required has been quite far-reaching, yet it has been implemented quickly and effectively, and with the evident support of enlightened opinion. It is encouraging to be able to report that most liberal commentators have tacitly endorsed the reform, while a growing number – so far mostly in the United States – actively defend it. Sadly, continental Europe – thoroughly corroded by moral relativism and lacking any deep commitment to the universality of liberal values – has been slow to accept the need for change.

No one can doubt the scale of the revolution that is under way throughout the world, but there may still be some who question that it is inspired by liberal values. The Iraq war is old-fashioned imperialism, they will say, not the next step in liberalism. There can be no doubt that Iraq's large oil reserves figured in the strategic calculations that were made in the White House in the run-up to war. The neo-conservatives who engineered American military intervention in Iraq have always made clear that securing control of the country's oil is a crucial part of their strategy of democratizing the Middle East, but this is far removed from anything resembling imperialism. Aside from exploiting them for their resources, European imperialists left the countries they conquered much as they were.

While they may have talked of spreading civilization, they did little in practice to alter the underlying societies. In contrast, America plans to transform Iraq into a freedom-loving democracy.

It is a task that must be completed in the fairly near future, or else support for the war may crumble in the US. Mr Bush would then be under pressure to declare victory and withdraw American forces before the job is done – an outcome Europeans have expected all along. The fragile interim regime would collapse and the country would descend into civil war and theocracy. Iraq's oil would pass out of US control – most likely into Iranian hands – and Saudi Arabia would face worsening instability, with potentially catastrophic consequences for the American economy. The entire American project in the Middle East would be endangered, and American power itself put at risk.

With these dangers in mind, Mr Bush may well decide to expand the war to Iran. Such a move will be risky. American forces are already somewhat stretched, and a further land invasion would pose some difficult logistical problems. Even if the US confines itself to bombing Iran it risks retaliation through an escalation of Iranian-supported unconventional warfare in Iraq.

However, the Bush administration's policy in the Middle East has never been one that seeks mere stability. In the words of the neo-conservatives who now more than ever shape its policies, the US aims to promote 'creative destruction' throughout the region. Iran's nuclear ambitions are in any case shifting the balance of power. In these conditions a widening of the war is the logic of events.

It is also the logic of liberal values. Liberalism is nothing if it is not a crusade, and the Middle East clearly needs conversion. The battle will be hard and long, and the hope of progress may sometimes be dim. Yet it will not be extinguished. It is burning even now, as Mr Bush and his neo-conservative strategists plan the next phase of the global democratic revolution.

2005

23

Evangelical atheism,
secular Christianity

An atmosphere of moral panic surrounds religion. Viewed not so long ago as a relic of superstition whose role in society was steadily declining, it is now demonized as the cause of many of the world's worst evils. As a result, there has been a sudden explosion in the literature of proselytizing atheism. A few years ago, it was difficult to persuade commercial publishers even to think of bringing out books on religion. Today, tracts against religion can be enormous money-spinners, with Richard Dawkins's *The God Delusion* and Christopher Hitchens's *God is Not Great* selling in the hundreds of thousands. For the first time in generations, scientists and philosophers, high-profile novelists and journalists are debating whether religion has a future. The intellectual traffic is not all one way. There have been counter-blasts for believers, such as *The Dawkins Delusion?* by the British theologian Alister McGrath and *The Secular Age* by the Canadian Catholic philosopher Charles Taylor. On the whole, however, the anti-God squad has dominated the sales charts, and it is worth asking why.

The abrupt shift in the perception of religion is only partly explained by terrorism. The 9/11 hijackers saw themselves as martyrs in a religious tradition, and Western opinion has accepted their self-image. And there are some who view the rise of Islamic fundamental-ism as a danger comparable with the worst that were faced by liberal societies in the twentieth century.

For Dawkins and Hitchens, Daniel Dennett and Martin Amis, Michel Onfray, Philip Pullman and others, religion in general is a poison that has fuelled violence and oppression throughout history, right up to the present day. The urgency with which they produce their anti-religious polemics suggests that a change has occurred as significant as the rise of terrorism: the tide of secularization has turned. These writers come from a generation schooled to think of religion as a throwback to an earlier stage of human development, which is bound to dwindle away as knowledge continues to increase. In the nineteenth century, when the scientific and industrial revolutions were changing society very quickly, this may not have been an unreasonable assumption. Dawkins, Hitchens and the rest may still believe that, over the long run, the advance of science will drive religion to the margins of human life, but this is now an article of faith rather than a theory based on evidence.

It is true that religion has declined sharply in a number of countries (Ireland is a recent example) and has not shaped everyday life for most people in Britain for many years. Much of Europe is clearly post-Christian. However, there is nothing to suggest that the move away from religion is irreversible, or that it is potentially universal. The US is no more secular today than it was 150 years ago, when de Tocqueville was amazed and baffled by its all-pervading religiosity. The secular era was in any case partly illusory. The mass political movements of the twentieth century were vehicles for myths inherited from religion, and it is no accident that religion is reviving now that these movements have collapsed. The current hostility to religion is a reaction against this turnabout. Secularization is in retreat, and the result is the appearance of an evangelical type of atheism not seen since Victorian times.

As in the past, this is a type of atheism that mirrors the faith it rejects. Philip Pullman's *Northern Lights* – a subtly allusive, multi-layered allegory, recently adapted into a Hollywood blockbuster, *The Golden Compass* – is a good example. Pullman's parable concerns far more than the dangers of authoritarianism. The issues it raises are essentially religious, and it is deeply indebted to the faith it attacks. Pullman has stated that his atheism was formed in the Anglican tradition, and there are many echoes of Milton and Blake in his work. His largest debt to this tradition is the notion of free will. The central thread of the story is the assertion of free will against faith. The young heroine Lyra Belacqua sets out to thwart the Magisterium – Pullman's metaphor for Christianity – because it aims to deprive humans of their ability to choose their own course in life, which she believes would destroy what is most human in them. But the idea of free will that informs liberal notions of personal autonomy is biblical in origin (think of the Genesis story). The belief that exercising free will is part of being human is a legacy of faith, and like most varieties of atheism today, Pullman's is a derivative of Christianity.

Proselytizing atheism renews some of the worst features of Christianity and Islam. Just as much as these religions, it is a project of universal conversion. Evangelical atheists never doubt that human life can be transformed if everyone accepts their view of things, and they are certain that one way of living – their own, suitably embellished – is right for everybody. To be sure, atheism need not be a missionary creed of this kind. It is entirely reasonable to have no religious beliefs, and yet be friendly to religion. It is a funny sort of humanism that condemns an impulse that is peculiarly human. Yet that is what evangelical atheists do when they demonize religion.

A curious feature of this kind of atheism is that some of its most fervent missionaries are philosophers. Daniel Dennett's *Breaking the Spell: Religion as a Natural Phenomenon* claims to sketch a general theory of religion. In fact, it is mostly a polemic against American Christianity. This parochial focus is reflected in Dennett's view of religion, which for him means the belief that some kind of supernatural agency (whose approval believers seek) is needed to explain the way things are in the world. For him, religions are efforts at doing something science does better – they are rudimentary or abortive theories, or else nonsense. 'The proposition that God exists', he writes severely, 'is not even a theory.' But religions do not consist of propositions struggling to become theories. The incomprehensibility of the divine is at the heart of Eastern Christianity, while in Orthodox Judaism practice tends to have priority over doctrine. Buddhism has always recognized that in spiritual matters truth is ineffable, as do Sufi traditions in Islam. Hinduism has never defined itself by anything as simplistic as a creed. It is only some Western Christian traditions, under the influence of Greek philosophy, which have tried to turn religion into an explanatory theory.

The notion that religion is a primitive version of science was popularized in the late nineteenth century in J. G. Frazer's survey of the myths of primitive peoples, *The Golden Bough: A Study in Magic and Religion.* For Frazer, religion and magical thinking were closely linked. Rooted in fear and ignorance, they were vestiges of human infancy that would disappear with the advance of knowledge. Dennett's atheism is not much more than a revamped version of Frazer's Positivism. The Positivists believed that with the development of transport and communication – in their day, canals and the telegraph – irrational thinking would wither way, along with the religions of the past. Despite the history of the past century, Dennett believes much the same. In an interview that appears on the website of the Edge Foundation (edge.org) under the title 'The Evaporation of the Powerful Mystique of Religion', he predicts that 'in about 25 years almost all religions will have evolved into very different phenomena, so much so that in most quarters religion will no longer command the awe that it does today.' He is confident that this will come about, he tells us, mainly because of 'the worldwide spread of information technology (not just the internet, but cell phones and portable radios and television)'. The philosopher has evidently not reflected on the ubiquity of mobile phones among the Taliban, or the emergence of a virtual al-Qaeda on the web.

The growth of knowledge is a fact only post-modern relativists deny. Science is the best tool we have for forming reliable beliefs about the world, but it does not differ from religion by revealing a bare truth that religions veil in dreams. Both science and religion are systems of symbols that serve human needs – in the case of science, for prediction and control. Religions have served many purposes, but at bottom they answer to a need for meaning that is met by myth rather than explanation. A great deal of modern thought consists of secular myths – hollowed-out religious narratives translated into pseudo-science. Dennett's notion that new communications technologies will fundamentally alter the way human beings think is just such a myth.

In *The God Delusion*, Dawkins attempts to explain the appeal of religion in terms of the theory of memes, vaguely defined conceptual units that compete with one another in a parody of natural selection. He recognizes that, because humans have a universal tendency to religious belief, it must have had some evolutionary advantage, but today, he argues, it is perpetuated mainly through bad education.

From a Darwinian standpoint, the crucial role Dawkins gives to education is puzzling. Human biology has not changed greatly over recorded history, and if religion is hardwired in the species, it is difficult to see how a different kind of education could alter this. Yet Dawkins seems convinced that, if it were not inculcated in schools and families, religion would die out. This is a view that has more in common with a certain type of fundamentalist theology than with Darwinian theory, and I cannot help being reminded of the evangelical Christian who assured me that children reared in a chaste environment would grow up without illicit sexual impulses.

Dawkins's 'memetic theory of religion' is a classic example of the nonsense that is spawned when Darwinian thinking is applied outside its proper sphere. Along with Dennett, who also holds to a version of the theory, Dawkins maintains that religious ideas survive because they would be able to survive in any 'meme pool', or else because they are part of a 'memeplex' that includes similar memes, such as the idea that, if you die as a martyr, you will enjoy seventy-two virgins. Unfortunately, the theory of memes is science only in the sense that Intelligent Design is science. Strictly speaking, it is not even a theory. Talk of memes is just the latest in a succession of ill-judged Darwinian metaphors.

Dawkins compares religion to a virus: religious ideas are memes that infect vulnerable minds, especially those of children. Biological metaphors may have their uses – the minds of evangelical atheists seem particularly prone to infection by religious memes, for example. At the same time, analogies of this kind are fraught with peril. Dawkins makes much of the oppression perpetrated by religion, which is real enough. He gives less attention to the fact that some of the worst atrocities of modern times were committed by regimes that claimed scientific sanction for their crimes. Nazi 'scientific racism' and Soviet 'dialectical materialism' reduced the unfathomable complexity of human lives to the deadly simplicity of a scientific formula. In each case, the science was bogus, but it was accepted as genuine at the time, and not only in the regimes in question. Science is as liable to be used for inhumane purposes as any other human institution. Indeed, given the enormous authority science enjoys, the risk of it being used in this way is greater.

Contemporary opponents of religion display a marked lack of interest in the historical record of atheist regimes. In *The End of Faith: Religion, Terror and the Future of Reason*, the American writer Sam Harris argues that religion has been the chief source of violence and oppression in history. He recognizes that secular despots such as Stalin and Mao inflicted terror on a grand scale, but maintains that the oppression they practised had nothing to do with their ideology of 'scientific atheism' – what was wrong with their regimes was that they were tyrannies. But might there not be a connection between the attempt to eradicate religion and the loss of freedom? It is unlikely that Mao, who launched his assault on the people and culture of Tibet with the slogan 'Religion is poison', would have agreed that his atheist worldview had no bearing on his policies. It is true he was worshipped as a semi-divine figure – as Stalin was in the Soviet Union. But, in developing these cults, Communist Russia and China were not backsliding from atheism. They were demonstrating what happens when atheism becomes a political project. The invariable result is an ersatz religion that can only be maintained by tyrannical means.

Something like this occurred in Nazi Germany. Dawkins dismisses any suggestion that the crimes of the Nazis could be linked with atheism. 'What matters', he declares in *The God Delusion*, 'is not whether Hitler and Stalin were atheists, but whether atheism systematically influences people to do bad things. There is not the smallest evidence that it does.' This is simple-minded reasoning. Always a tremendous booster of science, Hitler was much impressed by vulgarized Darwinism and by theories of eugenics that had developed from Enlightenment philosophies of materialism. He used Christian anti-Semitic demonology in his persecution of Jews, and the Churches collaborated with him to a horrifying degree. But it was the Nazi belief in race as a scientific category that opened the way to a crime without parallel in history. Hitler's worldview was that of many semi-literate people in inter-war Europe, a hotchpotch of counterfeit science and animus towards religion. There can be no reasonable doubt that this was a type of atheism, or that it helped make Nazi crimes possible.

Nowadays most atheists are avowed liberals. What they want – so they will tell you – is not an atheist regime, but a secular state in which religion has no role. They clearly believe that, in a state of this kind, religion will tend to decline. But America's secular constitution has not ensured a secular politics. Christian fundamentalism is more powerful in the US than in any other country, while it has very little influence in Britain, which has an established Church. Contemporary critics of religion go much further than demanding disestablishment. It is clear that Dawkins wants to eliminate all traces of religion from public institutions. Awkwardly, many of the concepts he deploys – including the idea of religion itself – have been shaped by monotheism. Lying behind secular fundamentalism is a conception of history that derives from religion.

A. C. Grayling provides an example of the persistence of religious categories in secular thinking in his *Towards the Light: The Story of the Struggles for Liberty and Rights that Made the Modern West*. As the title indicates, Grayling's book is a type of sermon. Its aim is to reaffirm what he calls 'a Whig view of the history of the modern west', the core of which is that 'the west displays progress'. The Whigs were pious Christians, who believed that divine providence arranged history to culminate in English institutions, and Grayling too believes that history is 'moving in the right direction'. No doubt there have been setbacks – he mentions Nazism and Communism in passing, devoting a few sentences to them. But these disasters were peripheral. They do not reflect on the central tradition of the modern West, which has always been devoted to liberty, and which – Grayling asserts – is inherently antagonistic to religion. 'The history of liberty', he writes, 'is another chapter – and perhaps the most important of all – in the great quarrel between religion and secularism.' The possibility that radical versions of secular thinking may have contributed to the development of Nazism and Communism is not mentioned. More even than the eighteenth-century Whigs, who were shaken by French Terror, Grayling has no doubt as to the direction of history.

But the belief that history is a directional process is as faith-based as anything in the Christian catechism. Secular thinkers such as Grayling reject the idea of providence, but they continue to think humankind is moving towards a universal goal – a civilization based on science that will eventually encompass the entire species. In pre-Christian

Europe, human life was understood as a series of cycles; history was seen as tragic or comic rather than redemptive. With the arrival of Christianity, it came to be believed that history had a predetermined goal, which was human salvation. Though they suppress their religious content, secular humanists continue to cling to similar beliefs. One does not want to deny anyone the consolations of a faith, but it is obvious that the idea of progress in history is a myth created by the need for meaning.

The problem with the secular narrative is not that it assumes progress is inevitable (in many versions, it does not). It is the belief that the sort of advance that has been achieved in science can be reproduced in ethics and politics. In fact, while scientific knowledge increases cumulatively, nothing of the kind happens in society. Slavery was abolished in much of the world during the nineteenth century, but it returned on a vast scale in Nazism and Communism, and still exists today. Torture was prohibited in international conventions after the Second World War, only to be adopted as an instrument of policy by the world's pre-eminent liberal regime at the beginning of the twenty-first century. Wealth has increased, but it has been repeatedly destroyed in wars and revolutions. People live longer and kill one another in larger numbers. Knowledge grows, but human beings remain much the same.

Belief in progress is a relic of the Christian view of history as a universal narrative, and an intellectually rigorous atheism would start by questioning it. This is what Nietzsche did when he developed his critique of Christianity in the late nineteenth century, but almost none of today's secular missionaries have followed his example. One need not be a great fan of Nietzsche to wonder why this is so. The reason, no doubt, is that he did not assume any connection between atheism and liberal values – on the contrary, he viewed liberal values as an offspring of Christianity and condemned them partly for that reason. In contrast, evangelical atheists have positioned themselves as defenders of liberal freedoms – rarely inquiring where these freedoms have come from, and never allowing that religion may have had a part in creating them.

Among contemporary anti-religious polemicists, only the French writer Michel Onfray has taken Nietzsche as his point of departure.

In some ways, Onfray's *In Defence of Atheism* is superior to anything English-speaking writers have published on the subject. Refreshingly, he recognizes that evangelical atheism is an unwitting imitation of traditional religion: 'Many militants of the secular cause look astonishingly like clergy. Worse: like caricatures of clergy.' More clearly than his Anglo-Saxon counterparts, Onfray understands the formative influence of religion on secular thinking. Yet he seems not to notice that the liberal values he takes for granted were partly shaped by Christianity and Judaism. The key liberal theorists of toleration are John Locke, who defended religious freedom in explicitly Christian terms, and Benedict Spinoza, a Jewish rationalist who was also a mystic. Yet Onfray has nothing but contempt for the traditions from which these thinkers emerged – particularly Jewish monotheism: 'We do not possess an official certificate of birth for worship of one God,' he writes. 'But the family line is clear: the Jews invented it to ensure the coherence, cohesion and existence of their small, threatened people.' Here Onfray passes over an important distinction. It may be true that Jews first developed monotheism, but Judaism has never been a missionary faith. In seeking universal conversion, evangelical atheism belongs with Christianity and Islam.

In today's anxiety about religion, it has been forgotten that most of the faith-based violence of the past century was secular in nature. To some extent, this is also true of the current wave of terrorism. Islamism is a patchwork of movements, not all violently jihadist and some strongly opposed to al-Qaeda, most of them partly fundamentalist and aiming to recover the lost purity of Islamic traditions, while at the same time taking some of their guiding ideas from radical secular ideology. There is a deal of fashionable talk of Islamo-Fascism, and Islamist parties have some features in common with inter-war Fascist movements, including anti-Semitism. But Islamists owe as much, if not more, to the far left, and it would be more accurate to describe many of them as Islamo-Leninists. Islamist techniques of terror also have a pedigree in secular revolutionary movements. The executions of hostages in Iraq are copied in exact theatrical detail from European 'revolutionary tribunals' in the 1970s, such as that staged by the Red Brigades when they murdered the former Italian Prime Minister Aldo Moro in 1978.

The influence of secular revolutionary movements on terrorism extends well beyond Islamists. In *God is Not Great*, Christopher Hitchens notes that, long before Hizbullah and al-Qaeda, the Tamil Tigers of Sri Lanka pioneered what he rightly calls 'the disgusting tactic of suicide murder'. He omits to mention that the Tigers are Marxist-Leninists who, while recruiting mainly from the island's Hindu population, reject religion in all its varieties. Tiger suicide bombers do not go to certain death in the belief that they will be rewarded in any post-mortem paradise. Nor did the suicide bombers who drove American and French forces out of Lebanon in the 1980s, most of whom belonged to organizations of the left such as the Lebanese Communist Party. These secular terrorists believed they were expediting an historical process from which will come a world better than any that has ever existed. It is a view of things more remote from human realities, and more reliably lethal in its consequences, than most religious myths.

It is not necessary to believe in any narrative of progress to think liberal societies are worth resolutely defending. No one can doubt that they are superior to the tyranny imposed by the Taliban on Afghanistan, for example. The issue is one of proportion. Ridden with conflicts and lacking the industrial base of Communism and Nazism, Islamism is nowhere near a danger of the magnitude of those that were faced down in the twentieth century. A greater menace is posed by North Korea, which far surpasses any Islamist regime in its record of repression and clearly does possess some kind of nuclear capability. Evangelical atheists rarely mention it. Hitchens is an exception, but when he describes his visit to the country it is only to conclude that the regime embodies 'a debased yet refined form of Confucianism and ancestor worship'. As in Russia and China, the noble humanist philosophy of Marxist-Leninism is innocent of any responsibility.

Writing of the Trotskyite–Luxemburgist sect to which he once belonged, Hitchens confesses sadly: 'There are days when I miss my old convictions as if they were an amputated limb.' He need not worry. His record on Iraq shows he has not lost the will to believe. The effect of the American-led invasion has been to deliver most of the country outside the Kurdish zone into the hands of an Islamist elective theocracy, in which women, gays and religious minorities are more oppressed than at any time in Iraq's history. The idea that Iraq could become a secular democracy – which Hitchens ardently promoted – was possible only as an act of faith.

In *The Second Plane*, Martin Amis writes: 'Opposition to religion already occupies the high ground, intellectually and morally.' Amis is sure religion is a bad thing, and that it has no future in the West. In the author of *Koba the Dread: Laughter and the Twenty Million* – a forensic examination of self-delusion in the pro-Soviet Western intelligentsia – such confidence is surprising. The intellectuals whose folly Amis dissects turned to Communism in some sense as a surrogate for religion, and ended up making excuses for Stalin. Are there really no comparable follies today? Some neo-cons – such as Tony Blair, who will soon be teaching religion and politics at Yale – combine their belligerent progressivism with religious belief, though of a kind Augustine and Pascal might find hard to recognize. Most are secular utopians, who justify pre-emptive war and excuse torture as leading to a radiant future in which democracy will be adopted universally. Even on the high ground of the West, messianic politics has not lost its dangerous appeal.

Religion has not gone away. Repressing it is like repressing sex, a self-defeating enterprise. In the twentieth century, when it commanded powerful states and mass movements, it helped engender totalitarianism. Today, the result is a climate of hysteria. Not everything in religion is precious or deserving of reverence. There is an inheritance of anthropocentrism, the ugly fantasy that the Earth exists to serve humans, which most secular humanists share. There is the claim of religious authorities, also made by atheist regimes, to decide how people can express their sexuality, control their fertility and end their lives, which should be rejected categorically. Nobody should be allowed to curtail freedom in these ways, and no religion has the right to break the peace.

The attempt to eradicate religion, however, only leads to it reappearing in grotesque and degraded forms. A credulous belief in world revolution, universal democracy or the occult powers of mobile phones is more offensive to reason than the mysteries of religion, and less likely to survive in years to come. Victorian poet Matthew Arnold wrote of believers being left bereft as the tide of faith ebbs away. Today secular faith is ebbing, and it is the apostles of unbelief who are left stranded on the beach.

2008

PART FIVE

After Progress

24

An agenda for Green conservatism

INTRODUCTION

Man's conquest of nature, if the dreams of some scientific planners are realized, means the rule of a few hundreds of men over billions upon billions of men. There neither is nor can be any simple increase of power on man's side. Each power won by man is a power over man as well. Each advance leaves him weaker as well as stronger. In every victory, besides being the general who triumphs, he is also the prisoner who follows in the triumphal car. C. S. Lewis[1]

It is fair to say that, on the whole, conservative thought has been hostile to environmental concerns over the past decade or so in Britain, Europe and the United States. Especially in America, environmental concerns have been represented as anti-capitalist propaganda under another flag. In most Western countries, conservatives have accused environmentalists of misuse of science, of propagating an apocalyptic mentality, and of being enemies of the central institutions of modern civil society. Nor are these accusations always wide of the mark. Indeed, in considerable measure they show conservatives endorsing the self-image of the Greens as inheritors of the radical protest movements of earlier times, and as making common cause with contemporary radical movements, such as feminism and anti-colonialism. In other words, both the Greens themselves and their conservative critics have been happy to share the assumption that socialism and environmental concern go together.

The aim of this present argument is to contest that consensus. Far from having a natural home on the left, concern for the integrity of the common environment, human as well as ecological, is most in harmony with the outlook of traditional conservatism of the British and European varieties. Many of the central conceptions of traditional conservatism have a natural congruence with Green concerns: the Burkean idea of the social contract, not as an agreement among anonymous, ephemeral individuals, but as a compact between the generations of the living, the dead and those yet unborn; Tory scepticism about progress, and awareness of its ironies and illusions; conservative resistance to untried novelty and large-scale social experiments; and, perhaps most especially, the traditional conservative tenet that individual flourishing can occur only in the context of forms of common life. All of these and other conservative ideas have clear affinities with Green thought, when it is not merely another scourge of the inherited institutions of civil society. The inherent tendency of Green thought is thus not radical but the opposite: it is conservative. At the same time, the absorption of Green concerns into conservative thinking will necessitate some radical changes within conservative philosophy and policy, particularly within those strands of conservative thought that have, during the past decade or so, come to be animated by neo-liberal doctrines whose origins are, in fact, not conservative at all, but rather in the classical liberal rationalist and libertarian ideologies which were spawned in the wake of the Enlightenment.

In one of its thrusts, the argument advanced here is a further critique, building on earlier criticisms I have developed elsewhere,[2] of the neo-liberal doctrines of the New Right, within the particular context of environmental policy. This New Right ideology is, in effect, the most recent eruption of secular liberal utopianism, a species of rationalism in politics[3] which affirms that the dilemmas of political life can be resolved, once and for all, by the application of a system of first principles for the regulation of governmental activity. This rationalist dogma is here rejected, as novel problems arise for government from people's unanticipated interactions with the natural environment. But the conception of human nature, and of human well-being, that underlies this species of liberal rationalism is also rejected. On the view developed here, though human beings need a sphere of independent action, and so of liberty, if they are to flourish, their deepest need is a home, a network of common practices and inherited traditions that confers on them the blessing of a settled identity. Indeed, without the undergirding support of a framework of common culture, the freedom of the individual so cherished by liberalism is of little value, and will not long survive. Human beings are above all fragile creatures, for whom the meaning of life is a local matter that is easily dissipated: their freedom is worth while and meaningful to them only against a background of common cultural forms. Such forms cannot be created anew for each generation. We are not like the butterfly, whose generations are unknown to each other; we are a familial and historical species, for whom the past must have authority (that of memory) if we are to have identity, and whose lives are in part self-created narratives, woven from the received text of the common life. Where change is incessant or pluralism too insistent, where the links between the generations are broken or the shared raiment of the common culture is in tatters, human beings will not flourish. They will wither, or else fall into anomic violence. Insofar as neo-liberalism has been an ideology of radical change, whose debts are to liberal individualism rather than to traditional conservatism, it has tended to reinforce the disintegrative processes of modernist societies. Understanding this fact may help to restore a balance within conservative philosophy which has in recent years shown signs of being lost.

It is also an attempt to correct some of the radical excesses of Green theory. On the whole, Green theory is inspired by an anti-capitalist mentality that neglects the environmental benefits of market institutions and suppresses the ecological costs of central planning. In the real world, environmental degradation has been at its most catastrophic where, as under the institutions of the former Soviet system, planners are unconstrained in their activities by clearly defined property rights or by the scarcities embodied in a properly functioning price mechanism. (The situation appears to be little different, or worse, in the People's Republic of China.) For reasons that are perfectly general, and which will be explored in greater detail later in the argument, environmental despoliation on a vast scale is an inexorable result of industrial development in the absence of the core institutions of a market economy, private property and the price mechanism. This is a vital truth as yet little understood by Green theorists, even though it is all too plain in the post-Communist countries.

Green theorists also harbour an animus, very often, to the distinctive technological and social forms of modern life, which is quixotic and counter-productive. It is eminently sensible for Green theorists to seek for forms of technology and of productive association which are less environmentally invasive, and so more sustainable over the long term, than many of those that characterize the highly industrialized societies of our age; but it is absurd to suppose that we can return to the technologies or the productive associations of pre-industrial societies, and it is unreasonable to stigmatize some of the least invasive modern technologies, such as nuclear power, as especially environmentally hazardous. It is reasonable to be concerned about the growth of mega-cities, such as Shanghai and Mexico City, in which vast aggregations of human beings are concentrated, without the amenities or the public spaces that distinguished the historic European cities. This is not a reason for hostility to cities – one of humankind's most civilized institutional inventions – or for rural nostalgia, but rather a ground for a project of restoration of the city in something akin to its classical historic forms. There is much that is amiss in modernity, and much to reject in modernism; but we can hope only to temper the modern age and its ills, not to abolish them, as some of the Green theorists suppose.

As against the neo-liberal strand within recent conservatism, on the other hand, my argument is that market institutions, although they are indispensably necessary, are insufficient as guarantors of the integrity of the environment, human as well as natural. They must be supplemented by governmental activity when, as with the restoration or preservation of the historic European city, private investment cannot by itself sustain the public environment of the common life. The environmental case against doctrinal neo-liberalism is yet stronger than this. The unfettered workings of market institutions may damage the natural and human environments, even if it is true (as I argue later) that in most cases they act to protect them. Though there is in many Western countries a good case for freer immigration, a policy of *laissez-faire* in immigration, by undoing settled communities, mixing inassimilable cultures and thereby triggering dormant racisms, would serve only to undermine the political stability on which successful market institutions depend for their existence; yet such a policy continues to be advocated by fundamentalist liberals who cannot, or will not, perceive that labour is a factor of production which is categorically distinct from others, inasmuch as it is wholly constituted by human beings, whose relations with each other are not at all like those of different sorts of assets in a global portfolio. Equally, despite the economic rationality of global free trade, the real evils of trade war, and the fact that multilateral free trade pacts remain often beneficial, global free trade as envisaged, say, in recent GATT discussions can often have disastrous effects on local and regional communities, wiping out entire ways of life while supplying no sustainable alternatives. Mechanical application of the simplistic panaceas of neo-liberalism spells ruin for communities in many parts of the world and, parenthetically, it is a recipe for disaster throughout the post-Communist world.

Neo-liberal ideas have been attractive to conservatives in many Western countries, and in parts of the post-Communist world, partly in virtue of the real excesses of twentieth-century statism, to which they provide a healthy corrective. They are nevertheless a distraction from the central concerns of traditional conservatism, and they inhibit conservatives in addressing the problems that arise for them in an age in which economic growth on conventional lines has begun to come up against genuine environmental constraints. Conservative policy in the post-war world has been governed by the strategy of securing legitimacy for market institutions by so aligning the electoral and the economic cycles as to yield uninterrupted economic growth. This is a strategy which, in neglecting the deeper sources of allegiance, is risky when the economy turns sour. It offers nothing in an age – not so far off, and perhaps imminent in some Western countries – when economic growth on the old model is not sustainable, and has in any case come to a shuddering halt.

The prospect of open-ended growth in the quantity of goods, services and people is in any case hardly a conservative vision. Though the eradication of involuntary poverty remains a noble cause, the project of promoting maximal economic growth is, perhaps, the most vulgar ideal ever put before suffering humankind. The myth of open-ended progress is not an ennobling myth, and it should form no part of conservative philosophy. The task of conservative policy is not to spread the malady of infinite aspiration, to which our species is in any case all too prone, but to keep in good repair those institutions and practices whereby human beings come to be reconciled with their circumstances, and so can live and die in dignified and meaningful fashion, despite the imperfections of their condition. Chief among all of the objects of conservative policy, for this reason, is the replenishment of the common life; the shared environment in which, as members of communities and practitioners of a common culture, people can find enjoyment and consolation.

As against the values and policies of neo-liberalism, which tend to deplete further and even to destroy the resources of this common life, a Green conservatism animated by the concerns of traditional Toryism would seek, wherever this is feasible, to repair and renew the common life. It would acknowledge the vital role of the core institutions of civil society, private property and contractual liberty under the rule of law, in any civilized modern state, and, more particularly, in any polity which seeks to protect the common environment, human and natural. It would recognize that unlimited government has been the greatest destroyer of the common environment in our age, and would accordingly support measures for the limitation of government, often by the devolution or hiving off of its activities. It would affirm that governmental monopoly, or near-monopoly, in a variety of vital services – perhaps even in the supply of money – has proved an evil against which the extension of market institutions may be the best remedy. It would nevertheless resist making a fetish of market institutions: it would be ready to extend them where their absence is a cause of environmental degradation (as when environmental depletion takes place through the occurrence of tragedies of the commons); but it would also be ready to curb them, when their workings are demonstrably harmful to the common life, and when the costs of such curbs are not prohibitive. It would recognize that the introduction into such services as education and health care of market institutions might often be an appropriate measure, helping to correct their tendencies to bureaucratization, and to make them more responsive to the needs of individuals.

At the same time, it would not follow the neo-liberals in supposing that marketization is the sovereign remedy for the failures of modern education and health care, which derive, in large part at least, from their ever more pronounced character as industries, conceived as adjuncts to governmental economic policies, rather than as forms of practice each having its own *telos*. The most profound failings of modern education and of health care require remedies more radical than any that neo-liberals have proposed, and they demand the adoption towards current educational and medical practice of an attitude that is far removed from uncritical reverence or unreflective conservatism. There is nothing at all unreasonable about a contemporary conservative adopting such radical attitudes to contemporary institutions, since these are in substantial part the results of very recent, and often very ill-considered, innovations. In respect of education and health, in particular, my argument will be that the conservative goal of restoring to them a distinctive *telos* and a traditional ethos will demand rather radical reforms in current practice, going well beyond the extension into them of market processes which, though it may enhance individual choice and the quality of service, does not by itself make of contemporary educational and medical institutions guardians of conservative values. Achieving this latter goal may require the radical remedies of disestablishing the school and curtailing the professional monopoly of doctors; just as conserving and restoring the historic European city may demand drastic controls on the private passenger car, or recovering personal responsibility for health may demand conferring on patients the responsibility of choosing when it is best that life be ended. These are only a few instances of an ancient paradox, with which the modern world abounds in examples, that conservatives cannot help becoming radicals, when current practice embodies the hubristic and careless projects of recent generations, or has been distorted by technological innovations whose consequences for human well-being we have not weighed. This is a paradox that a Green conservatism will often confront. It will confront it at a most fundamental level, inasmuch as Green thought – especially that variety of Green thought that is associated with the theory of deep ecology and with the Gaia hypothesis – embodies a challenge to the ruling worldview of the age, which is a sort of scientific fundamentalism allied with liberal humanism. This is a worldview which is thoroughly alien to conservative philosophy in virtue of the nihilism that it breeds in relations with nature and with fellow humans but which conservatives are nevertheless hesitant to resist, since it is associated with the prestige of science as the animating force of modernity. This scientific worldview must be brought into question among conservatives, as it has already been among Greens, and it is part of the agenda of Green conservatism that it be so questioned. Green conservatism will, first and last, repudiate the hubristic rationalist ideology that suffuses neo-liberal thought and policy, which has captured and subjugated recent conservatism, but which is merely the most recent excrescence of modernist humanism – a creed that both genuine conservatives and Greens have every reason to reject.

THEORY

Ecological Functions of Market Institutions

> *The rational herdsman concludes that the only sensible course for him to pursue is to add another animal to his herd. And another; and another ... But this is the conclusion reached by each and every rational herdsman sharing a commons. Therein is the tragedy. Each man is locked into a system that compels him to increase his herd without limit – in a world that is limited. Ruin is the destination toward which all men rush, each pursuing his own best interest in a society that believes in the freedom of the commons. Freedom in the commons brings ruin to all.*
>
> Garret Hardin[4]

The central ecological function of market institutions is in the avoidance of the tragedy of the commons.[5] This occurs when, in the absence of private or several property rights in a valuable natural resource, separate economic actors – individuals, families, corporations or even sovereign states – are constrained to deplete the resource by over-use, given their realization that, if they do not do so, others will. Tragedies of the commons occur because, in the absence of the institutions of private property, no one has an incentive to adopt a long-term view of the utilization of resources. Tragedies of the commons also have features akin to those of Prisoner's Dilemmas,[6] in that each has an overriding incentive to do what is not in his or her own interest – in this case, to run down the resource to extinction. Examples of such tragedies are manifold in environmental literature, unfortunately, but two may suffice to illuminate the central point about them. If a forest, say, belongs to no one, then no one will have an interest in planting the next generation of trees, or, for that matter, in developing logging techniques that leave saplings standing. Since no one stands to benefit from such foresight, no one will exercise it. Hence the reckless deforestation, for agricultural and other purposes, including timber harvesting, that has occurred in parts of Latin America and South-East Asia. Or consider natural resources in fish. Insofar as shoals of fish are in the commons – unowned assets in a state of nature – they will be harvested to extinction, since the only operative incentives on fisherfolk will be to catch the fish and reap a fast profit on them, before their competitors do. True, where fisherfolk live in isolated communities without competitors for their resources, they may develop traditions which limit the overexploitation of fish; but these will always go by the board when competitive fishing communities, or enterprises, come on to the scene. The moral of this example is a perfectly general one. Competition for natural resources, living or otherwise, in the absence of private property rights in them, spells inexorable ruin for such resources. The commons will always be doomed, and its resources fated to disappear, when there is a diversity of competing demands upon them. The lesson – rightly drawn by free market economists – is that the extension of private property institutions to cover resources, such as shoals of fish, hitherto in the commons, is a potent corrective to the over-exploitation of the natural environment.

Market institutions have another crucial ecological virtue: that of reflecting through the price mechanism shifting patterns of resource-scarcities. In the broadest terms, market pricing overcomes, at least partially, the otherwise insuperable epistemic dilemma facing all economic agents: that of utilizing information which is dispersed throughout society and which, in virtue of its often fleeting and circumstantial nature, and the fact that it is sometimes embodied in dispositions and traditions whose content is not fully articulable, cannot be collected or gathered together by any planning agency.[7] By allowing this, often tacit and embodied, knowledge to be expressed in price information available to all, market institutions mitigate the ignorance in which we must all act in our capacity as economic agents. They in this way allow for a measure of rationality in the allocation of resources, and of efficiency in their uses, that is unavoidably denied to central planners and their agents. The point may be put differently. Critics of central planning often focus on the perverse incentives that socialist institutions create for planners, bureaucrats, managers and workers. They point to the political factors that skew the allocation of capital into unproductive enterprises, the reinforcement of risk-aversion (and consequent low levels of technological innovation) that planning institutions yield via their inability to attach costs to unexploited opportunities, the disastrous state of labour morale in the absence of rewards for real productivity, and so on. All of these observations are pertinent, but they miss the mark in failing to note that resource-allocation would be immensely wasteful and chaotic under socialist institutions even if they did not have this perverse impact on incentives, simply in virtue of the fact that planners, managers and workers would still lack the information regarding resource-scarcities that only market pricing can make available to them. Even perfect servants of the plan could not help but generate economic chaos. In so doing, they would also, no less inexorably, produce environmental catastrophe.

Socialist Planning and Environmental Destruction: The Case of the USSR

The Soviet record after over seventy years of central planning is instructive for anyone who supposes that socialist institutions have any advantage over market institutions in ecological terms. Let us consider a few figures. According to Andrei Yablokov, the Russian government's adviser on the environment, life expectancy in Russia has, because of pollution, declined from 70.4 years in 1964 to 69.3 in 1990. In some especially badly polluted cities, it has fallen to 44 years.[8] Yablokov asserts that about 20 per cent of the population of the former Soviet Union lives in ecological disaster areas, while 30–40 per cent live in areas of 'ecological stress'.[9] An official report in 1988 admitted that in 103 industrial cities, with a total population of about 40 million, air pollution levels are more than ten times the official limit; in sixteen cities they are fifty times the limit.[10] The mortality rate of native peoples in the former Soviet Union is even lower than that of the average citizen. According to Stefan Hedlund,[11] the death rate among these peoples is two to three times higher than among Russians, and one group of native people – the Evenks – have a life expectancy of only 32 years. The human cost of environmental degradation in the former Soviet Union cannot be measured by such figures: it is incalculable. It is one of the blackest ironies of our age that, until very recently, the anti-capitalist mentality of Western Greens induced them to look to socialist institutions as solutions for the incomparably less serious environmental depredations of the Western European nations.

The destruction of nature in the former Soviet Union has consequences that go far beyond the regime that brought it to pass. It will affect the whole world for centuries to come. The dangers of the Soviet nuclear industry, though enormous, are perhaps only the best known of the threats that the Soviet ecological catastrophe pose for the environmental integrity of large parts of the planet.

Radioactive lakes, created over the years by waste from the Soviet nuclear weapons programme, are at risk from earth tremors which may send the polluted waters into the Caspian sea . . . and cause an environmental disaster comparable to, or even greater than, the Chernobyl accident . . . Lakes around the Urals city of Chelyabinsk, the centre of the Soviet nuclear industry, are oozing with plutonium.[12]

Built by slave labour immediately after the Second World War, Chelyabinsk – the name of the city as well as the province in which the long-secret nuclear complex, officially called Mayak, is sited – has been the scene of three nuclear disasters, each comparable with, or worse than, the Chernobyl meltdown of April 1986.[13] Further, the first of these nuclear disasters was not, like Chernobyl, an accident, but instead a result of conscious, deliberate policy: 'From 1940, when the Mayak complex produced its first nuclear weapon, to 1956, Mayak officials poured nuclear waste directly into the nearby Techa River.'[14] The effect of 'the unrestrained nature of Soviet "economic development"' has been that 'Both morbidity and mortality rates (in Chelyabinsk) rocketed during the Eighties. Growth in diseases of the blood circulation system . . . grew some 31% during the last decade, while bronchial asthma increased by 43%, congenital anomalies by 23% and gastro-intestinal tract illness by 35%.' These were figures acknowledged even in an official report commissioned by Gorbachev.[15] It is clear that it is not alarmist to describe the Chernobyl incident as one of a number that have occurred in the Soviet Union; and one of a much larger number that are still likely to occur. The situation in China is still largely unknown, but is very likely to be comparable or, if ominous reports from Tibet (where part of the Chinese nuclear arsenal is sited and tested) are at all well founded, even worse.[16]

The nuclear hazards of Soviet institutions are the most dramatic, but not necessarily the most serious, evidences of what has recently been termed 'ecocide in the USSR'.[17] 'Normal' policies of economic development may yet take a greater toll on the global environment. As Hedlund has observed,

In Soviet Central Asia, irrigation and overfertilisation to support a senseless cotton mono-culture has led to the virtual disappearance of the Aral Sea, once the world's fourth largest inland water . . . Desertification is comparable to the Sahel, and health indicators compare to those of Bangladesh . . . Giant herds of sheep, grazing in numbers 20 times greater than the land can sustain, have caused a disaster in the Kalmuck region between Stavropol . . . and the Caspian . . . the result has been the creation of a sand desert . . . This desert is spreading by 10% annually and is forecast to reach the southern Ukraine within five years . . .

Europe is threatened both by its first sand desert and by massive waves of ecological refugees.[18]

The inheritance of Soviet institutions is environmental destruction on an almost apocalyptic scale. And the environmental destruction has not ceased with the collapse of the Soviet Union. According to a recent report by the Lithuanian Department of the Environment, fifty years of Soviet military occupation have incurred environmental degradation that will cost at least 150 billion dollars to repair.[19] The collapse of the Soviet state has revealed an environmental wasteland, which the remnants of the Soviet system are further despoiling.

The causes of this catastrophe are not to be found in the wickedness of Soviet bureaucrats, in the backwardness of Soviet peoples or in errors in the implementation of economic planning, but in the nature of the system itself. Soviet institutions explain the Soviet ecological apocalypse, because they contained no mechanisms for accountability of the planners or their servants, no institutions for the transmission of negative popular feedback on the adverse effects and hazards of the plans, and for that matter no provision for monitoring those adverse effects. The fundamental explanation for the Soviet destruction of the environment, however, is that it occurred in a Hobbesian state of nature – a lawless condition without property rights in which human life was (and indeed is) 'nasty, brutish and short'. Apart from the complete absence of institutions of democratic accountability, the lack of a law of property meant (and means) that no one can in general know, even with the best will, who might have responsibility for which aspect of the environment; and, of course, every incentive of the system tends to suppress such knowledge, even where it exists.

The lesson of the Soviet example is the same as that of the broader theory of the role of market institutions in protecting the environment. The destruction of the environment proceeds most swiftly, and often most irreversibly, in a state of nature lacking in law and property rights. The institutions of a civil society, in which these lacks are remedied and a market economy built up, though long derided by Western Greens, are a vitally important necessary condition not only of human well-being but also of the conservation of the natural environment. This is a truth well understood by the Green movements of the post-Communist world, but yet to be absorbed (or accepted) by Western Greens, with a few noteworthy exceptions.

Ecological Limitations of Market Institutions

The ecological case for market institutions is undoubtedly a very strong one. If private property provides incentives for conservation of scarce resources, the price mechanism supplies a measure of the relative scarcity of different resources. Further, the price mechanism will encourage the search for alternative resources when existing resources of a certain sort grow too expensive, just as it will spur technological innovation in respect of the extraction and use of known resources. In these ways, market institutions embody the least irrational of available mechanisms for the allocation of resources, and, by comparison with socialist planning institutions, they are highly environmentally friendly.

Market institutions have, nevertheless, very serious ecological limitations. As they are described and defended by their most ideological advocates, market institutions are a sort of perpetual-motion machine, an engine of unlimited growth, which only the ill-conceived interventions of government stall. This conception is defective for several reasons. There are, at first glance, forms of environmental market failure that it fails to capture. Consider the phenomenon of global warming. (From the point of view of my argument here, it does not matter whether this phenomenon exists, whether the evidence shows it to be a real danger, or whether the evidence suggests that it is humanly caused. It could be merely a hypothetical danger and still do the work I want it to do in my argument.) Global warming reveals the limits of market institutions, from an environmental perspective, in that it is a threshold phenomenon, coming about via billions of separate acts, each of which individually is innocuous or even imperceptible. Market pricing of each of these acts will not prevent the totality of them generating the phenomenon. In this, and in similar cases of a pure public bad, only prohibitive governmental intervention can prevent or alleviate the problem. The class of environmental market failures may be a larger one than the example of global warming suggests, if (as is surely plausible) there are areas where the extension of property rights is inviable or merely too costly to be reasonably envisaged. This may be true of endangered species that are migratory over vast distances and across several legal jurisdictions: only an intergovernmentally agreed and enforced ban, or a quota system similarly set up, can protect them from extinction. In other words, even where a pure public bad is not at issue, the public good of protection of endangered species will be underprovided whenever market institutions cannot sensibly be extended to create property rights in the species in question, and where market institutions are not supplemented by governmental institutions and policies.

It will often not be enough to supplement market institutions for the sake of environmental protection. Their workings will have to be constrained. Global markets, left to themselves, will often decimate local trades and modes of production and will destroy the ways of life that they support. (Conventional programmes of 'aid' to 'developing countries' often have the same effect.) Global markets in food, along with dumping from developed countries with artificial and unnecessary agricultural surpluses, have destroyed agrarian ways of life in many poor countries, promoting migration into unsustainably gigantist cities, with all of their familiar costs and hazards. Ending economic aid that is self-defeating or counter-productive, and curtailing agricultural protectionism in the developed countries, as advocated by free-marketeers, is *not* an adequate response to the dilemma of protecting otherwise sustainable agrarian communities in poor countries, even if such measures are part of the solution. Such countries may need protection (in the form of tariffs and subsidies) for their peasant farmers – whatever GATT, the IMF or the World Bank may dictate. In this, and other contexts, market institutions must be restricted in their workings, and not merely supplemented.

We find another limitation of market institutions in their insensitivity to inherently public goods.[20] These are goods which do not necessarily satisfy the technical requirements of an economic public good, such as indivisibility and non-excludability, but which are ingredients in a worthwhile form of common life. Consider public parks in the context of a modern city – an example to which I shall return towards the end of this chapter, when I consider the implications for conservatives of a Green agenda for urban policy. There are, of course, no insuperable technical obstacles to turning urban parks into private consumption goods. Fences can be set up, electronic ID cards printed for subscribing members, private security patrols hired, litter collected by profit-making agencies, and so on. Public parks are not, in the conventional economic sense, public goods. However, they are inherently public goods in the sense that I intend, inasmuch as public parks that are safe, well tended, pleasing to the senses and easily accessible to urban dwellers are elements in the common form of life of the historic European city. The point is generalizable. Public spaces for recreation and for lingering, whether streets, squares or parks, are necessary ingredients in the common life of cities, as conceived in the European tradition, and elsewhere. Where such public places atrophy or disappear, become too dangerous or too unsightly to be occupied, and so vanish into a state of nature, the common life of the city has been compromised or lost. This is a nemesis, long reached in many American urban settlements and not far off in some British and European cities, which market institutions can do little to prevent. It is only one example, though perhaps a peculiarly compelling one, of the indifference of market institutions to inherently public goods.

If their workings are not to compromise the integrity of the environment, human as well as natural, market institutions must be both supplemented and constrained. They need such constraint and supplementation, in any case, if they and their various environmental benefits are to survive. Market institutions, except in their most rudimentary forms, are not natural phenomena, the spontaneous results of human action, but artefacts of law and creatures of government. They are as frail and as vulnerable to the onslaughts of war, revolution and dictatorship as any other civilized institution. This is an especially important point, insofar as market institutions may throw up problems which they cannot themselves solve, and which sometimes threaten their very stability. We do not need to look far for examples of this hazard. Left to themselves, no doubt, market institutions would throw up a cornucopia of narcotic designer drugs, even larger than that which has grown up underground and beyond the reach of law; in this, and in other areas of policy, a strategy of legal prohibition, though not without its own costs, has in many countries (though not, apparently, in the United States) contained the problem within a manageable compass. Again, unhampered market institutions may generate forms of entertainment, such as violent or horrific video films, whose general availability is manifestly harmful to the common life. Here, as elsewhere, market institutions must be curbed, or at least restrained in their workings, if a civilized and peaceful form of common life is to be preserved and transmitted across the generations.

On a larger scale, if market institutions generate demands which they cannot themselves satisfy, they will be swept away by revolution or popular dictatorship – as may happen in countries, such as some in Latin America, where the spread of market-generated prosperity has not been accompanied by a demographic transition and where overpopulation has supervened. Free-marketeers who repose their faith in market institutions forget that they are artefacts of human actions which human action can undo. In this they forget a crucial Hobbesian truth: that the integrity of market institutions, and ultimately their very survival, depend on the efficiency of coercive authority, in the absence of which market institutions collapse or else suffer capture by exploitative predators. Market institutions depend, in other words, on a Hobbesian peace for their very existence. The office of government, in this connection, is the superintendence of market institutions, with the aim of ensuring that their workings are not self-defeating or such as to endanger themselves. This is a rudimentary tenet of conservative philosophy of which many contemporary conservatives, whose vision has been occluded by the empty vistas of neo-liberal dogma, appear ignorant.

Ecological Theory and Conservative Philosophy

Change is a threat to identity, and every change is an emblem of extinction. But a man's identity (or that of a community) is nothing more than an unbroken rehearsal of contingencies, each at the mercy of circumstances and each significant in proportion to its familiarity. It is not a fortress into which we may retire, and the only means we have of defending it (that is, ourselves) against the hostile forces of change is in the open field of experience; by throwing our weight upon the foot which for the time being is more firmly placed, by cleaving to whatever familiarities are not

immediately threatened and thus assimilating what is new
without becoming unrecognizable to ourselves. The Masai,
when they were moved from their old country to the present
Masai reserve in Kenya, took with them the names of their
hills and plains and rivers and gave them to the hills and
plains and rivers of the new country. And it is by some
such subterfuge of conservatism that every man or people
compelled to suffer a notable change avoids the shame of
extinction.   Michael Oakeshott[21]

Green thought and conservative philosophy converge at several crucial points, the very points at which they most diverge from fundamentalist liberalism. There are at least three deep affinities between Green thought and conservative philosophy that are important to my argument. There is first the fact that both conservatism and Green theory see the life of humans in a multi-generational perspective that distinguishes them from liberalism and socialism alike. Liberal individualism, with its disabling fiction of society as a contract among strangers, is a one-generational philosophy, which has forgotten, or never known, the truth invoked by David Hume against Thomas Hobbes: that, in our species, wherein sexual and parental love are intertwined, the generations overlap, so that we are *au fond* social and historical creatures, whose identities are always in part constituted by memories (such as those which are deposited in the languages that we speak) which cross the generations.[22] The forms of common life in which we find our identities are the environments in which we live and have our being: they are our human ecology.[23] Again, contrary to the antinomian impulse that animates Marxian and other socialist liberationist movements, the traditions that we inherit from our forebears are not fetters on our identities, shackles which repress our self-expression, but the necessary conditions of having selves to express. We may sometimes legitimately seek to amend our historical inheritance, when it no longer meets human needs, but never to emancipate ourselves from it: that project, the project of making the world over anew, is the gnostic delusion that beset Paine, Robespierre and Lenin. For conservative philosophy, therefore, as for ecological theory, the life of our species is never to be understood from the standpoint of a single generation of its members; each generation is what it is in virtue of its inheritance from earlier generations and what it contributes to its successors. Insofar as one-generation philosophies prosper, the links between the past and the future are weakened, the natural and human patrimony is squandered and the present is laid waste. The modernist idea that each of us is here only once, so we had better make the most of it, is a popular embodiment of the one-generational worldview, which finds expression in much liberal and socialist thought.

A second, connected idea, shared by conservative philosophy and Green theory, is the primacy of the common life. Both conservative and Green thinkers repudiate the shibboleth of liberal individualism, the sovereign subject, the autonomous agent whose choices are the origin of all that has value. They reject this conception, to begin with, because it is a fiction. Human individuals are not natural data, such as pebbles or apples, but are artefacts of social life, cultural and historical achievements: they are, in short, exfoliations of the common life itself.[24] Without common forms of life, there are no individuals: to think otherwise is to be misled by the vulgarized Kantian idea of the person which, shorn of the metaphysics that is its matrix in Kant and that gives it all the (slight) meaning it has, dominates recent liberal thought.[25] But liberal individualism also embodies a mistaken conception of the human good. For conservatives, as for Green thinkers, it is clear that choice-making has in itself little or no value: what has value are the choices that are made, and the options that are available – in short, what is chosen, provided it is good. As I have already argued elsewhere,[26] individual well-being presupposes an array of choiceworthy options which can only be supplied by worthwhile forms of common life. It is from the options provided by such forms of life that choices, however autonomous, derive all of their value. The ultimate locus of value in the human world is not, therefore, in individual choices. This should lead us to qualify, even to abandon, the ideal of the autonomous chooser (which I have myself elsewhere endorsed)[27] in favour of the recognition that the good life for human beings – as for many kindred animal species – necessarily presupposes embeddedness in communities. It is an implication of this point that Green theorists who extend to other animal species the legalist categories of individual rights are moving in precisely the wrong direction: what is required is the recognition that, among human beings, it is not individual rights but often forms of life that need most protection, if only because it is upon them that individual well-being ultimately depends.

A third idea shared by conservative and Green thinkers is the danger of novelty, in particular the sorts of innovation that go with large-scale social (and technological) experimentation. It is not that conservatives (or sensible Green thinkers) seek to arrest change: that would be to confuse stability, which is achieved through changes that are responsive to the cycle of life and to the shifting environment, with fixity. It is rather that both Greens and conservatives consider risk-aversion the path of prudence when new technologies, or new social practices, have consequences that are large and unpredictable, and, most especially, when they are unquantifiable but potentially catastrophic risks associated with innovation. It is an irony that conservatives, whose official philosophy emphasizes reliance on the tried and tested, should often embrace technological innovation, as if it were a good in itself. To be sure, there is little likelihood that the flood of technological innovation can in our time be stemmed; but that is no reason to welcome it or to refrain from curbing it, where this is feasible and there are clear dangers attached to it. It is at least questionable, for example, whether experimental advances in genetic engineering will on balance add to the sum of human well-being; whether their prohibition in any one country, or group of countries, can successfully halt their development, however, is another matter. It is more than questionable whether current high-tech policies in farming are defensible from a conservative perspective that is prudently risk-averse, since current farming technology, like other branches of industrial food technology, encompasses a myriad of interventions in natural processes, each of which has consequences that are unknown and whose effects, when taken together, are incalculable and unknowable.

A sound conservative maxim in all areas of policy, but especially of policy having large environmental implications, is that we should be very cautious of innovations, technological or otherwise, that have serious downside risks – even if the evidence suggestive of these risks is inconclusive, if the risks are small or if their magnitudes cannot be known. A tiny chance of catastrophe may be a risk that can prudently be assumed, if all that is at stake is a human life or a few human lives. It is hard to see how any genuinely conservative philosophy can warrant risk-taking of this sort when the catastrophe that is being hazarded is environmental and millennial in its consequences. This is a truth which is acknowledged – and acknowledged as an element in a sane conservatism – by at least some Green thinkers.[28]

The conservative and Green aversion to risky change does not, of course, entail any policy of immobilism. It may indeed entail radical alternatives in current policy, if such policy encompasses substantial and unwarranted risks. Such alternatives will not, however, be animated by any conception of open-ended progress. It is a cardinal element in my argument for the consilience of conservative philosophy with Green thought that both reject the modernist myth of progress, and for very similar reasons. It is rejected by Green thought because it incorporates the idea of infinite growth – an idea alien to every tenet of ecology.[29] The characteristic that best distinguishes flourishing ecosystems is never growth, but rather stability (a conservative virtue in its own right). This is a truth which is acknowledged in the discipline of ecology in all of its varieties, but which is expressed most beautifully in James Lovelock's idea of Gaia:[30] the idea of life on the Earth as constituting a single organism, one which regulates the species and environments of which life on Earth is composed so as to maintain its stability as a whole. This is an idea, resisted by scientific fundamentalists on the ground that it restores teleology to nature, which should commend itself both to Green thinkers who seek to escape from anthropocentric conceptions of the place of the human species in the biosphere, and to conservatives who have not lost the sense of nature (preserved in the Judeo-Christian tradition) as an order or *cosmos*. Both Green and conservative thinkers should welcome the idea of Gaia, not least as a counterweight to the dominant humanist heresies of modernism. Modernist political faiths which advocate the unlimited growth of population, production and knowledge – political religions such as Marxism and liberalism – are effectively in rebellion against every truth we have established about order in the natural world. Only a sort of secular, humanistic fideism – not any rational assessment of the human lot – could support the otherwise groundless conviction that our species is exempt from the natural constraints that govern every other species of which we have knowledge. The idea of progress is rightly anathema to the most reflective Green thinkers, one of whom has stigmatized it as expressive of 'the anti-way', the way downwards, to entropic disorder and final extinction.[31]

Conservatives have, or should have, their own good reasons for rejecting the idea of progress. Several come at once to mind. The idea of progress is particularly pernicious when it acts to suppress awareness of mystery and tragedy in human life. The broken lives of those who have been ruined by injustice or by sheer misfortune are not mended by the fact – if it were a fact – that future generations will live ever less under these evils. Meliorism, as embodied in the idea of progress, corrupts our perception of human life, in which the fate of each individual is – for him or her – an ultimate fact, which no improvement in the life of the species can alter or redeem. Again, the idea of progress presupposes a measure of improvement in human affairs which, except in limiting cases, we lack.[32] This is not to deny that we can meaningfully judge there to have been improvements in specific spheres of human life: no one who has read Thomas de Quincey's *Confessions of an English Opium-eater* can doubt that anaesthetic dentistry has made a not inconsiderable contribution to human well-being. But improvements in one sphere are accompanied by new evils in others: who is bold enough to affirm that the technological advances of modern medicine have, on balance, promoted human well-being? The facts of iatrogenic illness, of meaningless longevity and of the medicalization of the human environment, well documented by Illich,[33] are telling evidences to the contrary. The deeper truth, however, is that, when assessing goods and evils across very different spheres of human life, we are trying to weigh incommensurables – longevity against the absence of pain, security against adventure, and so on. Although there are generically human evils – of torture, of constant danger of violent death, of human lives cut off in their prime – which are obstacles to any sort of human flourishing, even these universal evils cannot be weighed in the scales against each other. Like the goods of a flourishing human life, they are incommensurables. The conception of human history as a project of universal improvement, insofar as it is at all meaningful, is questionable, given that the eradication of one evil typically spawns others, and many goods are dependent for their existence on evils. At root, however, the idea of history as progressive amelioration is not so much debatable as incoherent; as Herder perceived when, acknowledging the incommensurability of the goods that are distinctive of different forms of cultural life, he rejected even the qualified meliorism of the Kantian philosophy of history.[34]

If the idea of history as the progress of the species is without meaning, it cannot afford a meaning to human life. And here we have the root of the conservative objection to the notion of progress: that it serves as a surrogate for spiritual meaning for those whose lives would otherwise be manifestly devoid of sense. The idea of progress is detrimental to the life of the spirit, because it encourages us to view our lives, not under the aspect of eternity, but as moments in a universal process of betterment. We do not, therefore, accept our lives for what they are, but instead consider them always for what they might someday become. In this way the idea of progress reinforces the restless discontent that is one of the diseases of modernity, a disease symptomatically expressed in Hayek's nihilistic and characteristically candid statement that 'Progress is movement for movement's sake.'[35] No view of human life could be further from either Green thought or genuine conservative philosophy.

The modern conception of progress is only one symptom of the hubristic humanism that is the real religion of our age. As against that debased faith, both conservative and Green thought have as their ideal peace and stability. They seek a form of society that is sufficiently at ease with itself that its legitimacy does not depend on the illusory promise of unending growth. Neither Greens nor conservatives, if they are wise, are in any doubt as to the magnitude of the obstacles in the way of such a society. There can be no doubt that the project of a social order that does not rest on the prospect of indefinite future betterment creates problems for policy that have as yet been barely addressed by conventional thought, including the mainstream of conservative philosophy. Securing the legitimacy of political and economic institutions in a stationary-state society, which is without open-ended growth in population or production, is a hard and central problem for policy, which ought to concern Green thinkers as deeply as it should conservatives.

POLICY

The Stationary State

> *It is perhaps only in transmissible arts that human progress can be maintained or recognized. But in developing themselves and developing human nature these arts shift their ground; and in proportion as the ground is shifted, and human nature itself is transformed, the criterion of progress ceases to be moral to become only physical, a question of increased complexity or bulk or power. We all feel at this time the moral ambiguity of mechanical progress. It seems to multiply opportunity, but it destroys the possibility of simple, rural or independent life. It lavishes information, but it abolishes mastery except in trivial or mechanical efficiency. We learn many languages, but degrade our own. Our philosophy is highly critical and thinks itself enlightened, but it is a Babel of mutually unintelligible artificial tongues.*
> George Santayana[36]

If the project of unbounded progress is to be rejected as a sensible social and political ideal, both in virtue of the ecological limits that it will soon meet and because of its spiritual emptiness, is there an alternative conception of the good society to which conservatives and Greens can alike repair? One may be found, I submit, in J. S. Mill, in his conception of a stationary-state economy, which he describes canonically as follows:

in contemplating any progressive movement, not in its nature unlimited, the mind is not satisfied with merely tracing the laws of its movement; it cannot but ask the further question, to what goal? . . .

It must always have been seen, more or less distinctly, by political economists, that the increase in wealth is not boundless: that at the end of what they term the progressive state lies the stationary state, that all progress in wealth is but a postponement of this, and that each step in advance is an approach to it ... if we have not reached it long ago, it is because the goal itself flies before us [as a result of technical progress].

I cannot ... regard the stationary state of capital and wealth with the unaffected aversion so generally manifested towards it by political economists of the old school. I am inclined to believe that it would be, on the whole, a very considerable improvement on our present condition. I confess I am not charmed with the ideal of life held out by those who think that the normal state of human beings is that of struggling to get on; that the trampling, crushing, elbowing, and treading on each other's heels which form the existing type of social life, are the most desirable lot of human kind, or anything but the disagreeable symptoms of one of the phases of industrial progress. The northern and middle states of America are a specimen of this stage of civilization in very favourable circumstances ... and all that these advantages seem to have yet done for them (notwithstanding some incipient signs of a better tendency) is that the life of the whole of one sex is devoted to dollar-hunting, and of the other to breeding dollar-hunters ...

Those who do not accept the present very early stage of human improvement as its ultimate type may be excused for being comparatively indifferent to the kind of economical progress which excites the congratulations of ordinary politicians; the mere increase of production and accumulation ... I know not why it should be a matter of congratulation that persons who are already richer than anyone needs to be, should have doubled their means of consuming things which give little or no pleasure except as representative of wealth ... It is only in the backward countries of the world that increased production is still an important object: in those most advanced, what is economically needed is a better distribution, of which one indispensable means is a stricter restraint on population.

There is room in the world, no doubt, and even in old countries, for a great increase in population, supposing the arts of life to go on improving, and capital to increase. But even if innocuous, I confess I see very little reason for desiring it. The density of population necessary to enable mankind to obtain, in the greatest degree, all the advantages both of cooperation and of social intercourse, has, in all the most populous countries, been attained. A population may be too crowded, though all be amply supplied with food and raiment. It is not good for a man to be kept perforce at all times in the presence of his species ... Nor is there much satisfaction in contemplating the world with nothing left to the spontaneous activity of nature; with every rood of land brought into cultivation, which is capable of growing food for human beings; every flowery waste or natural pasture plowed up, all quadrupeds, or birds which are not domesticated for man's use exterminated as his rivals for food, every hedgerow or superfluous tree rooted out, and scarcely a place left where a wild shrub or flower could grow without being eradicated as a weed in the name of improved agriculture. If the earth must lose that great portion of its pleasantness which it owes to things that the unlimited increase of wealth and population would extirpate from it, for the mere purpose of enabling it to support a larger, but not a happier or a better population, I sincerely hope, for the sake of posterity, that they will be content to be stationary, long before necessity compels them to it.

It is scarcely necessary to remark that a stationary condition of capital and population implies no stationary state of human improvement. There would be as much scope as ever for all kinds of mental culture, and moral and social progress; as much room for improving the Art of Living and much more likelihood of its being improved, when minds cease to be engrossed by the art of getting on. Even the industrial arts might be as earnestly and as successfully cultivated, with this sole difference, that instead of serving no purpose but the increase of wealth, industrial improvements would produce their legitimate effect, that of abridging labour.[37]

A universal stationary state may well be a utopia; but it is a better measuring-rod for attainable improvement in the human lot than the wholly unrealizable fantasy of infinite growth. It captures the core of what is often described as sustainable development, and, because it respects the varieties of finitude by which we are surrounded, it should commend itself not only to Green theorists, but also to conservatives. It has a vital element, however, which many conservatives and Greens find offensive, although it is eminently sensible, namely the neo-Malthusian commitment to the control of human population. Such a commitment, I shall argue, is indispensable to any policy seeking to avert regional and global ecological degradation; and the idea that market institutions and their matrices, civil societies, can flourish, or even hope to survive, in a world of rapidly but unevenly increasing populations is, in truth, sheer fantasy. It is to this global perspective on population, and to related topics of sustainable development, that I turn first in my consideration of policy. I proceed then to consider what might be an agenda of policy for Green conservatives as applied to the common environment at the national level in Britain, focusing on six related policy areas: energy and agriculture, urban and transport policy, and education and health. In all, I shall argue, conservative values dictate radical departures from current practice – changes that can also be seen as congenial to Green concerns.

The Global Perspective: Population

If there were only 500 million people on earth, almost nothing that we are now doing to the environment would perturb Gaia. James Lovelock[38]

In the days before Pasteur man's population was maintained approximately constant from generation to generation by a cybernetic system in which the principal feedback element at the upper limit was disease. The crowd-diseases – smallpox, cholera, typhoid, plague, etc. – are, by the ecologist, labelled 'density-dependent factors', whose effectiveness in reducing population is a power function of the density of the population. No growth of population could get out of hand as long as the crowd-diseases were unconquered ... With the development of bacteriological medicine, all this has been changed. Now, the feedback control is man himself. The reality of this truth is temporarily obscured by the increasing size of the feast, through technological advances, but this is only a passing phase which must soon come to an end ... Having eliminated all other enemies, man is his own worst enemy. Having disposed of all his predators, man preys on himself. Garrett Hardin[39]

The single greatest threat to global ecological stability comes from human population growth. According to United Nations estimates, there are around 5.5 billion people in the world today. Within thirty years, this number will have increased to 8.5 billion, and by the middle of the twenty-first century it will – barring demographic collapses of one sort or another – have topped 10 billion. These latter extrapolative figures take account of the demographic transition: the point in economic and social development at which families (in many, but not by any means all, poorer countries) begin to shrink in size. Even given that the rate of increase of world population fell from 2.04 per cent per annum in 1970 to around 1.8 per cent at present, it is worth noting that an annual growth rate of the latter figure will double the number of parents every thirty-nine years. Nor does the story end there. Even given the very large and doubtful supposition that a demographic transition occurs everywhere and at a similar rate, the world's total population will swell for a long time. The age-structure alone of many populations, such as that of Bangladesh, in which perhaps a majority are under fifteen, guarantees this further increase. The prospect is of a doubling of the world's human population in under sixty years. Is there anyone who can reasonably suppose that the world's ecological balance can cope with this unprecedented demographic growth? Or that it will occur unattended by vast economic and political (and military) convulsions?

It may be salutary to review briefly the principal reasons why population pressures are likely, unless sensible policies are adopted, to render the coming century one of wars and migrations even greater and yet more terrible than those of the twentieth century. To begin with, the growth of populations is very uneven as between different countries, and different parts of the world. In the former Soviet Union, for example, the population of Russians is in steep decline, whereas the Muslim population is, in general, increasing rapidly. The huge differences in size of different populations further increase the absolute magnitudes resulting from these different rates of growth. The population of mainland China, perhaps around twelve hundred million at present, is roughly ten times that of neighbouring Japan, whose population is static or declining. The population of Indonesia is such (well over a hundred million) that it would find no difficulty in fielding a land army larger than the entire population of New Zealand. Such examples could easily be multiplied. It requires a faith in the resilience of human institutions that borders on the absurd to imagine that discrepancies of these magnitudes will not occasion migrations and wars of the classical Malthusian varieties.

Nor is the celebrated demographic transition occurring evenly in all parts of the world. The theory itself, though it has a measure of leverage on historical and contemporary evidence, is a piece of economic imperialism. Like other applications of the model of *Homo economicus*, it neglects the crucial variable of culture. The theory tells us that families will shrink in size when parents, themselves growing richer and so able to provide for their old age, or sheltered from destitution by welfare programmes, cease to regard their children as investment goods and come to view them as consumer goods. Family size will then fall. This desiccated model leaves out the influence on fertility of very diverse moral and religious traditions. The demographic transition is likely to be most pronounced where – as in Taiwan and Japan – mores are such that birth control is unproblematic and abortion not a moral issue; and this is borne out by evidence from these countries. Where the local religion puts a premium on large family size, and anathematizes contraception and abortion, as with some varieties both of Roman Catholicism and of Islam, we may expect the demographic transition to be slow and slight, or else indefinitely delayed – as appears to be the case in parts of Latin America and North Africa. Such differences in the rate of demographic transition will magnify existing disparities in population size. They will generate waves of illegal immigration – of the sort already occurring from the Maghreb in Africa to Southern and Western Europe – that are likely to have highly destabilizing effects on both the recipient societies and the societies subject to such haemorrhagings of population. It is not difficult to foresee major military conflicts occurring as a result of actual or prospective population movements of this sort.

Resistance to population policy among conservatives is deep and widespread, and it is paralleled by Maoist attitudes among radical Greens, who see calls for population control as veiled policies of genocide on poor peoples. Such resistance is folly of the worst sort, from the standpoint both of conservative philosophy and of Green thought (not to mention common sense). For Greens, it must surely be clear that a vast uncontrolled expansion of human population will endanger and disrupt the biological community of which our species is only a part: it is a recipe for instability, or, if not, for the sort of stability that, if the Gaian hypothesis is at all well founded, comes about via catastrophic reduction in human numbers.[40] And such a reduction is most likely, in the absence of a well-conceived policy of population control, to occur in the poorest countries.

For conservatives, the sheer inordinacy, the defiance of natural finitude that is involved in open-ended population growth, and the hazards that it poses to civilized economic and political institutions, should be sufficient to caution them against that species of technological optimism about our capacity to cope with ever growing human populations that is found in such nineteenth-century thinkers as Herbert Spencer and Karl Marx. Such technological hubris – advocated, or presupposed, in our own time by thinkers such as Julian Simon and, in some of his later writings, by F. A. Hayek – is objectionable, in the first place, because of its overestimation of human inventiveness and its underestimation of the fragility of any natural or Gaian order that has a place in it for humans. It is to be resisted, secondly, because, even if human technology had the virtuosity attributed to it by these forms of Positivism and scientism, human institutions would break down long before technology could develop to such levels of virtuosity, or be applied in practice. Or, to put it another way: the growth of technology itself depends on human institutions that are always unstable and often desperately fragile; it is disrupted, or retarded, when human institutions break down. For this reason, the growth of technology cannot be guaranteed, and a technical fix for the problems of humankind, even supposing it to be possible, will always be beyond its reach.

If such philosophical considerations prove insufficiently compelling, perhaps the threat to liberty posed by human population growth will be persuasive. Overpopulation is itself an encroachment on individual liberty, as more and more of our activities are constrained by the density of human settlements.[41] The sudden and dramatic increase in human numbers has been identified by at least one twentieth-century conservative thinker[42] as but an aspect of the ascendancy of mass humanity which is the chief threat to individuality in our age. It is scarcely a conservative point of view to value the quantity of human beings in the world over the quality of their lives; to prefer a crowded world choked with noise and filth to a world of space and amenity that is peopled on a smaller scale; or to deny the human need for solitude and wilderness. All of these conservative considerations mandate a policy for population when, as now in most parts of the world, medical progress has removed natural constraints on over-population. The forms of population policy will naturally vary from time to time and place to place; and, for a conservative, it is important that they should conform, so far as they can do so feasibly, with local customs and beliefs. There will nevertheless be occasions when, unless local beliefs and values – about the sanctity of human life, say, or the evils of contraception – are radically reformed, the deeper conservative values of the stability and integrity of the common environment will be compromised, perhaps irreversibly. This is only one example of a truth to which my argument will recur: that, in our age of cataclysmic change, conservative values can sometimes be renewed only by radical revisions in current thought and practice.

Economic Development

Man's continuous tapping of natural resources is not an activity that makes no history. On the contrary, it is the most important long-run element of mankind's fate. It is because of the irreversibility of the entropic degradation of matter – energy – that, for instance, the peoples from the Asian steppes, whose economy was based on sheep-raising, began their Great Migration over the entire European continent at the beginning of the first millennium. The same element – the pressure on natural resources – had, no doubt, a role in other migrations, including that from Europe to the New World . . . Nothing could be further from the truth than the notion that the economic process is an isolated, circular affair – as Marxist and standard analysis represent it. The

> *economic process is solidly anchored to a material base*
> *which is subject to definite constraints. It is because of these*
> *constraints that the economic process has a unidirectional*
> *irrevocable evolution.*   Nicholas Georgescu-Roegen[43]

> *The economic activities of modern man are interfering ever*
> *more dramatically with the most fundamental Gaian cycles*
> *– water, carbon, sulphur, phosphorus – thus disrupting the*
> *critical order of the biosphere and reducing its capacity to*
> *support life. This is unfortunately inevitable if economic*
> *development remains modern man's overriding goal. For it*
> *is a one-way process, in which the Biosphere is systemati-*
> *cally transformed into the technosphere and technospheric*
> *waste – a process that cannot continue indefinitely.*
>   Edward Goldsmith[44]

The ideal of a stationary-state society implies stable levels of human population throughout the world; in most parts of the world, stability at levels lower than at present. In some Western countries, the ageing of current populations may support more liberal selective immigration policies; but the population of the world as a whole, and of most of the countries in it, is by any sensible standard far too high. Alleviation of the human lot lies not in a further growth in human numbers, but in stability at much reduced levels. To this end, attitudes and policies in regard to fertility and procreation will need to alter radically. If they do not, human numbers will be curtailed by other, more traditionally Malthusian means.

It is no less important to stress that economic development cannot proceed much longer on the traditional lines of indefinitely expanding output. Such policies carry with them an indefinite expansion of the toxic side-effects of hyper-industrialization, in pollution, ozone depletion, the disappearance of wilderness, and so on. Certainly, the proposition that the 'developing' world can ever hope to have the levels of production of the most industrialized nations is thoroughly absurd – but only slightly more so than the idea that the so-called First World can expect to return to the trajectory of uninterrupted economic growth that it enjoyed in the 1960s and 1980s. Both propositions underestimate the fragility of the world's ecological balance, and the impact on its stability of ever higher levels of industrial activity. Most absurd of all is the notion that a population around twice that of the world at present could ever expect to generate the industrial production that the world's richest nations presently exhibit.

The industrialization of the world on the model of its richest nations is a dystopian fantasy. It probably exaggerates even the capacity of the First World to renew itself on the conventional path of economic growth. The past few years have seen the abortion of the Reaganite and Thatcherite 'dashes for growth', and the stubborn resistance of the world's most advanced economies to a resumption of expansion on the old lines. In the United States, the artificial lowering of short-term interest rates to levels unknown for nearly thirty years, and probably in real terms negative, has so far failed to rekindle economic activity. In Europe and Japan, neither monetarist nor Keynesian strategies of the old sorts appear efficacious in restarting the engine of growth, and asset values are in ominous decline. The prospect for the First World – fraught with terrible implications for the rest of the world – may be a Great Depression, akin to that of the 1930s (or worse) in that it is accompanied by trade wars, financial meltdowns and geopolitical convulsions. This is not a prospect to be welcomed by any sensible conservative or Green, or by any sane observer; but it is one that should at least pose a question mark over the feasibility, if not the desirability, of a resumption of economic growth along the lines – almost certainly unrepeatable – of the 1960s and 1980s.

Even if the real prospect for the First World is one of continued stagnation rather than of cataclysmic depression, it bodes ill for the future of the transitional post-Communist countries. It is in any case highly contestable whether – as the conventional wisdom would have us believe – that future lies in a replication of the central institutions of Western democratic capitalism. As I have argued in detail elsewhere,[45] such a transplantation of Western institutions to the post-Communist countries is, in general, neither desirable nor possible. Except in a few areas, where development can piggy-back on the innovations of the military–industrial complex, it is fantastic to suppose that the future for Russia, say – whose environment is already virtually ruined by Faustian projects of industrialization – lies in further industrial growth: it is much more likely to be in the renewal of agriculture, if that can still be achieved. In any case, except perhaps in the Czech lands of Bohemia and Moravia, in Hungary, in Slovenia, in Estonia and possibly Lithuania, and in the Silesian parts of Poland, where Germany, Austria and Finland have historic interests and the capacity for investment, there is likely to be insufficient Western inputs of capital to finance the reconstruction of the post-Communist economies on any Western model. Most of the post-Communist peoples will therefore be compelled, by force of sheer economic stringency, to consider other paths to development.

The model of First World affluence and industrial productivity is, perhaps, especially pernicious in its applications to the world's poorest countries, in most of which it will be forever unrealizable. It may well be feasible, at least for a while, for small countries, such as Taiwan and Singapore, to follow in the tracks of Japan and to catch up with, and overtake in affluence and productivity, formerly First World countries, such as New Zealand; it is very doubtful whether a country of the size, geography, resources and population of mainland China can do likewise. (It is worth recalling that average levels of wages in mainland China are a fraction of those in Japan.) In this connection, whatever the other aspects of the present Chinese government, one cannot withhold admiration from their recent policies which initiated economic reform first in agriculture, where it reaped the boon of a surviving peasant tradition that the Bolsheviks, and Stalinist collectivization, destroyed in Russia. In countries such as China, the renewal of agriculture, along with population control and the search for light, intermediate technologies having the least destructive impact on the natural environment, should be cornerstones of policy, rather than the futile project of emulating Western industrial societies which are already in evident decline, and which may be headed for a fall.

Policies of emulation of First World economic development are pernicious, also, because of their adverse effects on local ways of life. In some instances, at least, there are ways of life that have long achieved an ecological balance with their environmental niche, in which poverty is unknown or even unthought of, and in which all the evidences of human flourishing are present. Modernization of a culture such as that of Ladakh, say, has thus far been an almost unmitigated disaster,[46] encompassing the ruination of ancient traditions that had served the Ladakhis well for many centuries. This is not to say that modernization can realistically be halted, since the introduction of Western medical technologies, with their explosive consequences for population growth, is already probably irreversible. In the case of Ladakh, as of that of analogous Bhutan (where the situation is complicated by ethnic strife between Nepali immigrants and native Bhutanese which threatens to resemble the conflicts that have decimated Sri Lanka), the precipitate introduction of Western medicine alone spells ruin for the people and their culture, unless countervailing modernizing measures – such as the introduction of birth control – are also soon adopted. Even assuming that the demographic crises of countries such as these can somehow be averted, they face the daunting task of negotiating a highly selective assimilation of Western technologies at a time when all of the international organizations, such as the World Bank and the United Nations, favour development on the First World model. If there are any safe bets in this field, one may be found in the prediction that such policies, which aim for unsustainable economic development at the cost of the irreversible destruction of traditional cultures, will end in tragedy. This is a wager that the post-colonial history of Africa, no less than the history of Western cultural imperialism that preceded it there, already amply supports. The result of such policies in Africa has so far been only the deracination of local peoples from their traditional tribal cultures and their impoverishment by a global market that drives out their local products. It is hard to see by what rationale this scenario should be replicated in other parts of the world.

Western models of economic development for poor countries should be objectionable both to conservatives and to Green thinkers. Where Western development has taken root, as in Japan, it has been able to do so precisely because (and insofar as) indigenous traditions have not been displaced: a fact which should reinforce the conservative precept that development policy should always conform with local traditions, and never amount to an attempt at a wholesale transplantation of an alien culture. For Greens, the very notion of universalizing Western affluence should be suspect, given its costs to the natural environment, and its unsustainability over the long term. Even conservatives who judge the imperatives of economic growth in an industrial society to be irresistible need not sanctify the fiction that such growth has furthered the cause of human happiness. Is any conservative ready to affirm that the city-dweller complete with ghetto-blaster is happier than the destitute Eskimo (prior to the fatal contact with Western culture), or the pious and cheerful Tibetan? Human experience suggests otherwise. We are led to the absurd view of economic growth as an inherently desirable phenomenon, partly by the fetish of calculability that has overtaken the social studies, and partly because we have few decent measures for the costs of economic growth.[47] This will prove a dangerous folly for policy-makers to persist in.

Western advice that poor countries abandon the First World model of development is often, and not always without reason, viewed as hypocritical. It is not unreasonably asked: what alterations are the First World peoples (so called) willing to make in their form of life for the sake of the integrity of the environment? If modernization on a First World model is to be resisted, how are the First World countries to reform themselves? More to my present purpose, how are conservatives to respond to the challenge posed by the fact that Western affluence cannot be made universal or enduring? What, in particular, are the implications for policy of a Green conservatism for an industrial society such as that of Britain? Let us consider what such an agenda of policy ought to be if it had as its object, not the resumption of economic growth on conventional lines, but instead the conservation and renovation of the common environment.

The National Perspective: An Agenda for Green Conservatism in Britain

Two caveats are in order before we explore the implications of a convergence of Green and conservative perspectives at a national level in Britain. It is far from clear that the nation-state is the appropriate unit for environmental policy, since some policy issues transcend it, while others are most manageable at regional and local levels. Nor is it at all self-evident that the nation-state is an institution that accords well either with conservative or with Green values (insofar as they are ultimately distinguishable). The nation-state is a very recent institution, a construction of the nineteenth-century classical liberal political elites, who were animated by Romantic thought rather than by conservative philosophy. Further, it has in the twentieth century, under institutions of mass democracy, been the arena for rival political elites whose one point of convergence in thought and policy has been a Promethean attitude to nature and a commitment to indefinite economic growth. These latter are hardly Green values. It is not clear that there is anything deep in either conservative or Green thought that commits them to the sanctity of the nation-state as we know it at present.

The nation-state is also, in some important respects, an inappropriate vehicle for environmental concern. Many environmental problems are global: they have effects that spill across territorial jurisdictions. This is true not only of phenomena such as ozone depletion and global warming but also of acid-rain pollution, and of many other injurious impacts on the natural environment. There is also a difficulty for Green theorists, which few, if any of them, have as yet confronted: the difficulty created by the ecological terrorism and environmental destruction that is wrought by bandit states. Here is meant not only deliberate acts of ecological vandalism of the sort that were committed in Kuwait by Saddam Hussein, which are increasingly likely in the future, but also the phenomenon of environmental holocausts, having global or regional spillover effects, which are wreaked by lawless states. The former Soviet Union and present mainland China probably fall into this latter category. These phenomena lead by a clear train of reasoning to another set of vast hazards to the natural and human environments, which is typically neglected or very inadequately treated in Green thought: the hazards generated by the ever more rapid development, proliferation and deployment of military technologies of mass destruction. This is an issue to which I will return at the end of this chapter. Here I wish only to note that the proliferation of such technologies is not halted, or even significantly retarded, by unilateral acts of national renunciation; and it is of very little profit to anyone to have installed exhaust controls on cars, or to have curtailed the peaceful development of nuclear energy, if we are thereafter subject to the lethality of biological, chemical, conventional and nuclear weapons technologies. The proliferation of such technologies throughout an increasingly anarchic world that contains a growing number of terrorist states casts a lengthening shadow over the future of our species, and over all of the others that it presently dominates, which should inform all serious projects of environmental conservation. In this area, above all, as in many others, unilateral action by nation-states is bound to be typically ineffectual: what is needed is effective concerted action by national governments.

The contemporary nation-state has been, and continues to be, an agency of centralization; as such, it is an institution that should be endorsed by conservatives and Greens only with considerable reserve and suspicion. Much environmental destruction has occurred because national governments have acted with indifference or ignorance upon local ecologies, natural and human. Again, there are many activities of existing nation-states that need not, and often should not, be performed by national governments, and that sometimes can be done most effectively without any action by government beyond the provision of a legal framework for private initiative. One of the most radical suggestions of neo-liberal thought has been that even the monopoly on the supply of moneys by national governments may be unnecessary and indeed undesirable from the standpoint of price stability.[48] This is a thought that should be congenial to Greens, since it opens up the possibility of local communities having their own local moneys, issued by local banks that are independent of central governments. Again, much welfare policy has been filtered through national government, when it is often best made and implemented at lower levels, closer to local communities, and often by intermediary and voluntary institutions. Though (as I shall argue) the contemporary nation-state is now the only political institution to retain legitimacy and, for that reason, cannot responsibly be dismantled, there can be no doubt that its responsibilities are currently massively overextended.

In general, policies toward local environmental issues are best made at local level, if only because, in the human world, all policies turn on the stability and vitality of local communities. Here a further caveat needs issuing. Returning environmental initiative to regions and localities need not, and typically (at least in Britain) should not, mean a multiplication of tiers of local and regional government. In Britain, local government has often been in the forefront of environmental vandalism – wrecking working-class communities by hubristic projects of urban renewal, demolishing serviceable buildings and despoiling countryside. What is needed is rather the strengthening of local and regional non-governmental institutions, the enabling of local communities – a task that may often require the intervention of national government to break the power of local bureaucracies and entrenched interests.

We see here a paradox from which neither conservative nor Green thought can escape: whereas there is nothing sacred in the nation-state that we are bound to revere, still less (after the fashion of modernist humanism) to worship, it remains nonetheless the only effective agency of environmental action. It acts by making and policing intergovernmental agreements and by conferring Hobbesian protection on local communities and regional ecologies that would otherwise surely be objects of predation by criminal states. And it uses its coercive powers to curb forces, such as uncontrolled migration, and to limit organizations, such as the transnational corporation, which might otherwise endanger local communities and environments. (I do not mean here to stigmatize the transnational corporations, which can sometimes take a larger view than national governments; merely to affirm that the activities of transnational corporations need to be subject to a monitoring that only national governments often can supply.) The nation-state can discharge this task, not only in virtue of its coercive powers, but because of that upon which they rest, namely, the fact that nation-states are in our time the only political institutions that retain authority in a world that has otherwise lost it. It is a lesson which wise conservative philosophy has to teach Green theory that only by working with and in institutions, such as the nation-state, which possess authority and legitimacy, can environmental problems be stably resolved.

The Political Economy of the Stationary State:
The Limits of Market Capitalism

> *There is nothing in front but a flat wilderness of standardis-*
> *ation either by Bolshevism or Big Business. But it is strange*
> *that some of us should have seen sanity, if only in a vision,*
> *while the rest go forward chained eternally to enlargement*
> *without liberty and progress without hope.*
>
> G. K. Chesterton[49]

> *The capitalist state is unstable, and indeed more properly a*
> *transitory phase lying between two permanent and stable*
> *states of society.*   Hilaire Belloc[50]

One of the central facts of our time is the historical vindication of market institutions. Central planning has not achieved economic security at the price of individual liberty; it has assured general poverty and sustained tyranny. By the conventional standard of its contribution to economic growth, central planning has been a comprehensive failure except in the strategic–military sector. As we have already seen, the inability of central planning institutions to deliver prosperity has not prevented them from devastating the environment. On the contrary, central planning has accomplished a near-ecocide[51] in the former Soviet Union without even a temporary compensating growth in prosperity, and with most of its gigantic industrial projects being ventures in absurdist pyramid-building which lack the aesthetic appeal and spiritual significance of their Egyptian prototypes.

The historical vindication of market institutions has been, popularly and wrongly, perceived as expressive of the triumph of Western capitalism. It is true enough that such absurd variants on a 'Third Way' as market socialism are utopian (or dystopian)[52] fantasies; but this is not to say that Western capitalism has triumphed, that it will or should be adopted throughout the post-Communist world, that it is a single set of institutions without distinctive varieties, or even that some of its varieties – those found in the Anglo-American world, especially – may not now be in steep decline. The simple fact is that market institutions come in an immense diversity of forms, of which Western capitalism is only one and is not necessarily the most stable.

From a standpoint that is acceptable to authentic conservatives and Greens alike, Western capitalism, at least as it is found in a country such as Britain, has two large and connected disadvantages, which disable it in ecological terms. The first is that Western capitalism – like socialist central planning but unlike medieval feudalism, say – is predicated upon indefinite economic growth. For Western capitalism, the stationary state represents the nemesis of secular stagnation, dreaded by mainstream economists from Ricardo to Hansen: any faltering in growth, any disruption of rising living standards is perceived – as indeed it is correct so to do – as a defect in the prevailing economic system. For Green theorists, accordingly, Western capitalism is predicated upon an ecological impossibility, and it is for that reason doomed to instability and ephemerality. The second disadvantage flows from the first. This is that the political legitimacy of Western capitalist market institutions depends upon incessant economic growth; it is endangered whenever growth falters. This is a feature of Western institutions that should be profoundly distasteful to all true conservatives, for whom the legitimacy of institutions, and the authority of government, has (or should have) ethical and spiritual foundations, whereby they can weather even protracted periods of economic hardship. The dependency of Western capitalism on uninterrupted economic growth for its political legitimacy has allowed it to evade addressing its chief defects, which account for its systemic tendency to instability: the insecurity that it generates for ordinary people by its prodigious technological virtuosity and inherently innovative character; and the maldistribution of capital whereby this insecurity is compounded. There are, indeed, varieties of market institutions in which this endemic insecurity is addressed, such as that of Japan, in which at least a substantial proportion of the working population enjoys lifetime job security in a company. (It is the stability which such practices confer on Japanese market institutions that addresses one reason among many others why Japan is very wise to resist emulating Western, and especially Anglo-American, models for business enterprise, which bear all the marks of bankruptcy.) In most capitalist countries, however, the insecurities of the economic system are at best mitigated by a range of welfare institutions, which foster a culture of dependency and do nothing to spread the advantages and responsibilities of ownership.

Such welfare institutions, when they are not confined to their proper function of assisting those incapable of productive employment to lead lives that are nevertheless dignified, abound with moral hazards and self-defeating effects. It is, in fact, hard (but essential) to envisage reforms of our inherited capitalist institutions which would obviate the necessity for a welfare state that has, on the whole, done little to emancipate its supposed beneficiaries from poverty and dependency, but has instead institutionalized these conditions. I have suggested elsewhere[53] reforms of current welfare institutions and policies which might go some distance towards achieving their original intent and rendering less significant their counter-productive side-effects. Here I want to argue that only a radical extension of the benefits of ownership will sufficiently mitigate market-generated insecurity for market institutions on a roughly capitalist model to be stable in the context of a stationary-state economy. In Britain, policies for the dispersion of wealth have been destructively perverse in the extreme. On inheritance, they have encouraged not wider ownership, but the transfer of wealth to the state.[54] In tax policy, the absurd fetish of home-ownership has been subsidized, while savings, dividends and capital gains have been subject to double taxation. Schemes for wider dispersion of wealth have taken the form of encouraging investment in highly volatile equities arising from privatizations. The combination of progressive income taxation with virulent inflation has rendered the accumulation of capital from earnings an impossibility for virtually everyone. The result has been the Servile State described by Belloc, which is little different from the new serfdom (one wholly lacking the redeeming features of its medieval predecessor) diagnosed by Hayek.[55]

Tax and welfare policies must urgently be reformed, so as to promote reskilling and to enhance the opportunities for the private accumulation of capital – itself a necessary condition of the Green virtue of social stability and the conservative values of harmony and independence. In addition, consideration should be given to a negative capital tax[56] whereby each citizen would receive at maturity a patrimony of capital that would confer on him or her the possibility of independence and of self-provision against most forms of market-generated insecurity. In Britain, such a patrimony could be denominated in government bonds, perhaps index-linked against inflation and tax-exempt, which were redeemable on stated terms for purposes of investment, saving, provision for retirement, and so on. The aim would be to guarantee a minimum of capital as a patrimony for each and all. (To be sure, such a scheme could not guarantee that the patrimony would not be wasted or malinvested, and so it could not obviate the need for all welfare institutions; but we are dealing here, as always, with exercises in imperfection, not utopias.) Such a distributivist measure in no way mandates egalitarian levelling (since it could easily be financed from proportional income taxation) and it needs for its justification none of the dubious notions of social justice rightly criticized by neo-liberals. In truth, it probably embodies one of the few viable means of reducing the systemic instabilities of market capitalism while substantially dismantling the elephantine apparatus of the welfare state.[57] It is vastly preferable to hare-brained neo-liberal schemes for a negative income tax, which I have criticized elsewhere.[58] And it might conceivably engender that fund of legitimacy that would enable market institutions to renew themselves stably across the generations in a stationary-state economy, in which only individual effort or the lottery of the market, but not an engine of forced economic growth, can alter individual positions in society.

New institutions and policies of other sorts will doubtless be necessary if market institutions are to adapt themselves to the constraints of a stationary-state economy. Daly has suggested, as an alternative to pollution taxes which attempt to cost the externalities of industrial production, depletion quotas on natural resources, which would be set by government but would be auctioned off as marketable assets. He commends this radical policy proposal on the grounds that 'It does not expropriate land and capital, but does further restrict their use at an across-the-board level. It provides the necessary macroeconomic control with the minimum sacrifice of microeconomic freedom. It minimizes centralized, quantitative planning and maximizes reliance on decentralized, market decision-making.'[59] Similar proposals have been made for the control of population.[60] It does not matter, for the purposes of my argument, whether these proposals are acceptable as appropriate responses to current environmental concerns. They have the merits (not always possessed by policies advocated by Greens) of seeking to turn to advantage the workings of market institutions, rather than to repress them; and in that respect, they accord maximal feasible respect to individual liberty. They accept that the task of Green policy is that of reforming civil society and its market institutions, not abolishing them. In this such policy proposals are exemplary. Even if the proposed measures were to prove defective, they will be less delusive than attempts to kick-start economic growth on the old models; and they will have some prospect of generating the legitimacy for market institutions that they have in recent times borrowed spuriously from an unsustainable expansion in material living standards.

ISSUES ON THE NATIONAL POLICY AGENDA

It is no part of the object of this chapter to address every issue in national political debate in Britain in order to identify a convergence of conservative and Green perspectives on it. Instead I shall, from the shifting and inevitably indeterminate subject matter of public discourse in Britain, address six broad policy areas – energy and agriculture, urban and transport policy, and health and education – to see how a Green conservative agenda might be applied. In every case, we will find a substantial convergence of perspectives, along with significant revisions in both standard conservative and conventional Green thinking.

Energy and Agriculture

> *The natural energy of the Universe, the power that lights the stars in the sky, is nuclear. Chemical energy, wind and water wheels: such sources of energy are, from the viewpoint of a manager of the Universe, almost as rare as a coal-burning star. If this is so, and if God's universe is nuclear-powered, why then are so many of us prepared to*

*march in protest against its use to provide us with elec-
tricity?*

*The very concept of pollution is anthropocentric and it
may even be irrelevant in the Gaian context.*

James Lovelock[61]

A feature of Green thought has been its opposition to novel technologies for the production of energy, most particularly its opposition to
nuclear power. At first glance this may appear to be one of the
many points of convergence between Green thought and conservative
philosophy which it is the purpose of this chapter to exhibit. After
all, conservative philosophy insists that it is collectively imprudent to
incur even tiny risks, if they are risks of catastrophe and are avoidable;
and we have had more than one instance thus far (as the opponents
of nuclear power never cease to remind us) of serious accidents in
nuclear power plants. Are not the Greens therefore in conformity
with conservative philosophy in opposing nuclear power, in virtue of
its novelty and its potentially vast hazards to the environment?

Almost all of the commonly accepted arguments against nuclear
power are substantially spurious, elements of a pseudo-Green conventional wisdom, part Luddite, which is suspicious of new technologies,
however benign they may be, and attached to old technology, no
matter how demonstrably environmentally pernicious. It is true, of
course, that there are in the world unsafe (because now obsolete)
nuclear power stations, especially in the post-Soviet world, and, very
probably, in China: the risk of further Chernobyls amounts, for that
reason, to a likelihood. These dangers are good arguments against
unsafe reactors, and therefore for the closure of such reactors; they
are not arguments against nuclear power. The fact is that, by comparison with older energy-producing technologies, nuclear power is
environmentally benign, and not especially hazardous. As Lovelock
has observed:

It is true that calculations have been made of the cancer deaths across
Europe that might come from Chernobyl, but if we were consistent, we
might wonder also about the cancer deaths from breathing the smoke fogs

of London coal and look on a piece of coal with the same fear now reserved for uranium. How different is the fear of death from nuclear accidents from the commonplace and boring death toll of the roads, of cigarette smoking, or of mining – which taken together are equivalent to thousands of Chernobyls a day?[62]

The public perception of nuclear power as peculiarly risky is an illusion, partly created by the failure to compare its hazards with those forms of power with which we are familiar. (Compare the frequency and devastating impact on the natural environment of oil spills – of which only the worst are reported – with the publicity given to nuclear accidents; or the havoc wrought on nature by the antediluvian, pre-nuclear industrial technologies of the former Soviet bloc – virtually screened out from Western perceptions – with the global publicity accorded to the Chernobyl meltdown.) Indeed, if time travel were possible, a visitor from an earlier period of industrial society – say, the nineteenth century in Britain – would most likely be astonished by the cleanliness and integrity of our environment, which early industrialism ravaged. There is a lesson here for Green thought, which is that, whereas the reckless adoption of novel technologies without due consideration of their consequences is imprudence or folly, new technologies are not always maleficent. Sometimes, as is arguably the case with nuclear power, they are a major improvement on the cumbrous, costly and ecologically invasive technologies of the past (such as coal-mining). In any event, nuclear power is with us; it behooves us to make the best of it. As Lovelock has put it:

If we cannot disinvent nuclear power, I hope that it stays as it is. The power sources are vast and slow to be built, and the low cost of the power itself is offset by the size of the capital investment required . . . I have never regarded nuclear radiation or nuclear power as anything other than a normal and inevitable part of the environment.[63]

This is not an argument for the indiscriminate adoption of nuclear power, or for everything that has been done by the nuclear industry or said on its behalf. It is, rather, an argument for a rational energy policy, formulated at national level, in which nuclear power, along with other forms of energy-production, would have an important role. That there is need for a national energy policy is questioned, I take it, only by free-market doctrinaires, whose positions are grounded in a metaphysical faith in market institutions rather than empirical reasonings about their operations and limitations. As in a good many other respects, we can take a cue here from Japan, which responded to the oil-shock of the 1970s by a host of governmentally sponsored energy-saving initiatives, including further development of its nuclear power programme. We will also be sensible if we treat the progressive curtailment of the role of the private passenger car as being, among other things, an element in a reasonable national energy policy.

After the size of the world's human population, the greatest threat to the integrity of our common environment is to be found not in the peaceful uses of nuclear energy, but most probably in current farming practices. Once again, the Green conventional wisdom, with its nostalgia for a lost rural arcadia and its contempt for the contrivances of city living, neglects or misperceives the real threats to our common life, and that of the planet. The impact on global ecological stability of even the world's most bloated cities is a trifle by comparison with that of the agricultural technologies that have been adapted to feed a swollen human population. As Lovelock again puts it:

we are moving towards eight billion people with more than ten billion sheep and cattle, and six billion poultry. We use much of the productive soil to grow a very limited range of crop plants, and process far too much of this food inefficiently through cattle. Moreover, our capacity to modify the environment is greatly increased by the use of fertilizers, ecocidal chemicals, and earth-moving and tree-cutting machinery ... Bad farming is probably the greatest threat to Gaia's health.[64]

Or, as Edward Goldsmith has observed:

The rapid degradation of the world's remaining agricultural lands is invariably attributed by governments and international agencies to traditional agricultural techniques. Thus US Aid attributes the rapid deterioration of 'the soil resource base' in arid lands to mismanagement, based on the use of 'traditional technology and agricultural practices' – though these technologies have been used sustainably for thousands of years ...

Malnutrition and famine are also attributed to archaic agricultural practices, and, in particular, to low inputs of fertiliser. A report based on a 20-year study jointly undertaken by the Food and Agricultural Organisation (FAO) and other organisations insists that the amount of food produced in the world is a direct function of fertiliser use, without mentioning the diminishing returns on excessive applications of fertiliser experienced whenever farmers have adopted modern agricultural methods.[65]

What does this mean for farming policy in a country such as Britain? Writing over twenty years ago, Robert Waller observed that:

The whole framework of prices, grants, subsidies and incentives within which he [the farmer] will be working will ... favour intensification. It developed basically within the 1947 Agricultural Act. This well-intentioned Act was designed to shield the farmer against the forces of the free market by fixing prices and subsidies that would assure him a reasonable livelihood. In practice it has had the opposite effect.[66]

Commenting on the ecological effects of intensive farming practices, Waller notes that:

Each one of the different technologies used to increase intensification is subject to a fundamental law of diminishing returns. Slowly the countless disadvantages resulting from each new input of machinery, fertiliser, pesticides, etc., will begin to outweigh their initial advantages. This process must render each further increment of growth achieved by these means progressively less profitable, until such time as negative returns set in.[67]

Intensive farming practices of this sort have been further reinforced by the provisions of the European Community's Common Agricultural Policy, which subsidizes overproduction. The question arises as to what policy framework for agriculture in Britain can be commended on grounds common to both Green and conservative perspectives, and by what standards current practices are to be assessed.

It is plain that the iniquitous Common Agricultural Policy must be phased out. At the same time, it is no less evident that subjecting farming, in Britain or in similar countries, to the exigencies of global markets is a recipe for environmental short-termism. (It is possible that the market reform of agriculture in New Zealand constitutes an exception to this generalization; but I cannot pursue the point here.) Wherever there remain small and medium-sized farms which are embedded in local communities to whose viability they make a decisive contribution, they deserve support and shelter from the global market if they cannot otherwise survive. The policy of subsidizing highly intensive, 'efficient' farming is precisely the opposite of that which is appropriate, when less 'efficient' farms, which have perhaps renewed themselves over several generations in contexts of markets that were not globalized, are at risk. The general function of tariffs and subsidies in relation to agriculture should be to act as an incentive to move away from high-intensive 'efficiency', rather than the contrary. (Agricultural subsidies may have, also, a strategic military justification, as in the Swiss and Japanese examples. This provides a further reason against the adoption of unrestrained free markets in farming.) In Britain, it is at least arguable that current CAP subsidies should be redirected to the support of organic farming methods which have a low impact on the soil and its related ecosystems, including a less intensive and more humane regime of life for breeding and caring for farm animals. It is not only arguable but also manifestly sensible, from any point of view which can be shared by genuine conservatives and Greens, that the destruction of small farms in the present economic depression should be arrested by reforms of current subsidy arrangements which take proper account both of the impact of farming practices on the natural environment and of the contribution of farming to the maintenance of rural community life.

It is no part of my brief here to try to specify the details of a sensible policy for agriculture in Britain. The goal of the argument is the simpler one of urging the repudiation of any agricultural policy which applies to farming norms of industrial productivity that neglect the non-renewability of many of the natural resources that enter into farming, which promote the further industrialization of farming, and which do not recognize the contribution that farming makes to the renewal of rural communities as one of its larger social benefits. It is this general framework of thought that must be applied to the details of policy as they pertain to the different varieties of farming which currently exist in Britain.

Urban and Transport Policy

A village or small town must . . . be arranged so as to confer on it a feeling of wholeness and oneness. In south-west France, the two neighbouring towns of Marmande and Villeneuve-sur-Lot are said to exert very different influences on their inhabitants. The former is stretched out along a main road, the latter, an ancient hastille, *is built round a central square. Of the two, it is the latter which is known for its spirited community.*

Cities . . . should also be designed on similar principles if they are to satisfy social needs. The central square is a very important feature, offering a place where the citizens can gather to run their affairs. The Greeks could not conceive a city without its agora. *Significantly, in the industrial cities of the West, as economic concerns take over from social ones, it is the shopping precinct with its multi-storied car park that is the focal point.*   Edward Goldsmith[68]

The typical American male devotes more than 1,600 hours to his car . . . He spends four of his sixteen waking hours on the road or gathering his resources for it. And this figure does not take into account the time consumed by other activities dictated by transport: time spent in hospitals, traffic courts and garages . . . The model American puts in 1,600 hours to get 7,500 miles: less than five miles per hour. In countries deprived of a transportation industry, people manage to do the same, walking wherever they want to go, and they allocate only three to eight per cent of their society's time budget to traffic instead of 29 per cent. What distinguishes the traffic in rich countries from the traffic in poor countries is not more mileage per hour of life-time for the majority, but more hours of compulsory consumption of high doses of energy, packaged and unequally distributed by the transportation industry.   Ivan Illich[69]

One feature of the Green conservative agenda that is central to my case has been intimated already, at several stages of the argument: namely, the rejection of a Green nostalgist hostility to the city, and of the corresponding arcadian conception of country life. To be sure, our discussion of agricultural policy has stressed the vital need to preserve rural communities, and to resist their destruction by crass development programmes and by the unfettered global market; and it will not be suggested that the good life can only be lived in cities. Green nostalgism for a lost (and, no doubt, substantially delusive) rural idyll is dangerous, nevertheless, in that it tends to obscure the real threats that now exist to one of humankind's most civilized institutional inventions, the city. It is the overdevelopment of the city, its deformation as a megalopolis, and its increasing insensitivity to the needs of those who labour and dwell in it that should be at the heart of an agenda of policy which is held in common by Greens and conservatives alike. In truth, the death of the city – an accomplished fact in parts of the United States – should be seen as a disaster in human ecology. The real and present danger is that it is occurring, in many modern countries, slowly and all but imperceptibly, but with ultimate effects on human social order which are all too visible in the limiting case of Detroit.

Urban policy and transport policy are, of course, closely interlinked – so closely that it may be worth looking at some of the absurdities of current transport policies (and the lack of them) before proceeding, with London as our exemplar, to try to say something on the larger issues of urban conservation and reconstruction. Since transport policy is a large and complex subject, my aim here, as elsewhere in this essay, is not to prescribe in detail; such a task would be not only beyond my competence but also profitless, given the very different policy dilemmas in different countries, and even within Britain. Instead, my aim is to sketch a rough outline of thought for policy which is animated by values of conservation and concern for the common life. The inevitable point of departure for critical reflection in the arena of transport policy, in Britain and in many Western countries, is its fatal domination by the private motor car and its requirements. The private motor car will always have a place in transport, and the argument I shall develop against it does not aim to eliminate that role; instead, my goal is to question the dominant place of the car in modern transport, and to do so by showing that its dominance is prejudicial to the common environment.

It may be worth glancing at a few global facts about cars and their effect on the environment before we look at their national and local impact. In under forty years (1950–88) the number of cars on the road across the world has multiplied by nearly ten times, from 53 million to 500 million. Cars account for about one-half of all air pollution, with three hundred pounds of 'greenhouse gas', carbon dioxide, being eventually released into the atmosphere for every fifteen gallons filled up. Worldwide, car accidents each year kill around a quarter of a million people, and seriously injure three million. The number of passenger cars rose by five times between the 1950s and the late 1980s. In Britain, each mile of a British motorway demands 25 acres of land, and each year up to 4,000 acres of rural land are paved over to be used as roads. Further, cars are extremely inefficient as a mode of transportation, both in terms of the number of people they carry, and because cars efficiently convert only 2–3 per cent of the potential energy in the oil refined for their use. The case against the private passenger car as a mode of transportation, stated solely in terms of its effects on the physical environment, is overwhelming.[70]

It is not the physical costs of over-reliance on the car but its impact on the life of urban (and other) communities that I want to focus on here. The impact of the car on cities is to destroy them as human settlements in which generations of people live and work together. It is well to recall that cities have not, traditionally, been concrete wastelands to which people repair only to work, and then flee; they have not been segregated by occupation or age, or carved up into residential and business areas; and they have, in consequence, been communities, not traffic intersections for transients whose lives are elsewhere and which at night have the funereal character of a deserted stage-set. Yet, at any rate in Britain today, this is what cities are fast becoming. As has recently been observed, 'London is becoming more mono-functional, increasingly divided into ghettos of poverty and affluence disrupted by traffic noise and pollution.'[71] And the reason for this degeneration is, in substantial part, to be found in the tyranny of the car: 'Leaving aside the costs of lost productivity caused by congestion, and the toll of deaths, injury and ill health, road traffic does more than anything else to undermine city neighbourhoods. Streets meant for shopping and meeting, green areas designed as places of recreation and relaxation become, respectively, trunk roads and roundabouts.'[72] The restoration of cities as public places for the enaction of the common life demands, first and foremost, policies for the drastic curtailment within cities of the motor car, a policy objective that is in any case justified by the deleterious effect on the health of city dwellers of car-related pollution.

No doubt an extension of market institutions into traffic control will be helpful to this end. Road-pricing, which has been technically feasible for some time but remains politically disfavoured, is a good example of the imaginative use in urban contexts of the price mechanism in the service of environmental concerns. It is hard to see how market solutions, by themselves, can be of much further use. An increase in petrol taxation might be defensible, though it is a blunt instrument of policy. Emission taxes on larger, less efficient cars are more worthy of serious consideration. Most importantly, however, is the recognition by policy-makers that only a massive expansion of public transport in Britain will diminish the role of the private car, with all of its environmental costs. One feature of such an expansion would undoubtedly be the enhancement of facilities for walkers and cyclists: in Britain, 37 per cent of passenger journeys and 32 per cent of travel time occur via walking or cycling, but these basic freedoms of mobility are very poorly planned for. The expansion of bus, railway and (in London and similar cities) underground services is a vital part of a policy aiming to curb the appetite (and the need) for the private car. Here we need to note that public transport may be privately owned and operated, and may (as with the growth of jitney services since coach deregulation in Britain) benefit from measures of economic liberalization. In transport, as elsewhere, there may well be a case for public funding of privately operated services, and so for privatization, where this does not create a private monopoly but rather promotes market competition. What cannot be shirked is the necessity in many areas of transport policy – rural buses being an obvious example – of governmental subsidy for environmental purposes. (In this connection, current proposals for the privatization of

British Rail are, at best, an exercise in irrelevance.) In transport, as in urban policy, few things are more pernicious than the market model of private persons making their several decisions. Such a model is bound to result in the running down of infrastructure – except for elements of it which benefit powerful interest groups, such as the motor industry – and the further erosion of communities and of cities as human settlements that contain communities.

The renewal and development of infrastructure in cities, at least in those built on the classic European model, requires decision-making by strategic planning authorities of a sort that can only be unthinkable to doctrinaire advocates of *laissez-faire*. This is not to say that intervention in the life of cities by governments has always been, or is ever likely to be, invariably beneficial: in Britain it involved the destruction of working-class communities by municipal housing programmes, and in the United States the further marginalization of black communities by urban-renewal policies.[73] The risks of further policy mistakes of this sort are unavoidable but against these we must set the certainty that uncontrolled private development will evacuate cities of their common life, and produce a common environment that is anomic, chaotic and aesthetically repellent. Both conservatives and Greens must acknowledge that only strategic planning authorities, of the sorts that are active in all of the other major European cities, can preserve British cities as places of aesthetic integrity and human amenity, as human settlements in which the inherently public goods of common life are protected.

Concern for the aesthetic integrity of cities confers on planning authorities another important responsibility: that of preserving the city as a place of pleasing buildings, in harmonious styles, and of composing a beautiful landscape and living-place. In part, the task of such authorities will reasonably be conservative and restrictive, that of denying planning permission to developments which would disrupt local architectural styles or would diminish the city as a setting for common life. An excellent example is that of the municipal authorities in Salzburg, who granted permission for a McDonald's outlet in that city only on condition that its architecture conform to the traditional style of the city. Such authorities will also reasonably concern themselves with restoration: with removing the uninhabited ruins of architectural modernism and replacing them with buildings which are worth living in and looking at. That this is not a utopian vision is shown by the real examples that we have in such European cities as Siena and Barcelona. Throughout much of Europe, but as yet very intermittently in Britain where planning institutions remain weak, cities have been renewed and conserved by imaginative and resourceful planning. Such planning will be rejected by *laissez-faire* dogmatists, who cannot grasp that the city is a form of life in itself, and not an individualist congeries of strangers; but the conservative pedigree of such planning policies for cities is impeccable, reaching back in Europe for centuries.

Such policies are radical in effect, but conservative in inspiration. Limiting the private passenger car – which one American conservative has called 'the mechanical Jacobin'[74] – is a potent corrective against the further weakening of the ties of street and local communities. Restoring cities as public places which are safe and pleasing, and in which we may take pride, gives an occasion for civic virtue, in the absence of which we are a society of transients. Even where, as will often be the case, national governmental funding is necessary for urban regeneration, it is best disbursed at local level, where it will be most responsive to the feedback of local people. Wherever market institutions can be introduced which facilitate this feedback, there is a strong case for their adoption. On this basis, it may well be worth considering charging for local services, when these are not elements in inherently public goods and so aspects of the common life, and where the price is genuinely responsive to consumers. However, for conservatives who are not mesmerized by the delusive harmonies of neo-liberalism and for Greens, the task of protecting and renewing the city cannot be envisaged, let alone achieved, without strategic planning by local authorities of infrastructural development, which reproduces the common environment within which cities can renew themselves as living human settlements whose members span the generations.

Education and Health

When cities are built around vehicles, they devalue human feet; when schools pre-empt learning, they devalue the auto-didact; when hospitals draft all those who are in critical condition, they impose on society a new form of dying.

Ivan Illich[75]

It is obvious that the current condition of educational institutions in Britain, and still more in the United States, offers little of comfort to conservatives. Schools regularly fail to achieve their most basic goals of inculcating literacy and numeracy in children; they are staffed by teachers whose competence and performance are not monitored, and who often cleave to outmoded progressive teaching methods that have long proved demonstrably ineffective; and, in the inner cities, they are plagued by mass truancy. Higher education is a bastion of an antinomian counter-culture whose relationship to the rest of society is one of ingrained hostility. It is plain that educational institutions are transmitting neither the skills nor the values whereby a stable society renews itself.

The response to this predicament by neo-liberals has been to advocate the privatization of schools and other educational institutions, or at least the introduction into them of market institutions. I have elsewhere criticized the commonest variation on this neo-liberal response, the proposal of a voucher scheme for schools, on a variety of grounds.[76] It should be said that actual conservative policy on education in Britain has not followed the voucher route, but has instead focused on releasing state schools from the control of local educational authorities by giving them the freedom to 'opt out' and become centrally funded but self-governing institutions, constrained only by the provisions of the national curriculum. This is a framework for policy in schooling that neo-liberals predictably attack, despite the fact that bringing state schools under the national funding umbrella emancipates them from far more invasive local authorities, and to that extent insulates them from political influence. The resultant situation can hardly be worse than that which preceded it, and may well in some respects be significantly better.

Voucher schemes do not in any case go to the root of the problems of modern schooling in a country such as Britain, which arise from the transformation of education into an arm of industry, and from the institutional monopoly which schools themselves have over learning. Schooling as we know it in Britain today is not much more than a century old. Literacy and numeracy were spreading quickly and widely among ordinary people in the nineteenth century well before compulsory schooling was instituted,[77] and the contribution of schools to their further promotion – like that of medical care to the prevention of disease – is easily exaggerated. The decline that has occurred in educational standards in Britain since the 1960s, say, has further limited the role of schools in transmitting essential skills and values. It has done so, pretty well across the board of the different varieties of schools, with some private schools doing less well than some state schools when measured by traditional standards. Doubtless the reckless experimentation with teaching methods and curricula in the state schools in the 1960s, the headlong rush into comprehensivation and the near-abolition of selective state schools during that period, all contributed to the erosion of educational standards. It is noteworthy, however, that it is the adoption of progressive methods of teaching which seems the decisive variable here, and that this was spread across both state and private schools. Privatization of itself would accordingly be no remedy for this decline, which has deeper institutional and cultural roots. From this point of view, neo-liberal voucher schemes are merely an irrelevance.

The chief defect of voucher schemes, from the standpoint of a conservative (or a Green) who is concerned with the renewal of community, is that they fail to address the institutional monopoly of learning by schools. Such a monopoly was tolerable, when teaching in schools was governed by a tacit curriculum of inherited skills, values and cultural understandings that expressed the traditions of local communities; it becomes insupportable when schools are estranged from the communities that they are supposed to serve, and reproduce themselves (rather than their communities) in alienated unemployables. Though Britain contains many good schools, in the state as well as in the private sector, in which something akin to a traditional education is still offered, it is increasingly plain that schools as institutions have, on the whole, become insensitive to the skills and traditions that they exist to transmit, and often indifferent to the communities that they serve. Voucher schemes have the merit of extending to the poor a range of choice which is currently enjoyed by the affluent, and of ending the inequity whereby families of modest means, who nevertheless scrape together the funds to finance private education for their children, end up paying twice. It is unclear that voucher schemes, as currently advocated by neo-liberals, would do much, if anything, to remedy the failings that belong generically to the majority of contemporary schools, state-supported and private.

One solution to this dilemma may be in a system of educational credits for all, which is not tied to attendance at schools but instead to measured achievement in literacy and numeracy, the two most basic skills which present schooling inculcates least successfully. The basic content of such a scheme has been set out by Illich, programmatically:

Right now educational credit good at any skill center could be provided in limited amounts for people of all ages, and not just to the poor. I envisage such credit in the form of an educational passport or an 'edu-credit card' provided to each citizen at birth. In order to favour the poor, who would probably not use their yearly grants early in life, a provision could be made that interest accrue to later users of cumulated 'entitlements'. Such credits would permit most people to acquire the skills most in demand, at their convenience, better, faster, cheaper and with fewer undesirable side effects than in school.[78]

There is little doubt that enabling pupils, or their families, to choose among a range of venues and methods of learning, which were not restricted to the institution of the school, would result in a blossoming in many fields of teaching of traditional teaching methods. As Illich notes:

The strongly motivated student who is faced with the task of acquiring a new and complex skill may benefit greatly from the discipline now associated with the old-fashioned schoolmaster who taught reading, Hebrew, catechism or multiplication by rote. School has now made this kind of drill teaching rare and disreputable, yet there are many skills which a motivated student with normal aptitudes can master in a matter of a few months if taught in the traditional way. This is as true of codes as of their encipherment; of second and third languages as of reading and writing; and equally of special languages such as algebra, computer programming, chemical analysis, or of manual skills like typing, watchmaking, plumbing, wiring, TV repair; or, for that matter, dancing, drawing and diving . . . At present schools pre-empt most educational funds. Drill instruction which costs less than comparable schooling is now a privilege of those rich enough to bypass the schools, and those whom either the army or big business sends through in-service training.[79]

The central idea of such a proposal is akin to that of the voucher, in that it confers purchasing power on individuals for the acquisition (in a context of market competition for their provision) of a specified range of services; but it differs radically from the voucher scheme, as it figures in recent neo-liberal policy proposals, in not requiring that the services be provided in a specific institutional setting (the school) and therefore in not presupposing attendance in schools. In this way it goes much further than any neo-liberal measure could: it not only severs public financing of a good from its market provision but also severs its provision from the narrow context of any specific institution – in this case, the declining institution of the school. It thereby cuts a Gordian knot in neo-liberal policy: that surrounding compulsory schooling and the definition of schools themselves. In this proposal, education credit could be used in any institutional context (including that of schools) which could show a record of achievement in transmitting specific skills. The obligation on families would not be to assure school attendance by their children, but to enable them (with the use of the educational credits) to acquire specified basic skills. These latter could be subject to assessment by state examinations (as proposed over a century ago by J. S. Mill)[80] and the institutions, or 'skill centres', which taught them would also be subject to governmental accreditation, based on objective performance criteria for the transmission of the skills; both of these would be legitimate uses of governmental activity. (Of course, the obligations of families in bringing up their children to specified levels of literacy and numeracy would need to be qualified with respect to disability and retardation; but this is, I think, a matter of detail in the overall proposal, which does not affect its major thrust.) At the same time, the compulsory element in schooling would have been removed, and the privileging of schools with governmental finance (an objectionable feature of all current voucher schemes) would have been ended: school would have been disestablished. One predictable result of exposing schools in this way to competition by non-school institutions would be a drastic and rapid improvement in the quality of schooling itself.

The educational credit proposal, like the voucher schemes it is designed to supplant, need not come in only one form; it could have many variations and be introduced in a series of incremental steps. For the vast majority where incomes are adequate, it could take the form of a tax credit for each child, to be spent at any accredited school, state or private, and at any accredited, non-school 'skill centre'. For those whose incomes are too low for tax credits to be feasible, an educational credit card (akin to the voucher) would be needed, usable on the same liberal terms as tax credits. Providing that a poverty trap was not thereby created, there is no reason why, in the interests of opening up opportunities for the worst-off, such a credit card for learning purposes need not be worth significantly more than the tax credits of more affluent families. Equally, as Illich indicates, there is no reason why such a learning credit card should be restricted to children: it could, and should, be available as a means of reskilling (or skilling for the first time) those who discover, later in life, that schools have failed them, or whose existing skills have been rendered obsolete by economic or social change. In this proposal, learning is conceived as a lifelong engagement whose limits are not those of the institution of the school, but only of the lives of learners. The basic skills specified for children would, by necessity, be different from (and far more uniform than) those needed by most people later in life, and monitoring and accreditation procedures would differ accordingly. The device of an educational credit would link learning at all levels, nevertheless, while freeing it from the disabling confines of an institution from which traditional understandings of learning and teaching have often vanished.

From a conservative perspective, a radical proposal on the lines sketched has the advantage of promising to revivify traditions of learning in all of their variety. From a Green perspective that is shared by conservatives, it should be welcomed as rendering more permeable the barriers between learning and working, between work and leisure, that disfigure modernist societies. The prospect opened up by such a proposal is that of learning occurring in the context of a common life which harbours flourishing schools, but in which the school is no longer a hermetic institution, whose funding and legal status separate it from the vernacular transactions of its supporting communities. Of course, the disestablishment of school does not mean that there will be no schools, any more than the disestablishment of Churches means that there are to be no more Churches; nor, in the proposal here advanced (as distinct, perhaps, from that of Illich) does it mean that people may not use their educational credits to acquire an education in schools. The proposal is designed to foster greater institutional pluralism in learning and, as a likely result of such diversity, to restore or save otherwise disappearing (but nonetheless highly effective) traditions in education. It may be that the disestablishment of school is now, in some countries such as Britain and the United States, the only measure that can rescue traditional understandings of teaching and learning. Arguably, and ironically, it may be the only way to save schools from what is otherwise their manifest fate – that of becoming adjuncts to an industrial economy, for which, no less ironically, they produce workers lacking in most of the skills and moral capacities that are demanded by work in the conditions of late industrial society. It is in order to deliver schools from this fate of becoming a hybrid institution, part prison, part playground, part outdoor poor relief, that the radical measure of disestablishment is contemplated.

It is not envisaged that a radical measure of this sort could or should be introduced rapidly in Britain, or similar countries. Incremental and gradualist measures are clearly appropriate. A reduction (rather than outright abolition) of the compulsory school leaving age, together with the provision of educational credit for those who choose this option, is one such incremental measure. No doubt there are many others which might be conceived. A weighty consideration in framing all such gradualist measures is that they enhance the capacity for exit

– currently zero, aside from that afforded by truancy – of the poorest members of our society, who are worst served by schools. Accordingly, if vouchers are to figure as an element in a phased policy of school disestablishment, they should begin by being conferred upon the poorest families, who have most need for them. No measure could do more to prevent the further growth in Britain of an estranged underclass, unemployable across several generations, which – as the American experience graphically illustrates – constitutes one of the greatest impediments to a harmonious common life in our cities. And, in any case, no measure can be justified, in this or other areas of policy, which does not enhance the well-being of those positioned in the underclass as the direct result of their being trapped in ghettos created by the misconceived interventionist policies of an earlier generation.

Sensible reflection on a conservative policy for health care begins with the recognition that ideally acceptable institutions for the promotion of health and the care of the sick exist nowhere in the world. Countries, such as those of the post-Communist bloc, which have attempted a full-scale, comprehensive socialization of medical care have produced a morass of corruption in which medical resources are scarce and very inequitably distributed. They embody a model for health that no sane conservative (or Green) would wish to emulate. However, the American market-driven system of medical care is hardly a model that any sane conservative would adopt either. With costs climbing inexorably towards a sixth of US gross domestic product, plagued by litigation and defensive medicine, straitjacketed by the worst drug-testing bureaucracy in the world, and leaving nearly forty million of its citizens without medical coverage of any systematic sort, the American system of medical care performs extremely poorly by comparison with the systems of countries such as Britain and Greece which, unlike the USA, spend only a fraction of their GDP on medical care. In fact, the British National Health Service performs remarkably well, both in terms of cost-containment and in terms of its adequacy as perceived by its users in many areas of care. Indeed, current reform measures, aiming at the creation within the NHS of markets through the transformation of hospitals into independent trusts, may well prove costly remedies for tolerable ills in the old system, which a genuine conservative policy should probably have left alone. (This is not to say that current reform measures can or should be reversed; any future administration has no option but to try to make them work.) Certainly, no policy for the National Health Service could be worse conceived than one of privatization or marketization on the American model, given its record.

Reform of the National Health Service in Britain, like reform of other systems of health care in other countries, begins by accepting a few truisms which are denied by many in the current Pelagian climate of opinion but which are central to both conservative and Green outlooks on human life. There must first be acceptance of the limits of medical care. We are all going to die, and it cannot be the proper office of medical care to thwart the course of nature – rather, to assist and smooth its way. Many, if not most, episodic ailments are self-limiting: either the healing resources of the body cope with them or else death supervenes. Medical care can help in moments of crisis and can assist in adapting to chronic illness; it cannot wipe out sickness or conjure away our mortality. When it attempts to do so, iatrogenic illness becomes a worse affliction than those that befall us in the natural course of things. Much modern medicine is pathological in its denial of death and reflects the broader culture of which it is a part in refusing to recognize that we may thrive in dying, just as our souls may wither in senseless longevity. Virtually all of modern medical care resists this implication, but it is an inexorable result of existing medical technology, which can keep us 'alive' almost indefinitely, that death must henceforth be for us – except in the context of catastrophic accident – a chosen option, if we are to be spared the death-in-life that follows from many forms of illness, disability and senility. This is a crucial point to which I shall return.

Medicine can do little about the frailties of our condition, and nothing about our mortality; these remain subject to fortune and genetic fate. It must be accepted, also, that medical care has contributed comparatively little to the improvement of health that has undoubtedly occurred in recent times. This, as Illich and others have amply shown,[81] arises far more from improvements in sanitation and other aspects of the environment, in diet and in lifestyle, than from any sort of medical intervention. The task of medicine, which is understood in Britain by wise general practitioners, is often, if not typically, to help patients to cope with ailments which arise from their lives as a whole and which medical intervention cannot hope to cure. For the most part, our ailments arise from the way in which we live (or the genes that we have acquired in the genetic lottery); we cannot hope for a medical cure for them, we can hope only, at best, for their alleviation. This is a truth which is obscured by popular discourse of 'the war against cancer' – as if death were an enemy that could be vanquished rather than, at last, a friend to be welcomed – and which is denied in macabre high-tech medicine involving organ transplantation. The major phases in the human life-cycle are not necessarily occasions for medical intervention. For millennia, people have been born, have suffered pain and illness and have died, without these occurrences being understood as treatable disorders. There remain many who wish their children to be born at home, their illnesses and old age to be lived through at home, and who want to die at home. The medicalization of human life, which has occurred in all modern societies, increasingly denies us these options. As Illich has put it, describing one end of the spectrum of this medicalization of the human life-cycle: 'Only the very rich and the very independent can choose to avoid that medicalisation of the end to which the poor must submit and which becomes increasingly intense and universal as the society they live in becomes richer.'[82] The question remains, what is to be done to reverse this trend to ever greater medicalization of human life? And how might such an objective be achieved, while preserving (or extending) access to basic, decent medical care, where this is a manifest human need? Illich has stated, in the most general terms, what needs to be done:

In several nations, the public is now ready for a review of its health-care system. Although there is a serious danger that the forthcoming debate will reinforce the present frustrating medicalisation of life, the debate could still become fruitful if attention were focused on medical nemesis, if the recovery of personal responsibility for health care were made the central issue, and if limitations on professional monopolies were made the major goal of legislation.[83]

Let us see how this programmatic statement might be applied in the context of a country such as Britain.

It must be acknowledged, first of all, that many medical procedures, which are currently restricted to members of the medical profession, can be performed safely and intelligently by trained laypeople. The tendency to further professionalization of medical care must be resisted and reversed, professional monopolies curbed or broken, and competency in a variety of medical tasks allowed to para-medical personnel. Even the licensure of physicians itself – the corner-stone of the privilege of the medical guild in the United States, but important in Britain also – must come under critical questioning, as should the ever increasing designation of medicines as prescription-only medications. It would, of course, be absurd to propose, in the fashion of radical libertarian critics of contemporary institutions such as Thomas Szasz, that all legal limitations on medical practice and on pharmaceutical freedom be abolished forthwith; that is a measure that no conservative or Green thinker could sensibly support. There is nevertheless every reason for professional monopolies to be curtailed and pharmaceutical freedoms enhanced, in order to achieve the recovery of personal responsibility for health and the reversal of the dehumanizing medicalization of life. The contemporary world contains a variety of regimes for the medical profession: pharmaceutical freedom is significantly greater in continental Europe and in Latin America than in English-speaking countries (of which the United States is, by far, the most restrictive); the freedoms and competencies of nurses, midwives, pharmacists, opticians and others in the medical professions vary widely across jurisdictions; and different countries are at different stages on the road to the medicalization of life that the omnicompetent authority of the medical guild carries with it. There is no reason why a policy of restoring personal responsibility for health should not borrow eclectically from these differing regimes for the medical profession, with a view to relaxing and, perhaps, eventually curtailing the professional monopoly of doctors.

In this connection, the recovery of personal responsibility for health would be assisted by reforms in the funding of health services. In Britain, where the National Health Service will remain the cornerstone of health care, there is a good case for a hypothecated health tax, with an exit option for those who prefer private arrangements solely. Such an exit option should be framed to permit those who exercise it to use the resources so released not only on conventional medical care but also on alternative therapies which are, at present, only rarely available within the NHS. Two further fundamental points must here be recognized: first, the relative performance and the epistemological credentials of conventional medicine, as compared with many alternative therapies, are far less impressive than mainstream opinion allows; second, the choice among therapies, conventional or alternative, should so far as is practicable be that of the patient him/herself. An enabling condition of such freedom among therapeutic regimes, however, is a revision of the neo-liberal health voucher, analogous to that proposed earlier for the education voucher, such that it covers alternative traditions of medicine and not only that of conventional, scientistic Western medicine. To be sure, there will always be a shifting borderline between what is counted as medical care and what is regarded as a genuine alternative tradition of medical theory and practice. In part, this arises from our irremediable ignorance – obscured by much mainstream medical authority – of what is best for our health. As Illich observes,

Nobody knows how much health care will be worth to him in terms of money and pain. In addition, nobody knows if the most advantageous form of health care is obtained from medical producers, from a travel agent, or by renouncing work on the night shift. The family that forgoes a car to move to a Manhattan apartment can foresee how the substitution of rent for gas will affect their available time; but the person who, upon the diagnosis of cancer, chooses an operation over a binge in the Bahamas does not know what effect his choice will have on his remaining time of grace. The economics of health is a curious discipline, somewhat reminiscent of the theology of indulgences that flourished before Luther. You can count what the friars collect, you can look at the temples they build, you can take part in the liturgies they indulge in, but you can only guess what the traffic in remission from purgatory does to the soul after death. Models developed to account for the willingness of taxpayers to foot rising medical bills constitute similar scholastic guesswork about the new world-spanning church of medicine.[84]

Our ignorance as to what are the best remedies for our ailments justifies the most liberal form of voucher, or health credit scheme, for those who wish to opt out of the NHS. (It also supports moves towards greater diversity in medical traditions within the NHS, as I shall argue later.) Of course, this amended voucher proposal could not escape all of the difficulties of standard neo-liberal proposals: difficulties created by disability, uninsurability, and so on. It would therefore be a serious error to regard it – as neo-liberals regard their own pet measures – as a panacea for all of the dilemmas of health care. In promoting choice and pluralism in health care, however, it would also do its bit for the recovery of personal responsibility for health that should be the aim of conservatives and Greens alike. Recognizing that both the perception of health and the definition of illness are personal judgements rooted in cultural traditions, it would devolve health-care decisions to the level of specific individuals in definite communities. The aim would be to promote individual choice of medical services in the context of a pluralistic diversity of medical institutions and traditions, with professional monopoly being progressively relaxed, so that an ever greater variety of practitioners – herbalists, homeopaths, acupuncturists, holistic and traditional doctors, and so forth – could, through the unfettered choice of individuals in their communities, receive support from an extended health credit system. (As noted above, such credits would need to be fine-tuned, so as to be significantly greater for those – the disabled, the chronic sick, and so on – with greater medical needs. The problems that are raised by such fine-tuning do not seem to me to be insoluble or to affect the proposal decisively.) The proposal which is advanced would have the inestimable advantage, not possessed by standard neo-liberal measures, of promoting competition not only between the NHS and private practice but also between orthodox and alternative medical practices and traditions.

All systems of health care, including one containing an extended medical credit scheme of the sort sketched above, are systems for the rationing of medical resources. Not all medical needs are insatiable (contrary to neo-liberal dogma); but enough of them have the property of insatiability to make rationing – by price, formula or clinical discretion – unavoidable. Often such rationing involves decisions of life or death, or decisions which dictate the future quality of life of patients irreversibly. Any reform of medical care aiming to promote responsibility and enhance dignity must encompass measures enabling patients to reject medical care, and to prevent their unwilling survival. No scheme of reform of health care is adequate which does not contain measures for enabling and empowering patients as agents in these decisions. This entails the legal empowerment of patients, or of those whom they have assigned as their guardians, to request euthanasia, under conditions specified by the patient. Conservatives who resist arguments for euthanasia have not noticed that a natural death is, perhaps, rarer now than at any time in human history. It is threatened, for those in the highly industrialized societies, not (as hitherto in our history) by war or civil violence but instead by the medicalization of human life: 'The technical and the non-technical consequences of institutional medicine coalesce and generate a new kind of suffering: anaesthetised, impotent and solitary survival in a world turned into a hospital ward.'[85] Only the legal availability of euthanasia, physician-assisted where necessary, as provided for in a version of the Living Will mandating termination of life under specified conditions, can end the absurdity and moral horror in which we currently warehouse for survival those who would, often enough, vastly prefer to exercise the ultimate form of exit option. Where natural death is an uncovenanted blessing which is denied to virtually all of us, resistance to the death-by-choice of voluntary euthanasia is not wisdom, conservative or otherwise, but rather a fetishization of physical survival, which is condemned by all of the world's religions and offensive to human dignity. If patients are not in this most crucial of all decisions empowered as agents, then we transfer authority from responsible persons to the servants of medical institutions, themselves increasingly conceived as industries for the maintenance of human machines. We are then not far from the transforming of the patient into an object, and of medicine itself from a humane profession into a branch of biological engineering, whose ultimate output is soulless survival.

Reform of contemporary medical institutions and practice – in Britain, and in similar countries – cannot avoid taking the road of deprofessionalization, of curbing and limiting professional monopoly over health care. An extended health voucher or health credit scheme of the sort proposed, though not without its difficulties, could assist in promoting this objective in the context of legal reforms to break down professional monopoly. No doubt there will always be a place for governmental involvement in health care, even in countries where health care is entirely privately provided, if only to guarantee that children's health be protected and public health safeguarded. In respect of adults, however, considerations of personal responsibility for health, and of our ignorance as to what is best for our health (shared by the medical profession in many cases), argue for the greatest feasible individual freedom. The extended health voucher, as discussed so far, together with provision for the ultimate exit option of euthanasia (in many circumstances, though not all, itself merely a refusal of further treatment) would go a very considerable distance toward this goal. A health credit which was usable in a diversity of medical traditions would meet Paul Feyerabend's desideratum that 'health and sickness are to be determined by the traditions to which the healthy or sick person belongs and within this tradition again by the particular ideal of life a person has formed for himself.'[86] Of course, there will always be a question, which can never be decided *a priori*, as to what is to count as a *bona fide* tradition of medical treatment and what as a medical service. It may be, for this reason, that individual freedom can be safeguarded (the interests of children and the problems of public health aside) only if the extended health credit, which is advanced here as part of an exit option from the National Health Service in Britain but which is applicable in other, similar countries, be returnable entirely to the individual as free purchasing power. This appears to be the logic of returning health care to personal responsibility.

It is not my argument that deprofessionalization and the enhancement of personal freedom in medical care be applied solely in the context of an exit option from the NHS. On the contrary, the aim – as with an educational credit for non-school institutions, one of whose aims is the revitalization of schooling – is to encourage these developments within the NHS also. This reflects my belief that, though a hypothecated health tax with an exit option that is in the end redeemable as free purchasing power is defensible on grounds of personal freedom, the crucial considerations in the reform of health care are not whether its funding or organization is public or private, but instead the degree of professional monopoly within it, the diversity of medical traditions available to the patient, and his or her opportunities for controlling the care offered to him or her. These are the decisive considerations that should govern health-care reform in countries such as Britain, not narrow concerns about funding. The mix of funding and organizational arrangements for health care will, inevitably and desirably, vary considerably from country to country, and from time to time. Even in the case of Britain, there is no *a priori* way of determining the institutional mix that will be most appropriate for medical care in the future, except to say that the NHS will remain the point of departure for sensible reform, even if (as proposed here) there be instituted an exit option from it. No doubt the best institutional framework for health care in Britain is one that allows for the maximum of diversity in a setting that allows for, and has incentives for, further unplanned developments; but there is a variety of forms that this institutional framework might take, and I have not tried to settle here the issues between them. It is no part of the argument here to try to settle which of these arrangements is to be adopted, since none will be universally desirable and the relevant reasonings are always circumstantial, not applications of first principles. The general thesis remains: that conservative values of respect for individuals and for the communities in which they live their lives mandate a reform of health care which is aimed at limiting professional monopoly within it and promoting the recovery of personal responsibility for health. This – together with the recognition that frailty and mortality are parts of our condition, not treatable disorders in it – should be a framework of thought that is eminently acceptable to Greens.

CONCLUSION

The project of science, as I understand it, is to solve the mystery, to wake us from our dream, to destroy the myth; and were this project fully achieved, not only should we find ourselves awake in a profound darkness, but a dreadful insomnia would settle upon mankind, not less intolerable for being only a nightmare. Michael Oakeshott[87]

We know now that a completely planned heaven is either impossible or unbearable. We know that it is not true that design can come only out of planning. Out of luxuriant waste, unmoved by selection, come designs more beautiful and in greater variety than man could plan.

Garrett Hardin[88]

My argument has been that there are many natural affinities between conservative philosophy and Green thought, from which both may profit. Conservatives must learn from Green thought that the promise of open-ended global growth, held out by today's neo-liberal descendants of Herbert Spencer, is delusive; instead they must turn their attention to the sources of legitimacy by which social institutions could be sustained in a stationary-state economy. In repudiating the fashionable heresies of neo-liberalism, conservatives are merely returning to an older and sounder Tory tradition, which perceived the illusoriness of the sovereign, autonomous chooser of liberal theory, and so insisted on the primacy of the common life. The importance of Green thought for conservatives today is that it recalls them to their historic task of giving shelter to communities and reproducing them across the generations – in a context of finite resources which dictates stability, not growth, as the pre-eminent conservative value.

An encounter between conservative and Green thought compels important revisions in some standard conservative positions. It is unreasonable for conservatives to disregard the dangers inherent in the present growth of human population, and perverse for them to resist measures for its control. Conservatives must learn to be open to radical criticism of current institutions of market capitalism and of the health and education professions, insofar as they are predicated on spurious promises of indefinite growth or open-ended progress, and so depart both from Green thought and from genuine conservative philosophy. Conservatives need to explore, with Greens and others, as yet unthought-of dilemmas of life in societies which are no longer buoyed up by the prospect of incessant economic growth or by modernist pseudo-religions of endless world-improvement.

On the other hand, Greens need from conservatives a vital tincture of realism without which their thought, and so their policy proposals, become merely utopian. It is supremely pointless for Greens to insist that the alternatives before our species are only a total transformation of our condition or oblivion. If that is so, we may confidently predict oblivion as our fate. In this, we would only be applying an aspect of the Gaia hypothesis, well stated by Lovelock:

Gaia, as I see her, is no doting mother, tolerant of misdemeanours, nor is she some fragile and delicate damsel in danger from brutal mankind. She is stern and tough, always keeping the world warm and comfortable for those who obey the rules, but ruthless in her destruction of those who transgress. Her unconscious goal is a planet fit for life. If humans stand in the way of this, we shall be eliminated with as little pity as would be shown by the micro-brain of an intercontinental ballistic missile in full flight to its target.[89]

The prospect of a Gaian decimation of the world's human population has indeed been welcomed by the most radical supporters of the *wild-politik*, such as John Aspinall:

Some of us are now drawn to believe that a demo-catastrophe will be an eco-bonanza. In other words, a population readjustment on a planetary scale from 4,000 million to something in the nature of 200 million would be the only possible solution for the survival of our species and of the eco-system or systems that nurtured us.

But Aspinall goes on immediately to ask what might the price be in terms of the well-being of other species, of such a catastrophic curtailment of human hubris:

The next great death might last a millennium, but during it, and indeed before it, who knows how many genera of plant and bird and beast would be swept away? . . . What will be left? What will survive the holocaust? The surviving world must be a diminished world; at its worst, a world in apocalyptic, irreversible decline; at its best, one savagely mutilated, even dismembered.[90]

Only Panglossians – Marxist, neo-liberal, humanist or Pelagian – will gainsay Aspinall's apocalyptic vision. If there is any consolation, it comes from the Gaian hypothesis itself, which suggests that a reduction in biodiversity might be the route to stability for the remaining life-forms on earth.

Lest these prospects seem overly apocalyptic, it is well to remind ourselves of one of the facts of our age that is rarely addressed by Greens, save in a spirit of pacifist wish-fulfilment: that is, the apparently inexorable proliferation of ever cheaper technologies of mass destruction. It is worth recalling that the international order in which, for the while, we live, is a Hobbesian state of nature, an anarchy containing well over a hundred sovereign states. Of these states, many are desperately unstable, riven by internal ethnic and other conflicts; some, like Bangladesh or Indonesia, confront large Malthusian problems; others, such as some African, Middle Eastern and Balkan states, are ruled by criminals or fanatics. To all of these states there is an uncontrollable leakage of weaponries of spiralling lethality – a leakage that has been massively increased in speed, magnitude and danger by the collapse of order in the former Soviet Union. It beggars belief to suppose that these weapons will not be used in the coming decades, with incalculable cost to human and other life. In former Yugoslavia, ethnic war of the sort that is likely to dominate the coming century has already endangered a fragile and precious part of the human environment, the city of Dubrovnik, and is degrading much of what is left of the natural environment. It is difficult not to foresee military convulsions, far vaster in scale than those in former Yugoslavia and using far more destructive technologies, wreaking irreparable harm on the environment in the years to come. If, for our species, the coming century looks like being one of wars, massacres and forced migrations, of which the holocausts of our own century are but precursors, for the other species with which we share a common environment the prospect looks hardly less bleak.

Such sobering prospects – whose realism will be doubted only by fundamentalist believers in progress – should occasion in both conservative and Green thinkers a mood of almost desperate humility. There will be no conversion to an ecological worldview that will deliver us from ourselves: we must make what little we can of the human animal as we find it. This means recognizing that local environmental improvement can always be swept away by bandit states, by ecological terrorism or by Malthusian invasion: it is always precarious and ever endangered. In turn, for Greens, this should compel a revision of attitude to some recent technologies, including (hardest of all for Greens who see themselves as inheritors of earlier protest movements) the technologies involved in space-based defence systems. Fallible as the latter are, they are probably the best defence that we have in an intractably anarchic world against environmental catastrophes produced by weaponries of mass destruction. (Given the speed with which nuclear weapons systems can be reassembled, proposals for multilateral nuclear disarmament, like most arms-control proposals, are of little avail. This is true even supposing – what is plainly false – that inspection and enforcement are always feasible. Such measures may have limited uses in specific contexts, as perhaps currently in negotiating between Russia and the Western allies; they do not solve problems of proliferation or obviate the need for space-based defence systems.) Green resistance to serious thought about the possibilities of such systems is only the clearest symptom of their refusal to contemplate the strategic–military dimensions of environmental conservation in our time. It is also an exemplar of the uncritically and unselectively hostile attitude of many Greens to new technologies with which, like them or not, we are saddled, and which we cannot hope to disinvent.

In part, such technologies as are involved in space-based defence systems are, like many others, prophylactic devices against other technologies which are otherwise uncontrollable. The task of using technology to tame itself is one that fate forces upon us. In this, as in so much else, Greens should heed the wise words of Lovelock, when he tells us that 'there can be no voluntary resignation from technology. We are so inextricably part of the technosphere that giving it up is as unrealistic as jumping off a ship in mid-Atlantic to swim the rest of the journey in glorious independence.'[91] Equally, Green hostility to the urban–industrial environment that modern humans have contrived for themselves misidentifies the real threats to their natural environment, which come from proliferating technologies of mass destruction, from farming, and, above all, from the growing deadweight of human numbers. As Lovelock has concluded: 'It seems therefore that the principal dangers to our planet arising from man's activities may not be the special and singular evils of his urbanized industrial existence.'[92] There can be no turning back from our current mode of life in cities, with its complex technologies; only a radical reform of them, with ecological stability as its aim. Protecting the environment from further human depredations will demand better technologies; it cannot be achieved by the Quixotist posture of trying to remove technology or abandon industrialism. Any people who attempted such a renunciation would soon be destroyed or conquered by others who had retained modern technology in its most invasive and destructive forms. This is a predicament that no ecological conversion can escape.

Green thought can learn from conservative philosophy the basic lesson of not looking after ultimate outcomes but, instead, of improvising humbly in order to avoid catastrophe and to stave off calamity. Green theory is an invaluable corrective of the Whiggish, anthropocentric, technological optimism by which all the modernist political religions are animated and which has, in the form of neo-liberalism, even infected most of what passes today as conservatism. From conservative philosophy, Greens must learn that the institutions of civil society are hard-won achievements, not to be casually thrown away for the sake of any ecological utopia. With all of their limitations and the needs that I have identified, which mandate their supplementation and restriction, the institutions of civil society – including market institutions, suitably amended – are the only set of institutions whereby any civilization can in our age renew itself. The alternative to civil society – to an order of private property and contractual liberty, defined (and constrained) by a rule of a law that demarcates the spheres, and sets the boundaries, of autonomous social institutions – is only barbarism, in which both the human and the natural environments are laid waste. Our century is littered with the debris of political variations on Pascal's wager, in which people have gambled that the familiar conveniences of civil society can be transcended, and supplanted, by another order, whose outlines they could as yet only dimly perceive. All such wagers have proved to be bad bets. Greens would be more consistent, and more prudent, if they regarded the institutions of civil society, including the market economy, as elements in a social ecology or spontaneous order,[93] akin to those found in the ecologies of natural environments, which human reason can barely understand, let alone redesign. This is not to say that human environments – such as cities, or markets, for that matter – are invariably self-regulating, or that their workings cannot sometimes be improved upon by judicious intervention; but rather that intervention should typically take the form of alterations in the framework within which spontaneous activity occurs and which defines and limits property rights and contractual liberties, taxes and subsidies, and so on. In society, as in nature, we depend always on an order that we did not invent, and cannot re-create; our task can only be to remove the obstacles that we have ourselves put in the way of its natural healing, and, where this is not enough, to provide prophylaxis against hazards generated by our own virtuosity.

This may appear too humble a task for those who dream of ecological utopias, or who remain epigones of unlimited progress. In fact, the task of negotiating sensibly the transition to a stable social order is crucial. For latter-day Pelagians, it involves shedding the protective illusion of infinite improvement; for Greens, it means resisting the allures of arcadianism and utopianism. It is far from obvious that either the intelligence or the will exists among us in sufficient measure to make such a transition feasible. Behind the meliorist superstitions of the modern political religions and the Pelagianism that has conquered all of the traditional faiths, at least in the West, lies nihilism which, in becoming for the first time a mass philosophy, has also evoked its dialectical negation, fundamentalism, in many parts of the world. Further, contemporary science has itself assumed a fundamentalist form which – in the works of Monod[94] and Dawkins, for example – propagates a species of nihilism about nature and humanity's place in it. It is this species of scientism, in which fundamentalism and nihilism are conjoined, which allies itself with a sentimental humanism to give us the distinctive modernist worldview. Lovelock has justly characterized this view of things, and its narrow limitations, when he observes: 'Our humanist concerns about the poor of the inner cities or the Third World, and our near-obscene obsession with death, suffering, and pain as if these were evils in themselves – these thoughts divert the mind from our gross and excessive domination of the natural world.'[95] Certainly, ridding ourselves of a humanism that not only closes off any sense of transcendence but also lacks the reverence for nature and the tragic sense of life of genuine paganism is a precondition for any judicious assessment of our current environmental circumstances and prospects. It may indeed be that the Gaian vision, being free from the anthropocentrism which privileges humans in the universe and which even models the universe on humans, is the most appropriate antidote to this malady of the spirit that parades as enlightenment. It remains doubtful whether so subtle a vision can fill the spiritual emptiness of the masses of human beings who are lacking in transcendental faith and in respect for nature and for whom the promise of progress is proving a cruel joke.

Such a general condition of profound spiritual debility is ill suited to the task of preserving the common environment that we inherit from our forebears and from nature itself. It may well be that a Gaian correction of the place of the human species in planetary ecology is the most likely outcome – even, perhaps, the least undesirable outcome – of current environmental trends. In the meantime, however, we are well occupied in doing good in minute particulars, in preserving what is left of beauty and wilderness in the natural world, and in doing what we can to tend and renew amenity and stability in the common environment of human settlements.

1993

25

Joseph Conrad, our contemporary

'The sacrosanct fetish of today is science.' Mr Vladimir, first secretary at the Russian embassy in Joseph Conrad's novel *The Secret Agent*, believes that if terrorism is to be truly effective, it must be directed against the spirit of the age. In order to have any real impact, a bomb outrage must be purely destructive – an attack on society's most deeply cherished beliefs. Believing it to be 'in some mysterious way at the source of their material prosperity', both bourgeois public opinion and society's most radical critics regard science with deep reverence. Accordingly, Mr Vladimir instructs his *agent provocateur*, Adolf Verloc, to blow up the Royal Observatory at Greenwich: 'Go for the first meridian. You don't know the middle classes as well as I do. Their sensibilities are jaded. The first meridian. Nothing better, and nothing easier, I should think.' Attacking a building dedicated to the science of astronomy would be 'an act of destructive ferocity so absurd as to be incomprehensible, inexplicable, almost unthinkable', but it would be effective for that very reason: 'Madness alone is truly terrifying, inasmuch as you cannot placate it either by threats, persuasion or bribes.'

In *The Secret Agent*, Conrad makes use of an actual terrorist attempt on the Royal Observatory in 1894, when a French anarchist accidentally blew himself up in Greenwich Park before reaching his target. At the start of the twenty-first century, science remains a sacrosanct fetish. We believe the Internet is the source of our prosperity, linking up economic life everywhere in a network of beneficial exchange. At the same time, in a development that attests to the power of Conrad's darkly ironic vision, the symbols of trade and new technology have come under terrorist attack. On 11 September 2001, the suicide-warriors of al-Qaeda carried off a terrifying assault on the spirit of the age of precisely the kind that Mr Vladimir recommended.

Conrad published *The Secret Agent* in 1907. He took his subject matter from the anxieties of his time: the ambiguities of progress and civilization; the sense of the blind drift of history that preceded the First World War; and the break-up of personal identity that comes with loss of faith in the future. For much of the past hundred years, these seemed dated themes, with little bearing on the great political transformations that preoccupied novelists such as George Orwell and Arthur Koestler. Whatever horrors they chronicled, Orwell and Koestler never gave up the hope that humankind could have a better future. It did not occur to them that history might be cyclical, not progressive, with the struggles of earlier eras returning and being played out against a background of increased scientific knowledge and technological power. For all their dystopian forebodings, neither anticipated the twenty-first-century reality, in which ethnic and religious wars have supplanted secular ideological conflicts, terror has returned to the most advanced societies and empire is being reinvented.

Conrad, by contrast, scorned the nineteenth- and twentieth-century faith in revolutionary political change. Yet precisely because he never accepted that collective action could fundamentally transform the conditions of human life, he anticipated more clearly than any twentieth-century writer the dilemmas that face us today. He can be read as the first great political novelist of the twenty-first century.

Conrad spurned the idea of progress. Writing to Bertrand Russell, who had pinned his hopes for the future on international socialism, he declared that it was 'the sort of thing to which I cannot attach any definite meaning. I have never been able to find in any man's book or any man's talk anything convincing enough to stand up for a moment against my deep-seated sense of fatality governing this man-inhabited world.' This sense of the fated character of human life was reflected in Conrad's portrayal of revolutionaries, whom he viewed as shams who renew the crimes and delusions of the society they seek to destroy.

Verloc, in *The Secret Agent*, thinks of himself as a respectable family man. A dealer in pornography, a police informer and a spy working for a foreign embassy, he believes his work contributes to social and political stability. In this, he is no different from his controller, Vladimir, who directs him to commit bomb outrages so as to force the English (whom he views as over-tolerant to the point of decadence) to defend the social order by repression. Yet Verloc is murdered by his wife, Winnie, after she discovers he has caused the death of her brother, the mentally retarded and hypersensitive Stevie, by using him to place the bomb at Greenwich.

Conrad's scorn for revolutionaries is comprehensive and unremitting. He represents Verloc as a man whose life is ruled by indolence and a perversely refined notion of respectability. Much the same is true of Verloc's revolutionary comrade Ossipon, who is described as a weakling who lives by exploiting the vulnerability of women. All of these professed revolutionaries are shown as being hopelessly compromised by the same vices that permeate the society they reject.

Even the book's most sympathetically portrayed anarchist, the Professor, is presented in terms that are half comic. His beliefs are a ragbag of the pseudo-scientific superstitions of the time, such as Lombroso's theories of inherited criminal degeneracy and the bastardization of Darwinian ideas to supply a rationale for exterminating the weak. Like many progressive thinkers, the Professor affects a lucidity of thought that is devoid of sentimentality. In fact, his thinking is credulous and self-indulgent, shaped by a naive Positivist belief in science not much different from the faith in progress that animated the Victorian social order he despised. His fate goes unrecorded, but it seems likely that, like the weaker Comrade Ossipon, he will end 'marching in the gutter as if in training for the task of an inevitable future', shoulders bowed, 'ready to receive the leather yoke of the sandwich board'.

Unlike Dostoyevsky, by whom he was much influenced, but whose Christianity he found repugnant, Conrad saw no redemption for revolutionists. To him, revolutionary violence was vain, deluded and inherently criminal. But nor did he believe in the fundamental health of the society that revolutionaries tried to disturb. In Conrad's radically Hobbesian view, social institutions are themselves tainted with criminality. Society is a dim battleground of predatory and fragmentary egos, in which self-interest and self-deception leave nothing untouched. Thus, in *The Secret Agent*, Conrad portrays London as a sightless wasteland, where 'the dust of humanity settles inert and hopeless out of the stream of life', and human hopes are consumed in the everyday struggle for survival. But his most direct statement of the inherently criminal aspect of every social enterprise is in *Heart of Darkness*, his celebrated fable of imperialism.

A great deal of ink has been spilt attacking Conrad's views on colonialism, but it is safe to say that few, if any, of his twentieth-century critics had the imagination to anticipate that the age of empire could return. With an irony Conrad would have appreciated, however, that is what is happening today. Partly as a matter of self-defence and partly for familiar reasons that have to do with the control of natural resources, the world's great powers are reviving the imperial projects of the nineteenth century. There are differences between then and now, some of them vast. Today's great powers include countries that were subject to Western rule in Conrad's day, notably China and India, and, though it is at present economically weak, Japan remains potentially hugely powerful. These parts of the world will not return to European or Western hegemony. The new imperialism centres on regions where states have collapsed, with damaging spill-over effects on migration, crime and terrorism.

Equally significantly, the Great Game seems to have become less dangerously competitive. With the shared goals of countering terrorism and securing control of Central Asia's reserves of oil and natural gas, Russia and the US appear to have entered a long-term strategic partnership. Furthermore, the great powers are now to some degree inhibited by the danger of exposure in the mass media, and by the need to legitimize intervention through transnational organizations. These differences have led some to argue that the new imperialism will not revive the exploitative rule of a century ago: rather, it will supply desperately needed benefits, otherwise beyond reach, to people living in failed states. This is the view expressed by Robert Cooper, an adviser to the Prime Minister, in a recent pamphlet for the Blairite Foreign Policy Centre.

The merit of his line of thought is that it candidly faces the realities of state failure that have for too long been evaded. But it is impossible to suppress a sense of irony about the prospects of the new imperialism: not the fashionable kind of irony that takes nothing seriously,

but the irony explored in Conrad's writings – the unintended consequences and inevitable moral ambiguity of all our enterprises. This is
a pervasive feature of his interpretation of imperialism. As Conrad
pictures him, Kurtz – the ivory trader at the Inner Station in *Heart of
Darkness* – is corrupt, power-obsessed and hardly sane. Yet Conrad
also describes him as 'essentially a great musician', and wrote: 'All
Europe contributed to the making of Kurtz.'

Conrad had no illusions about the civilizing mission that was
invoked to justify imperialism in the nineteenth century. He knew
that European expansion into Africa was fuelled by much baser
motives. Yet Conrad also shows how it emerged from, and worked
to undermine, the European sense of self. The dissolution of civilized
values that occurred in the Belgian Congo was a disaster for its
inhabitants. At the same time, it exposed the illusions – of progress,
enlightenment and universal humanity – that shape the modern
European self-image.

What is truly distinctive about Conrad's perspective is that he does
not view this development as somehow liberating. Taking their cue
from Christianity, European progressives imagine that perceiving the
darker side of civilization enables us to move on to higher levels of
enlightenment. Conrad accepts no such redemption. Always finding
Christianity distasteful (he once described it as an 'absurd oriental
fable'), he rejects the idea that we can improve our condition by
understanding it better. For him, this humanist faith is only Christianity dressed up in the language of reason and world-improvement. His
was a more austere view, a modern renewal of the ancient pagan
sense of fate that is given voice in Greek tragedy.

The political religions of the twentieth century were at one in
rejecting the idea that history is fated. Marxism and market liberalism
both promised a time when its tragedies could be left behind. Both
saw history as a process of progressive emancipation ending in a
universal civilization. Both believed that, with the growth of knowledge, all of humanity would come to share the same values. This is
the Enlightenment faith in progress that Conrad rejected. Nowadays,
our thinking made lax by a constant emphasis on feeling, we imagine
that the idea of progress expresses an attitude of optimism, and its
rejection pessimism. In fact, the idea of progress does more than

express an attitude: it embodies a theory – one that has never had much to support it, and which was falsified in the century that has just ended.

The core of the belief in progress is that human values and goals converge in parallel with our increasing knowledge. The twentieth century shows the contrary. Human beings use the power of scientific knowledge to assert and defend the values and goals they already have. New technologies can be used to alleviate suffering and enhance freedom. They can, and will, also be used to wage war and strengthen tyranny. Science made possible the technologies that powered the industrial revolution. In the twentieth century, these technologies were used to implement state terror and genocide on an unprecedented scale. Ethics and politics do not advance in line with the growth of knowledge – not even in the long run.

It is no accident that nothing approaching a great political novel appeared in the last decades of the twentieth century. The shallow orthodoxies of the time were not propitious. Not only the right, but also the centre left, had made a sacred fetish of science – not, as in *The Secret Agent*, the science of astronomy, but the rather shakier discipline of economics. Practically every part of the political spectrum accepted the ridiculous notion that the secret of unending prosperity had been found. Free markets, balanced budgets, the correct supply of the correctly measured money, a judicious modicum of state spending – with such modest devices, the riddle of history had at last been solved.

The savants who announced the end of history took for granted that the globalization of markets would lead to peace. They did not notice that savage wars were being fought in many parts of the world. The economists who bored on about a weightless economy, which had dispensed with the need for natural resources, contrived to pass over the twentieth century's last big military conflict, the Gulf war, which was fought to protect oil supplies. None of this mattered much so long as the boom continued, and the illusion of peace was preserved. Yet the price of living on these fictions was a hollowing out not only of politics, but also of literature. It is a telling fact about the closing decades of the twentieth century that the closest approximation to a notable political novel was probably *The Bonfire of the Vanities*.

Conrad is our contemporary because, almost alone among nine-teenth- and twentieth-century novelists, he writes of the realities in which we live. At bottom, we know the dilemmas we face are not wholly soluble; but we prefer not to dwell on that fact. In order to avoid ethnic and religious enmities interacting with the rising scarcity of oil, water and other necessities, we need a worldwide programme of restraint and conservation; but such a programme is difficult to imagine at the best of times, and impossible while crucial regions of the world are at war. The realistic prospect is that the most we can do is stave off disaster, a task that demands stoicism and fortitude, not the utopian imagination. Which other novelist can school us so well in these forgotten virtues?

Conrad's greatness is that he brings us back to our actual life. The callow, rationalistic philosophies of the twentieth century, promising world peace and a universal civilization, are poor guides to a time in which war, terror and empire have returned. It falls to a novelist without much faith in the power of reason to enlighten us how to live reasonably in these circumstances. As to the ideologues of the end of history, prophets of a new world united under the sign of the market, their day is done. It will surely not be long before we find them, like Ossipon, marching in the gutter in the leather yoke of the sandwich board.

2002

26

Theodore Powys and the life
of contemplation

The last full-length novel of T. F. Powys, *Unclay*, is the summation of his life's work. Though not without precedents, the manner and the substance of this strange, compelling, not always comfortable book are uniquely his own. Written in his inimitable style – poetic and aphoristic, pared down and at the same time highly allusive – *Unclay* was published in 1931. It has remained one of the least read books of a great English writer, and one reason for this strange state of affairs may be the picture of human life it presents. Presented with lapidary finality in *Unclay*, Powys's vision is deeply at odds with contemporary sensibility. Theodore Powys is a religious writer without any vestige of orthodox belief, a dark poet who celebrates passing beauty and a stark realist who is also a supreme fabulist. Unless one unlocks these paradoxes one cannot fully understand his work, or appreciate the rare delights it contains.

Achieving such an understanding is no simple matter, for while Powys writes with exquisite clarity his way of thinking is gnomic and often hard to decipher. In what may be the most penetrating assessment of this elusive mind, Alyse Gregory wrote that Powys 'sees Man's place in the universe as ephemeral, inconsequential and doomed. He is a combination of the Baron d'Holbach, John Bunyan, Schopenhauer and Traherne with a sprinkling of Sterne. Who will understand him or do justice to him?'[1] The incongruous mix of writers mentioned by Gregory underscores the difficulty. Other seemingly ill-assorted authors could be added. Jeremy Taylor, the seventeenth-century Anglican divine and author of *The Rule and Exercises of Holy Dying*, was a powerful influence; the word 'unclay' that gave the title to Powys's novel comes from a poem of Taylor's. But Nietzsche –

a furious atheist – was also a commanding presence throughout Powys's life as a writer. Powys's intense ambivalence towards religion is one of the keys to his work. One sometimes has the feeling that he views religion in the manner of the eighteenth-century arch-materialist Holbach – as a fantasy distracting humans from clear awareness of their true situation. Yet it is unthinkable that Powys could have shared Holbach's dream of a world without religion. Like Freud – whose writings he read and admired – he saw humans as creatures animated by illusion: if they give up religion it is usually only to run after other fantasies. In any case – he asks – what would a human life without illusions be like?

Though Powys is a religious writer, for him religion was not about belief. As he put it in *Soliloquies of a Hermit*, an early volume first published in America in 1916 in which many of the themes of his mature fictions are prefigured, 'I am without a belief; – a belief is too easy a road to God.'[2] Religion – 'the only subject I know anything about' – is not, for him, a set of propositions or creed. It is a mood, or a shifting pattern of moods, whose intimations are fleeting. Spiritual truth was best approached by silence – or else by the indirect art that Powys employs in his wonderful *Fables* (1929),[3] where pots and pans converse with fleas and corpses. If Powys had any religious beliefs they were – in the terms of conventional Christianity – highly heterodox, even heretical. Except in the shape of mortality – which, in the figure of John Death, is the central protagonist of *Unclay* – there is nothing of salvation to be found in his writings. Far from death being the supreme evil – as it was for his brother Llewelyn, a consumptive from the age of twenty-five who spent his life battling his illness – it enters the world to make the burdens of human life lighter. In *Unclay*, John Death is God's messenger, instructed to 'scythe' or 'unclay' two inhabitants of the village of Dodder. Losing the parchment that contains their names, he determines to spend the summer in the village. Throughout his stay he gives and receives joy, relishing sexual encounters with the village women and rejoicing in his mission of bringing release to suffering humanity. John Death is a gay, wanton figure, one of the few among Powys's characters to pass through the human world with something akin to pleasure (though, Death confesses, the experience has taught him to weep).

For Powys the longing to live for ever is a mark of human misery, while death cancels all sorrow. 'Perhaps I am an illusion,' Death ruminates towards the end of the book. 'But, whether real or no, I am no enemy to man.' Here we see the first of Powys's striking reversals of orthodox religious belief. The lust for everlasting life, which conventional religion expresses, is for Powys the greatest human vice – a weakness that finds expression in greed, ambition and the love of glory. We can live more peacefully, he seems to be suggesting, if we befriend our own mortality.

To endure for ever is the worst of fates in Powys's eyes, and even God, who appears as Mr Weston the wine salesman in his other great fable, *Mr Weston's Good Wine* (1927), ends by seeking oblivion. Mr Weston arrives in the village of Folly Down in an old Ford, knocking down a child he then brings miraculously back to life. Selling the light wine of love and the dark wine of death, he finds that in the end they go together. He recognizes that his comic and lovely creation – the village of Folly Down, which is the human world in miniature – is irretrievably flawed. At the end of the book he asks his assistant, Michael, to drop a burning match into the Ford's petrol tank:

Michael did as he was told. In a moment a fierce tongue of flame leaped up from the car; a pillar of smoke rose above the flame and ascended into the heavens. The fire died down, smouldered and went out.

Mr Weston was gone.[4]

The theme of God seeking annihilation is echoed in Powys's *The Only Penitent*, a shorter work published in the same year as *Unclay*. Mr Hayhoe, the vicar of Maids Madder, is a man of simple faith who does not doubt the goodness of his parishioners; he is sure they will welcome the opportunity to confess and repent their sins. Accordingly he makes himself available for confession, but no one seeks his absolution and he comes to doubt his faith. At last a solitary penitent turns up – Tinker Jar, a mysterious person Mr Hayhoe 'thought he knew', and of whom it was said that 'when the tinker wasn't walking upon the everlasting hills, he would use the storm-clouds as a chariot.' Tinker Jar confesses his sins:

'I crucified my son . . .'Twas I who created every terror in the earth, the rack, the plague, all despair, all torment . . . I destroy all men with a sword. I cast them down in a pit, they become nothing.'

'Hold!' cried Mr Hayhoe. 'Is that last word true?'

'It is,' answered Jar.

'Then, in the name of Man,' said Mr Hayhoe boldly, 'I forgive your sin; I pardon and deliver you from all evil; confirm and strengthen you in all goodness, and bring you to everlasting death.'[5]

Along with the Reverend Hayhoe, Mr Jar reappears in *Unclay*, where the Reverend describes him as 'the chief of sinners'. Mr Jar, who is clearly another of God's alter egos, confesses: 'I have done too much harm already.' As in *The Only Penitent*, God is held responsible for all the evil in the world. In *The Left Leg* (1923), a novella of Powys's early maturity, Jar appears as an old man who lives in a rough hut under the shelter of Madder Hills. He is also described poetically, in terms that make clear his role as one of God's alter egos:

'E be the leaf that do drift in the wind. 'E be the cloud that do cross the moon at night-time. 'E be the stone that a poor man do take up in road to throw at 'is dog. 'E be the pond weeds where do bide the wold toad. 'E be the bastard child before 'tis born.[6]

It is evident that Powys's God was never the all-powerful, all-loving deity of Christianity. 'One would think almost', he writes in *Unclay*, 'that at the bottom of the well of being one may discover, instead of a mighty God, only the cap and bells of a mad fool.' It is tempting to think that Powys may have entertained the Gnostic notion that the world was created by a demiurge, but it is questionable whether he had any notion of a creator-god. Certainly his writings are saturated with Christian symbolism and can hardly be understood without some familiarity with Christian traditions, but to my mind they stand outside these traditions. In a wise assessment, William Hunter wrote that in Powys's work 'Christian myth is used to express a pagan philosophy.'[7] The spare lives Powys chronicles show no traces of redemption, and the rural landscape he uses for his fictions is chosen not only because it was intimately familiar to him but also because it represented the unchanging conditions of human existence.

Powys spent many years living in the Dorset village of East Chaldon, where he settled for the seclusion he believed he could enjoy there. As things turned out he received a stream of literary visitors – including some of the luminaries of the Bloomsbury group – and in his latter years, when his health had weakened, he moved to the even greater seclusion of Mappowder. There Powys took part in a regular religious service in the church next to his cottage, but it seems he did so mainly for the quietude of the ceremony and at the end of his life he declined communion from the Rector.[8] Yet Theodore Powys was shaped by the religion of his father even as he rejected it, and in this he is at one with his brothers John and Llewelyn. Coming from a family that traced its lineage back to John Donne and William Cowper, all three were sons of a clergyman who spent much of their lives seeking an alternative to his Christian faith. The alternatives they found were different, though not perhaps as different as they believed. John Cowper described himself in *Autobiography* (1934) as 'a natural-born disciple of the greatest of all philosophers. I refer, of course, to the philosopher, Pyrrho, who when asked, at the end, whether he was alive or dead, replied "I do not know." '[9] Pyrrho was the founder of Greek Scepticism, and throughout his long life John Cowper viewed religions and philosophies as works of art to be appreciated for their aesthetic qualities as much as for any truth they might contain. While he became increasingly hostile to Christianity – especially the Christian cult of 'love' – he never ceased to regard religion as being like poetry, an irreplaceable creation of the human imagination. In the most complete exposition of his outlook, *Impassioned Clay*, Llewelyn Powys presents himself as a disciple of Lucretius, though his celebration of the pleasures of sex has more in common with the *fin-de-siècle* attitudes of Wilde than it does with the ascetic hedonism of the Roman poet.[10] Unlike his brothers, Llewelyn was for most of his life an ardent campaigner against religion in all its varieties.

Llewelyn, John and Theodore found different successors to the faith of their father, but when writing about how a human life is best spent they spoke with a single voice. For all of them contemplation was superior to action. Llewelyn wrote of Theodore: 'Never for a single moment, since he reached the age of discretion, has my brother given so much as a sunflower-seed for the busy practical life of our Western World.' In this, however, the three brothers were at one. Whether contemplation meant the static enjoyment of sensation as it did for John Cowper or included the active pleasures of the body, as advocated and practised by Llewelyn, it demanded a type of life in which practical activity took second place. In seeking peace in the quiet paths and secret valleys of Dorset, Theodore lived such a life.

Steeped in the greatest works of English literature,[11] the writings of Theodore Powys present a vision that goes against the modern grain, which – when one sets aside the conceit that fancies human action can alter the terms on which we live in the world – is profoundly refreshing. 'Life and Death do not quarrel in the fields. They are always changing places in the slow dance. Alive here and dead there. So the evening is devoured by the night, and the dawn by the day.'

2008

27

Homo rapiens and mass extinction

According to the Darwinian Edward O. Wilson, the earth is entering a new evolutionary era. We are on the brink of a great extinction the like of which has not been seen since the dinosaurs disappeared at the end of the Mesozoic Era, sixty-five million years ago. Species are vanishing at a rate of a hundred to a thousand times faster than they did before the arrival of humans. On current trends, our children will be practically alone in the world. As Wilson has put it, humanity is leaving the Cenozoic, the age of mammals, and entering the Eremozoic – the era of solitude.

The last mass extinction has not yet been fully explained. Many scientists believe it to have been the result of meteorites whose impact suddenly altered the global climate, but no one can be sure. In contrast, the cause of the current mass extinction is not in doubt: human expansion. As humans invade and exploit the last vestiges of wilderness, they destroy or destabilize the habitat of tens of thousands of species of plants, insects and animals. *Homo rapiens* is gutting the earth of biodiversity.

The lush natural world in which humans evolved is being rapidly transformed into a largely prosthetic environment. Crucially, in any time-span that is humanly relevant, this loss of biodiversity is irreversible. True, life on earth recovered its richness after the last great extinction; but only after some ten million years had passed. Unless something occurs to disrupt the trends that are under way, all future generations of human beings will live in a world that is more impoverished biologically than it has been for aeons.

Given the magnitude of this change, one would expect it to be at the centre of public debate. In fact, it is very little discussed.

Organizations such as the World Wildlife Fund press on with their invaluable work, and there are occasional reports of the destruction of wilderness; but, for the most part, politics and media debates go on as if nothing is happening. There are many reasons for this peculiar state of affairs, including the ingrained human habit of denying danger until its impact is imminent; but the chief reason is that it has become fashionable to deny the reality of overpopulation.

In truth, the root cause of mass extinction is too many people. As Wilson puts it: 'Population growth can justly be called the monster on the land.' Yet according to all the mainstream parties and most environmental organizations, the despoliation of the environment is mainly the result of flaws in human *institutions*. If we are entering a desolate world, the reason is not that humans have become too numerous; it is because injustice prevents proper use of the earth's resources. There is no such thing as overpopulation.

Interestingly, this view is not accepted in many of the world's poor countries. China, India, Egypt and Iran all have population programmes, as have many other developing nations. Opposition to population control is concentrated in rich parts of the world, notably the US, where the Bush administration pursues a fundamentalist vendetta against international agencies that provide family planning. It is understandable that rich countries should reject the idea of overpopulation. In their use of resources, they are themselves the most overpopulated. Their affluence depends on their appropriating a hugely disproportionate share of the world's non-renewable resources. If they ever face up to that reality, they will have to admit that their affluence is unsustainable.

Another reason for denying the reality of overpopulation is that the growth in human numbers is extremely uneven. In some parts of the world, population is actually declining. This is strikingly true in post-Communist Russia. A precipitate fall in public health and living standards has led to a virtually unprecedented population collapse, which is set to accelerate further as an African-style AIDS die-off triggered by the country's enormous numbers of intravenous drug users begins to take hold. In other countries, such as Japan, Italy and Spain, declining fertility is leading to zero or negative population growth. Such examples have given currency to the silly notion that overpopulation is no longer an issue – that, if anything, it is a slow-down in the growth of human numbers that we should be worrying about.

But while human numbers are falling in some parts of the world, in others they are exploding. Globally, the human population will continue to rise for at least a century – even if worldwide fertility falls to replacement level tomorrow. In 1940, there were around two billion humans on the planet. Today, there are about six billion. Even on conservative projections, there will be some eight billion by 2050.

Eight billion people cannot be maintained without desolating the earth. Today, everyone aspires to live after the fashion of the world's affluent minority. That requires worldwide industrialization – as a result of which the human ecological footprint on the earth will be deeper than it has ever been.

Rainforests are the last great reservoirs of biodiversity, but they will have to be cleared and turned over to human settlement or food production. What is left of wilderness in the world will be made over to green desert. This is a bleak enough prospect, but what's worse is that it is a path from which there is no turning back. If a human population of this size is to be kept in existence, it must exploit the planet's dwindling resources ever more intensively. In effect, humans will turn the planet into an extension of themselves. When they look about the world, they will find nothing but their own detritus.

There are many who profess to be unfazed by this prospect. Marxists and free-market economists never tire of ridiculing the idea that other living things have intrinsic value. In their view, other species are just means to the satisfaction of human wants, and the earth itself is a site for the realization of human ambitions. These self-professed rationalists are prone to the conceit that theirs is a purely secular view of the world; but in thinking this way about the relationship of humans to the earth, they are in the grip of a religious dogma. The belief that the earth belongs to humans is a residue of theism. For Christians, humans are unique among animals because they alone are created in the image of God. For the same reason, they are uniquely valuable. It follows that humanity can behave as lord of creation, treating the earth's natural wealth and other animals as tools, mere instruments for the achievement of human purposes.

To my mind, such religious beliefs have caused an immense amount of harm, but at least they are coherent. It is perfectly reasonable to think humans are the only source of value in the scheme of things – so long as you retain the theological framework in which they are held to be categorically different from all other animals. But once you have given up theism, this sort of anthropocentrism makes no sense. Outside monotheistic religions, it is practically unknown. The view of things in which we are separate from the rest of nature and can live with minimal concern for the biosphere is not a conclusion of rational inquiry; it is an inheritance from a humanly aberrant religious tradition.

The fashionable belief that there is no such thing as overpopulation is part of an anthropocentric worldview that has nothing to do with science. At the same time, there is more than a hint of anthropocentrism in Wilson's suggestion that we are entering an age of solitude. The idea that, unlike any other animal, humans can take the planet into a new evolutionary era assumes that the earth will patiently submit to their inordinate demands. Yet there is already evidence that human activity is altering the balance of the global climate – and in ways that are unlikely to be comfortable for its human population. The long-term effects of global warming cannot be known with any certainty. But in a worst-case scenario that is being taken increasingly seriously, the greenhouse effect could wipe out densely populated coastal countries such as Bangladesh within the present century, while massively dislocating food production elsewhere in the world.

The result could be a disaster for billions of people. The idea that we are entering an era of solitude makes sense only if it is assumed that such a world would be stable, and hospitable to humans. Yet we know that the closer an ecosystem comes to being a monoculture, the more fragile it becomes. The world's rainforests are part of the earth's self-regulatory system. As James Lovelock has observed, they sweat to keep us cool. With their disappearance, we will be increasingly at risk. A world overcrowded with humans that has been denuded of its biodiversity will be extremely fragile – far more vulnerable to large, destabilizing accidents than the complex biosphere we have inherited. Such a world is too delicate to last for long.

There are good reasons for thinking that an era of solitude will not come about at all. Lovelock has written that the human species is now so numerous that it constitutes a serious planetary malady. The earth is suffering from disseminated primatemaia – a plague of people. He sees four possible outcomes of the people plague: 'destruction of the invading disease organisms; chronic infection; destruction of the host; or symbiosis, a lasting relationship of mutual benefit to the host and the invader'.

The last two can be definitely ruled out. Humankind cannot destroy its planetary host. The earth is much older and stronger than humans will ever be. At the same time, humans will never initiate a relationship of mutually beneficial symbiosis with it. The advance of *Homo rapiens* has always gone with the destruction of other species and ecological devastation. Of the remaining outcomes, the second – in which over-numerous humans colonize the earth at the cost of weakening the biosphere – corresponds most closely to Wilson's bleak vision. But it is the first that is most likely. The present spike in human numbers will not last.

If it is not forestalled by changes in the planet's climate, we can be pretty sure that Wilson's era of solitude will be derailed by the side-effects of human strife. Resource-scarcity is already emerging as a factor aggravating tension in several regions of the world. In the coming century, it is set to be one of the primary causes of war. A world of eight billion people competing for vital necessities is highly unlikely to be at peace. On the contrary, it is programmed for endemic conflict. New technologies may blunt the edge of scarcity by allowing resources to be extracted and used more efficiently. But their key use will be to secure control over dwindling supplies of oil, natural gas, water and other essential inputs of industrial society.

The Internet originated in the military sector. Information technology is at the heart of the revolution in military affairs that is changing the face of war by powering the new generations of computer-guided missiles and unmanned planes. Only a couple of years ago, a host of air-headed publicists was proclaiming the arrival of a weightless world. The reality is just the opposite. The Gulf war was won with computers, and they will be critically important in any future war. In that sense, it is true that information technology will be the basis of prosperity in the twenty-first century. But its main contribution will not be to create a hypermodern, knowledge-driven economy; it will be to enable advanced industrial states to retain control of the most ancient sources of wealth – the world's shrinking supplies of non-renewable resources.

In the past, war has rarely resulted in a long-lasting decline in human numbers. But in a highly globalized world it could have a new and more devastating impact. With a hugely increased population reliant on far-flung supply networks, large-scale war in the twenty-first century could do what it has frequently done in the past: trigger food shortages, even famine. Globalization no more engenders world peace than it guarantees an unending boom. It simply magnifies instability.

As we are now learning, globalization makes it harder to control the knock-on effects of stock-market crashes. It may not be long before we learn that the same is true of war.

Summing up his view of the future in his book *Consilience*, Wilson writes:

At best, an environmental bottleneck is coming in the twenty-first century. It will cause the unfolding of a new kind of history driven by environmental change. Or perhaps an unfolding on a global scale of the old kind of history, which saw the collapse of regional civilizations, going back to the earliest in history, in northern Mesopotamia, and subsequently Egypt, then the Mayan and many others scattered across all the inhabited continents except Australia.

Wilson's 'new kind of history' would involve a worldwide revolution in attitudes and policies. This would include universal access by women to the means of controlling their fertility, abandonment of the belief that there is a natural right to have as many children as you like, and a basic shift in attitudes to the environment in which it is accepted that our fate and that of the rest of life on earth are inseparably linked. These are the minimum conditions for Wilson's new kind of history.

Unfortunately, one has only to list these conditions to see that they are unrealizable. There cannot be a sustainable balance between natural resources and human needs so long as the number of people continues to increase, but a growing population can be seen as a weapon. Many Palestinians and Kurds view having large families as a survival strategy. In a world containing many intractable ethnic conflicts, there is unlikely to be a benign demographic transition to a lower birth rate.

The examples we have of societies in which population has declined in the absence of a big social crisis cannot be replicated worldwide. A policy of zero population growth requires universal availability of contraception and abortion, and limits on the freedom to breed; but the authority that could impose these conditions does not exist.

Homo rapiens has a long history of mass killing, but it has rarely chosen to regulate its numbers intelligently and humanely. If population declines, it will be as a result of war, genocide or the kind of generalized social collapse that has taken place in post-Communist Russia.

The increase in human population that is currently under way is unprecedented and unsustainable. It cannot be projected into the future. More than likely, it will be cut short by the classical Malthusian forces of 'old history'. From a human point of view, this may be a discomfiting prospect; but at least it dispels the nightmare of an age of solitude.

2002

28

A report to the Academy

In Kafka's story 'A Report to an Academy', an ape called Red Peter delivers a lecture to a learned society in which he gives an account of the life he led before he acquired human ways. Captured on the Gold Coast (now Ghana), Red Peter was transported in a cage to Hamburg. In that city, he reports, he faced two alternatives: the zoological gardens or the variety stage. Life in the zoological gardens meant only another cage, so he chose the stage. It was not easy to get into the variety hall, but once there Red Peter was an enormous success. Soon he learnt to talk like a human, and it was not long before he achieved what he termed 'the cultural level of an average European'. His stage performances enabled him to enjoy a distinctly human way of life. As he described it in his report to the academy: 'When I come home late at night from banquets, from scientific receptions, from social gatherings, there sits waiting for me a half-trained little chimpanzee, and I take comfort from her as apes do.'

Kafka's story is cited in J. M. Coetzee's *The Lives of Animals*, a profound fictional meditation on the contradictions that beset our attitudes to other animal species. The story of Red Peter is a fantastical version of the fate that befell many apes, and, as one of Coetzee's characters notes, there were real-life prototypes of Red Peter. In 1912, the Prussian Academy established a research centre on the island of Tenerife to study the mental powers of apes; and in 1917, the director of the centre, Wolfgang Kohler, published some of the results of this in his celebrated study *The Mentality of Apes*. Like Red Peter, Kohler's apes underwent a period of training designed to induce them to adopt human ways. Among the pedagogic methods used was slow starvation, with the apes being repeatedly shown and denied food until they developed something resembling human faculties.

It is not clear how researchers today would assess the results of this experiment, but Kohler, one of the founders of cognitive psychology, seems to have seen it as a success, noting with satisfaction how the captive chimpanzees ran in a circle round their compound, some draped in old strips of cloth and others carrying pieces of rubbish, 'for all the world like a military band'.

Kohler's experiments were cruel and demeaning to the animals on which they were inflicted, but they are chiefly notable for the deep confusion they exhibit in his, and our, view of our closest evolutionary kin. We have come to view apes as proto-humans, yet we subject them to treatment we would not dream of inflicting on members of our own species. If apes were not similar to us in important respects, many of the experiments to which they are subjected would be imposs- ible or pointless. Few now deny that apes share much of our intellec- tual and emotional inheritance. They have many of our own capacities and vulnerabilities: they can think and plan, and they feel fear and love. Without these similarities, Kohler's experiments would not have been possible. Yet these very similarities undercut the ethical basis of such experimentation.

We do not put humans into captivity and starve them in order to test their intellectual abilities because we know that such treatment would cause severe suffering. How can we justify such experimenta- tion on apes, knowing that it can work only to the extent that their capacities, including the capacity to suffer, are much like our own? Can there be any compelling ethical defence of using creatures so like ourselves in ways that we would find unbearable? Or is the answer that the animals used in such experiments are simply unfortunate, that we have them in our power and their suffering is a regrettable but unavoidable result of our using them for our benefit?

The last of these options appears to have been taken recently by a spokesman for Cambridge University. Responding to protests against plans to establish a primate research centre there, he observed that it is an unfortunate fact that only primates have brains like our own. The implication is that it is precisely because apes have many of the capacities of humans that they are used for experimentation. It is true that experimenting on primates is a productive research technique; but if their similarities with us justify using apes in this way, it would surely be even more effective to use humans. The argument for experimenting on primates leads inexorably to the conclusion that it is permissible – in fact, preferable – to experimenting on humans.

Quite rightly, the idea that humans should be used in painful or dangerous medical experiments evokes intense moral horror; but this has not always been so. Powerless and marginal people in prisons and mental hospitals, for example, have in the past often been used as guinea pigs, and it is all too easy to imagine the forcible use of humans in scientific research practised on a far wider scale. The Nazis saw nothing wrong in subjecting members of what they considered to be inferior populations to the most horrible experiments; and there can be little doubt that had the outcome of the Second World War been different, the use of humans for scientific research would have been institutionalized across Europe. No doubt it would have been condemned by a dedicated few, but the historical experience of occupied Europe suggests that the majority of the population would have accepted the practice.

It will be objected that there is a vital difference between using animals for scientific research and using humans: humans have the capacity for consent, whereas animals do not. It is true that adult humans can express their wishes to other humans in ways that even our closest animal kin cannot; but consent is not the heart of the matter. Even if they agreed, it would be morally intolerable to use prison inmates in dangerous medical experiments. No form of consent they might give could make the injury done to them less real; it would only reflect their powerlessness. Similarly, it is not the inability of human infants to give their consent that justifies an absolute ban on experimenting on them. It is the terrible damage we would inflict on them merely to produce benefits for ourselves.

The same is true of experiments on animals. It is not the capacity for consent that is most relevant, but the capacity for suffering. I am no Utilitarian, but Jeremy Bentham hit the spot when he wrote of animals that the crucial question is not 'Can they speak?' Rather, it is 'Can they suffer?'

At this point, those who support animal experimentation have a habit of wheeling out some extremely familiar arguments. Animals lack the capacity for personal autonomy, they tell us, and so cannot recognize duties to others. For the same reason, they cannot have rights. Humans have the power of choice, and this entitles them to a moral status denied to other animal species.

We hear this tired refrain whenever the subject of animals is discussed, but it is significant not so much for any intellectual content it may have, but for what it shows about the lingering influence of religious belief. If you are a Christian, it makes perfect sense to think of humans as standing in a different category from other animals. Humans have free will and an immortal soul, and these attributes confer an incomparable importance on human life. No doubt we should refrain from gratuitous cruelty to other creatures, but they have no claim to value in their own right; they are instruments for achieving human ends. Humans have dominion over animals because humans alone are made in the image of God.

Secular thinkers find it extremely difficult to come up with reasons for thinking that the human species has some kind of unique standing in the world. Darwin showed that we share a common lineage with other animals, and subsequent genetic research has shown the closeness of these evolutionary links. Insofar as humans do have morally relevant attributes that other animals lack, it is right to treat them differently. But within a purely secular perspective there can be no good reason for thinking the human species is supremely valuable.

In the context of their beliefs about animals, as in many other areas, secular humanists parrot a Christian hymn of human uniqueness. They prattle on about the supreme value of human personality as if it were a self-evident truth. Yet it is not accepted in most of the world's religions, and is strikingly absent in some, such as Buddhism, that have never thought of other species as mere instruments of human purposes. Secular humanists are adopting the anthropocentric viewpoint of Christianity, while abandoning the theistic belief system from which it sprang, and without which it is meaningless.

Once Christianity and humanism have been set aside, it becomes clear that the chief difference between humans and other animals is simply that humans have acquired enormous power. In evolutionary terms, the human species has been an astonishing success. In the space of a few thousand years, it has achieved a seeming mastery over its environment, which is reflected in a vast increase in human population. At the same time, humans have had a huge, and almost entirely harmful, impact on other animal species. The mass extinction of wildlife we are seeing throughout the world comes from the destruction of habitat, itself largely a result of rising human numbers. The damage done to the welfare of other animal species by human expansion is on an incomparably larger scale than anything that is done in scientific laboratories. This does not mean vivisection is unimportant or that it should not be prohibited. After all, no one thinks that since millions of people are slaughtered in wars it does not matter if some die as a result of murder. It does mean that anyone who focuses narrowly on animal experimentation is missing the big picture.

The chief threat to animal welfare today comes from the unchecked expansion of *Homo rapiens*. Wherever humans have entered a new environment the result has been a wave of extinctions. This is what happened when Polynesian settlers arrived in New Zealand a few hundred years ago, and it was the arrival of humans in North America around 12,000 years ago that accounts for the disappearance of about 70 per cent of its large mammals. Though some hunter–gatherer cultures may have reached a precarious balance with the natural world and a number of Buddhist peoples have displayed remarkable self-restraint in their treatment of animals, the history of human relations with other species is a record of almost unbroken rapacity. Wrecking the environment seems to be in the nature of the beast.

This may seem a despairing conclusion, but for anyone whose horizons are not confined to the human world, there are grounds for hope. While humans have enormous power over the environment, their capacity to control it is strictly limited. The present level of human population depends on maintaining high levels of industrial production, but global warming will prevent worldwide industrialization on anything resembling the dominant Western model. There is no way that eight billion people can have the lifestyle that has come into being in a few countries over the past century or so.

Most Green thinkers believe that this transition can come about as a result of political action, and there are some policies that would help. By far the most effective way of limiting human numbers is giving women control of their own fertility. Making contraception and abortion universally available enhances human well-being and at the same time reduces the pressures that are destroying animal habitat. Population control should be central in any programme of transition to a more stable world and, in fact, many developing countries have population policies. However, the subject is surrounded with an aura of political incorrectness. As a result, it has become fashionable to talk as if a sustainable way of life can be achieved simply by shifting to a different economic system. In reality, finite resources impose insuperable limits on the growth of human numbers and the Earth's carrying capacity has probably already been breached.

One way or another, human expansion will be curbed; and a plausible scenario is that this will occur as a by-product of war. Globalization supports the present high levels of human population, but its logic is to intensify the struggle for scarce natural resources. Resource wars, such as the two Gulf wars, look set to dominate the coming century. Such conflicts would be damaging to animals as well as humans, but because of their disruptive effect on the global supply chain, their impact on humans could well be much more severe. The end result could be a less crowded world in which other species have room to breathe. *Homo rapiens* is a ferociously destructive creature, but its capacity for self-destruction is even greater. The human behaviour that Wolfgang Kohler was so pleased to observe being parodied by his captive apes may yet prove to be the ultimate guarantee of animal liberation.

2004

29

The body disassembled in Damien Hirst

The poet Thomas Lovell Beddoes, in his revenge tragedy *Death's Jest-Book*, which was begun in 1828 but not published until after his suicide in 1849, has one of the characters declaim:

> Nature's polluted
> There's man in every secret corner of her
> Doing damned wicked deeds. Thou art, old world,
> A hoary, atheistic, murdering star.

It is a curiously premonitory statement, and one that returns to me when viewing the art of Damien Hirst. It is not that Hirst's art is in any way misanthropist, or nihilistic. He has said that he wants to give those who look at his work – paintings, drawings, installations, sculptures and the rest – the energy to go away and think about their lives again, and for many people that is the effect of his work. The impact is not at all negative: we are returned to life with fresh eyes. At the same time there is a powerfully deconstructive impulse at work in Hirst's art, and it is applied most relentlessly to that most cherished modern icon – the human species.

Much of Hirst's work is a labour of denudation in which humans are revealed as adventitious assemblages, bits and pieces knocked almost randomly together: look at *The Hat Makes the Man* (2004). Or human life is pared down to its bare rudiments – Eliot's 'birth, copulation and death' – as in *From the Cradle to the Grave* (2000). The impulse that drives these works, and much else that Hirst has done, is a desire to peel away the layers of history and memory that cover the human animal – to de-anthropomorphize our picture of ourselves.

Hirst's work has been seen as an exercise in *détournement*, a subversively witty reordering of the late modern spectacle. That it is this in part cannot be denied, and there are obvious affinities with Duchamp – for example in the dot paintings, some of which are exhibited here. Yet it seems to me that the spirit of Hirst's work is quite unlike that of Dada. Of course Dada was a channel for many different currents, but the stance of negation that many of its practitioners sustained until they lapsed into comic poses of political engagement is at odds with Hirst's underlying seriousness. Their coupling of the playful destruction of anti-art with the simple pieties of progressive politics was ridiculous in a way these connoisseurs of absurdity seem not to have noticed. If such Dadaists were nihilists it was not without the hope of finding redemption in the destruction of meaning. When that was not forthcoming many of them – Breton and Aragon, for example – turned to the most banal and fraudulent of secular faiths.

Nothing of this kind can be found in Hirst. There is plenty of wit – just look at *Adam and Eve Exposed* (2004) – but it serves a forensic clarity that is uncharacteristic of Dada, which rarely exposed its hopes to the light of day. The destructive impulse that Dada expressed was, in effect, a humanist version of the mystic's *via negativa*. If Dada demolished the bourgeois image of humankind it did so in order to uncover the unknown god it supposedly concealed. In contrast Hirst disassembles that image in order to look at the result – whatever it might be.

This divergence between Hirst and Dada suggests another – between Hirst and Bacon. Once again the affinities are clear, and freely avowed. The difference is that whereas Bacon, as a disbelieving Christian, painted from a sense of loss, Hirst takes the passing of religion as given even as he continues to deploy its symbols. The debts of Bacon to Velázquez are not just iconographic. Both painters belong in a tradition in which human life is seen as needing – but in Bacon's case not finding – a transcendental meaning. Consciously or otherwise Bacon seemed to want to shock the viewer into some kind of epiphany. Hirst – so it seems to me – wants us to try the experiment of looking at what is in front of our noses.

Hirst's strategy of deconstruction is methodical, even scientific in a way that Duchamp's and Bacon's were not. Nothing is spared. That does not mean he disdains the symbolic forms that have been inherited from religion. On the contrary his use of these ciphers – in his *The Martyrdom of Saint Andrew* and *The Martyrdom of Saint Peter* (2002), for example – points to an unexpected affinity with a religious artist. William Blake was a heretical Christian who put the human imagination at the centre of the world. No one could be more determinedly anthropocentric, and in this and other respects Blake and Hirst are radically different kinds of artist.

Yet it is hard to resist the suspicion that Hirst is doing today something akin to what Blake was doing in his time. Blake's poetry and engravings had as their target a materialist worldview, which he rejected because it left humans as accidents in the world. Hirst's art accepts this fact, even celebrates it, while refusing the sentimental consolations of humanism. Blake worked at a time when science was fused with hope; his originality comes from his resistance to this hope, and his attempt to return to a kind of aboriginal humanity. Hirst's work is done in a time when science is linked with fear, and the prodigious fecundity of technology has left man in every corner of the world; his originality is in his use of the imagery of science to recall the lost ciphers of religion, in an effort to see what comes from their interaction and dissolution. Both aim to disclose the lineaments of humanity by tearing away the systems of belief in which they are presently clothed. The belief-systems may be different but what is revealed is the same: the ghost of a flea; like flies, like people.

The art of Damien Hirst seems to me an experiment whose aim is to uncover the human form. Where it differs from other such artistic investigations is in its rigorous empiricism. There is no attempt to ascend into freedom; the impossibility of escape is taken for granted. There is a strong preference for the brutality of fact. The human form may turn out to be as inhuman as that Leviathan, the shark. The upshot is left open. In a time when everyone thinks they know what it means to be human Hirst demands that we look and think again.

2007

30

As it is

*Should the truth about the world exist, it's bound to be
nonhuman.*   Jospeh Brodsky

I
THE CONSOLATIONS OF ACTION

In his novel *Nostromo*, Joseph Conrad wrote: 'Action is consolatory.
It is the enemy of thought and the friend of flattering illusions.'

For those for whom life means action, the world is a stage on which
to enact their dreams. Over the past few hundred years, at least in
Europe, religion has waned, but we have not become less obsessed
with imprinting a human meaning on things. A thin secular idealism
has become the dominant attitude to life. The world has come to be
seen as something to be remade in our own image. The idea that the
aim of life is not action but contemplation has almost disappeared.

Those who struggle to change the world see themselves as noble,
even tragic figures. Yet most of those who work for world betterment
are not rebels against the scheme of things. They seek consolation for
a truth they are too weak to bear. At bottom, their faith that the
world can be transformed by human will is a denial of their own
mortality.

Wyndham Lewis described the idea of progress as 'time-worship'
– the belief that things are valuable not for what they are but for what
they may someday become. In fact it is the opposite. Progress promises
release from time – the hope that, in the spiralling ascent of the
species, we can somehow preserve ourselves from oblivion.

Action preserves a sense of self-identity that reflection dispels. When we are at work in the world we have a seeming solidity. Action gives us consolation for our inexistence. It is not the idle dreamer who escapes from reality. It is practical men and women, who turn to a life of action as a refuge from insignificance.

Today the good life means making full use of science and technology – without succumbing to the illusion that they can make us free, reasonable or even sane. It means seeking peace – without hoping for a world without war. It means cherishing freedom – in the knowledge that it is an interval between anarchy and tyranny.

The good life is not found in dreams of progress, but in coping with tragic contingencies. We have been reared on religions and philosophies that deny the experience of tragedy. Can we imagine a life that is not founded on the consolations of action? Or are we too lax and coarse even to dream of living without them?

2
SISYPHUS' PROGRESS

Nothing is more alien to the present age than idleness. If we think of resting from our labours, it is only in order to return to them.

In thinking so highly of work we are aberrant. Few other cultures have ever done so. For nearly all of history and all prehistory, work was an indignity.

Among Christians, only Protestants have ever believed that work smacks of salvation; the work and prayer of medieval Christendom were interspersed with festivals. The ancient Greeks sought salvation in philosophy, the Indians in meditation, the Chinese in poetry and the love of nature. The pygmies of the African rainforests – now nearly extinct – work only to meet the needs of the day, and spend most of their lives idling.

Progress condemns idleness. The work needed to deliver humanity is vast. Indeed it is limitless, since as one plateau of achievement is reached another looms up. Of course this is only a mirage; but the worst of progress is not that it is an illusion. It is that it is endless.

In Greek myth, Sisyphus struggles to roll a stone to the top of a hill so that it will then roll down the other side. Robert Graves tells his story thus:

He has never yet succeeded in doing so. As soon as he has almost reached the summit, he is forced back by the weight of the shameless stone, which bounces to the very bottom once more; where he wearily retrieves it and must begin all over again, though sweat bathes his limbs, and a cloud of dust rises above his head.

For the ancients, unending labour was the mark of a slave. The labours of Sisyphus are a punishment. In working for progress we submit to a labour no less servile.

3
PLAYING WITH FATE

Gamblers wager for the sake of playing. Among those who fish for pleasure, the best fisherman is not the one who catches the most fish but the one who enjoys fishing the most. The point of playing is that play has no point.

How can there be play in a time where nothing has meaning unless it leads to something else? In our eyes, *Homo ludens* lives a life without purpose. Since play is beyond us, we have given ourselves over to a life of purposeless work instead. To labour as Sisyphus does is our fate.

But can we make our labours more playful? At present we think of science and technology as means of mastering the world. But the self that struggles to master the world is only a shimmer on the surface of things. The new technologies that are springing up around us seem to be inventions that serve our ends, when they and we are moves in a game that has no end.

Technology obeys no one's will. Can we play along with it without labouring to master it?

4
TURNING BACK

Searching for a meaning in life may be useful therapy, but it has nothing to do with the life of the spirit. Spiritual life is not a search for meaning but a release from it.

Plato believed the end of life was contemplation. Action had value only in making contemplation possible; but contemplation meant communing with a human idea. Like many mystical thinkers, Plato thought of the world disclosed by the senses as a realm of shadows. Values were the ultimate realities. In contemplation Plato sought union with the highest value – the Good.

For Plato, as for the Christians who followed him, reality and the Good were one. But the Good is a makeshift of hope and desire, not the truth of things. Values are only human needs, or the needs of other animals, turned into abstractions. They have no reality in themselves, as George Santayana points out:

All animals have within them a principle by which to distinguish good from evil, since their existence and welfare are furthered by some circumstances and acts and are hindered by others. Self-knowledge, with a little experience of the world, will then easily set up the Socratic standard of values natural and inevitable to any man or to any society. These values each society will disentangle in proportion to its intelligence and will defend in proportion to its vitality. But who would dream that *spiritual life* was at all concerned in asserting these human and local values, or in supposing that they were especially divine, or bound to dominate the universe for ever?[1]

Through fasting, concentration and prayer, mystics shut out the shifting world of the senses in order to reach a timeless reality. Quite often they find what they seek – but it is only a shadow play, an arabesque of their own anxieties, projected on to an inner screen. They end as they began, stuck fast in the personal time of memory and regret.

In modern times, the immortal longings of the mystics are expressed in a cult of incessant activity. Infinite progress . . . infinite tedium. What could be more dreary than the perfection of mankind? The idea of progress is only the longing for immortality given a techno-futurist twist. Sanity is not found here, nor in the moth-eaten eternities of the mystics.

Other animals do not pine for a deathless life. They are already in it. Even a caged tiger passes its life half out of time. Humans cannot enter that never-ending moment. They can find a respite from time when – like Odysseus, who refused Calypso's offer of everlasting life on an enchanted island so he could return to his beloved home – they no longer dream of immortality.

Contemplation is not the willed stillness of the mystics but a willing surrender to never-returning moments. When we turn away from our all-too-human yearnings we turn back to mortal things. Not moral hopes or mystical dreams but groundless facts are the true objects of contemplation.

5
SIMPLY TO SEE

Other animals do not need a purpose in life. A contradiction to itself, the human animal cannot do without one. Can we not think of the aim of life as being simply to see?

2002

Notes

INTRODUCTION

1. Wallace Stevens, *The Collected Poems* (New York: Vintage Books, 1990), 'Extracts from Addresses to the Academy of Fine Ideas', p. 255.
2. Joseph Conrad, *Heart of Darkness and Other Stories*, World's Classics edn (Oxford and New York: Oxford University Press, 1990), pp. 151–2.
3. Loren Eiseley, *The Invisible Pyramid* (Lincoln, Nebr.: University of Nebraska Press, 1998), p. 65.

CHAPTER 1: *MODUS VIVENDI*

1. The pervasive dependency of Locke's political thought on a particular version of the Christian religion has been shown in John Dunn's classic study *The Political Thought of John Locke: An Historical Account of the Argument of the 'Two Treatises of Government'* (Cambridge: Cambridge University Press, 1969).
2. For an interpretation of Hobbes as a thinker who returns to a pagan tradition in which it is not belief but practice which is primary, see Michael Oakeshott, *Hobbes on Civil Association* (Oxford: Basil Blackwell, 1975), pp. 69–72.
3. Voltaire, *Philosophical Dictionary* (London: J. and H. L. Hunt, 1824), vol. 6: *Toleration*, p. 272.
4. See Alasdair MacIntyre: *After Virtue: A Study in Moral Theory* (London: Duckworth, 1981); *Whose Justice? Which Rationality?* (London: Duckworth, 1988); *Three Rival Versions of Moral Enquiry* (London: Duckworth, 1990); *Dependent Rational Animals: Why Human Beings Need the Virtues* (London: Duckworth, 1999).
5. I have considered the inadequacies of Hayek's treatment of social justice in my *Hayek on Liberty*, 3rd edn (London and New York: Routledge,

1998), 'Postscript: Hayek and the Dissolution of Classical Liberalism', pp. 146–61.

6. On the anti-political character of Rawlsian liberalism, see 'Rawls's Anti-Political Liberalism', in my *Endgames: Questions in Late Modern Political Thought* (Cambridge: Polity Press, 1997), pp. 51–4.

7. I noted the continuation in his later work of Rawls's early agenda regarding the strong determinacy and finality of his principles of justice in 'Contractarian Method, Private Property and the Market Economy', in my *Liberalisms: Essays in Political Philosophy* (London and New York: Routledge, 1989), pp. 161–98.

8. The early Robert Nozick may be taken as a spokesman of the view that market freedoms are derivations from fundamental human rights. See Robert Nozick, *Anarchy, State and Utopia* (Oxford and New York: Basil Blackwell, 1974).

9. For an argument against both egalitarian and libertarian versions of liberal legalism, see my *Beyond the New Right: Markets, Government and the Common Environment* (London and New York: Routledge, 1993), pp. 76–92. For an argument that market institutions best advance personal autonomy when they are complemented by enabling welfare institutions, see ibid., pp. 99–110.

10. For a statement of Rawls's views that may be definitive, see John Rawls, *Collected Papers*, ed. Samuel Freeman (Cambridge, Mass., and London: Harvard University Press, 1999).

11. I am indebted to Dr Henry Hardy for conversation on the conflict between value-pluralism and the claims of universal religions.

12. For a critique of social democracy from the standpoint of value-pluralism, see 'After Social Democracy', in my *Endgames*, pp. 11–50.

13. For a thoughtful contrary view, see Richard Rorty, *Contingency, Irony and Solidarity* (Cambridge: Cambridge University Press, 1989), especially chs 3 and 4, and *Truth and Progress: Philosophical Papers* (Cambridge: Cambridge University Press, 1998), particularly chs 9 and 10.

14. Stuart Hampshire, 'Justice is Strife', *Proceedings and Addresses of the American Philosophical Association*, vol. 65, no. 3, November 1991, pp. 24–5.

15. On the contemporary cult of the free market, see my *False Dawn: The Delusions of Global Capitalism* (London and New York: Granta Books, 1998, and New Press, 1999).

16. For an argument that much in the Enlightenment is a secularization of Christian hopes, see my *Enlightenment's Wake: Politics and Culture at the Close of the Modern Age* (London and New York: Routledge, 1995), ch. 10.

17. I consider some of the difficulties of defining and delimiting the liberal tradition in the Postscript to my *Liberalism*, 2nd edn (Buckingham: Open University Press, 1995).

18. See F. A. Hayek, *The Constitution of Liberty* (London: Routledge & Kegan Paul, 1960; Chicago: Henry Regnery Company, 1960), pp. 174ff. For a statement of a view antithetical to Hayek's that is relevant today, despite having been first published in 1911, see L. T. Hobhouse, *Liberalism* (New York: Oxford University Press, 1964).

19. An invaluable account of the new Pyrrhonism is to be found in Richard H. Popkin's *The History of Scepticism from Erasmus to Spinoza*, 4th edn (Berkeley: University of California Press, 1979). See also Popkin's *The High Road to Pyrrhonism*, ed. R. A. Watson and J. E. Force (Indianapolis and Cambridge: Hackett Publishing, 1980).

20. Hayek, *Constitution of Liberty*, p. 56.

21. For an admirable recent study of Smith that does full justice to the subtlety and complexity of his thought, see Charles L. Griswold Jr, *Adam Smith and the Virtues of Enlightenment* (Cambridge: Cambridge University Press, 1999). For a study of Smith's highly complex relations with 'liberalism', see Donald Winch, *Adam Smith's Politics* (Cambridge: Cambridge University Press, 1978).

22. See James Fitzjames Stephen, *Liberty, Equality, Fraternity*, ed. Stuart D. Warner (Indianapolis: Liberty Fund, 1993).

23. See Oakeshott, *Hobbes on Civil Association*, p. 63. For two other distinguished interpretations of Hobbes as one of the chief authors of the liberal tradition, see Leo Strauss, *The Political Philosophy of Thomas Hobbes* (Chicago: University of Chicago Press, 1952), and C. B. Macpherson, *The Political Theory of Possessive Individualism* (Oxford: Clarendon Press, 1962).

Two more recent studies in which Hobbes appears as a proto-liberal are Gregory S. Kavka, *Hobbesian Moral and Political Theory* (Princeton, NJ: Princeton University Press, 1986), and Jean Hampton, *Hobbes and the Social Contract Tradition* (Cambridge: Cambridge University Press, 1986).

24. For a powerful and highly original interpretation of Hume as a philosopher of common life, see Donald W. Livingstone, *Hume's Philosophy of Common Life* (Chicago: University of Chicago Press, 1984).

I considered the relations of Pyrrhonism with politics in 'After Liberalism', the Postscript to my *Liberalisms*, pp. 261–4.

25. On the emergence of Romanticism, see Isaiah Berlin, *The Roots of Romanticism*, ed. Henry Hardy (London: Chatto & Windus, 1999), especially chs 2 and 3.

26. See Wilhelm von Humboldt, *The Limits of State Action*, ed. J. W. Burrow (Indianapolis: Liberty Fund, 1993). John Burrow's Introduction (pp. xvii–lviii) is itself a notable contribution to thought on liberalism.

27. J. S. Mill, *On Liberty and Other Essays*, ed. John Gray, World's Classics edn (Oxford: Oxford University Press, 2008), pp. 69–70.

28. I have discussed some of the tensions in Mill's thought in the Postscript to my *Mill on Liberty: A Defence*, 2nd edn (London and New York: Routledge, 1996), pp. 130–58.

29. For Mill's arguments against the illiberal tendencies in French Positivism, see his *Auguste Comte and Positivism* (Ann Arbor: University of Michigan Press, 1973). A useful selection from *Auguste Comte and Positivism* can be found in John Stuart Mill, *Utilitarianism, On Liberty and Considerations on Representative Government*, ed. H. B. Acton (London: J. M. Dent, 1972), pp. 395–413.

30. See 'John Stuart Mill and the Ends of Life', in Isaiah Berlin, *Four Essays on Liberty* (Oxford: Oxford University Press, 1969), p. 188.

31. I discuss Berlin's agonistic liberalism in my *Isaiah Berlin* (London: HarperCollins, 1996; Princeton, NJ: Princeton University Press, 1996), ch. 6.

32. Michael Oakeshott, *Rationalism in Politics and Other Essays* (London and New York: Methuen, 1977), p. 136.

33. Mill, *On Liberty and Other Essays*, pp. 13–14.

34. I argued that Oakeshott's thought issues in an ideal of *modus vivendi* in 'Oakeshott on Law, Liberty and Civil Association', in my *Liberalisms*, pp. 199–216. I advanced an interpretation of Oakeshott as a liberal thinker in 'Oakeshott as a Liberal', in my *Post-Liberalism: Studies in Political Thought* (London and New York: Routledge, 1993), ch. 4, reprinted as Chapter 4 of the present volume.

A similar interpretation of Oakeshott is presented by Wendell John Coats Jr, 'Michael Oakeshott as Liberal Theorist', *Canadian Journal of Political Science*, vol. XVIII, no. 4, December 1985, pp. 773–87. I owe this reference to Oakeshott, who expressed his admiration of Coats's paper in conversation with me.

I discuss some affinities and contrasts between Oakeshott and Berlin in 'Berlin, Oakeshott and Enlightenment', in my *Endgames*, pp. 84–96.

CHAPTER 2: JOHN STUART MILL AND THE
IDEA OF PROGRESS

1. Some dissenters from this consensus are: Alan Ryan, 'John Stuart Mill's Art of Living', *Listener*, 21 October 1965; 'John Stuart Mill and the Open Society', *Listener*, 17 May 1973; Antony Flew, 'J. S. Mill – Socialist or Libertarian?', in Michael Ivens (ed.), *Prophets of Freedom and Enterprise* (London: Kogan Page for Aims of Industry, 1975), pp. 21–7; Ian Bradley, 'John Stuart Mill – A Victorian's Message for Modern Liberals', *The Times*, 8 May 1973.

2. For example: Jack Parsons, *Population versus Liberty* (London: Pemberton Books, 1971), with forewords by Douglas Houghton, Sir David Renton and Lord Beaumont.

3. See Thomas Szasz, *Law, Liberty and Psychiatry* (London: Routledge & Kegan Paul, 1974) and other writings.

4. See especially chapter 3 of *On Liberty*, in J. S. Mill, *On Liberty and Other Essays*, ed. John Gray, World's Classics edn (Oxford: Oxford University Press, 2008).

5. Ibid., p. 118.

6. For example, Milton Friedman, *Capitalism and Freedom* (Chicago: University of Chicago Press, 1974); A. T. Peacock and C. K. Rowley, *Welfare Economics – A Liberal Restatement* (London: Martin Robertson, 1975).

7. The suggestion is made by Flew, 'J. S. Mill'.

8. See, for example: Professor J. E. Meade's *Intelligent Radical's Guide to Economic Policy* (London: George Allen & Unwin, 1975) for a reform programme very much in the Millian tradition.

9. *Principles of Political Economy* (Harmondsworth: Penguin, 1970), p. 133.

10. Ibid., pp. 114–15.

11. Ibid., p. 116.

12. See Mill's proposals for a proportional or personal representation in *Considerations on Representative Government*, in *On Liberty and Other Essays*, pp. 353–69.

CHAPTER 3: SANTAYANA'S ALTERNATIVE

1. See T. L. S. Sprigge, *Santayana: An Examination of his Philosophy* (London and Boston: Routledge & Kegan Paul, 1974), p. 1.

2. First published by Charles Scribner's Sons (New York), republished by Dover Publications (New York, 1955).

3. *Life of Reason, or The Phases of Human Progress*, 5 vols (New York: Charles Scribner's Sons, 1905–6).

4. *Realms of Being*, 4 vols (New York: Charles Scribner's Sons, 1927–42).

5. *Winds of Doctrine: Studies in Contemporary Opinion* (New York: Charles Scribner's Sons, 1913).

6. *Soliloquies in England and Later Soliloquies* (New York: Charles Scribner's Sons, 1922).

7. *Winds of Doctrine*, p. 146.

8. *Soliloquies in England and Later Soliloquies*, pp. 165–6.

9. Ibid.

10. Ibid., pp. 207–8.

11. *Dominations and Powers: Reflections on Liberty, Society and Government* (New York: Charles Scribner's Sons, 1951), p. 340.

12. *Soliloquies in England and Later Soliloquies*, p. 189.

13. *Dominations and Powers*, p. 438.

14. Ibid., p. vii.

15. Ibid., p. 158.

16. 'Alternatives to Liberalism', in Santayana's *The Birth of Reason and Other Essays* (New York: Columbia University Press, 1968), p. 114.

17. *Dominations and Powers*, pp. 211–12.

18. Ibid., p. 450.

19. Ibid., p. 452.

20. Ibid., see p. 440.

21. Ibid., pp. 454–6.

22. 'Alternatives to Liberalism', pp. 108–9.

23. P. S. Schilpp, *The Philosophy of George Santayana* (New York: Tudor Publishing, 1951), p. 559.

24. 'A Long Way Round to Nirvana', in Santayana's *Some Turns of Thought in Modern Philosophy* (Cambridge: Cambridge University Press, 1935), p. 94.

25. 'Alternatives to Liberalism', p. 115.

CHAPTER 4: OAKESHOTT AS A LIBERAL

1. *Rationalism in Politics and Other Essays* (Indianapolis: Liberty Press, 1991), pp. 439–40.

2. The paper is Wendell John Coats Jr, 'Michael Oakeshott as Liberal Theorist', *Canadian Journal of Political Science*, vol. XVIII, no. 4, December 1985, pp. 773–87.

3. The two books are: Robert Grant, *Oakeshott* (London: Claridge Press, 1990) and Paul Franco, *The Political Philosophy of Michael Oakeshott* (New Haven and London: Yale University Press, 1990).

4. John Rawls, *A Theory of Justice* (Cambridge, Mass.: Harvard University Press, 1971); Ronald Dworkin, *Taking Rights Seriously* (London: Duckworth, 1978).

5. Michael Oakeshott, *Rationalism in Politics and Other Essays*, new and expanded edn, ed. Timothy Fuller (Indianapolis: Liberty Press, 1991).

6. Coats, 'Michael Oakeshott'.

7. *Rationalism in Politics and Other Essays*, p. 452.

8. Grant, *Oakeshott*, p. 85.

9. See *Rationalism in Politics and Other Essays*, pp. 384–406.

10. Henry C. Simon, *Economic Policy for a Free Society* (Chicago: University of Chicago Press, 1948; Cambridge: Cambridge University Press, 1948).

11. *Rationalism in Politics and Other Essays*, p. 443.

12. See Oakeshott, *The Voice of Liberal Learning* (New Haven: Yale University Press, 1989).

13. Franco, *Political Philosophy of Michael Oakeshott*.

CHAPTER 5: NOTES TOWARDS A DEFINITION OF THE POLITICAL THOUGHT OF TLÖN

1. R. Goodin and P. Pettit (eds), *A Companion to Contemporary Political Philosophy* (Oxford: Basil Blackwell, 1993).

2. Ibid., p. 176.

CHAPTER 6: ISAIAH BERLIN: THE VALUE OF DECENCY

1. Isaiah Berlin, *Political Ideas in the Romantic Age: Their Rise and Influence on Modern Thought*, ed. Henry Hardy, with an Introduction by Joshua L. Cherniss (Princeton, NJ: Princeton University Press, 2006).

2. 'The Apotheosis of the Romantic Will', in Henry Hardy (ed.), *The Proper Study of Mankind* (New York: Farrar, Straus & Giroux, 1998), p. 580.

3. Berlin examines the roots of utopianism in 'The Decline of Utopian Ideas in the West', in *The Crooked Timber of Humanity: Chapters in the History of Ideas* (London: John Murray, 1990; New York: Alfred A. Knopf, 1991), pp. 20–48.

4. For Berlin's criticism of ideas of autonomy, see his 'From Hope and Fear Set Free', in *The Proper Study of Mankind*, pp. 91–118.

5. William A. Galston has written an elegant and resourceful pluralist defence of liberalism in *Liberal Pluralism: The Implications of Value Pluralism for Political Theory and Practice* (Cambridge: Cambridge University Press, 2002). A survey of the literature on the issue is given in George Crowder, *Liberalism and Value Pluralism* (London: Continuum, 2002).

6. Avishai Margalit presents a powerful defence of the idea of a decent society as one that seeks to eradicate practices that involve the humiliation of any of its members in his book *The Decent Society*, trans. Naomi Goldblum (Cambridge, Mass.: Harvard University Press, 1996).

7. Isaiah Berlin and Beata Polanowska-Sygulska, *Unfinished Dialogue*, with a foreword by Henry Hardy (Amherst, NY: Prometheus Books, 2006).

8. 'Russia, Poland and Marxism: Isaiah Berlin to Andrzej Walicki, 1962–1996', *Dialogue and Universalism*, vol. 15, no. 9–10, 2005, pp. 53–173.

9. Lev Shestov, *Athens and Jerusalem* (New York: Simon & Schuster, 1968), p. 431.

CHAPTER 7: GEORGE SOROS AND THE OPEN SOCIETY

1. George Soros, *The Age of Fallibility: The Consequences of the War on Terror* (New York: PublicAffairs, 2006).

2. Tivador Soros recounts his experiences in *Masquerade: Dancing around Death in Nazi-Occupied Hungary* (Edinburgh: Canongate Books, 2000; New York: Arcade, 2001).

3. George Soros, 'The Capitalist Threat', *Atlantic Monthly*, February 1997, pp. 45–58.

4. Robert M. Solow, 'The Amateur', *New Republic*, 8 February 1999, p. 29.

5. In *The Age of Fallibility*, Soros acknowledges that a number of important twentieth-century economists 'recognized that knowledge is imperfect and that this leads to fundamental difficulties in defining economic rationality', and mentions F. A. Hayek, J. M. Keynes and Frank Knight as examples.

6. The text of the mission statement, signed by Dick Cheney, Paul Wolfowitz and Donald Rumsfeld, is printed in *The Bubble of American Supremacy: Correcting the Misuse of American Power* (New York: PublicAffairs, 2004), pp. 5–7.

7. The document can be viewed at *www.globalsecurity.org/security/library/report/2004/hsc-planning-scenarios-jul04intro.htm*.

8. For the role of evangelical Christianity in Bush's rise to the presidency, see Kevin P. Phillips, *American Theocracy: The Peril and Politics of Radical Religions, Oil, and Borrowed Money in the Twenty-first Century* (New York: Viking, 2006); and Michael Lind, *Made in Texas: George W. Bush and the Southern Takeover of American Politics* (New York: Basic Books, 2003).

9. Norman Cohn, *The Pursuit of the Millennium: Revolutionary Millenarians and Mystical Anarchists of the Middle Ages*, revised and expanded edn (Oxford: Oxford University Press, 1970). Cohn also analysed the role of apocalyptic myths in fuelling anti-Semitism. See his *Warrant for Genocide: The Myth of the Jewish World Conspiracy and the Protocols of the Elders of Zion* (London: Serif, 1996).

10. See Lakoff's recent book, *Whose Freedom?: The Battle over America's Most Important Idea* (New York: Farrar, Straus & Giroux, 2006).

CHAPTER 8: HAYEK AS A CONSERVATIVE

1. F. A. Hayek, *The Constitution of Liberty* (London: Routledge & Kegan Paul, 1960; Chicago: Henry Regnery Company, 1960).

2. F. A. Hayek, *Law, Legislation and Liberty*, one-vol. edn (London and New York: Routledge & Kegan Paul, 1982), vol. 2: *The Mirage of Social Justice*.

3. Hayek's epistemology is most systematically presented in his treatise on philosophical psychology, *The Sensory Order: An Inquiry into the Foundations of Theoretical Psychology* (London: Routledge & Kegan Paul,

1952), and in the earlier essays collected in his *Studies in Philosophy, Politics and Economics* (London: Routledge & Kegan Paul, 1967).

4. For the intriguing idea of a meta-conscious rule, see Hayek's *Studies in Philosophy, Politics and Economics*, pp. 60–63.

5. Saul Kripke, *Wittgenstein on Rules and Private Language* (Oxford: Basil Blackwell, 1982), p. 88n.

6. Hayek acknowledges the inevitability of legislation in the modern state in his response to the most interesting and original criticism of his views in Bruno Leoni's *Freedom and the Law* (Princeton, NJ: D. Van Nostrand, 1961). See Hayek, *Law, Legislation and Liberty*, vol. 1: *Rules and Order*, pp. 168, 35n.

7. F. A. Hayek, *The Road to Serfdom* (London: George Routledge & Sons, 1944).

8. I refer, most especially, to Oakeshott's *Human Conduct* (Oxford: Clarendon Press, 1975), pp. 274–8, for its masterly evocation of the sources and character of the modern European sense of individuality.

9. For Hayek's conception of an unviable morality, see *Law, Legislation and Liberty*, vol. 2: *The Mirage of Social Justice*, ch. 11.

10. On the Platonist and Christian roots of Marxism, see L. Kolakowski, *Main Currents of Marxism* (New York and London: W. W. Norton, 2005), vol. 1: *The Founders*, ch. 1.

11. For a conservative criticism of Hayek's Mandevillian argument, see Irving Kristol, 'When Virtue Loses All her Loveliness – Some Reflections on Capitalism and "The Free Society" ', *Public Interest*, Fall 1970, pp. 3–15.

12. For a profound interpretation of contemporary moral inversion, see Michael Polanyi's *Personal Knowledge: Towards a Post-Critical Philosophy* (Chicago: University of Chicago Press, 1958), ch. 7, sections 9–16.

CHAPTER 9: A CONSERVATIVE DISPOSITION

1. Michael Oakeshott, 'On being Conservative', in *Rationalism in Politics and Other Essays* (London and New York: Methuen, 1977), p. 183.

2. Thomas Hobbes, *Leviathan*, Everyman edn (London: Dent, 1949), pt 2, ch. 17, pp. 88–9.

3. W. B. Yeats, *Selected Poems* (London: Pan Books, 1980), p. 179.

4. See Roger Scruton, 'In Defence of the Nation', in J. C. D. Clark (ed.), *Ideas and Politics in Modern Britain* (London: Macmillan, 1990), pp. 53–86. I have criticized Scruton's view in the same volume in my 'Conservatism, Individualism and the Political Thought of the New Right',

pp. 81–102, reprinted as chapter 19 of my book, *Post-Liberalism: Studies in Political Thought* (London and New York: Routledge, 1993). An excellent statement of conservative communitarianism, to which I am much indebted, may be found in Robin Harris's *The Conservative Community: The Roots of Thatcherism – and its Future* (London: Centre for Policy Studies, 1989).

5. John Stuart Mill, *On Liberty and Other Essays*, ed. John Gray, World's Classics edn (Oxford: Oxford University Press, 2008).

6. See F. A. Hayek, *Law, Legislation and Liberty*, one-vol. edn (London and New York: Routledge & Kegan Paul, 1982), vol. 2: *The Mirage of Social Justice*, p. 112: 'the only ties which hold together the whole of a Great Society are purely "economic".'

7. The term Areopagitic refers, of course, to Milton, and is used in a political context to characterize ideal liberalism by J. R. Lucas in his *Principles of Politics* (Oxford: Clarendon Press, 1966).

8. Philip Larkin, 'Days', in *Collected Poems* (London: Marvell Press and Faber & Faber, 1988), p. 67.

9. I have elsewhere suggested how the NHS in Britain might by an evolutionary development turn into a system of private care for all who seek it. See my *Limited Government: A Positive Agenda* (London: Institute for Economic Affairs, 1989). That argument should not be interpreted as a rationale for under-funding the NHS in its present, or likely future, form.

10. For evidence that individualism is in England immemorial, see Alan Macfarlane, *Origins of English Individualism: The Family, Property and Social Transition* (Oxford: Basil Blackwell, 1978).

11. The term 'radically situated selves' originates, so far as I know, in Michael Sandel's *Liberalism and the Limits of Justice* (Cambridge: Cambridge University Press, 1982).

12. Oakeshott, 'The Tower of Babel', in *Rationalism in Politics and Other Essays*, p. 65.

13. On this, see *Correct Core: Simple Curricula for English, Maths and Science*, prepared by Sheila Lawlor, Policy Study 93 (London: Centre for Policy Studies, 1988).

14. *Community Care: Agenda for Action*, Report to the Secretary of State for Social Services by Sir Roy Griffiths (London: HMSO, 1988).

15. Isaiah Berlin, *The Crooked Timber of Humanity: Chapters in the History of Ideas* (London: John Murray, 1990; New York: Alfred A. Knopf, 1991), especially 'The Pursuit of the Ideal'.

16. G. L. S. Shackle, *Epistemics and Economics: A Critique of Economic Doctrines* (Cambridge: Cambridge University Press, 1972), p. 239.

17. See Joseph A. Schumpeter, *Capitalism, Socialism and Democracy*, 4th edn (London: George Allen & Unwin, 1952).

18. See P. Smith (ed.), *Lord Salisbury on Politics* (Cambridge: Cambridge University Press, 1972).

19. This is a point illuminatingly explored in George Santayana's neglected conservative classic, *Dominations and Powers: Reflections on Liberty, Society and Government* (New York: Charles Scribner's Sons, 1951).

20. I owe the expression 'the politics of imperfection' to Anthony Quinton's book, *The Politics of Imperfection: The Religious and Secular Traditions of Conservative Thought in England from Hooker to Oakeshott* (London: Macmillan, 1976).

21. See Donald W. Livingstone's excellent book, *Hume's Philosophy of Common Life* (Chicago: University of Chicago Press, 1984).

22. David Hume, *A Treatise of Human Nature* (London: Penguin, 1969), p. 319.

CHAPTER 10: THE STRANGE DEATH OF TORY ENGLAND

1. I have considered the decay of the post-war British settlement during the Callaghan Labour government in more detail in my monograph, *The Undoing of Conservatism* (London: Social Market Foundation, 1994), reprinted as ch. 7 of my book, *Enlightenment's Wake: Politics and Culture at the Close of the Modern Age* (London and New York: Routledge, 2007). I examined the contradictions of neo-liberal ideology in the Introduction to my *Beyond the New Right: Markets, Government and the Common Environment* (London and New York: Routledge, 1993).

2. An exception might be made for the thought of Michael Oakeshott, in which a criticism of the Enlightenment is obliquely pursued. However, though Oakeshott's thought was an object of reverence in the New Right think-tanks, particularly the Centre for Policy Studies, it was never an influence on policy – in the way that Hayek's was, say – and, no doubt wisely, he held himself aloof from quotidian politics. Analogously, Roger Scruton's *Salisbury Review* adopted a stance of Jacobitic or quixotic resistance to the spirit of the age, which sometimes encompassed opposition to aspects of economic liberalism; and its influence on practising Conservative politicians was correspondingly negligible.

3. I do not mean to imply that Popper's and Hayek's thought were at all

points convergent, but only that neither of them belonged to a recognizable tradition of British or European *conservative* thought.

4. Not all British classical liberals were, or are, opposed to European federalism. Sir Samuel Brittan, the distinguished economic commentator, is perhaps the most noteworthy among several exceptions.

5. A significant part of this new insecurity among the middle classes in Britain no doubt derives from the globalization of the economy and new technologies rather than from any impact of domestic policy. This does not mean that the neo-liberal policies of the past seventeen years have not worsened insecurity for the Tories' core supporters – and it certainly will not stop the Tories being held to electoral account for doing nothing to make the new job insecurity more humanly tolerable.

CHAPTER 11: TONY BLAIR, NEO-CON

1. Blair's statement was made to the Labour Party conference in September 2004 as part of a defence of his role in the Iraq war. See *Guardian*, 29 September 2004.

2. For samples of neo-conservative thinking, see Irwin Stelzer (ed.), *Neoconservatism* (London: Atlantic Books, 2005), which contains a contribution by Tony Blair; and Irving Kristol, *Neoconservatism: The Autobiography of an Idea* (New York: Free Press, 1995).

3. John Kampfner, *Blair's Wars* (London and New York: Free Press, 2004), p. 173.

4. Tony Blair, Prime Minister's speeches, http://www.number-10.gov.uk/output/Page1297.asp.

5. Ibid.

6. Tony Blair, speech to the World Affairs Council in Los Angeles, 1 August 2006.

7. Tony Blair, 'Defence – Our Nation's Future', 12 January 2007, http://www.pm.gov.uk/output/Page10735.asp.

8. For a penetrating account of political lying in the Blair era, see Peter Oborne, *The Rise of Political Lying* (London and New York: Free Press, 2005).

9. Raymond Aron, Foreword to Alain Besançon, *The Soviet Syndrome*, trans. Patricia Ranum (New York: Harcourt Brace Jovanovich, 1978), pp. xvii–xviii.

CHAPTER 12: MARGARET THATCHER AND THE EUTHANASIA OF CONSERVATISM

1. Thatcher's remark is cited by Jason Burke in 'The History Man: A Profile of Francis Fukuyama', *Observer*, 27 June 2004.

2. For an account of how *laissez-faire* was engineered in early Victorian England, see my *False Dawn: The Delusions of Global Capitalism* (London and New York: Granta Books, 1998, and New Press, 1999), pp. 7–17.

3. Hoskyns's paper was presented at a private dinner in late 1977. So far as I know it has not been published. It is archived at the Margaret Thatcher Foundation.

4. Hugo Young, *One of Us: A Biography of Margaret Thatcher* (London, Pan Books, 1993), p. 113.

5. For a brilliantly perceptive account of the rise and dominance of Thatcherism, see Simon Jenkins, *Thatcher and Sons: A Revolution in Three Acts* (London: Allen Lane, 2006).

CHAPTER 13: THE SYSTEM OF RUINS

1. Eugen von Böhm-Bawerk, *Karl Marx and the Close of his System* (Clifton, NJ: A. M. Kelly Publishers, 1973).

2. Tom Bottomore (ed.), *A Dictionary of Marxist Thought* (Oxford: Basil Blackwell, 1983).

3. Gérard Bekerman, *Marx and Engels: A Conceptual Concordance*, trans. Terrell Carver (Oxford: Basil Blackwell, 1983).

4. David Felix, *Marx as Politician* (Carbondale: Southern Illinois University Press, 1983).

5. Ernest Nolte, *Marxism, Fascism, Cold War* (Asson, Netherlands: Van Gorcum, 1983).

6. Ernest Nolte, *Three Faces of Fascism* (London: Macmillan, 1965).

7. Nolte, *Marxism, Fascism, Cold War*.

8. Ibid., p. 84.

9. Alan Macfarlane, *Origins of English Individualism: The Family, Property and Social Transition* (Oxford: Basil Blackwell, 1978).

10. G. A. Cohen, *Karl Marx's Theory of History: A Defence* (Oxford: Clarendon Press, 1978).

11. Alex Callinicos, *The Revolutionary Ideas of Karl Marx* (London: Bookmarks, 1983).

12. Alex Callinicos, *Marxism and Philosophy* (Oxford: Oxford University Press, 1983).

13. David McLellan (ed.), *Marx: The First Hundred Years* (London: Fontana, 1983).

14. Paul Craig Roberts, *Alienation and the Soviet Economy* (Albuquerque, N. Mex.: University of Mexico Press, 1971, 1st edn; New York and London: Holmes & Meier Publishers, 1991, 2nd edn).

15. Norman Fischer, Louis Patsouras and N. Georgopoulos (eds), *Continuity and Change in Marxism* (Brighton: Harvester, 1983).

16. Susan M. Easton, *Humanist Marxism and Wittgensteinian Social Philosophy* (Manchester: Manchester University Press, 1983).

17. Jorge Larrain, *Marxism and Ideology* (London: Macmillan, 1983).

18. Jean L. Cohen, *Class and Civil Society: The Limits of Marxian Critical Theory* (Oxford: Martin Robertson, 1983).

19. Michael Burawoy and Theda Skocpol, *Marxist Inquiries: Studies of Labor, Class, and States* (Chicago: University of Chicago Press, 1983).

20. Barry Smart, *Foucault, Marxism and Critique* (Routledge & Kegan Paul, 1983).

21. George G. Brenkert, *Marx's Ethics of Freedom* (Routledge & Kegan Paul, 1983).

CHAPTER 14: CULTURAL ORIGINS OF SOVIET COMMUNISM

1. L. Kolakowski, *Main Currents of Marxism* (New York and London: W. W. Norton, 2005), vol. 1: *The Founders*, ch. 1.

2. See Eric Voegelin, *The New Science of Politics* (Chicago: University of Chicago Press, 1952), pp. 107 et seq.

3. Michael Polanyi, *The Logic of Liberty* (Chicago: University of Chicago Press, 1951), p. 93.

4. See N. Berdyaev, *The Origin of Russian Communism* (London: Centenary Press, 1837).

5. See Alain Besançon, *The Rise of the Gulag: Intellectual Origins of Leninism* (New York: Continuum, 1981).

6. See A. Solzhenitsyn, *The Red Wheel* (London: Bodley Head, 1989; New York: Farrar, Straus & Giroux, 1989).

7. See, especially, Dostoyevsky's great novel, *The Possessed* (1871–2).

8. For a brilliant demystification of the French Revolution, see René Sédillot, *Le Coût de la Révolution Française* (Paris: Perrin, 1987).

9. See Besançon, *Rise of the Gulag*, ch. 12 on the Jacobin aspect of Leninism. J. L. Talmon's *The Origins of Totalitarian Democracy* (London: Secker & Warburg, 1952) is also relevant here.

10. Theodore H. von Laue, *Why Lenin? Why Stalin? A Reappraisal of the Russian Revolution, 1900–1930* (New York: Lippincott Company, 1971), p. 213.

11. For their comments on this paper, I am indebted to Fred Miller, Zbigniew Rau, Roger Scruton, Stefan Sencerz, Andrzej Walicki. I am particularly indebted to Ellen Paul for her detailed written comments.

CHAPTER 15: WESTERN MARXISM: A FICTIONALIST DECONSTRUCTION

1. L. Revai, *The Word as Deed: Studies in the Labour Theory of Meaning*, ed. G. Olsen and J. Kahn (Helsinki: Praxis Press, 1988).

2. L. Wittgenstein, *Philosophical Investigations* (Oxford: Basil Blackwell, 1972), 5e, section 2.

3. *Concerning Marxism in Linguistics*, IV, 1, 3.

4. G. Olsen, *Sense and Reference in Marxian Semantics* (Oxford: Oxford University Press, 1980).

5. P. Reimer, *Analytical Foundations of Marxian Microlinguistics* (Berkeley: Praxis Press, 1982).

CHAPTER 16: THE END OF HISTORY, AGAIN?

1. Francis Fukuyama, *National Interest*, Summer 1989.

2. John Gray, *Liberalisms: Essays in Political Philosophy* (London and New York: Routledge, 1989).

CHAPTER 17: WHAT GLOBALIZATION IS NOT

1. Joseph Schumpeter, 'The Instability of Capitalism', *Economic Journal*, vol. 38, September 1928, p. 368.

2. David Held, David Goldblatt, Anthony McGrew and Jonathan Perraton, 'The Globalization of Economic Activity', *New Political Economy*, vol. 2, no. 2, July 1997, pp. 257–77, p. 258. See also, by the same authors, *Global Flows, Global Transformations: Concepts, Theories and Evidence* (Cambridge: Polity Press, 1997). I am much indebted to David Held for

making the pathbreaking paper to which I have referred above available to me prior to publication.

3. Anthony Giddens, *The Consequences of Modernity* (Cambridge: Polity Press, 1990), p. 64.

4. John Micklethwaite and Adrian Wooldridge, *The Witch Doctors* (London: William Heinemann, 1996), p. 294.

5. Tom Nierop, *Systems and Regions in Global Politics* (London: John Wiley, 1994), ch. 3.

6. Micklethwaite and Wooldridge, *Witch Doctors*, p. 245.

7. See Paul Krugman, 'Growing World Trade: Causes and Consequences', *Brookings Paper on Economic Activity*, no. 1 (1995).

8. For evidence on this point, see J. Frankel, *The Internationalization of Equity Markets* (Chicago: University of Chicago Press, 1994); H. Akdogan, *The Integration of International Capital Markets* (London: Edward Elgar, 1995).

9. On the trend to global pricing of equities, see Lowell Bryan and Diana Farrell, *Market Unbound: Unleashing Global Capitalism* (New York: John Wiley, 1996), ch. 2.

10. GATT, *International Trade 1993–4*, vol. 1 (Geneva: GATT, 1994); UN Development Programme, *Human Development Report 1994* (Oxford: Oxford University Press, 1994); UNCTAD, *World Investment Report 1994* (Geneva: UNCTAD, 1994).

11. *Wall Street Journal*, 24 October 1995; Bank of International Settlements, Annual Report, 1995.

12. Michel Albert, *Capitalism against Capitalism* (London: Whurr Publishers, 1993), p. 188.

13. UNCTAD, *World Investment Report 1994*.

14. Micklethwaite and Wooldridge, *Witch Doctors*, p. 246.

15. W. Ruigrok and R. van Tulder, *The Logic of International Restructuring* (London: Routledge, 1995).

16. Paul Hirst and Grahame Thompson, 'Globalization', *Soundings*, issue 4, Autumn 1996, p. 56.

17. See Micklethwaite and Wooldridge, *Witch Doctors*, pp. 243–4.

18. Kenichi Ohmae, *The End of the Nation-State: The Rise of Regional Economies* (London: HarperCollins, 1995), p. 7.

19. Paul Hirst and Grahame Thompson, *Globalization in Question* (Cambridge: Polity Press, 1996), p. 6. Similar sceptical arguments about globalization may be found in P. Bairoch, 'Globalization, Myths and Realities', in R. Boyer and D. Drache (eds), *States against Markets – The Limits of Globalization* (London: Routledge, 1996). See also P. Bairoch and R. Kozul-

Wright, *Globalization Myths: Some Historical Reflections on Integration, Industrialization and Growth in the World Economy*, UNCTAD Discussion Paper No. 113, March 1996.

20. Hirst and Thompson, *Globalization in Question*, p. 31.

21. Held et al., 'Globalization of Economic Activity', p. 6.

22. Hirst and Thompson, *Globalization in Question*, p. 10.

23. Ibid., p. 163 et seq.

24. Held et al., 'Globalization of Economic Activity'.

25. Ohmae, *The End of the Nation-State*, pp. 15, 19–20.

26. Nicholas Negroponte, *Being Digital* (London: Hodder & Stoughton, 1995).

27. Bryan and Farrell, *Market Unbound*, p. 1.

28. Robert B. Reich, *The Work of Nations: Preparing Ourselves for 21st Century Capitalism* (New York: Alfred A. Knopf, 1991).

29. John Naisbitt, *Global Paradox* (London: Nicholas Brealey Publishing, 1995), p. 40.

30. Ruigrok and van Tulder, *Logic of International Restructuring*.

31. Hirst and Thompson, *Globalization in Question*, p. 12.

32. I am indebted to some aspects of the analysis of Scott Lash and John Urry, in their book *The End of Organized Capitalism* (Cambridge: Polity Press, 1987).

33. See Susan Strange, *Casino Capitalism* (Oxford: Basil Blackwell, 1986).

34. See Martin van Craveld, *On Future War* (London: Brassey, 1991), for a brilliant exposition of the decline of Clausewitzian war.

35. An interesting study of business organization as epistemic, knowledge-creating devices is Ikujiro Nonaka and Hirotaka Takeuchi, *The Knowledge-Creating Company: How Japanese Companies Create the Dynamics of Innovation* (New York and Oxford: Oxford University Press, 1995).

36. On the contemporary interaction between resource-scarcity and military conflict, see T. Homer-Dixon, 'On the Threshold: Environmental Changes as Causes of Acute Conflict', *International Security*, Fall 1991.

CHAPTER 18: THE WORLD IS ROUND

1. Thomas L. Friedman, *The World is Flat: A Brief History of the Twenty-first Century* (New York: Farrar, Straus & Giroux, 2005; London: Penguin, 2005).

2. For an analysis of the failures and social costs of Western-sponsored

'market reform' in post-Communist Russia and an assessment of alternative policies, see Peter Reddaway and Dmitri Glinski, *The Tragedy of Russia's Reforms: Market Bolshevism against Democracy* (Washington, DC: United States Institute of Peace Press, 2001).

3. For an interesting view of the role of nationalism in the emergence of capitalism, see Liah Greenfield, *Nationalism: Five Roads to Modernity* (Cambridge, Mass.: Harvard University Press, 1992).

4. See Michael T. Klare, *Resource Wars: The New Landscape of Global Conflict* (New York: Metropolitan, 2001).

5. See Kenneth S. Deffeyes, *Hubbert's Peak: The Impending World Oil Shortage* (Princeton, NJ: Princeton University Press, 2001).

CHAPTER 19: THE ORIGINAL MODERNIZERS

1. L. Kolakowski, *Modernity on Endless Trial* (Chicago and London: University of Chicago Press, 1990), p. 67.

2. For a thorough study of Saint-Simon, see Frank Manuel, *The New World of Henri Saint-Simon* (Cambridge, Mass.: Harvard University Press, 1956). Manuel presents a fascinating account of the leading Positivist savants and their milieu in his later book, *The Prophets of Paris* (Cambridge, Mass.: Harvard University Press, 1962).

3. Mary Pickering, *Auguste Comte: An Intellectual Biography*, vol. 1 (Cambridge: Cambridge University Press, 1993), p. 79.

4. *Henri Saint-Simon: Selected Writings on Science, Industry and Social Organisation*, ed. and trans. with an Introduction and Notes by Keith Taylor (London: Croom Helm, 1975), pp. 78, 101.

5. Manuel, *Prophets of Paris*, p. 256.

6. The quote comes from Comte's French biographer Henri Gouhier, *La Jeunesse d'Auguste Comte* (Paris: Vrin, 1933–41), vol. 1, p. 146, and is quoted in Kenneth Thompson, *Auguste Comte: The Foundations of Sociology* (London: Nelson, 1976), p. 9.

7. Manuel, *Prophets of Paris*, p. 265.

8. Auguste Comte, *The Catechism of Positive Religion*, trans. Richard Congreve (London: John Chapman, 1858), pp. 303–4.

9. For John Stuart Mill's assessment of Comte, see his interesting short book, *Auguste Comte and Positivism* (Ann Arbor: University of Michigan Press, 1973).

10. The quote from Condorcet comes from Emma Rothschild, *Economic Sentiments: Adam Smith, Condorcet and the Enlightenment* (Cambridge,

Mass., and London: Harvard University Press, 2001), p. 203. Rothschild's book contains a brilliant reinterpretation of Condorcet's thought.

11. *Henri Saint-Simon*, p. 124.

12. Thompson, *Auguste Comte*, p. 44.

13. *Henri Saint-Simon*, p. 123.

14. Thompson, *Auguste Comte*, p. 43.

15. Ibid., p. 58.

16. *Collected Writings of John Maynard Keynes*, vol. 7: *The General Theory of Employment, Interest and Money* (London: Macmillan/ St Martin's Press, 1973), p. 383.

CHAPTER 24: AN AGENDA FOR GREEN CONSERVATISM

1. C. S. Lewis, *The Abolition of Man* (London: Macmillan, 1947). The citation occurs in Herman E. Daly (ed.), *Toward a Steady-State Economy* (San Francisco: W. H. Freeman, 1973), p. 323.

2. See my *Beyond the New Right: Markets, Government and the Common Environment* (London and New York, Routledge, 1993), chs 2 and 3.

3. The expression 'rationalism in politics' is, of course, Michael Oakeshott's.

4. Garret Hardin, 'The Tragedy of the Commons', *Science*, vol. 162, 13 December 1968, pp. 1243–8. The citation occurs in Daly, *Toward a Steady-State Economy*, pp. 137–8.

5. This is acknowledged in Hardin's book, *Nature and Man's Fate* (New York: Mentor Books, 1959), ch. 11.

6. For a discussion of the Prisoner's Dilemma, see Russell Hardin, *Collective Choice* (Chicago: University of Chicago Press, 1987).

7. The best version of this argument for market institutions is to be found in Michael Polanyi, *The Logic of Liberty* (Chicago: University of Chicago Press, 1951), ch. 8.

8. Yablokov's estimates were reported in the London *Independent* of 24 January 1992.

9. As quoted in the London *Sunday Times*, 7 July 1991.

10. Ibid.

11. Stefan Hedlund is an Associate Professor of Soviet and East European Studies at Uppsala, Sweden, who presented a paper on Soviet environmental degradation to the Washington-based National Security Information Center in June 1991.

12. *Independent*, 24 January 1992. The *Independent on Sunday* of 15 December 1991 contains a much more detailed account by Mark Hertsgaard of the secret Mayak nuclear complex at Chelyabinsk; it mentions the cover-up by both Soviet and Western authorities of the nuclear disaster at the Mayak waste dump in 1957, during which around twenty million curies of radioactivity – four times the amount released at Hiroshima – were released into the local environment.

13. See Hertsgaard's report in the *Independent on Sunday* for details.

14. Ibid.

15. Ibid.

16. See Vanya Kewley, *Tibet: Behind the Ice Curtain* (London: Grafton Books, 1990).

17. See Murray Feisbach, *Ecocide in the USSR* (New York: Basic Books, 1992).

18. Stefan Hedlund, 'Red Dust', London *Sunday Times*, 7 July 1991.

19. As reported in the *New York Times*, 2 August 1992.

20. The term 'inherently public goods' I owe to Joseph Raz, who explains it in his *The Morality of Freedom* (Oxford: Clarendon Press, 1986), pp. 198–9.

21. Michael Oakeshott, *Rationalism in Politics and Other Essays* (London and New York: Methuen, 1977), p. 171.

22. There are some penetrating observations of the consequences of this point for moral and political thought in Stuart Hampshire, *Innocence and Experience* (London: Penguin, 1989).

23. That human individuals are tokens of which forms of life are the types is argued in the last chapter of my book, *Post-Liberalism: Studies in Political Thought* (London and New York: Routledge, 1993).

24. See ibid.

25. I have criticized the use of the Kantian conception of the person in recent Anglo-American political philosophy in my 'Against the New Liberalism', *Times Literary Supplement*, 3 July 1992.

26. See my *Beyond the New Right*, ch. 3.

27. Ibid.

28. See Arne Naess, 'Green Conservatism', in Andrew Dobson (ed.), *The Green Reader* (London: André Deutsch, 1991), pp. 253–4.

29. For a good statement of this truth, see Edward Goldsmith, *The Way: An Ecological World-View* (London: Rider, 1992), chs 22, 64 especially.

30. James Lovelock, *The Ages of Gaia* (Oxford: Oxford University Press, 1988).

31. Goldsmith, *The Way*, pp. 367–8.

32. I discuss the incoherence of the idea of progress, in the context of incommensurabilities among human goods and evils, in chapter 20 of my *Post-Liberalism*.

33. See Ivan Illich, *Limits to Medicine: Medical Nemesis: The Expropriation of Health* (London: Penguin, 1976), chs 1–3.

34. I have discussed Herder's rejection of the melioristic interpretation of human history in my *Post-Liberalism*, especially in chs 6, 20.

35. F. A. Hayek, *The Constitution of Liberty* (London: Routledge & Kegan Paul, 1960; Chicago: Henry Regnery Company, 1960).

36. George Santayana, *Dominations and Powers: Reflections on Liberty, Society and Government* (New York: Charles Scribner & Sons, 1951), p. 340.

37. J. S. Mill, *Principles of Political Economy*, vol. 2 (London: John W. Parker & Son, 1848), pp. 320–26. The citation is reproduced in Daly, *Toward a Steady-State Economy*, pp. 12–13.

38. Lovelock, *Ages of Gaia*, p. 178.

39. Hardin, *Nature and Man's Fate*, pp. 289–90.

40. On this possibility, see Lovelock, *Ages of Gaia*, p. 178ff.

41. On the conflict between high population density and individual liberty, see Jack Parsons, *Population versus Liberty* (London: Pemberton Books, 1971).

42. I refer to José Ortega y Gasset, and his book *The Revolt of the Masses* (New York: W. W. Norton, 1957).

43. Nicholas Georgescu-Roegen, 'The Entropy Law and the Economic Problem', in Daly, *Toward a Steady-State Economy*, pp. 37–49.

44. Goldsmith, *The Way*, p. 300.

45. See my paper, 'From Post-Communism to Civil Society: The Re-emergence of History and the Decline of the Western Model', *Social Philosophy and Policy*, vol. 10, no. 2, Summer 1993, pp. 26–50.

46. For an excellent account of the introduction of poverty into Ladakh via development programmes which were animated by conceptions of modernization, see Helena Norberg-Hodge, *Ancient Futures: Learning from Ladakh* (London: Rider, 1991).

47. This is a point well discussed by E. J. Mishan in his *Costs of Economic Growth* (London: Pelican, 1967).

48. On this, see F. A. Hayek, *Denationalisation of Money: An Analysis of the Theory and Practice of Concurrent Currencies*, Hobart Paper 70, 2nd edn, revised and enlarged (London: Institute for Economic Affairs, 1978); and Kevin Dowd, *The State and the Monetary System* (New York: St Martin's Press, 1989).

49. G. K. Chesterton. The citation appears in Daly, *Toward a Steady-State Economy*, p. 148. No source is given, but I believe that it comes from Chesterton's book, *The Outline of Sanity* (London: Methuen, 1926).

50. Hilaire Belloc, *The Servile State* (Indianapolis: Liberty Press, 1977), p. 107.

51. The reference is to Feisbach's study, *Ecocide in the USSR*.

52. I have argued, in *Beyond the New Right*, ch. 3, that market socialism, as a 'Third Way' between capitalist and socialist institutions, is systemically unstable.

53. See ibid., chs 1, 3.

54. I have discussed reform of inheritance taxation in ibid., ch. 1.

55. F. A. Hayek, *The Road to Serfdom* (London and Henley: Routledge & Kegan Paul, 1944).

56. I believe that the idea of a negative capital tax was advanced by A. B. Atkinson but I have been unable to trace the source.

57. I have argued, in *Beyond the New Right*, ch. 3, that the current apparatus of the welfare state could in most countries be substantially dismantled, while the needs of the most disadvantaged and vulnerable were satisfied better than at present.

58. See ibid., chs 1, 3.

59. Daly, *Toward a Steady-State Economy*, pp. 160–63.

60. Ibid., p. 158. The proposal for 'child licenses' which Daly discusses originates with Kenneth Boulding, in the latter's *Economics as a Science* (New York: McGraw-Hill, 1970), p. 149.

61. Lovelock, *Ages of Gaia*, pp. 171, 110.

62. Ibid., p. 173.

63. Ibid., p. 174.

64. Ibid., p. 178.

65. Goldsmith, *The Way*, p. 373.

66. Robert Waller, 'Prospects for British Agriculture', in Edward Goldsmith (ed.), *Can Britain Survive?* (London: Sphere, 1971), p. 133.

67. Ibid., p. 135.

68. Goldsmith, *The Way*, p. 291.

69. Ivan Illich, *Energy and Equity* (London: Calder & Boyars, 1974), pp. 30–31.

70. I owe these figures to Wolfgang Zuckerman's *The End of the Road* (London: Lutterworth Press, 1991).

71. See Richard Rogers and Mark Fisher, *A New London* (London: Penguin, 1992). The quote comes from the London *Sunday Times*, 14 February 1992.

72. Rogers and Fisher, *New London*.

73. See, on this, Jane Jacobs's book *The Death and Life of Great American Cities* (New York: Vantage Books, 1963).

74. I have not traced the expression but I believe that it originates with Russell Kirk.

75. Illich, *Limits to Medicine*, p. 50.

76. See *Beyond the New Right*, ch. 3.

77. On this see the writings of E. G. West.

78. Ivan Illich, *Deschooling Society* (London and New York: Harper & Row, 1970), pp. 20–21.

79. Ibid., p. 19.

80. For Mill's suggestion, see J. S. Mill, *On Liberty and Other Essays*, ed. John Gray, World's Classics edn (Oxford: Oxford University Press, 2008), pp. 117–19.

81. See Illich, *Limits to Medicine*.

82. Ibid., p. 92.

83. Ibid., p. 272.

84. Ibid., p. 235.

85. Ibid., pp. 271–2.

86. Paul Feyerabend, *Three Dialogues on Knowledge* (Oxford: Basil Blackwell, 1991), p. 75.

87. Michael Oakeshott, *Hobbes on Civil Association* (Oxford: Basil Blackwell, 1975), p. 151.

88. Hardin, *Nature and Man's Fate*, pp. 296–7.

89. Lovelock, *Ages of Gaia*, p. 212.

90. John Aspinall, *The Best of Friends* (London and New York: Harper & Row, 1976), pp. 132–4.

91. Lovelock, *Ages of Gaia*, p. 138.

92. Ibid., p. 121.

93. I do not mean here to endorse the Hayekian conception of spontaneous order, with its attendant erroneous theory of cultural evolution. I refer instead to Polanyi's account of it in his book, *The Logic of Liberty*.

94. For J. Monod's views, see his book *Chance and Necessity* (London: Collins, 1972).

95. Lovelock, *Ages of Gaia*, p. 211.

CHAPTER 26: THEODORE POWYS AND THE LIFE OF CONTEMPLATION

1. Alyse Gregory, *The Cry of a Gull: Journals 1923–48*, ed. Michael Adam (Brushford: Ark Press, 1973), p. 122.

2. T. F. Powys, *Soliloquies of a Hermit* (London: Village Press, 1975), p. 1.

3. T. F. Powys, *Fables* (New York: Viking, 1929; republished Brighton: Hieroglyph, 1993).

4. T. F. Powys, *Mr Weston's Good Wine* (London: Hogarth Press, 1927), p. 316.

5. T. F. Powys, *The Only Penitent* (London: Chatto & Windus, 1931), pp. 56–7.

6. T. F. Powys, *The Left Leg* (London: Chatto & Windus, 1968), p. 81.

7. William Hunter, *The Novels and Stories of T. F. Powys* (Beckenham, Kent: Trigon Press, 1977).

8. See J. Lawrence Mitchell, *T. F. Powys: Aspects of a Life* (Bishopstone, Herefordshire: Brynmill Press, 2005).

9. John Cowper Powys, *Autobiography* (London: Macdonald, 1967), p. 446.

10. Llewelyn was aware of his differences with ancient Epicureanism. See his essay 'Lucretius' in L. Powys, *Rats in the Sacristy* (London: Watts, 1937).

11. For a detailed examination of Powys's literary allusions, see Marius Buning, *T. F. Powys: A Modern Allegorist* (Amsterdam: Rodopi, 1986). Elaine Mencher's Introduction to *T. F. Powys: Selected Early Works*, 2 vols (Bishopstone, Herefordshire: Brynmill Press, 2003), is an indispensable guide to Powys's work.

CHAPTER 30: AS IT IS

1. George Santayana, *Platonism and the Spiritual Life* (New York: Charles Scribner's Sons, 1927), p. 30.

Acknowledgements

The writings collected here record my attempt to make sense of the past few decades. They are republished without any alteration apart from their titles, some stylistic conventions that have been modified for purposes of consistency and some updating in the citations. They do not pretend to compose any kind of system. Yet they seem to me to express a line of thinking, pursued over the years, which can be systematically defended, and anyone who is interested can consult *The Political Theory of John Gray*, edited by John Horton and Glen Newey (London: Routledge, 2007), where I set out my standpoint in more academic terms.

Conversations stretching over many years stirred many of the thoughts in this volume. Among the people who contributed to these writings I would like to mention Bryan Appleyard, John Aspinall, J. G. Ballard, John Banville, Isaiah Berlin, Jim Blance, Nick Butler, Norman Cohn, Bob Colls, Charles Constable, Yehuda Elkana, James Goldsmith, Henry Hardy, Dick Holt, John Horton, Charles King, Marcin Krol, Michael Lind, James Lovelock, Steven Lukes, Pankaj Mishra, Geoffrey Neate, Gary Newman, Michael Oakeshott, John O'Sullivan, Adam Phillips, Joseph Raz, David Rieff, Paul Schutze, Will Self, Geoffrey Smith, Albyn Snowdon, George Soros, Masahiro Takeya, Ernest van den Haag and George Walden. Responsibility for the thoughts expressed here remains mine.

I am grateful to Richard Reeves for suggesting the book's title, and to Simon Winder, my editor at Penguin, for his advice on the selection. Alice Dawson of Penguin has assisted me in assembling the book, and Peter James as copy-editor has improved the text in many ways. Tracy Bohan of the Wylie Agency has given me help and encouragement at every stage of the book's production.

My greatest debt is to Mieko, without whose devotion this and much else would not have been possible.

John Gray

Permissions

The pieces collected here appeared first in the following publications, and I am grateful to the publishers for granting me permission to reprint them: 'Modus vivendi', taken from my Two Faces of Liberalism, Polity Press (in conjunction with Blackwell Publishers), 2000; 'John Stuart Mill and the idea of progress', Contemporary Review, September 1976; 'Santayana's alternative', The World and I, February 1989; 'Oakeshott as a liberal', Salisbury Review, January 1992; 'Notes towards a definition of the political thought of Tlön', Times Literary Supplement, 15 October 1993; 'Isaiah Berlin: the value of decency', New York Review of Books, 13 July 2006; 'George Soros and the open society', New York Review of Books, 5 October 2006; 'Hayek as a conservative', Salisbury Review, July 1983; A conservative disposition, Centre for Policy Studies, February 1991; 'The strange death of Tory England', Dissent, Fall 1995; 'Tony Blair, neo-con', taken from my Black Mass: Apocalyptic Religion and the Death of Utopia, Penguin, 2007; 'The system of ruins', Times Literary Supplement, 30 December 1983; 'Cultural origins of Soviet Communism', taken from my 'Totalitarianism, reform and civil society', in Totalitarianism at the Crossroads, ed. E. F. Paul, Transaction Books, 1990; 'Western Marxism: a fictionalist deconstruction', Philosophy, Royal Institute of Philosophy, no. 64, July 1989; 'The end of history, again?', National Review, 27 October 1989; 'What globalization is not', taken from False Dawn: The Delusions of Global Capitalism, Granta Books, 1998; 'The world is round', New York Review of Books, 11 August 2005; 'The original modernizers', taken from Al Qaeda and What It Means to be Modern, Faber & Faber, 2003; 'The Jacobins of Washington', New Statesman, 11 March 2003; 'Torture: a modest proposal', New Statesman, 17 February 2003; 'A modest defence of George Bush', New Statesman, 17 January 2005; 'Evangelical atheism, secular Christianity', Guardian, 15 March 2008; 'An agenda for Green conservatism', taken from Beyond the New Right: Markets, Government

444

and the Common Environment, Routledge, 1993; 'Joseph Conrad, our contemporary', *New Statesman*, 29 April 2002; 'Theodore Powys and the life of contemplation', taken from the Introduction to a new edition of T. F. Powys's *Unclay*, Sundial Press, 2008; '*Homo rapiens* and mass extinction', *New Statesman*, 22 July 2002; 'A report to the Academy', *New Statesman*, 9 February 2004; 'The body disassembled', taken from *Re-object*, vol. 1, ed. Eckhard Schneider, Kunsthaus Bregenz, 2007; 'As it is', taken from *Straw Dogs: Thoughts on Humans and Other Animals*, Granta Books, 2002.

The lines from Wallace Stevens that appear as the epigraph to the Introduction were taken from 'Extracts from Addresses to the Academy of Fine Ideas', *The Collected Poems of Wallace Stevens*, Vintage Books (a Division of Random House), New York, 1990, p. 255.

INDEX

References to endnotes are indicated by 'n' (e.g. 426n9)

progress
  Conrad on 385, 388
  and conservatism 130, 136, 138,
    308, 329
  and deception 180–81, 328
  in ethics and politics 10, 112,
    119, 263, 265, 299, 389
  Hayek on 130, 329, 336
  and immortality 416–17
  and knowledge 110, 388–9
  and liberalism 67–8, 68–9,
    75–6, 82, 136, 327, 388–9
  and Marxism 327, 388
  meliorism 13, 328–9, 382
  Mill on 14, 53
  myth of 16, 312, 327–9
  and neo-conservatism 136
  Positivists' view of 263, 264–5,
    268–9, 295
  and religion 12–14, 299
  Santayana on 67–9, 75, 330
  in science and technology 1, 10,
    119, 136, 250, 263, 264–5,
    268, 299, 336, 389
  as 'time-worship' 68, 413
  and work 414–15
Project for the New American
    Century 112–13, 426n6
propaganda 115–16
property
  distribution of 56–61
  private 59, 74, 77, 183, 219,
    244, 312, 314–15, 320
  rights 35, 36, 74, 127, 309,
    314–15, 319–21, 382
protectionism 256, 321
Protestantism 414
Proudhon, Pierre-Joseph 70
Prussian Academy 404
psychology 112, 124, 193, 405

Pullman, Philip 292, 293–4
Putin, Vladimir 7, 108, 117–18,
    255
pygmies 414
Pyrrho 395
Pyrrhonism 45, 46, 420n19, 24

Quakers 30, 177
Quango State 161, 163, 168
quietism 46
Quinton, Anthony 91

racism 12, 188, 199, 270, 296,
    297, 311
radio 15, 295
railways 15, 252, 273, 359
rainforests 315, 399, 400, 414
Ramadi 288
rational consensus 21, 22, 23, 24,
    43, 47, 48, 49
rationalism
  Aristotelian 206
  Cartesian 45, 126
  constructivist 126
  and ideas of government 78–9,
    81
  and neo-liberalism 308–9
  Platonic 131
  in Popper's works 112
  secular 2–3, 15–16, 17, 137
Rawls, John 22, 33, 35–6, 37, 41,
    78, 79, 140, 218, 282,
    419nn6-7
Reagan, Ronald 5, 167, 250, 289
Reaganism 83, 166, 339
realism 16, 89, 103, 201, 378
Red Brigades (Italian) 300
reflexivity 110–12, 119
Reformation 206
regime change 10, 276, 283, 287

PENGUIN POLITICS

BLACK MASS
JOHN GRAY

From the bestselling author of *Straw Dogs*

Our conventional view of history and human progress is wrong. It is founded on a pernicious myth of an achievable utopia that in the last century alone caused the murder of tens of millions. In *Black Mass* John Gray tears down the religious, political and secular beliefs that we insist are fundamental to the human project and shows us how a misplaced faith in our ability to improve the world has actually made it far worse.

'The closest thing we have to a window-smashing French intellectual'
Andrew Marr

'Causes vertigo when it does not cause outrage' *Sunday Times*

'Brilliant, frightening, devastating' John Banville, *Guardian*

'Savage. Gray raises profound and valid doubts about the conventional "plot" of modern history' *Financial Times*

read more

PENGUIN SCIENCE

THE REVENGE OF GAIA:
WHY THE EARTH IS FIGHTING BACK AND HOW WE CAN STILL
SAVE HUMANITY

JAMES LOVELOCK

'The most important book for decades' Andrew Marr, *Daily Telegraph*

For millennia, humankind has exploited the Earth without counting the cost.
Now, as the world warms and weather patterns dramatically change, the Earth is
beginning to fight back. James Lovelock, one of the giants of environmental
thinking, argues passionately and poetically that, although global warming is now
inevitable, we are not yet too late to save at least part of human civilization.

'The most important book ever to be published on the environmental crisis …
Lovelock will go down in history as the scientist who changed our view of the
earth' John Gray, *Independent*

read more

PENGUIN HISTORY

EMPIRE: HOW BRITAIN MADE THE MODERN WORLD
NIALL FERGUSON

Once, vast swathes of the globe were coloured imperial red and Britannia ruled not just the waves, but the prairies of America, the plains of Asia, the jungles of Africa and the deserts of Arabia. Just how did a small, rainy island in the North Atlantic achieve all this? And why did the empire on which the sun literally never set finally decline and fall? Niall Ferguson's acclaimed *Empire* brilliantly unfolds the imperial story in all its splendours and its miseries, showing how a gang of buccaneers and gold-diggers planted the seed of the biggest empire in history – and set the world on the road to modernity.

'The most brilliant British historian of his generation ... Ferguson examines the roles of "pirates, planters, missionaries, mandarins, bankers and bankrupts" in the creation of history's largest empire ... he writes with splendid panache ... and a seemingly effortless, debonair wit' Andrew Roberts, *The Times*

'Thrilling ... an extraordinary story' *Daily Mail*

'A brilliant book ... full of energy, imagination and curiosity' *Evening Standard*

'A remarkably readable précis of the whole British imperial story – triumphs, deceits, decencies, kindnesses, cruelties and all' Jan Morris

'Dazzling ... wonderfully readable' *New York Review of Books*

'An enormous saga ... crammed with the kind of anecdotes that leave the reader wanting more' *Sunday Herald*

PENGUIN HISTORY

THE WAR OF THE WORLD: HISTORY'S AGE OF HATRED
NIALL FERGUSON

> The beginning of the twentieth century saw human civilization at its most
> enlightened, well-educated, globalized and wealthy.
> What turned it into a bloodbath?

In his sweeping, epic new book Niall Ferguson re-tells the story of history's most savage century as a continual war that raged for 100 years. From the plains of Poland to the killing fields of Cambodia, he reveals how economic boom-and-bust, decaying empires and, above all, poisonous ideas of race led men to treat each other as aliens. It was an age of hatred that ended with the twilight, not the triumph, of the West. And, he shows, it could happen all over again.

'The most brilliant British historian of his generation ... he writes with splendid panache and a seemingly effortless, debonair wit' *The Times*

'A heartbreaking, serious and thoughtful survey of human evil that is utterly fascinating and dramatic' Simon Sebag Montefiore, *The New York Times*

'A sweeping narrative in which he balances wide-screen storytelling and close-focus anecdote ... Even those who have read widely in twentieth-century history will find fresh, surprising details' *Boston Globe*

PENGUIN POLITICS

AL-QAEDA: THE TRUE STORY OF RADICAL ISLAM
JASON BURKE

'A must-read … Jason Burke's book is the one that will last. It's a triumph'
Guardian

'If you read one book about the troubles, make it Jason Burke's al-Qaeda'
Tony Parsons

Prize-winning journalist Jason Burke's al-Qaeda – now fully updated with new material on Iraq, Afghanistan and the July 2005 London bombings – is acknowledged to be the most accurate, readable and expert account yet of the complex nature of Islamic extremism.

Burke has spent a decade reporting from the heart of the Middle East and gaining unprecedented access to the world of radical Islam. Drawing on his frontline experience of recent events, on secret documents and astonishing interviews with intelligence officers, militants, mujahideen commanders and Osama bin Laden's associates, he reveals the full story of al-Qaeda.

Burke shows Islamic militancy to be a far broader – and thus more dangerous – phenomenon than previously thought, and by doing so demolishes the myths that underpin the 'war on terror'. Only by understanding the true, complex nature of al-Qaeda, he argues, can we address the real issues surrounding our security today.

'The most reliable and perceptive guide to the rise of militant Islam yet published'
William Dalrymple

PENGUIN DARWIN

DARWIN'S SACRED CAUSE
ADRIAN DESMOND AND JAMES MOORE

In this remarkable book Adrian Desmond and James Moore give a new explanation of how Darwin came to his famous view of evolution. His 'sacred cause' was the abolition of slavery, and at its core lay a belief in human racial unity. Desmond and Moore show how he extended to all life the idea of human brotherhood held by those who fought to abolish slavery, so developing our modern view of evolution.

Through a great deal of detective work among unpublished family correspondence, manuscripts and rare works, the authors back up their compelling claim. Leading apologists for slavery in Darwin's day argued that blacks and whites had originated as separate species with whites superior. Creationists too believed that 'man' was superior to other species. Darwin abhorred such 'arrogance'; he declared it 'more humble and ... true' to see humans 'created from animals'. Darwin gave *all* the races – blacks and whites, animals and plants – a common origin and freed them from creationist shackles. Evolution meant emancipation.

Darwin's Sacred Cause restores Darwin's humanitarianism, tarnished by atheistic efforts to hijack his reputation and creationist attempts to smear him. The result is an epoch-making study of this eminent Victorian.

By the authors of 'unquestionably the finest biography ever written about Darwin' (Stephen Jay Gould).

He just wanted a decent book to read ...

Not too much to ask, is it? It was in 1935 when Allen Lane, Managing Director of Bodley Head Publishers, stood on a platform at Exeter railway station looking for something good to read on his journey back to London. His choice was limited to popular magazines and poor-quality paperbacks – the same choice faced every day by the vast majority of readers, few of whom could afford hardbacks. Lane's disappointment and subsequent anger at the range of books generally available led him to found a company – and change the world.

'We believed in the existence in this country of a vast reading public for intelligent books at a low price, and staked everything on it'
Sir Allen Lane, 1902–1970, founder of Penguin Books

The quality paperback had arrived – and not just in bookshops. Lane was adamant that his Penguins should appear in chain stores and tobacconists, and should cost no more than a packet of cigarettes.

Reading habits (and cigarette prices) have changed since 1935, but Penguin still believes in publishing the best books for everybody to enjoy. We still believe that good design costs no more than bad design, and we still believe that quality books published passionately and responsibly make the world a better place.

So wherever you see the little bird – whether it's on a piece of prize-winning literary fiction or a celebrity autobiography, political tour de force or historical masterpiece, a serial-killer thriller, reference book, world classic or a piece of pure escapism – you can bet that it represents the very best that the genre has to offer.

Whatever you like to read – trust Penguin.

read more
www.penguin.co.uk